Acting Truths
And Fictions

Straight Talk!

about the Many Popular Acting Methodologies...
The Myths and Myth-Conceptions of Their Origins...
Comparing the Approaches of Leading American Teachers...
and The Individual Approach Items Most Widely Taught...
Some Reexaminations and Recent Adaptations of Their Use...
The Relative Values in Actors' Later Professional Careers
of the Complicated and Simpler Approaches!

A Recommended Library for Actors with Limited Budgets!...
Straight Talk Advice from Stars, Agents and Others
about the Professional Actor's Talent Marketplaces
in Hollywood Film and New York Theatre!...
and Definitions of Actors' Terms in
Film, Television and Theatre

by the noted American Acting Teacher
and Author of Best-Selling Books for The Actor
LAWRENCE PARKE

An Acting World Books Publication

Acknowledgements for quoted materials appear on pages 419-420, which shall be considered continuations of the copyright page.

Published by
Acting World Books
Post Office Box 3044
Hollywood, California 90078

Manufactured in the United States of America

First Printing 1995

Cover design: Dynamedia Design and Graphics, Inc.
Cover photo: Ed Whiting Photography (l. to r.): Agent Steven R. Stevens (Steven R. Stevens Talent Agency), Lawrence Parke, Milt Hamerman (longtime Vice President of Talent, Universal Pictures), conducting an Actors' Seminar sponsored by The Actors' Center, Albuquerque, New Mexico.

Publisher's Cataloging in Publication Data

Parke, Lawrence. 1922-
    Acting Truths And Fictions
    Includes Index and Glossary of Terms
    ISBN 0-9615288-7-7 (pbk) $22.50 (US), $29.95 (Canada)
l. Acting.   2. Acting - Vocational Guidance.   3. Acting - Study and teaching. 4. Method (Acting).   5. Stanislavsky, Konstantin, 1863-1938 - Criticism and interpretation. 6. Strasberg, Lee, 1901-1982 - Criticism and interpretation.   7. Actors Studio (New York, N.Y. l.. Title
PN2061.P37 1995
792'.028-dc20   95-75729

"Little known facts, myths and misunderstandings of actors about the Stanislaski System; the Strasberg Method, the Actors Studio; the approaches of other leading teachers; controversial approach items; reexamination, adaptation and updating of teaching; stars, top players, agents discussing practices encountered by the contemporary actor in Hollywood and New York; much career advice; recommended books; actors' film, television and theatre terms defined."

This book is dedicated to
the many hundreds of actors with whom I've worked
and who have contributed to the development of my teaching
with patience, insight, respect for the goals of our work
and their kind comments to others about me in spite of
my continually driving them to the limits of their endurance
toward ever greater achieving of the highest goals of acting art;
to my patient and loving wife, Virginia,
who understood and forgave the long days and nights
I spent away from her to be with "Frances", my computer;
to our son Mike for doing the many, many things
that left me free to spend time with Frances;
and to my dear, beloved friend Miriam, wherever she is now,
who sat beside my hospital bed day and night in 1961 when I was dying
and told me I had more work to do.

Contents

Myths and Myth-Conceptions About Acting..... **211**

The Author

Lawrence Parke has taught many of today's theatre, film and television stars, both in New York and Hollywood. In addition to his close to thirty-five years of teaching, he has himself appeared in hundreds of prominent roles in all three performing arts in New York theatre and in films; won two New York theatre awards for Acting and Directing in his twelve earlier years there; has appeared in theatre productions in France, Italy and Germany, and had his first film role under Roberto Rossellini's direction at the age of twenty-one. . .

. . . won top honors for his environmental theatre production *"Minus One"* at French and German International Theatre Festivals and critical acclaim for its long Paris engagement and its subsequent European theatre capitols tour, also received critical praise for his direction of a number of theatre productions Off Broadway in New York, six national touring productions, and the producing and directing of sixteen productions of *The Lawrence Parke Company of Actors* and *Theatre Today* in Hollywood.

The late Brooks Atkinson, the *New York Times'* Theatre Editor and Dean of New York Theatre critics, commented that *"His work is admirable, the results brilliant."* In Hollywood, James Powers, Editor of *The Hollywood Reporter,* wrote that *"He has the uncommon ability to give actors totality of character and to make the whole a balanced and pulsating organism."* Critic Deena Metzger of *The Los Angeles Free Press,* wrote that *"He awakens all the sleeping edges of talent;"* Dan Sullivan, the Theatre Editor of *The Los Angeles Times,* called him in print *"The Hollywood Acting Coach Guru;"* and *Hollywood Talent News'* Editor called him *"Hollywood's foremost career maker."*

Jack Lang, until recently France's Minister of Culture, stated in print that *"In his work are found the excitements of Artaud without falsification, of Grotowski without plagiarism, and of Stanislavski and Vakhtangov first and foremost."*

A leading industry organizer, in his New York years he spearheaded the formation of the Off Broadway League (now the League of Off Broadway Theatres) at the bidding of Brooks Atkinson and Vernon Rice, and formed the Entertainment and Sports Committee of the then new United Cerebral Palsy Foundation.

In Hollywood, he was the first three terms' president of *The Acting Coaches And Teachers Association*; was founder and first three terms' president of *The League of Los Angeles Theatres;* was co-founder of both *The ANTA Repertory Theatre West* and *Equity Library Theatre West* and was co-chairman of both of those organizations' inaugural seasons.

James Powers, former Editor of *The Hollywood Reporter,* stated that *"Parke is a man who detects a need and either finds or creates what's needed."* His history of forming the abovementioned organizations in response to obvious needs confirms that.

The same observation of a need inspired the writing of this book, just as surely as it prompted his originally becoming a teacher of actors. It also prompted his conducting and moderating, between 1964 and 1985, twenty annual *Actors' Career Guidance Seminars* in Hollywood, and several additional *Actors' Career Seminars* in other U. S. cities, featuring top industry casting directors, agents, producers and directors as panelists.

It was also the compelling motive for his suspending his teaching for a period to become a Screen Actors Guild franchised talent agency head to help some of his most exciting actors begin their careers on highest possible levels during times when the film industry was a fairly closed door to new talents.

Prior to teaching, his own studies included working with teachers of the Stanislavski and Vakhtangov Systems and study of the Strasberg Method for a time with Mr. Strasberg. He later in Hollywood taught side by side with Miriam Goldina, former student of Vakhtangov, who was also directed by him in Moscow, and who later edited and translated two books about him for America.

Information about his researching the Vakhtangov modifications of the Stanislavski System reaching Moscow through Goldina, he was invited to meet Yuri Zavadsky, another of Vakhtangov's former students, and discuss Vakhtangov's work lengthily with him while he was in New York lecturing and directing *"The Cherry Orchard"*. He was also privileged to have many discussions about Vakhtangov's influence upon the teaching and directing experience with Raikin Ben-Ari, another of Vakhtangov's students who later taught several stars in Hollywood.

From the latter two and his friend Miriam he was able to confirm some of the Vakhtangov revisionist theories of the Stanislavski System that are only touched upon in Stanislavski's writings, at least as published in English thus far.

In the 1960's Goldina, during a Moscow trip, lectured on Mr. Parke's teaching innovations before the Moscow Art Theatre School's faculty and student body at the Vakhtangov Theatre.

A number of teachers taught by him now teach in other major cities throughout the world. His earlier book, *"Since Stanislavski And Vakhtangov: The Method As A System For Today's Actor"*, is used as study and reference text in a number of colleges and universities.

Foreword

Of all professions, *acting* is the one that appears more often than any other career on young people's secret lists of "someday" choices. They all feel they have the talents, and they all probably do. Most people have talent.

Talent isn't something you learn. It's innately there, waiting to be developed and expanded. That's what this book is about. . . the *development* of talents . . . the encyclopedic confusions and problems that actors are sure to experience in that development . . .

. . . the also encyclopedic list of methods, techniques and approaches that are available from which to choose . . . the complex, years-taking study programs and the available alternatives that may produce equal results more quickly . . . the sometimes purely logical, objective and stunningly effective approaches, and other theories taught for realizing optimum functioning of actors' minds and bodies that have been broadly criticized as offering little if any teaching of role preparation approaches.

Lee Strasberg's work has been so voluminously documented, with both highest praise and hard criticism. Both views are discussed briefly because they need to be. And many actors don't yet know that the English versions of Stanislavski's books are recently reported as being first censored by Stalin and later incorrectly edited for America. More accurate versions of his writings have now been found in Moscow (uncensored by Stalin and unedited in English) and may be published in English, perhaps by the time this is read. This book can only deal with the approaches in the Stanislavski books as thus far published.

Also, the book presents advice from leading actors, agents and producers to clear up misapprehensions about today's film, television and theatre worlds and the manners in which actors can successfully function in those worlds . . . some stars' discussions of their own experiences in early study, later professional work and problems the actor encounters.

There are descriptions of books available for actors, with fervent recommendation of some, questioning of the comparable value of others.

The book's title makes a complete, no-holds-barred, straight-from-the-shoulder candor obligatory, and this author is known for that honesty and straightforwardness. That's exactly what has prompted the writing of this book.

I feel the time has come when many aspects of preparing to become an actor, entering the professional milieu and preparing and performing roles of all kinds in today's entertainment mediums' situations, need to be given some fresh air in evaluation terms---some acknowledging and facing of lingering questionmarks and criticism or praise where I feel they're deserved.

It's my hope that every reader will come away from the reading of this book with clearer concepts of the most often encountered approaches that have great and enduring value for actors, as well as clearer perception of the reasons for some other approaches creating questionmarks.

I've also included in this book many strictly career guidance items that have nothing to do with acting technique but that are equally important for actors career-wise once they enter the professional milieu. The professional world's many myths and myth-conceptions as they apply to actors involve many truths and fictions too!

My own life as an actor, director, teacher, playwright and sometimes talent executive in film, television and theatre has been rich and happy. I was taught by masters; my own teaching innovations have been lectured on at the Moscow Art Theatre; I've been invited to demonstrate my teachings in Paris; I've watched students of mine become stars and win awards and was honored with two awards myself; I've had three television series roles; I've had the honor of founding New York and Hollywood organizations and the joy of watching them grow. Along the way, I've enjoyed friendships with and received encouragement and help from many people I consider to be important. Also along the way, I've inevitably found myself in positions where I learned many things that many actors and others need to know. I've included as many as possible in this book.

This book will have served its purpose if it helps actors find new ideas that attract them; if it clears away some misconceptions; and if in the end it helps them make productive and rewarding choices for themselves throughout all of their professional lives.

Lawrence Parke

Acting Truths
And Fictions

"Acting" (in quotes) is something nobody should be caught doing. "Acting" (again in quotes) is lying. Nobody likes a liar. If an actor must "act" all of his or her roles without at least that amount of actual experiencing that's within his or her control, that actor doesn't deserve to be called an actor.

True, every role an actor plays is a created fiction, but the consummate actor is able to *believe in a fiction as if it were true.*

After analyzing a role to find the core of the personality created by the writer for the role---the psychology that lies behind the total of the character's actions, traits, attitudes, thoughts, mental states, etc., the good actor must be able to prepare whatever subtext approaches will generate *within himself* that total life, those feelings and those behavior patterns for all moments of the role . . .*without acting!*

The greatest minds involved with the study of acting have since time immemorial searched for the manners of accomplishing that. Of all the researchers whose pursuits of that ideal have been sufficiently documented, the name Constantin Stanislavski is the first that, certainly deservedly, comes to the contemporary actor's mind.

More than any others who've continually throughout their lifetimes explored with unceasing perseverence and unflagging ardor the principles that constitute acting as an art form, Stanislavski probed deep into all the facets of the actor's art and arrived at profound conclusions as to what actors could do in first preparing themselves through developing manners of controlling their minds, their wills and their feelings and then applying those developed resources to the preparation and performance of acting roles.

He created a system, later called it *The Method of Physical Action.* But even that system wasn't formed in a single moment, and Stanislavski can't with historical accuracy be credited with originating the total of its recommended approach items.

1

I'd wager that a lot of American actors, when referring to *The Stanislavski System,* haven't an inkling as to why that System could as aptly be called . . .

■ The Stanislavski / Sulerzhitski / Nemirovich-Danchenko / Vakhtangov / Stalin / Hapgood System

The very first theory destined to become a fixed item in Stanislavski's System was *Concentration on Objects*, which in 1907 became the first firmly laid foundation block of the system to come. Throughout 1907 he conducted continuous exercises with his classes in *Concentration on Objects*, recognizing their importance.

It's ironic that later, between 1915 and 1922, his most respected teacher, Eugene Vakhtangov, was urging him---after all the rest of the System was formed---to return *Concentration on Objects* to its cornerstone place in the System as the main concentration point. That was never to happen.

In 1907 Stanislavski also began adding other approach items of inner characterization.

The *Super Objective* credited to him was actually the discovery of Vladimir Ivanovich Nemirovich-Danchenko, the Literary Head and co-founder of the Moscow Art Theatre. Stanislavski simply incorporated it prominently in his own developing role preparation system. And many of the other approach items that were to be credited to him in the years to come were actually brought into focus, formed more fully and afforded approach titles in the daily discussions with his longtime close friend Leopold Sulerzhitsky, who taught by his side at the Moscow Art Theatre and constantly counselled him.

In 1909, during the four months of preparation of Ivan Turgenev's *"A Month In The Country"*, most of his system's other items were conceptualized and incorporated into the whole---by Stanislavski, but with Sulerzhitski's always persent counselling.

Improvisation, too, was not originally conceived of by Stanislavski, as so many believe today. In the same year that the Moscow Art Theatre officially adopted the Stanislavski System (1911), it was playwright Maxim Gorky who suggested improvisation to him. Throughout 1911 and 1912 especially, improvisation became a regular exploration in Stanislavski's work and remains today an often employed manner of exploration, like other approaches wholly credited to Stanislavski as their innovator.

The *Affective Memory*---which was to create the lasting controversies and questions about his system that still exist today--- was brought to his attention by, again, Sulerzhitski, who in 1911

2

brought him from Paris the newly published theory of the French psychologist Theodule Ribot, *"Problémes de Psychologie Affective (1910)"*. Stanislavski immediately tested the possible application of the *affective memory* for actors. For a time he believed it to be one of the more important items of his System, but he later discarded it as potentially harmful when used by actors in their performances. That item has haunted his System later!

By 1914 he had added the *Through Line Of Action* and *Spine* theories and approaches (originally inspired by and mere extensions of Nemirovich-Danchenko's *Super Objective*); the same year commenced the advocating of *Beats* (or *Bits*) for defining the smaller moments of roles and supplying his recommended *Psychological Intentions* for their individual experiencing.

One of the best kept secrets with respect to the Stanislavski System's development remains the contributions of Eugene Vakhtangov. Principal among them was his returning to the very first approach item formulated by Stanislavski, *Concentration on Objects*, as the key and the missing link in what he recognized and promoted as Stanislavski's otherwise so complete system---a key that Stanislavski himself failed to fully appreciate until quite late in his life and only infrequently recommended in his notes and writings that were later published. Fiercely supportive and publicly defensive of Stanislavski and his System, Vakhtangov's contributions to the System's further crystallization may never be given their due credit.

Stanislavski's System has survived the decades since its formulation and the several decades since his death. During his life it survived the censorship imposed by Stalin on all Russian writers of the time, a censorship constantly monitored by editor Lyubov Gurevich who constantly urged Stanislavski to conform to the imposed theories of dialectical materialism.

It survived the urgency of so hurriedly getting his writings into print in America, where he realized he must find the money he needed so desperately after losing his family's fortune and properties to the Stalinist government. His son was desperately ill. His writings were rushed. Also during that period his terminology had to be adjusted to suit the state.

And those writings survived the American versions that were required by Theatre Arts Books to be shortened in order to be printed. And they survived the inaccuracies in translation by his American editor that have later become apparent---inaccuracies which are now in the process of being corrected in the *"Collected Works"* being published by the Russian publisher *Iskusstvo* and, here in America, the ten volume *Collected Works* being prepared by Routledge.

3

New material found in the Moscow Art Theatre archives, that somehow eluded Stalin's watchdogs, will be included in both of those collections, shedding new light and certainly some revisionist illumination on the theories and approaches that most American actors and many American teachers have misunderstood for the foregoing reasons.

Stanislavski steadfastly maintained that *action* would create the desired experience for the actor.

But the more recent discoveries of the *behavioral stimuli that cause responsive action* must inevitably direct us to the considering of Vakhtangov's theory that *action should be prompted by concentration on an object---a behavioral stimuli*, in today's scientific terms. It was his theory that, therefore, *the object of whatever nature---simply physical or inner thought---should exist in the mind before a desired action is formed.*

He posited and suggested to Stanislavski that such objects might even be used in substitution for desired actions, or at least both before and during desired actions' being formed and taken. Stanislavski could not accept those suggestions until very late in his life, when he more and more spoke of *Objects*.

■ The "American Method" of Lee Strasberg

The *Lee Strasberg Method*, contrary to its critics, is, as claimed, *an updated interpretation of The Stanislavski and Vakhtangov Systems*. But so much of his work was on *the actor's processes and the strengthening of his ability to control those processes*, and on some exercises (like *affective memory*) that provoked controversy, that his important promoting of Vakhtangov's *Objects* as a substitute for Stanislavski's *Action* concepts was overlooked. He seldom mentioned *Actions and Intentions*, preferred Vakhtangov's *Objects* . (*Action* is mentioned just once in Robert Hethmon's selections of recordings of *"Strasberg At The Actors Studio"*.) The *Action/Intention* oriented teachers were following Stanislavski; Strasberg preferred Vakhtangov in that respect. That too brought him criticism.

Stanislavski emphasized *the character's experience*. Strasberg's approaches emphasized *the actor's own experience,* and his manner of combining the two---constituting one of the first major adoptions of Vakhtangov's *Object* persuasions, as opposed to Stanislavski's so strongly recommended *Action* theories--- will be argued about forever.

This book, while critical of some of Mr. Strasberg's teaching approaches, will stress the importance of a new recognition of Vakhtangov's version of the System. In that respect this author is totally in agreement with Lee Strasberg.

The Acting Theories
Most Widely Taught
in America Today

*The Methodologies, Further Discoveries
and Continued Searching*

The Stanislavski System,
Vakhtangov's Little Known Adaptations
and The Strasberg Method

Although there were acting theories long before those of Constantin Stanislavski, only a few have survived the passing of the many centuries. For today's actor, most acting relates to Stanislavski. Stanislavski created "a new beginning" and theatre historians are the few who look still further back and tell us of the many acting approaches of those still earlier times.

Were you ever told that you were studying *the complete Stanislavski System?* The Stanislavsky System was *never* complete. Stanislavsky himself said that. He recommended that actors find their own systems and adapt them to their own time, their own sensibilities and artistic goals, and their own ever-changing professional needs. He was honored to contribute.

Some of us who teach feel that his own system could have been *more* complete than it was at the time of his death if he could heve persuaded himself to publicly acknowledge his debt to his most respected teacher, Eugene Vakhtangov, for providing a vital missing link. He could never persuade himself to do that.

When Stanislavski died his *still incomplete* System was cast in bronze and taught in its unfinished form by many teachers in both Russia and America---all presenting it as a complete system, which he never claimed it to be. He was so close, though! And Vakhtangov may have been even closer.

Stanislavski's System has endured and will endure as the acting world's basic syllabus for actors because so many of his system's approaches are valid, ideally coordinated and essential for truth in acting.

There is no system for actors that is so complete and penetratingly effective. The individual steps in its development of actors' instruments and its progressive role preparation techniques can help today's actors in all acting. But there is still that missing link in many approaches---that giant hole that Stanislavski himself was never able to fill.

6

Vakhtangov supplied an answer and urged it upon Stanislavski, but he died too soon.   Except for the few who were blessed with enough details of Vakhtangov's research and discoveries through direct association with him at the Moscow Art Theatre and who later explained his adaptations of the system to some of us who have come later, most actors and teachers have had to come upon his adaptations through their own research if at all.

■ The Widely Publicized Method of Lee Strasberg

Maybe you've studied *"the Method" (The Lee Strasberg Method)*.   If you were told you were studying *Strasberg's version of the Stanislavski System,* you were probably studying the exercises devised by Mr. Strasberg---some being elaborations and further investigations of some of the items dealt with in Stanislavski's books---primarily those early explorations in the very first book, *"An Actor Prepares";*   also learning Mr. Strasberg's manner of establishing characters and the use of *Sense Memory, Affective Memory* and *Vakhtangovian Objects*; seldom the *Actions* and *Intentions* taught by many others.

Strasberg's teachings were inspired in the main by his early studies at the American Lab Theatre under Richard Boleslasky and Maria Ouspenskaya in 1924 and 1925. They had worked with Stanislavski before emigrating to America and commencing to teach here. Certain items of their teaching struck resounding response chords with Strasberg and when he himself began teaching (less than ten years later, as head of the training program at the Group Theatre) he began---and continued throughout his teaching life---emphasizing his own selections from the early Stanislavski System and Vakhtangov's variations.

If you were told that Mr. Strasberg's method was an updated and further developed version of the Stanislavski System---*even with some of the modifications recommended by Vakhtangov* (whom Strasberg stated that he considered equally and in some respects more insighted than Stanislavski), that was true to an extent, but so much of his work was devoted to *his own favorite, skillfully developed exercises* that he was inspired to develop from his own selections from among the Stanislavski and Vakhtangov approaches. He considered some of the approaches of Stanislavski too fixed and labeled, too limiting, and seldom dealt with them. That brought him much criticism.

If you were instead told that you were being taught *the Strasberg Instrument-Conditioning and Consciousness-Expanding Exercises* and some *basics for preparing roles,* you were being told the truth. The most virulent criticism leveled at him was mostly with regard to his *Affective Memory* work.

Said by some critics to *not have taught role preparation,* he did in fact teach a number of the basic role preparation approaches recommended by Vakhtangov (more than Stanislavski). He simply eschewed labeling some of them with the formal labels applied in their teaching by others. He regularly punctuated his discussions of acting with credit to Stanislavski's and Vakhtangov's determinations of what the actor needs, but he applied the formalized labels of *role preparation* approaches to mostly *Units* and *Objects.* preferring to discuss those other items *without labeling* them, feeling his real calling lay in developing the actors themselves---more specifically their instruments and their abilities to control their processes.

He seldom talked in terms of *Super Objectives* and *Through Lines Of Action* for entire characterizations. He preferred a more moment-to-moment manner of working, with *Sense Memory,* Vakhtangov's *Inner Objects* and *Thought Objects,* also the *Affective Memory* exercise toward use of what it produced for actual performance moments. The latter item produced most of the criticism of his work.

Some of the criticism has been very strong, just as there has been broad praise for his teaching over the years since the nineteen-thirties (when he was head of the training program at The Group Theatre) and the nineteen-forties when he began his own private classes and also taught at The American Theatre Wing until he was brought in as a teacher and quite soon thereafter became head of the actor training program at the Actors Studio.

Some of the harshest criticism of his teaching has come from former close associates from the old Theatre Guild and Group Theatre days---Harold Clurman, Stella Adler, Robert Lewis, Elia Kazan, Sanford Meisner and others who were to later become teachers themselves.

Strasberg's affection for *Affective Memory* and his dogged insistence on continuing his own work with it, even after he learned from Stella Adler that Stanislavski himself had abandoned it, caused a great breach between Ms. Adler and himself (at the Group Theatre) that never healed, eventually led to a rift between him and the rest of the Group Theatre, and led to his summary departure from the Group in 1937.

Harold Clurman---at first a staunch supporter, with whom he had earlier formed the brief-lived Theatre Guild Studio (1928-1929) and later (1931) formed The Group Theatre with Cheryl Crawford, became an especially vocal critic of Strasberg's understanding of the Stanislavski System. He's reported as having told actors in a seminar talk once, *"The Method should drop dead."* (He was referring to Strasberg's Method.)

8

■ Other Teachers Have Emphasized Stanislavski's *Actions*

If you've studied Stella Adler's techniques, or even simply read her book *"The Technique Of Acting"*, you've surely observed her apostolic emphasis on Stanislavski's *Action* and *Intention* precepts, but also her teaching of *Circumstances, Personalizations, Justifications, Substitutions, Atmospheres* and other qualifying items as originally labeled by Stanislavski to turn actors' chosen *Actions, Intentions* and *Objectives* into the more complete experiences for both characters and actors. She has presented Stanislavski's teachings pretty much to the letter. Strasberg 's *Objects* made some of those steps unnecessary.

If you've read Robert Lewis's books *"Method---Or Madness"* and (more recently) *"Advice To The Players"*, you've observed his equally complete and less approach-labeling, more handily simplified use of Stanislavski's *Intentions* through insisting on the adding of the *Objec ts* at which *Intentions* should be aimed.

In the books of Uta Hagen (*"Respect For Acting"* and *"A Challenge To The Players"*) and Sanford Meisner's book *"Sanford Meisner On Acting"*, those celebrated teachers' books involve *Actions* and other System labels along with their own.

The items taught by most teachers without exception remain *Actions, Intentions* and *Objectives*. Some teachers simply use more, some fewer, of Stanislavski's recommended terms.

Those who want to study the Stanislavki and Vakhtangov Systems in their most complete forms (although with some later adaptations) but without the *Strasberg Exercises* and with more of the standard labeling of the individual *role preparation* items advocated by Stanislavski can find them in the teaching programs of Robert Lewis, Stella Adler, Uta Hagen and Sanford Meisner, to name only a few.

In short, the teachings of Lee Strasberg shouldn't be misapprehended as being exclusively inspired by the Stanislavski System. His teaching stands apart, representing his own further developments based primarily on some of the theories written of in *"An Actor Prepares"* and the most significant of Vakhtangov's reformulations. Beyond the inspirations he received from those approach items, his broadly questioned but unquestionably important further explorative work has in reality been a unique method of his own creation.

In Chapters 8 and 9 of her book *"Strasberg's Method As Taught By Lorrie Hull"* that respected American teacher clearly describes the *role preparation* work Strasberg involved in his teaching in addition to his work on actors' instruments.

And Dr. Hull continues Strasberg's manner of teaching in her own classes---with less actual labeling of the items others prefer

9

to label, but covering what appears to be the same territory in Mr. Strasberg's and her own manners.

■ The Best Kept Secret of the System—Eugene Vakhtangov

The exploring for manners of adapting the basic *Action, Intention, Objective* approaches (as codified by Stanislavski) in order to make them ideal will probably never end.   It didn't end for Stanislavski---except, as some of us have gathered (from bits of Vakhtangov's less prolific writings, and from students and associates who were with both Stanislavski and Vakhtangov at the time) in those private sessions when Vakhtangov coached both Stanislavski and Michael Chekhov on their own roles.

Although Stanislavski later employed Vakhtangov's dynamic *Inner Objects* approach more and more in his own directing of actors---as is evidenced in his director comments to the cast of the opera *"Werther"*   late in life, he seldom mentioned Vakhtangov's suggested alternate approach (the placing of more emphasis on *Inner Objects* and *Thought Objects* than on *Action*) with any endorsement in his own writings.

It's generally known---at least to teachers in Hollywood and to some other coaches in New York and in various universities and colleges throughout this country, also at the School of The Moscow Art Theatre---that I propose, and have taught for many years, that the *Thought Objects and Inner Objects of Vakhtangov,* if given more importance than *Actions,* simplify and bring at least equal and (a growing handful of us now believe) much more depth and personal involvement to actors' work, and accomplish those desirable results in a vastly simplified manner.

The difference in end results for the actor between Stanislavski's *Actions* and Vakhtangov's *Objects* appearing so crystal clear to some of us who teach, we continue advocating the latter, and continue exploring the further avenues of their development and popularizing of their use.   (This book is one more manner of presenting what we consider to be one of the "truths" that, not yet sufficiently aired, needs wider promulgation.)

Stanislavski's System for *analyzing* characters is flawless. His preparing of a directed subtext experience based on that analysis is terribly important.   It's primarily in the determining of the individual approach tools for use in preparing the over-all characterization, and in what the actor can focus upon in the separate *Units* and *Beats* of roles, where Vakhtangov's reformulations differed importantly from Stanislavski's approaches.

It's the contention of some of us that Vakhtangov's *Objects* offer the complete circuit of experience---both incoming and outgoing, while desired *Actions, Intentions* and *Objectives* offer only

10

action (whether *inner, outer* or both) until a sufficient number of other particularizing approach items are applied to them. What still receives little acknowledgement by those who faithfully teach Stanislaski's *Actions and Intentions* is the fact that so many of those action-particularizing, action-justifying and action-personalizing preparation items would upon closer examination essentially be *Inner Objects and Thought Objects!*

Precisely as Vakhtangov posited, each of those conditioning preparation items already exist before the action or intention is planned by the actor. The resulting action or intention must be put into final form with those pre-existing conditions in mind.

One other leading teacher, Hollywood's Eric Morris (who teaches and lectures in New York and other cities as well) put it nicely when he explained in an interview with Eva Mekler for her book *"The New Generation Of Acting Teachers"* that in his opinion Objectives, being based on what the character wants to do, are essentially *after the fact* and relate only to what the character's doing, not what makes it do it; that actors using Objectives are starting at the tail end, not the beginning. Vakhtangov would applaud its being put so well. Strasberg would agree. So would I.

But *Actions* and *Intentions* (and *Objectives,* as some teachers call them) were, and still remain in most teaching, the basic preparation items around which all the rest of the Stanislavski System revolves. Vakhtangov's *Objects* have thus far become the primary approach item of only a few of us.

Throughout this book, therefore---in spite of my deep conviction that Vakhtangov's *Inner Objects,* even more his *Thought Objects,* are the keys to making the Stanislavski System still more complete than it is in many others' teachings, I'll continually acknowledge my respect for those who with equally deep conviction have taught Stanislavski's *action and intention* approaches and have done so with skill and dedication.

■ **The Search Continues**

Returning to *Theories* in general, the life work of Lee Strasberg and those who now teach that broadly publicized teacher's instrument-conditioning exercises, as well as others who conduct their own types of exercises for *the accessing of the actor's inner resources and his ability to control his processes*---and those who *also teach exclusively the Stanislavski manners for the preparing of roles*---are and will always be important.

The theories of Stanislaski and Vakhtangov, and the approaches they've inspired in others, have become the matrix of present day actors' development and use of their talents.

What the reader must of course remember is that all of us---teachers, actors alike---are still searching. Were he alive, Stanislavski would still be searching. So would Vakhtangov. And so, in his own specialized areas, would Mr. Strasberg. The actor should take from yesterday's and today's systems what he finds works for him . . . and join the continuing search for what's still to be found.

*The Individual
Approach Items And Steps
Taught by Many Of
Today's Acting Teachers*

Actors Must Prepare

The Phases Of The Actor's Work On Roles and Self

If an actor tells you he's learned all he needs to learn, feel sorry for him. The actor's involvement with *preparation* never stops. First there's the necessity of preparing to *be* an actor in the first place. That can take place easily and quickly under some tutelages, or it can require the devoting of many years of working with other teachers. Next, and continuously throughout the actor's professional life, there's the constant task of preparing role after role in the most productive manner the actor knows.

Preparing to *be* an actor is considered by some to be the hardest, so first I'll discuss the simpler of the two...

Preparing a Role

There are three easily distinguished phases of the actor's work in preparing a role: *The Internal Work, The External Work,* and finally *The Creative Work.* Regardless of the methodology favored by a teacher, most teaching is divided into these three areas.

The *Internal Work* involves some manner of analyzing the behavior of the character, thereafter determining the personality and conditioning of the character that justifies and moves its behavior, its traits, its attitudes, its thoughts and its mental states, and justifies what the writer has the character do.

Whatever approach an actor may by choice employ in analysis of what the author has created for the character, there remains the task of forming the conclusions the analysis produces into a multi-level approach to bring the psychology and primary concerns of the character to continuous life with as much acutely personal feeling of truth for the actor as is possible.

The *External Work* involves the physical embodiment and behavior that results from the character's personality---the character's physical appearance; what the character does; the manner in which it does what it does; the use of the external stimuli provided by the author that create the character's scripted experience, its reactions and its problems; and the conditions---the given cirumstances---that must impact upon and particularize the moment to moment experience.

The *Creative Work* is the means by which the actor can decide what to focus upon, how the continuing motivations for the char-

14

acter can be caused to kindle desired responses in the actor, and how individual steps in the character's progress from first moments to last can be organized to produce truthful and ideally satisfying experiences for the actor while also engrossingly conveying the character's moments for the viewer.

The Actor's Work on Himself

Stanislavski's trilogy of books about the actor's processes---"An Actor Prepares", "Building A Character" and "Creating A Role"---deals with these three phases and more, one after another, in terms of (1) the actor's work on himself (preparing himself and his instrument as an actor), (2) starting to prepare characterizations, and (3) analyzing authors' intentions, justifying characters' participations in stories and then continuing to supply subtext experiences for characters throughout their entire stories.

Stanislavski dealt with many explicitly "training" phase items. Those approaches are still duplicated in hundreds of acting teachers' classes. Most teachers throughout America, Europe and elsewhere who work with beginning actors essentially follow the Stanislavski formulae, from time to time perhaps discovering some of their own exercises and approaches for accomplishing the same and perhaps some additional ends more rapidly.

Admittedly, each item has its value for a beginner who wants to be an actor and must start somewhere. But that beginner may not need to spend months, perhaps years, on "kindergarten" items---primarily taught to remind him of the desirability of regularly using them, and an actor beyond the beginning stage often becomes impatient with them when they're the substance of class after class as they are still today in the progressive Beginning, Intermediate and Advanced classes of some of the most celebrated teachers.

Acording to some who worked with both Stanislavski and Vakhtangov, Vakhtangov moved more swiftly with his students than Stanislavski did, because he found the key beyond action and---while remaining loyal to Stanislavski's teachings---emphasized the use of Inner and Thought Objects to quicken the development of the actor. There are teachers and coaches today who use those Inner and Thought Objects instead of Actions and Intentions (or in support of them, as Vakhtangov originally advocated) for that quicker development purpose.

However, since the acceptance and following of Stanislavki's Action approach is so widespread in the early training of actors it'll be described here---not literally in Stanislavski's terms but in Vakhtangov's version of them, since Stanislavski himself said "You, Eugene, teach my System better than I do."

15

Vakhtangov was less prolix, more succinct and precise. His descriptions of Stanislavski's (and his own) separate items under the three headings---*Internal Work, External Work* and *Creative Work*---are simpler for new actors to understand. They're what appear here, partially in Vakhtangov's own words, partially in descriptions by this author.

Relaxation

Many teachers down through the ages since Stanislavski and Vakhtangov have endorsed the theory about *Relaxation* that Vakhtangov defined ideally:

"A relaxed performer is better able to follow the precise instructions of his director and not become involved in extraneous, nervous movement. Relaxation and Concentration are often inseparable. Complete attention on or absorption in an object---sound, smell, feeling or thought---will automatically free the body of self-consciousness and tension."

Different teachers' recommendations and exercises for actors' achieving of relaxation are many and varied---as were Stanislavski's and Vakhtangov's. The reader will find some of them discussed in this book's chapter on *Relaxation,* some more in the *Freeing Of The Instrument* chapter.

Concentration

Again quoting Vakhtangov: *"An actor must have an object of attention every moment that he is on the stage. Concentration exercises develop the actor's ability to find that object quickly and then be carried away by it."*

Stanislavski's own *Objects of Attention* were postulated by him as primarily physical objects. That's what they were in 1906 and 1907 when he first focused his own attention on their importance and began advocating their use. That's how they essentially remained. That in the final years of his life he was becoming more convinced of the importance and power of the *Inner and Thought Objects* (at Vakhtangov's urging) is only modestly documented in his own writings that thus far appear in English.

Still today, many teachers conduct exercises in which their actors deal with only physical objects. Their inclusion of the Vakhtangov types of *Inner Objects* is detectably on the increase, but they're called *Objects* explicitly by only a few. (They can of course be labeled any number of things. The important thing is that they be recognized and used.)

Over the years more and more respect and attention have come for Vakhtangov's missing link, whatever it may now be called and in whatever manner it may become more prominently incorporated in process.

Sense Memory exercises with only *physical* objects can be so habit-forming that, as Theodore Hoffman wrote in 1960, decrying some "Method" fetishes, *"When a piece of business like lighting a cigarette or pouring a drink comes up, the play seems to stop while the actor carefully examines the cigarette to find out what brand it is or looks for germs on the glass."*

Sense memory exercises of that kind (from a Strasberg or similar class) can lead to actor behavior that makes the exercise (with an *Object of Attention* of strictly physical nature) the end rather than the means. Hoffman's comment has been paralleled by the comments of many others.

Vakhtangov meant far more! He knew that no amount of attempt at *concentration* on a *purely physical* object can create the same *complete personal experience* for the actor as concentration on an *Inner or Thought Object!*

Justification

This item is self-defining. Each thing the writer requires of the character---each speech, each concentration, each action, each hesitation, each handling of something---should be *justified* by the personality of the character, given circumstances of the moment, relationships to other characters, time of day, physical condition, perhaps even religious belief or political persuasion. whatever. Vakhtangov simply suggested selecting the most important from among the many *Thought Objects* that could apply and using it as the dominant source of involvement.

In fact it was in Vakhtangov's search for something to justify *desired actions*---because it was his conviction that actions should always be somehow justified---that his focus was drawn to the *Objects of Concentration.*

The preparation step of choosing and wording a *Justification* is of course left up to the actor. That there should be some kind of justification for any action or non-action is obvious. If an *Action or Intention* is the actor's choice, then so must be some *Justification.*

Circle of Attention

This is used to develop the ability to concentate on a small *"circle"* of attention, so that external distractions can be more easily ignored---i.e., the audience, self-conscious thoughts, etc.

Affective Memory

Literally---not only in the sense of an *"Emotional Recall"* or *"Emotional Memory"* exercise, but involved in those also, this item involves *Sense Memory* of bodily experience also, and most often requires the developing of the actor's sensory awareness to recall physical sensations and physical objects in order to more easily access the purely feeling and emotional experiences the object implies for the right brain.

The Task

Call it what you like---in Stanislavski's terminology, *Action* or *Intention,* in the actor's training it's invariably involved with the step of choosing and supplying the primarily external *why* and *how* for things to be done, whatever its label. This item is most often presented in class training in the form of a sequence of small, changing *actions* or *intentions.*

But in classes where Vakhtangov's and later versions of *Objects* are emphasized, this "task" comes so easily, in all its facets---if it (an action) in fact should come naturally at all---as a result of the actor's concentration being more fixed on the *cause and stimulus* for whatever task may be defined and whatever action may be taken toward its accomplishing.

The *Action* exercises of some leading coaches include such basic action wordings as "To talk", "To dream", "To argue", "To persuade", etc. At the risk of offending some teachers, I have to comment that with endless class hours taken up with these so generalized *actions,* then with the next steps of adding *Justifications and what all* to make those actions more specific, those kinds of exercises can protract students' learning cycles ad infinitum. Such generalized *actions* are so hopelessly lifeless, as Vakhtangov discovered, that they could well be completely bypassed rather than take up hours of class time!

Actors who've been in classes that have devoted much time to such kindergartenish *actions (tasks)* study almost never continue this step's use in their preparation later in professional life. They've learned---perhaps on their own, outside such classes---to move directly forward into action and intention wordings that have so much more evocative substance in their wordings.

Tempo / Rhythm

It long ago became apparent that *tempo* is something that evolves naturally from characterization or more often from external circumstances and, further, it's usually determined by the director---which is essentially how Stanislavski and Vakhtan-

18

gov actually saw it even then, and *rhythm* is a natural result of a prevalent style, surroundings, psychology, family role, calling or occupation, body condition, concentration upon an object of any kind, national and regional characteristics, and nature of scenes.

Of course, both *Tempo* and *Rhythm* explorations in acting classes can be diverting and revealing for actors in their observing of the particular variations produced by a slower or more rapid speech or movement pattern, for instance, or even the variations that result from more rapid or slower breathing patterns, as awareness exercises.

But these items aren't that often consciously explored by today's actors as an actual step in role preparation processes. Again, they're two of those items that, because Stanislavski wouldn't totally accept Vakhtangov's theories about *Object preceding and qualifying Action,* he spent so much time exploring for an answer of his own.

Strasberg employed the *rhythm* concept in his *"Song And Dance"* exercise---to train the actor's will through making the body do things that would go against its grain---against its conceptual and habit behavior. But it's the opinion of many teachers that any actor possessing developed sensitivity falls into the natural tempos and rhythms of a style, an event, a location, a body condition, concentration on an object of any kind, etc.

Communication

The actor who needs extensive class exercising in *verbal* communication should not aspire to becoming an actor. That's a "given" with most teachers, and it's rare for even a new, beginning actor to be asked to practice the art of *verbal* comunication in today's acting classes.

Non-verbal comunication is another matter. Most current acting teachers agree with the early precepts that *non-verbal* communication is not only important for a character but is also important in training the actor.

So many different kinds of roles require it. It's an important part of the training of an actor whether that actor be a beginner or an experienced professional who needs more development in this area.

"The eyes are the windows of the soul" is a common quotation with which most of us are familiar. We communicate with our eyes. There's also body communication, both voluntary and involuntary. There are many books on today's bookstore shelves about body communication. *Non-verbal* communication exists in almost every moment of life.

Public Solitude

While the initial explorations of what has come to be known more generally as the *"Private Moment"* (Strasberg's term) may have been somewhat primitive, they, like the present day Strasberg and other exercises they've generated, focused the actor on the many facets, the many small activities, the many brief experiences, the many truths that occured when actors observed themselves doing so many fairly unconscious things in private moments that were overlooked or consciously bypassed when the same things were done under the observation of others.

Whether such training in the exploring of *Private Moments* is conducted in the same manner as Strasberg employed it regularly throughout his work with actors (primarily in his private classes)---having actors do *Private Moments* of their own choosing in front of classes---or in some other manner, it's an important class exploration toward developing the actor's awareness and use of many real-life facets of simple moments that might otherwise never appear in his work. Its value as a classroom exercise lies mainly in that area.

Many of Stanislavski's exercises of the same genre are regularly taught in a majority of the present day coaching sessions.

For instance, many coaches employ *Animal Imagery* in its strictly animal form (as Stanislavski, Vakhtangov and Chekhov did) to help actors find in themselves the emotional ranges and different forms of experience, characterization and expression in animals' private moments that they might not find otherwise.

Used as that kind of class exploration, the actor combines the movements and body formation of the animal in a *private moment*, prompting the finding of many animal moments that can inspire parallel activities and involvements for human counterparts. The animal's observable feeling gamut and the thought processes connected with those feelings are explored. For this use in class, there is no translation of the different aspects into what they can inspire in human terms . (Animate imagery is a valuable "tool" in creating characters' embodiments as well, but here it's discussed in terms of its *private moment* use.)

Some Newer Manners of Aiding The Actor's Development

There are many other developmental classwork approaches aimed at expanding actors' access to more of their resources that have been developed by individual teachers in the more recent decades.

The New York teacher and praticing psychologist Michael Shulman, after studying with and then teaching for Strasberg, and after observing the unintentionally confidence-assaulting aspects of some of Strasberg's approaches and the scathing critiques that followed some actors' attempts with them (according to Mr. Schulman), now employs more *"Confidence Stimulus Exercises"*, wherein the actors use objects, people or events from their pasts to make them feel strong and confident and help them eradicate tenseness produced by fear and achieve relaxation.

Eric Morris, a leading Hollywood teacher for many years, has formulated many, many exercises to free actors from what he terms their *Instrumental Blocks*. Just a few examples: For a conflict-shy person, an *"Accuse and Indict"* exercise, or a *"You Never Gave Me"* exercise. The actor picks a person out of the past or current life toward whom resentment is deeply felt, stands before the class and accuses the imaginary person. To free the emotions of someone who keeps deep feelings locked inside, there's Eric's *"Dump"* or one of his other original exercises, in which the actor expresses aloud his feelings of frustration and suppressed anger until he feels his emotions flowing out with no obstruction.

Like Michael Shulman and others of us, he recognizes the need of actors for a support system for the ego. He offers his *"Count Your Blessings"* exercise to counteract an actor's natural feelings of inadequacy or shorcomings. The actor recites before the class his good points, and in the process comes to value them more himself. And Mr. Morris has literally hundreds of other such exercises designed to effectively reduce or totally eliminate blockages and offer ego support.

Some of us periodically now use group sociological games of the self realization types recommended by noted psychologists, such as are conducted at Esalen Institute at Big Sur, California, and some of the Ford Foundation Psychotherapy Groups.

I personally favor one called *"I'm the best person in this room because..."* in which a group of people (who in my own judgment should know each other fairly well by the time this game is appropriate) sits around in a circle. One member says that phrase, finishing it with just a few brief words that state some attribute he or she feels offers justification for that *"best person"* distinction . . . perhaps *"I'm considerate of others."*

The person to the actor's right looks into the "best person's" eyes steadily as he or she tells the "best person" what he or she assumes (from acquaintance and observation over a period) the "best person" *really means behind those few words.* The *"best person"* doesn't respond, simply listens. The guessing by all participants continues around the circle, one after another, each participant looking steadily into the eyes of the *"best person"* as each new interpretation is offered of what *"I'm considerate of others"* means to the *"best person"*.

21

The *"best person"* hears many observations from others as to their insights into what he or she has claimed as his or her good point, those observations in some cases offering far more than he or she has thought others could possibly observe. When all in the circle have offered their observations the "best" person has received soul-gratifying assurance that often brings tears streaming from increased self acceptance during the more insighted of those individual observations.

I've found the opposite of the *"best person"* ---the *"worst person"*---just as ego-strengthening. The same procedure is followed. As others' interpretations are received, eye to eye, with the many different insights as to what the *"worst person"* really means in self-judging, often self-critical terms by the words stated, many reassurances are received by the confessor that (in their individual interpretations) others in the circle quite clearly see the self-misjudgment and needless concerns and easily accept them.

In New York, Terry Schreiber has said that he uses what he calls his *"Phrase Exercise"*, in which the actor stands on the stage and Terry, as he sees things on the actor's face, puts what they appear to indicate into phrases like *"I'm scared,"* *"I'm a little boy,"* *"I don't want to be here,"* etc. This often progresses to phrases like *"I don't know,"* *"I can't,"* etc. From that progressive point, as the mask is eroded, come expressions and experiences for the actor that produce phrases like *"Hold me, daddy,"* *"Love me, mommy,"* etc. The fear of self revelation is diminished.

Terry uses this exercise to help actors open up in front of others and share more of themselves, to find the freedom to do that without fear of being judged as weak or cowardly or a bad person. It's designed to give the actor courage.

The point of these class experiences, when they appear to be needed by a sufficient number of the class members, is that actors are vulnerable and self-doubting and those frailties are often exacerbated in the critical development processes of acting classes.

While Strasberg's exercises were so often aimed at the same result, his own fierce pedagogical control and even criticism of results when they did come (especially if he felt they were found in a manner not to his liking) produced the opposite result in many of the actors he was trying in his own way to help escape from their fears. (This comment is not solely this author's. It's been observed and spoken of by many others.)

There are many directly supportive teachers on the scene now who recognize that the actor's own unique and vulnerable experience and its discovery and release, rather than the manner of simply doing an exercise, is what's important. Those who observe this fact of actors' natures often devise their own exercises.

An approach this author has found wonderfully effective for helping actors rekindle and bring to the surface without fear of judgment those vulnerable, self-critical aspects that they've hidden for survival is to require them to work with self-critical *Objects* (of the Vakhtangov kind, but in contemporary street words) on the order of *"How weak I am," "My f---g clumsiness," "How f---ed up I am,"* etc., in improvising situations with other actors, after building their characters' personalities around those *Thought Objects* and then experiencing those unique personality colors while improvising.   (Note: Many of the actors who need this kind of work speak in the vocabularies indicated.)

In dredging up these inner experiences that they've shoved into hiding places in themselves for much of their mature lives many swaggering macho athletes and efficiency-expert hardheads have found easy tears and other habitually suppressed inner vulnerabilities in improvisations with personalities based on those hidden wellsprings of feeling, then have observed other class members' approval or acceptance of their hidden monsters, and quickly found for themselves the values of allowing to the surface some of the human imperfections that lie behind most of our facades.

In one of my classes devoted to releasing actors' suppressed vulnerabilities in that manner, one of the aforementioned macho type actors (who at the time played and still currently plays mostly hard and threatening characters in top roles) fell to his knees with tears streaming down his cheeks after such an improvisation, mumbling *"I haven't felt like that since I was a little kid."*

Another exceedingly tough nut to crack comes to mind. I'm sure my good friend "Boots" Southerland won't mind my telling of his experience in some of these classes.

A former stuntman and originally a bit player in films constantly sought by location directors when filming in his native New Mexico because he fearlessly risked life and limb in every job, "Boots" brought his tough, domineering and quick-on-the-trigger machoism into his classes with me for a long time before I could force him (by implying the threat of expulsion from class!) to work with those four-letter-word-sprinkled, self-critical and self-hating *Objects* mentioned above to encourage his finding and using his secret vulnerabilities to expand his role potentials.

The result was a swift and stunning freeing of those other dimensions of talent that he couldn't have found otherwise. Today his roles are continually enlarging, and they're acting roles. We both chuckle at the memories of his early period with me. He's still the same tough "Boots", but he enjoys bringing much more human vulnerability to his roles now too.

■ Here's a standard item that's only now being reconsidered by some . . . granted, not by many, but some!

Actions And Intentions

A Reexamination of Their Use

This chapter's title itself---implying that it's even remotely possible there might be some justification for any reexamination at all---will no doubt offend the actor who's been taught that an *Action* or *Intention* is the most important "tool" of an acting technique, as Stanislavski for most of his life considered it to be. The greatest number of acting teachers still accept that premise, so it's presumptuous to even suggest an alternative, but some of us now feel that the *Action's* superiority over all else among approaches is (unconsciously) fiction instead of fact.

Director-teacher Robert Lewis's short, to the point definition of *Intention* (his personally preferred term) is: *What you are really doing inside at any given moment, regardless of what you are saying or doing physically.* Slightly paraphrased here, M r. Lewis's definition is what an *Action* or *Intention* should certainly be.

M r. Lewis and others who advocate *Actions* or *Intentions* (as Stanislavski did) generally agree that in application it must be expressed in terms of a verb, perhaps following *"I wish to . . ."* He and others appropriately advise that the way in which you state the intention to yourself should derive from elements of the character. He and the best among other teachers also encourage actors to choose and put to themselves *imaginatively and interestingly worded* intentions. Excellent advice, all of it.

However, this book will offer both the conditioned skeptic and the willing listener a still revolutionary but wonderful alternative. It was urged upon Stanislavski by Eugene Vakhtangov--- *Objects.* A lot of us wish Stanislavski had himself finally championed it publicly.

An interesting footnote to the manner in which Robert Lewis teaches *Intentions* is expressed by him in essentially the following words: *"You must be sure you direct your intention toward some object, whether concrete or abstract . . . use transitive verbs (verbs that take objects)."*

You see? Those of us who advocate the more central use of *Objects* aren't really so different; we're simply more convinced that such *Objects* should precede the *Intention or Action* they occasion. To suggest action, they surely had to be there first.

24

Lee Strasberg is recorded on tape saying *"Objects can be mental or thought objects, or fantasy objects. They can be situations, or events, or relationships, or characters---or elements of these things---as created by the playwright. Through concentration the actor brings these things alive for himself . . . The properly trained actor learns to depend not just on technique or approach but on a variety and sequence of objects."*

Ever since the 1940's, in the classes of most of the most noted American teachers who most closely follow Stanislavski's codifications, actors have begun their study with actions like "To talk", "To chat," "To fight", "To explain," "To teach", "To advise", etc. Those teachers have spent many class sessions with actors exploring variations of those simplistic "beginner" tools. It's a "beginning step" that many of us have found unnecessary.

Also formulated by Stanislavski were *"Physical* Actions" and *"Psychological* Actions" . . . the former being tiny, very brief and quickly executed actions that (when strung together in sequence) were designed to move a character from Point A to Point B in a scene; the latter being goal-directed desires that linger in the mind and determine a character's behavior toward other characters and his surroundings throughout continuing sequences of those small Physical Actions.

The *"Through Line* Of Action", which Stanislavski first recognized with any impact in 1914, was prescribed by him for either an entire role (his most frequently advocated application of the tool)---to serve the author's intention throughout the role, or (less frequently recommended by him) for the separate Units of a role, where the basic given circumstances experience changes and one action after another, strung together in sequence, establish a *Through Line* for the duration of those Units.

"Action" became the key word and the hallmark of the Stanislavski System. One must grant that the overwhelming majority of teachers and actors, still today, consider it *the cornerstone of the Stanislavski System* and of their own systems. Some call it *"Intention"*, but by its nature it's the same tool.

There's an essential connecting link between an *Action* and an *Object,* certainly. As modern behavioral science confirms and Robert Lewis advocates, in the experience of the character even a *desired* action involves and should be the result of some tangible stimulus---some *feeling experience about something* that prompts the desire to take action.

Therefore, *what causes action* might more evocatively occur *before* action, often continuously *during* it, and equally often *instead of it.* An increasing number of us believe and teach the latter---that the *Object* should often be used for the total experience it provides *instead of* an *Action!* We observe some other teachers gradually coming around to the same conclusion, but *Action and Intention* remain thus far the dominant choices.

Vakhtangov simply postulated the use of *Objects before* Actions--as their stimuli. He understood that an action of any kind, unless it's a simple *re*-action or involuntary response, is certainly in all instances the result of a decision---of the actor in preparing it for use, therefore of the character too, but for the character it's generally made *as the result of a problem or other type of stimulus* that should (therefore) precede it!

Skipping the sometimes brief but more often protracted moments of enduring a problem that should *precede* any important action decision is skipping some of the actor's richest experience as his character. In the judgment of some of us, actions eventually decided and taken by the character offer so much less.

Vakhtangov taught that if the actor focused on the *problem, the experience,* both before any action at all could be decided and taken, and during whatever action results, the entire sequence--- including any action taken or intensely desired---would be illuminated with a more complete experiencing, since the problem would still be there as the primary experience for as long as the action needs to be attempted.

Also, what many who believe in and use the *Affective Memory* exercise (perhaps even ideally) apparently haven't correlated in their mind is the significance of the form of the *"key"* or *"trigger"* that's found to reevoke the *Affective Memory* (like other experiences) for them. Isn't it almost always, really, some *Object?* ---some aroma, some tactile sensation, some sound, etc.?

Over the many years since Vakhtangov's untimely death in 1922, most exclusively *"Action"*-trained actors have spent many years of their training and early professional work knowing deep down that "something was still missing"; that the right brain feeling of *true experience* too often remained untapped in their performances. Many have never found the solution.

An "action"---no matter how skillfully or even creatively prepared by the actor---is by its very nature *goal-directed.* It's worded so as to attempt to *do something.* By its very nature, it's aimed like an arrow at the bull's eye of a target. And in the straight line or arc of an arrow's flight or a bullet's trajectory *there's no time to experience much but the action!*

Also, the actor's "action" requires *continuous conscious direction* toward its desired result . . . mostly left brain direction(!), involving less the right brain where *feelings* could be generated and tapped for the richer human experience of the character.

26

Even with a bushel basketful of *Justifications, Circum-stances, Substitutions, Personalizations, Body Conditions, Urgent Situations* or whatever else a particular teacher chooses to call those qualifiers and particularizers that are required in order to breathe more specific and more meaningful life into the *Action,* in the choice of wording or in its use by a less sensitive actor it can fall far short of a complete experience if the *Action or Intention* itself remains the prime focus.

The "action"-trained actor also too often forms (in some teaching of its use)---and later can't rid himself of---the limiting habit of working *directly toward* and often *eye-to-eye* with other actors, simply because of trying to *get something from* or *do something to* others' characters. Such an acting habit has to be eradicated . . . if by then it's still possible . . . before even attempting any outstanding professional work.

Even in theatre roles---but still more definitely for film and television cameras, the actor must often work f*acing away from* other characters. Some *action*-trained actors aren't comfortable with those moments, feeling something lacking---the other person, since the other person is too often (in *Action* and *Intention* training) actually the *Object of the Action.*

In most roles there are many moments that require looking at problems (because they dominate the character's conscious thought and concentration), describing things (which ideally need to be looked at in the imagination in order to describe them), etc. Marlon Brando asserted that he preferred *"looking at my character's problems; they're more important."*

The "action" actor often has trouble with those moments---out of habit feeling the need of *ascribing some kind of action to those moments,* being so indoctrinated with the need to *take some kind of predetermined action*---in doing so, bypassing the moments of *experiencing.* These *aren't action moments!* They're strictly *"being done to"* moments, with which some action-trained actors aren't all that acquainted.

Haven't you also noted that some *action*-oriented actors are too often really in the *next moment* instead of even for a brief moment experiencing *this moment?* They're too often working determinedly to *get something done* or *find a solution* for something.

Their concentration is so often firmly fixed on the "target"---the result to be desired, the solution to be achieved---in the *next moment* that they're distracted from what's happening *right now.* What a barren and troubling wasteland this manner of working must be for the actor who hasn't devised his own way of giving these kinds of moments their life!

27

The best suggestion one can offer the too exclusively *action*-trained actor is that he or she start searching out the venues where some manner of *problem-experiencing via Objects,* rather than *problem-solving with Actions,* can be learned, practiced and developed as habit.

Whatever form of problem experience exists, I for one teach that it should productively dominate and overwhelm, affording the actor an experience, the character an opportunity to suffer it, and the viewer an opportunity to vicariously experience those facets which they know from their own life experiences accompany such moments more than does the taking of action.

Whether what dominates these moments is called a *Problem* (as it is in some coaches' terminologies), a *Given Circumstance* (as it is in some others'), an *Obstacle* (as it is in some) or an *Object* (as in still others'), or simply spelled out by the actor in whatever manner may be preferred for the focusing of his thoughts . . . . *it* provides the ultimate experience for the actor.

The *Object* provides in its ideal wording (1) *the character's unique personality colors,* (2) its *characteristic words and sentiments,* (3) its *reactive stimuli,* and (4) *opportunity to fully experience those frustrations, irritations, angers, suffocations, disorientations, etc. that it generates*---which many of us feel the simple situation and an *action* approach can't provide without the help of several additional preparation items.

■ **Following is an "Action" approach that almost all teachers agree actors should know about . . .**

Action Verbs

An Application of Action That Works Sensationally

Watching Jack Nicholson's unforgettable performance in the movie *"A Few Good Men"*---with his constantly violent, spitting, snapping domineering and overkill in the face of any confrontation or challenging of his authority, there's little possibility that he wasn't using some kind of inspired *Action Verb*---not just for individual moments of that role but probably also as a manner of bringing the total psychology of the character.

Mr. Nicholson is an actor who can take chances. Often they're far out chances. He's able to pull every one of them off admirably.

Nicholson defies categorization. That he apparently employs his own versions of many of the approaches that may have

28

been suggested by others is obvious, but through his own unique, extraordinarily brilliant and creative mind, body and feeling resources, they come to full bloom in every character he plays. "*A Few Good Men*" offered one more stunning example of his art.

His work epitomizes what can be achieved when an actor has planned a character so completely, so personally and so creatively that it can dare to let its wildest inner animals loose on its surface, running rampant without any apparent control.

But there *is* control in Nicholson's work. And in that performance of *"A Few Good Men"* there was something else---always there and apparently in conscious use as a manner of personifying the evil of the man in any confrontation.

Remember the unbelieveable amount of venom he spat at others in those moments? That's an example of what a specific *Action Verb* can accomplish. (Remember, we're not talking about simple *Action* here. An *Action Verb*---at least in the hands of a consummate actor like Nicholson---is something far more specific and far more creative in its results.)

Action-trained actors are early taught the difference between *generalized* verbs and their more specific, body-stimulating *Action Verb* forms. If they're sufficiently perceptive, they learn that if the character's mind wants to "get" something---even though that's also an action, the body will be moved more definitely if it's told to *suck in, grab out, squeeze up, yank in* or *sponge up* (action verbs) whatever is desired.

The same actors are taught that if the character wants to "keep from" something---though that too, although general, is an action, the body will be moved more definitely if told to *throw off, curl away, knock out* or *squeeze down* (action verbs) whatever it is the character wants to avoid.

Action verbs can be very illuminating as to characters' total inner responses to external stimuli in the individual, brief moments of roles----even as clear indications of psychology for entire roles---through the *body response stimuli* they provide. *Action Verbs* unquestionably indicate an *Object* being dealt with! They're the exceptions to our bias against pure *action* tools.

An *Action Verb* can admirably aid in creating the external, physical manifestation of an inner thought or feeling experience, but if an *Action Verb* is to serve the actor over any protracted period of time it should at least be combined with and aimed at some object---at least in the object's *literal* form---that it's chosen to deal with. One might "Squeeze out the shame" or "Yank up some recognition".

Better still, the *Action Verb* can be combined with a *definite Inner or FeelingThought Object,* resulting in a more feeling evoking and physically interesting "action"---yes, it's still an "action"---like *"Squeeze out the biting shadow"* or *"Curl in the sparkling perfume"* or some other *desired action* phrase that includes the *Feeling Thought Object* to create the complete experience in a more colorful form. (See the *Creative Psychological Objectives* chapter for action verb / inner object combinations.)

Adding a feeling-based *Inner Object*, the actor's mind can focus on the many facets of *it* and the body will respond organically in the action verb manner without distracting the actor from his scenic surroundings . . . because the *Object truly is* what the character is focusing upon in the scenic surroundings. An *Action or Intention* would mean far less without it!

Watching Nicholson's performance in the aforementioned film, one couldn't help noting that there appeared to be some kind of very specific object or image at which his action verb was characteristically directed---probably the same object or image, whether in some specific form or not, throughout the entire role. The actor should always know in his mind *what the action verb is aimed at!* (Remember Robert Lewis's apt quote.)

Whether recoiling from a rattlesnake or yearning toward a beautiful sunset, who among us would have our mind more on our recoiling than on the rattlesnake, or on our yearning more than on the beautiful sunset? Rattlesnakes and sunsets are *Objects.* They're also available and highly effective *Inner Objects* for other simply factual things.

In some circumstances the "action verb" has been found to be an expedient boon for directors, either when dealing with a less than ideally expressive actor or actress and wanting some visible manifestation which the actor can't otherwise provide or when simply desiring a physical response he himself has envisioned.

Paul Newman, some years ago, in describing his experience in directing Joanne Woodward (Mrs. Newman) in *"Rachel, Rachel"*, explained to an interviewer that if he suggested Joanne "squeeze in" the inner experience of a moment Miss Woodward was such an extraordinarily gifted actress that her lips would purse, her body would contract and even her toes would curl.

Other directors familiar with *Action Verbs* from early training often use them in similar manners when directing cast members in both theatre and film roles. They communicate quickly and directely to the point.

Most of us who appreciate the difference between the "Object" experience and the "Action" experience also abjure too much dependency upon action verbs as a whole because of their limiting effects on so many actors' total instruments (Jack Nicholson's instrument certainly excepted) and their being too often employed by action-trained actors *without the "Objects"*---whether you call them "Objects" or something else--- *that may have been the stimuli suggesting their use.*

■ **Another item that most teachers recommend enthusiastically. . .**

Activities

Both Conscious and Apparently Unconscious Ones can be Productive

How often we see a character played by an actor with everything so neatly and appropriately planned and executed, and with nothing happening in even a single moment of the performance that hasn't been supplied or suggested by the writer. In such a performance there's just one thing missing . . . *real life!*

The time is long past for such skeletal representation of life as was characteristic of many of the melodramas and many actors of the Victorian and Eduardian eras.

How much more interesting to observe---than an actor in a role simply standing or sitting in conversation exchange moments, whether they be quiet and calm or even highly agitated--- is an actor who's doing something that appears either totally unconscious or at least not story-furthering per se, and perhaps even appearing a bit distracting to the character itself.

Writers and Directors shouldn't have to think of all these truly human activities that are part of life. The actor can certainly come up with some of them very easily if the actor remembers that *this moment* is not only *this moment* for the character. There are the "magic three" realities ready and waiting for the actor to consider them for inspirations:

Some coaches call them *The Moment Before, This Moment and The Next Moment.* Others call them *Yesterday, Today and Tomorrow.* Still others, more literally oriented, call them *"Where I've just come from," "What I'm doing here,"* and *"What I'm going to do later."* They're still the "magic three", and all actors should consider them part of any total scenic reality.

There's no moment in life when all three or at least two of them aren't hovering at the edge of our concentration, tugging at out attention! *Yesterday* or *The Moment Before* can provide the actor with inspiration of a headache or backache from work, a letter in the pocket forgotten to be mailed, a car pool driver to be waved at when entering, irritation at being held up in a traffic jam, coming from an unpleasant experience or disturbing news,

31

coming in from jogging, stuffing change in a pocket after paying the taxi, out of breath from climbing the stairs. cleaning glasses after they've been fogged by smog, tired after the day's work, finishing a hot dog grabbed on the way home, etc.

In one of the progressive steps of his *"Repetition"* procedure Sandy Meisner supplies or has the actors come up with extremely urgent activities that they've arrived with and must accomplish as previous (usually calmer) improvisations are repeated with those urgent circumstances distracting and obstructing them.

Very productive for an actor are both *Today* and *Tomorrow; This Moment and the NextUpcoming Moment.* Writers don't always suggest so many of those possibilities.

A restaurant waitress, talking with her spouse after coming home from work at night, probably has tired feet in *this moment* that suggest taking off her shoes and rubbing them; has a tired body that needs to loosen its clothing to relax; has hair that wants to be let down out of the bun required at work; has a back that aches . . .

She might have coins and folding money in a pocket from tips received and not yet counted; maybe has a headache from the noisy restaurant; might find a spot from spilling something on her uniform; has a uniform that feels sticky to the body from perspiring at work; and many more possible items from *Today.*

For the same waitress, her uniform must be protected in *this moment* from wrinkle-pressing when she sits down because she's wearing it *tomorrow;* her shoes may need spit-polishing for *the next day;* she may need to put rollers into her hair for combing out *in the morning;* and there are any number of other things that *Tomorrow* can suggest.

The actor needs only consider the *Yesterday, Today* and *Tomorrow* of the character ---or some other three step label connoting the same items---to be inspired with so many seemingly unconscious activities to enrich the passing moments of a role!

■ **Still another approach that most of us offer in classes . . .**

Animate Images

and Other Available Non-Human Sources

of Experience and Inspiration

If the actor's ever been asked in an acting class to be a wormy apple, a cool glass of milk or a tree---any *inanimate* object, he or she should have been told that it was a *sensitizing, perhaps a sense memory or "communion with an object" exercise* first and foremost.

It probably wasn't being presented as a characterization tool in such an acting class experience, but instead was aimed to help the class members become the kind of people who wouldn't have to tell jokes about going to an acting class and being asked to be a wormy apple, a cool glass of milk or a tree.

Stanislavski tried *inanimate* imagery exercises of that sort in the beginning too. There's a section in his book of first explorations, *"An Actor Prepares"*, devoted to using a tree as an image. But he soon reduced the amount of exploration of such *inanimate* imagery and began to teach what's presently used on occasion by many fine actors and actresses for inspiration of specific character externals. Although they may be called *"Character Images"* or *"Animal Images"*, they should more aptly be called *"Animate Images"*. Such imagery isn't limited to only *animals!*

There are of course all kinds animals, but also amphibians, arachnids (spiders), reptiles, insects, crustaceans, feathered birds and fowl, marsupials, bats, etc.

Most readers who've attended any acting classes at all have encountered this item. It's one of the most universally used, still today, of all the *External Characterization* and *Awareness-Expanding* explorations.

Experiencing As The Animal Itself

One use of Animate Imagery is to devote classroom exercise time to exploring and miming the actual form and movements--- as closely as the human body's limitations allow---of one of these categories of animate beings (mammals, birds, insects, reptiles, crustaceans, arachnids, fish, rodents, amphibians, marsupials, etc.). The list of availables is almost limitless.

If you're taught to explore animate images in this manner it's probable that the teacher has in mind the expansion of your processes into feelings and behavior areas of more varied experience forms. The teacher may have felt that you needed to be reacquainted with some of the experience of the animal inside yourself. Perhaps you needed more survival-feeling intensification similar to the animal's feeling responses.

Or perhaps exercising in this manner was to help you find certain feelings which had been strange to you and not detected by the teacher in your work---feelings and emotions which you'd be able to more easily associate with the animate image and had not previously realized could be productive in your work as well.

33

A large number of us teach this item as an *External Characterization* tool too . . . and consider it one of the best.

As Source for External Characterization Inspirations

Many of us now teach that, perhaps at that point just beyond forming your character's personality, if you think an animate image may help inspire more interesting *external* colors for it you can decide upon one to use and, after itemizing all the characteristics you can think of that are common to that animate being, skillfully translate each item, or at least as many as possible, into an external that's appropriate for your human character.

A classic example, Charlie Chaplin's very apparent *penguin* image comes to mind. Also Groucho Marx's bent over walk with arms (wings) flying and with the cigar in his mouth (the bill of a duck)! Any who saw the old television show he headed remembers that after basing his externals on a duck he even conceived of the limp duck that would drop out of the air on cue. I'll use Charlie Chaplin's as an example, because it's such a good one:

The baggy pants inspired by the pear-shaped body of the penguin . . . The feet pointed outward duplicating the webbed feet also pointed outward and creating the waddling walk . . . The big, tattered old shoes taken from the large penguin feet and their webbing . . . The beak, with some ingenious thinking, became the cane and its pecular manner of being carried pointed forward, much like a beak . . . The little spit curls on the forehead were inspired by the nostrils on the side of the penguin's beak . . .

The wardrobe was chosen for the penguin's colors . . . The head movement resembled the penguin's . . . The "after-wiggling" upon sitting came from the penguin's habit of settling its feathers! A touch here, a touch there . . . all adding up to that unforgettable total image that made "the little tramp" so memorable!

There are a number of actors and actresses who claim that they often at least consider an animate image when they're conceptualizing the externals for a role. A few have gone so far as to say that they *always* use one to bring added inspirations for far more interesting colors for their portrayals than they might otherwise be able to think of.

Movements, wardrobe, sounds, makeup, hairstyle, props, body habits, little activities and manners of doing ordinary tasks in unique manners can all be inspired by a productive animate image. Even feelings themselves can be adapted, and if the image is well chosen thousands of mannerisms of the image will apply excellently with very little adaptation into human form if combined with good taste and good judgment by the actor.

The inspiration sources from an animate being used as the character's image can include *covering* (fur, feathers, scales, shell, etc.)---which may vary at different points on the image's body, remember . . . *extremities* (wings, claws, paws, fins, tendrils, tails, etc.); *head shape* (bills, jaws, teeth, facial markings, ears, hair, etc.); *characteristic body positions and movement patterns* (standing, sitting, walking, lying down); *typical pastimes and body habits* (preening, scratching fleas, etc.); *sounds, especially:* (clucking, growling, purring, crowing, hissing, etc.); even *items with which they're usually surrounded or with which they're usually involved* ; etc., etc.

While there's a tendency on the part of actors to more often think of applying animate imagery to classics such as Shakespeare, Moliere, Ibsen, some of Chekov, etc., there's no reason to limit its use to such style and period works. Contemporary characters of all kinds can often benefit equally from the use of animate images, as long as some subtlety is applied to the adapting of the characteristics of the image into strictly human form.

A word of caution: *Sounds* adapted from the image are often mishandled by people who are new to the use of this tool. We *shouldn't sound exactly like the image.* Instead we should use the snarl of the image, for example, to inspire a cold in the nose; the soft growl to inspire a tired groan that recurs; the woodpecker's pecking to inspire a tongue-clicking habit or fingernail-tapping; the dog's bark to suggest a hacking cough. Then sounds are no problem.   No audience member should ever be overheard saying "She's a hen" when she's supposed to be a nervous secretary!

It's always wise to practice all physical movements and any sounds adapted from the image, to tailor them into very believable human forms that don't even remotely suggest their source.

A Couple of Examples

Here are two examples of how many inspirations can be gleaned from the use of an animate image by first considering the image, then listing all the charateristics we can think of and then finally translating as many of its characteristics as are productive into human form.

Let's say a truck driver is to arrive home from the road one winter evening in a scene, sit around drinking beer, relaxing and listening to his wife telling the children's news. Maybe that's all the writer has provided. It could be pretty dull. But suppose the actor seeking the most appropriate and most productive animate image---knowing that the many inspirations to be found through its use can make the character much more interesting---decides to use a lazy brown bear in its zoo enclosure.

35

First, he lists all the characteristics, one after another, that he can think of. To avoid limiting himself to a few, he remains exclusively fixed on simply *listing the bear's characteristics* until he feels his list is complete with all possible items available for considering there in front of him. When that list of simply the animate image's characteristics is complete . . .

. . .he considers each and every item to find a possible adaptation of it into a *strictly human* attribute. The list, prepared totally first, and the inspirations gleaned one after another from the listed items later, might wind up like this:

Body Covering: Brown, Matted Fur . . . A thick brown pile jacket and dirty brown pants. *White Spot on Chest* . . . A thick white winter scarf. *Ruff around the Neck* . . . Jacket buttoned closed and a big collar turned up . . .

Extremities: Furry Legs and Claws . . . Thick gloves for driving, with some fingers tattered, inspired by the bear's claws; heavy boots inspired by the thick legs . . .

Head Conformation: Long, Pointed Nose . . . A billed cap, also brown. *Small, Pointed Ears* . . . The winter cap could be ear-flapped, with the flaps up from the ears as truckmen sometimes wear them. *Small, Beady Eyes* . . . Small eyeglasses for looking over the mail that's come since he left on the trip. *Messy Fur on Top of Head* . . . Greasy, mussed hair pulled back by the cap and scraggly-ended . . .

Body Positions and Movement Patterns: *Lying back with legs spread wide* . . . Sitting spraddle-legged and slumped in that position. *Holds Things in Both Paws*. . . Holding the beer can in that manner at times. *Lies on Side* . . . Position to lounge in some of the time to listen to his wife's account. *Heavy, Lumbering Walk*. . . Same for the driver. *Head Rolling From Side To Side* . . . A manner of reacting to what he hears about the children. *Swats with Paws* . . . An adapted gesture carefully used some of the time in reaction . . .

Sounds: The Growl and The Roar. . . Heavy "tired" and similar throat sounds. A throat-clearing habit. Noisy throat sound with nose-blowing. Soft growling or groaning as he checks some of the mail that's come or hears something about the children . . .

Body Habits: Scratching . . .Rubbing stomach. Rubbing the stubble on his unshaven face after several nights on the road . . .

Of course the bear's *Tail* would have been listed, and it might suggest for this role something like a greasy rag hanging from a rear pocket (maybe an amount showing as is suggested by the bear's tail), of the type truck drivers carry for handling the oily and greasy parts of their truck. But this tail and all other tails in imagery warrant special discussion:

Tails of the many different kinds often prompt new users of imagery (who don't know better) to have belts tied in back with an end hanging down or something of that sort. Since it's highly unusual for anyone to tie a sash or buckle a belt in the back---and especially to let an end hang down obviously---such use is ill-advised. Care should always be taken to turn a tail into something which is absolutely appropriate to be found in that same location for a human, just like all the other items. Again, the actor in the above case would not want an audience member to be overheard saying *"He's a bear!"*

A second character might be a perpetually busy and worried female clerk in an outer office. After some body improvising with the patterns and movements of hurried and nervous clerks, perhaps the actress preparing the role decides on a Plymouth Rock, henhouse breed of laying hen. The hen may have come to mind in the spread-winged, hurried movement pattern moments of the hen, not the moments of sitting on a nest, although those moments are available for inspiration source material as well. The following ideas, plus many more, might be found:

Body Covering: Mottled Grey Feathers . . . Grey or mottled sweater and skirt, or tiny print, grey-tones dress . . .

Body Conformation of a Hen . . . When sitting, doing so in a manner that makes her dress bunch up like a hen . . .

Extremities: Light Yellow, Scaly, Bumpy Legs . . . Light, maybe even yellow-toned stockings with a few wrinkles. Perhaps a wrist-length sleeved dress if not a sweater. If a sweater, it could be rolled up on the wrists to where the feathers might begin on legs. *The Spread-Clawed Feet* . . . All fingers spread with worry as the woman works under self-imposed pressure. *Wings* . . . Arms extended worriedly as she scurries around . . .

Head: The Beak . . .Perhaps a small yellow pencil stub in her mouth at times. *Red Crest on Top* . . . One or two ribbons or a red comb near the top of the hair. *Shorter Feathers on Top of Head* . . . Simple, short hairdo close to the head and maybe pompadoured back. *Small, Round Eyes* . . . Perhaps a pair of small granny glasses for working or some manner of eye makeup. . .

Body Positions and Movement Patterns: Head Looking Down for Grain . . . Head bent out over desk much of the time. *Head Cocks Up in Excitement* . . . Same. *Nest Sitting* . . . Leaned forward nervously with arms lowered to sides and a little to the rear, perhaps clasped on chair in nervousness, as she pores over papers anxiously or checks her paperwork. *Waddle Walk* . . . Waddling, but subtly adapted. *Running* . . . Arms out at sides. *Arranges Feathers when Sitting* . . . Nervous arranging of her dress when sitting down.

Pecking for Food . . . Bobbing head with others' talking or even in silent thinking moments; leaning far forward over the typewriter or paperwork like a hen searching for something to peck at; bobbing the head as papers are scanned word by word; perhaps nearsightedness from too much office work . . .

Sounds: Clucking . . . Private thinking sounds like palate-tonguing. *Cackle* . . . Sounds of detail paranoia occasionally. *Cackling when Disturbed* . . .When buzzed to come to the boss's office, making paranoid sounds from worry and insecurity about pencil, pad, work disturbed, etc.

Habits: Picking at Feathers . . . Constantly rearranging of a bodice or a pin and looking down at it, or using a chest-pocket pen or pencil and having to look for it often. *Constant Blinking of Eyes* . . . Occasional shutting of eyes, then opening them wide, cleared. *Cackling and Body Fidgeting when Laying an Egg and Just Afterward* . . . Little cackles when possible to provoke them legitimately, then self-conscious shifting of the body back into a settled position in chair out of embarassment . . .

Usual Surrounding Items: Straw Nest . . . Maybe a light colored pillow on chair for settling onto. *Chicken Feed Pan* . . . A planter on desk, which she mutters to occasionally and putters with absentmindedly, peering closely at each small plant one after another like a chicken selecting which morsel to pick at. It's good to not overlook these *Usual Surrounding Items.*

The imaginative actress might find even more little or big inspirations for character externals, and be very proud of the extra colorful aspects they would bring over and above the emotional preparation for the character's personality and moment to moment life.

The quality of result gained by the actor from the exploring and use of an *Animate Image* depends on the amount of close attention to available details and the quality of imagination the actor applies to the human form translations.

■ **There are effective and ineffective manners of handling . . .**

Beats
What They Are . . . and Aren't

In almost any class the actor attends the word *"Beats"* will be used. Simply, the word means the separate moments (half a page or two, three or more pages of script) which require the focusing of attention to some object of concentration.

38

The things that happen to the character, the experiences they create, any action taken in response, and the thoughts and feelings which dominate and cause those responses change from moment to moment throughout roles. Each changing moment, whether quite short or perhaps more elongated over several pages of script, requires a new shifting of the character's focused attention---perhaps to a situation problem, or another character, or to our character's personal experience.

To allow yourself and your character to let these changes remain vague---to dovetail them helter-skelter and without definition, to fuzzy them out with sameness throughout sequences--- would be defeating to each separate development step the author has created and to the separate ideas the actor wants to bring to each moment and its experiencing.

A *Beat* is not, as some actors think it, simply a beat of a bass drum because something happens that fades away again, leaving the actor and the character floundering aimlessly and disorganizedly throughout the next subsequent moment.

A *Beat* begins because something happens to change our character's focus, then ends when something new occurs that requires a new change of focus. These changes are almost always caused by some external stimulus---something someone else says; something unexpected occuring; something gratifying or annoying or frustrating happening that affects our character.

Some actors make the mistake of changing *Beats* at almost every line of dialogue. They've detected the slight differences in degrees of anger or pleading or frustration. But as they become more familiar with *Beats* they find that, even though the *degree of intensity* may have changed here and there---have grown more intense here, become less intense there, appeared to disappear altogether for a moment---*the Beat really hasn't changed.* Actors can profit from observing those continuations.

The character still has the same thought in its mind while those small variations come and go. In other words, actors soon learn the wisdom of considering *longer* beats, at least to the extent that they can apply productively.

They learn that, just as in life, the character shouldn't be so easily diverted from its one main concentration focus or the feeling substance of a longer moment. They learn that while a single *thought* exists for only one brief moment, *a feeling experience and its cause* exist for much longer timespans. This should be as true in acting as it is in real life.

After a heated argument with his wife, with his Beat's dominating thought and the feeling it sustains, the husband, as he runs out, slams the front door, runs down the walk to his car, guns the motor and drives away, even as he mopes in a nearby bar later, probably wouldn't changed Beats. The main focus remains.

By elongating *Beats* to the points to which they can be elongated *without forsaking one single reality of the experience*, we can more closely duplicate the processes of our own lives. Individual *thoughts* may come and go within the longer Beat, but the *Object of Attention and the feeling experience it evokes* for the Beat might well remain the same.

Some actors foolishly trust themselves to be able to bring clarity to single beats by simply making check marks at the points in their scripts where they detect that moments have changed. Some of the same actors who do little else with beats don't even bother to clarify for themselves *what the new beat's focus is!*

The actor who uses beats effectively knows that each change---precisely when and where it occurs---should stand out clearly on the pages of the script.

The late Geraldine Page, whose thoughts were always so clear, recommended an excellent manner of making sure that each beat change stands out clearly when and where it occurs, to make sure it won't be overlooked:

She recommended that, when a change occurs that signals a new beat's beginning, a heavy, dark line be drawn all the way across the page---not just in the dialogue line itself but extending out to the very edges of the page on both sides, before starting to choose the beginning and end of the next beat.

Then, when the tool for focusing the character's attention, thought and feeling within a beat has been chosen, she recommended writing it in bold, heavy print at the left margin at the start of the beat, to call attention to itself and its worded content as the actor begins to study the lines and actions of that beat.

Many actors have found her recommendation valuable. I'm personally convinced that her manner of so clearly outlining Beats and highlighting their contents contributed to the utter clarity with which she bared all her thoughts and feelings for those observing her wondrous talents.

The clarities which are brought by the actor to the chosen manners of experiencing the separate moments of roles by such handling of the Beats allow the spectator to observe and vicariously experience with those same clarities what's happening inside the character as it moves through the ever-changing moments in which it finds itself involved.

Now, since there are some actors who fail to appreciate the desirability of breaking down roles into *beats*, I'll quote an exchange from recorded notes of a critique discussion I had once with a former starring actor who was at the time approaching early middle age. He was considering studying with me after a lengthy professional career which at the moment had become reduced to smaller, less important roles.

The Actor: *"But I'd like to think that I've always brought all those changes----all those beats, you call them---without having to break them up so carefully. They're just there. You can't help noticing them. Isn't it just up to the actor to bring them out? Do you really have to spend a lot of time breaking scenes up into a thousand beats and planning them so definitely?"*

Parke: *"I've seen a lot of your work over the years, as you know. While I generally like it I've always felt that you had much more to give as an actor than you realized or knew how to use.*

The Actor: *"You told me that. It got me thinking, but I didn't do anything about it."*

Parke: *"Now, I'm going to tell you something that I hope will explain something you told me earlier has always troubled you. You told me producers and directors haven't really given you any chance to 'shine out' in recent years. . . those were your words . . . that you've had difficulty persuading them to give you those larger roles you had in your earlier years.*

"Here's something you didn't know. When I was a casting director you worked on my shows several times in somewhat smaller roles than you had played earlier, right? You wrote me a couple of times, thanking me . . . thank-you notes I didn't deserve, because you were never recommended by me for those roles. It was always the director or producer who knew your work and felt, in their words, 'He can do the job' . . . 'He looks right' . . . something like that. Never 'He'll be exciting' or 'He'll make the role shine out' or anything like that.

"You didn't realize that those moments you feel could simply be noticed and they'd be there, and the actor could simply 'bring them out,' as you say, weren't really defined in your preparation so that you could do anything with them beyond just what the author had already provided.

"I want to go a little further now, hopefully without offending you. Those times when your performances have been called 'adequate' . . . I'll bet you hate that word . . . or 'well cast,' which says nothing good beyond just that . . . those times and those words have meant that in people's opinions you were up to what the author's dialogue and action and character required . . . but no more. I think you must have known what they meant, and I'm sure those reviews bothered and hurt you.

"Beat breakdown isn't the total answer to your problem, but it could make a difference immediately, even in the roles you're doing now. Remember that nasty note you wrote me once when you were told by Alex that I'd called you a 'utility actor'?

"You didn't know that the star of the series, Dane Clark, had taken me to task for not trying to get someone who'd be exciting. I had to explain that you were not my choice, and that the director had requested you, and it turned out that Alex was in my office about a client when that phone call came from Dane. I'm sorry Alex was there listening, and told you of my comment, but I imagine he was in his own way trying to help you see what you were missing.

"The letter I wrote replying to your nasty one expressed my true feelings about you. For someone who had never sought any kind of acting coaching or formal training, yet worked as much as you did, your talent itself could certainly claim some credit. You had everything but technique. You had looks---which you still have. You had good, organic masculine appeal---which you still have. You had a good mind. And there were many roles you could easily serve, just as you were doing.

"I even told you that if you wanted to learn how to bring more depth, power and excitement into the way you did what you did I thought you could be an important actor. I believed that then, and I'm more sure of it now, since you're concerned that something's missing and concerned to find out what it is.

"We both know that you're customarily hired for your handsomeness and that fine personality you bring to roles. The next step for you---even at this later time in your career---is the clear and productive breaking down of beats and deciding what to do with each one to make it 'shine out.'

"You're right . . . it does take some work. But it's worth all that work later when the result gets you praise you've never gotten before and you start climbing back into those larger roles you're not getting anymore."

The Actor went to work immediately. New, clear and more interesting colors began appearing in all his moment to moment work, finally attracting the support of a director of a major motion picture which brought him back to starring billing. He's done a number of excellent, highly praised top starring roles and two television series starring roles since.

Some years later he's told me that he'd always realized that it was apparently his basic personality which had always been the thing he'd been hired for in roles, whether motion picture or television, but that it took *Beats* (and *Beat Objects*, which I taught him) to bring him back to top attention and to the beautiful hill-

42

top mansion overlooking Hollywood in which we were sitting as we talked. This is an example of how important Beats are.

Choosing the Content of Each Individual Beat is the Challenge!

There are many, many teachers who recommend the use of an *action* or *intention* for each beat (as Stanislavski did); others who recommend a *sense memory* for each beat; others who advocate an *objective;* still a few others who might recommend a *substitution* of the type taught by Uta Hagen as well; and a few advocate the use of an *affective memory* for use during a beat.

While those separate approach items are discussed individually in other chapters of this book (under their individual titles), I personally feel, as Stanislavski appears to have quite possibly begun to feel in his last few years between 1936 and 1938---and as Vakhtangov felt long before that, that *Objects* are equally ideal content for beats.

In Stanislavski's recorded comments to the cast of the opera "Werther" in Paris at a late point in his teaching career, there's his comment that *"The actor's attention should be moving from one Object to another."* That's what separate beats are for---to *clarify where one feeling thought starts and ends*, and to firmly decide *what the focus of the character's attention shall be* within each beat. In my estimation, shared with a growing number of other teachers, there's no other focal point for the actor's attention in Beats that brings more clarity and life than an *Object.*

■ **Many of us agree in theory, but as mentioned in the foregoing simply disagree as to manners of preparing. . .**

Beats' Contents

The Three Kinds of Objects of Attention (also of Actions)

The actor has available *three different points of attention* from which to choose when forming the content of beats. In simplest terms, they're (1) *other person(s),* (2) *the situation,* and (3) *personal experience.* Those *points of attention* apply as certainly for actors using *Actions* or *Intentions* as they do for actors using *Objects.*

Although I keep pressing my own persuasion that *Objects* are vastly superior to *Actions and Intentions,* I also respect those who teach action tools for use within *Beats* and firmly believe in them as Stanislavski proposed and believed in them. But I especially respect those who recognize, as Robert Lewis does, the importance of those tools too at least being *directed at some object*.

It's to the credit of *Beat Objects* that they can magnetically focus the attention of the actor on any one of these three choices and produce a clear and vibrant experience with each, even when no *inner action* is chosen. I'm one who believes and teaches that the *action and intention* approaches can't do that so dependably and so effectively. Others can disagree, and do.

Focusing on The Other Person(s) . . .

Some actors have the ridiculous habit of continually working directly into the eyes of other characters when focused on them; are even moved to work nose-to-nose with them some of the time! Those actors bring primarily *action* in such moments, with only a negligible amount of experience of "being done to" or much if any other *personal experience* that should be caused their characters by those other persons. That our focus should in those moments be magnetized by the problem or pleasant prospect they're causing for us escapes many such actors.

It's much fuller and more true to life in using an "other person" beat to of course *some* of the time work directly into the other person's eyes but, just as importantly, much of the time *not feel any need or inclination to look at them.*

It's equally true to life---because of the body's natural response to a behavioral stimulus---to some of the time shut one's eyes tightly to *keep from seeing* another person's suffering, or their stupidity, or their meanness, their vulgarity, etc.

It's also not an uncommon behavior for us to some of the time look off into the air space of the imagination to focus on the *happy or pleasant* things those other persons are causing us to experience---even when in their presence.

First and foremost, even for an intense argument or a moment of trying to do something to another character ---to change, correct or teach them (if one is using an *action*); to appeal or plead to them; to be accepted or appreciated by them; to interrelate with them in any way---it's best to be sure that *what they're doing to us* is incorporated more than anything else in our choice of our *other person(s)* beat content.

Focusing on The Situation . . .

When a character is focused (by the actor's choice and by his directed and controlled attention) on *the situation* during a beat, *that's often all the character should see, no matter where it looks!* Even in appearing to interact with other characters, the

44

character most often sees only the problem. Eyes ranging the entire space around it frantically, the character can imagine the problem coming at it from all directions. It can shut its eyes tightly, to keep from seeing the problem, but can't escape from it even then.

A productive bonus of concentration on *the situation* is the fact that it offers the feeling that there is *no solution* for the problem---at least for the duration of the beat in which it's used.

Remember, *solution*-finding is the *writer's* province, not the character's. An actor accustomed to using *actions* as the content of beats will sometimes be *looking for a solution*, in fact be in the next moment instead of this one---and be less interesting throughout those moments (beats) when *the situation itself----- that problem that won't go away, for which no solution can be found , and which must be suffered for a prolonged period*---can afford the actor a fuller, more feeling-generating and a vastly more interesting experience throughout the beat.

Focusing on Our Character's Personal Experience . . .

This is the kind of concentration and feeling focus that Marlon Brando was discussing some years ago in a magazine article interview about him which later appeared in *Playboy*. He was asked in the interview why he spent so little time *looking at other actors*. His response, not quite in these words: *"Why should I look at other actors? I look at my character's problems. They're more important."*

Now, some actors make the mistake in *personal experience* beats of *totally and continually isolating themselves* from other characters and situations around them. This is of course a mistake. In doing that, they miss the "pull" of situations that intrude upon their concentration and demand at least a modicum of participation and interaction. But a modicum is often enough.

A more full and more lifelike manner of working in a *personal experience* beat is to of course *some* of the time *appear* to be participating in the situation while still *looking at our character's problem* and encouraging the body responses that are generated by that *personal experience* rather than by the situation or the other person(s) involved.

Even when relating with other characters and some amount of "situation-playing" is demanded, the *personal experience* as the content of a beat is what will generate *more body responses than any other attention focus! No* moment of *any* role should be experienced without *some* personal experience being caused for our character, by another person, by a situation, or by direct concentration on the *personal experience itself* as the problem.

One of the leading West Coast acting teachers, Jeff Corey, expressed himself on the subject, saying that he never tells an actor to listen to other actors; that a more complete conversation is experienced when, instead, your attention should be on all the things that you're listening to *inside yourself* ; that it's more iportant to listen to the unspoken messages behind the words as they affect you.

I believe Jeff, from the foregoing comment made in an interview with Eva Mekler for her book *"The New Generation Of Acting Teachers"* (mentioned earlier), is agreeing with my own precept . . . that all incoming experience must be filtered through *our character's own experiencing* of it. Jeff's classes are among those which, since he wasn't a member of the Acting Coaches And Teachers Association when I was its president, I wasn't invited to observe, so I'm not sure my interpretation of his comment is correct, but to me it makes sense.

■ **Regardless of what kind of** *Object of Attention* **or** *Action or Intention* **may be chosen for an individual** *Beat,* **for the purpose of more fully experiencing its chosen involvement later in actual performance the actor will have to make his or her own decision about the following manners of working, which are continuing "bones of contention" among teachers . . .**

Beats / Their Use During Line Study
Their Planned Involvements May Get Lost Otherwise!

Some teachers recommend doing all your planning of what should be the focus of your attention during a beat, then simply setting all that planning aside and getting to studying and memorizing your lines by rote or whatever other process. *"Put it all together later,"* I actually heard one teacher advise.

Some teachers advocate going into a theatre rehearsal, or into last minute rehearsals for film scenes *without even planning the focus of attention with any approach items (Action, Intention or Object)* because they feel you should wait until you find out what you're going to get from other actors in the scenes with you.

Both of these recommendations are pure rot! With the first approach, there's no way in hell you can later blend your planning with the simple dialogue and action of a scene if your lines have been studied and memorized without the focus and experience that results from your planned involvements for the beat.

With the second approach, you'll be arriving for rehearsal (whether film or theatre) with no substantive contribution of your own to determine what will occur. In theatre, the director will immediately start supplying his own version of your subtext. In film, you should be sent home and replaced with another actor! There's no time under film conditions for this nonsense.

The importance of using whatever technique tool you've prepared for the separate beats while memorizing your lines can't be too strongly stressed. The lines shouldn't be learned simply by rote, without the prepared thought and feeling patterns providing at least those early experiencings of the emotion, feeling and mood realities for which they've been painstakingly created.

Having broken down your script into beats, instead of ignoring your preliminary planning of the beats' involvements (feeling you can *"put it all together later,"* after line study), center your concentration on the Object, Action or Intention or whatever other tool you've planned for the beat as you begin and continue to memorize your lines in each beat!

Also, working *beat by beat,* one beat at a time, is important. Work on one beat until its lines are secure, all the time maintaining the focus and feelings of the prepared involvement tool, whatever it may be, throughout the memorizing process.

Finish that beat's memorizing before going on to the following one. If you maintain the beat's prepared inner experience throughout the line study the particular concentration and the particular feeling depth you desire will become firmly associated with that beat as the role is studied and will remain into the performance without your having to think the actual tool at a time when you should be living the character's experience.

Especially for film and television roles' line study, this practice of studying one beat at a time while remaining in the planned feeling for that beat is doubly important!

Those who've worked in motion pictures especially know that if a beat's action is to move from one room to another, or from an exterior scene directly to the entrance and into the interior of a building, those different locations of that beat's duration will be shot hours or even weeks or months apart.

The running up to the front door may be shot in Malibu or in an Afghanistan marketplace a week or ten weeks before the same running entrance, hopefully with its same feelings of the character, bursts into the interior of the building on a sound stage back on the Universal lot!

The actor who doesn't have a definite plan, a definite Object or other tool, firmly in mind at both times, may well have his footage cut from the picture because when the interior shots were made on a soundstage on a Hollywood studio lot so long a time later he may have forgotten the level of intensity or even the exact focus of his thoughts and feelings which were so evident in the exterior footage shot so long before!

Having an actor's footage in a film cut from the picture in the Editing Room for that reason is an example of being done to! . . .

■ **There's a lot of disagreement among teachers on this . . .**

Being Done To

vs. Doing To

Why do we call an actor's total being his or her "instrument"? Because to make its most stirring music it should be "played upon".

Examining and practicing the fuller experience of the "being done to" concept, rather than any "doing to" dogma, points up the difference and promotes the habit quickly and effectively. There's no comparison.

In real life, aren't we more often concerned with what others are thinking about us, how others are treating us, what they're doing to us, etc.? Don't we devote more time to brooding about unpleasantness, hurt, annoyance, ridicule, pressures and all the other things that other people cause us than to planning specific responsive actions against others?

Top New York veteran acting teacher Sanford Meisner has expressed this ideally, saying that *"What an actor does doesn't depend on him, but on what the other actor does to him."* He has stated that he believes this is the foundation from which all acting training should begin. A lot, including myself, agree!

In real life, we feel "done to" much more often and for periods of longer duration than we find ourselves "doing to others". In our private life problems are dwelt on for much longer periods than their solutions. Why should it be different in acting roles?

What's more important for the actor, though, is recognizing which of the two is a more total experience. Taking action--- doing something to others, if it consumes the total of our concentration---is so often single-dimensioned. The "target" is usually *outside ourself*. *"Being done to"*, on the other hand, creates the many-dimensioned experience it does because the target is *you* in real life, *your character* in a role.

This is borne out by present day behavioral scientists and psychologists. It'd be ridiculous for a therapist or analyst to decide that a patient's problems were initially conditioned by something the patient did to others! The only difference between the psychologist and the actor is that, while the psychologist is intent upon observing the behavior of others, the actor's only subject is himself. He must study which stimuli he can apply to himself to experience the desired feeling and responses for characters.

There are three main classes of behavioral response stimuli: *Unconditioned, Conditioned* and *Discriminative.*

Unconditioned response stimuli are those unexpected occurrences that produce the natural, often simply automatic responses of the body when stimulated by something happening to it. It's almost purely left brain, the response being easily and immediately reflexive and objective, usually without much if any emotional involvement at all.

For example, when the body suddenly encounters unanticipated touch, pain, cold or heat its response is often visibly body-moving in a simply reflexive, perhaps even barely conscious manner. Another example: A commuter on a subway, if the car sways or jerks, will probably grab a nearby strap or pole without thinking. The *body* is "being done to" and simply responds mechanically and logically at the urging of the left brain.

Conditioned response (called by some *Respondent*) stimuli are those which, like Pavlov's dog salivating at the sight of food, the smell of food, or the ringing of a bell signalling food, produce either or both physical and emotional responses because expectation has been created, a desire is formed, and a remembered feeling is being kindled. Real or imaginary stimuli of the *conditioned response* type may be visual (an object or person seen), olfactory (an odor or scent), auditory (a sound or word or phrase), tactile (the sensation of something touched---its surface, conformation, temperature, etc.) or taste.

The sensory images of *Conditioned Response* stimuli are valuable for actors in that they can, and most often do, bring with them conditioned feeling responses of pleasant or unpleasant nature. Some actors even use particular *Sense Memory* and *Affective (Emotional) Memory* images to bring personally experienced feelings and emotional truths in moments of their roles. In conditioned response, the *body* and often also the *right brain's memory bank* are "being done to."

Discriminative response stimuli are those that---because they don't evoke *unconditioned* (simple, purely automatic for the body) responses, involve the *left brain* more than the body in determining response.

49

These are stimuli that, either because of common knowledge or because of an existing feeling about, or a justifiable reaction to, or an unflinching attitude about something that occurs and affects us, produce responses that generally involve decisions, conscious manipulation, objective coping, etc.

If someone insults us, we might *consciously opt* to simply walk away or might *consciously opt* to deliver a worse insult in return. If someone demands our car keys in a bar to drive us home because we're drunk, we might *consciously opt* to surrender the keys or might scoff at the assumption and decide for ourselves whether we're capable or not.

All three types of the now universally recognized *Behavioral Response Stimuli* are examples of our constantly *"Being done to"* by someone or something.

In moments of "being done to", *our character* is the one being hurt, embarrassed, ridiculed and pressured---sometimes all those in the same moment. Or frustrated, blocked, angered, rendered helpless, made to hate its own inadequacy and inability to cope--- perhaps all those in another single moment. Or ignored, left out, lonely, put down, unappreciated or some other feeling experiences----again, all those colors perhaps in a single moment. The bottom line is that those many-dimensioned experiences can't occur for your character when it's already into the next moment and is already busy *doing something to another character.*

Over the years, in first interviews with actors seeking admission to my classes, I've observed so many of them---either instinctively or as a result of training---continually using the "doing to" manner of working opposite me in a sample reading exercise. This happened so often that I devised an illustration of the alternative. I've often stopped them and used this single moment to illustrate the "being done to" difference:

As an example, I suggest to those actors that a line in a script might be *"Get the hell out of my office!"* Now, there's a line that would probably trap the action-oriented, "doing to" actor into leaning forward ridiculously, yelling directly into the face of the other character and pointing to the door. I illustrate the "being done to" point by first delivering the line in that totally cliché manner---with little or no "being done to".

Then I've asked the interviewee to consider for a moment where the audience member, the viewer who's seeking to share an *experience*, would immediately look. The one yelling and pointing isn't the one having an *experience!* . . . he's simply an *event happening to the other character.* All eyes will flash to the character *being done to* . . . *it's* the one having the experience, not the event creator!

50

In a second, *"being done to"* version of the same scripted line, to illustrate the vastly more desirable alternative, I've shut my eyes tight to shut out the disgusting, irritating sight of the other character, turned away to not even have to look in the other character's direction, cringed back bodily to get away as far as the chair would allow and, first waving my hand before my face---again to protect myself from having to see the other person, then putting my hand to my stomach---because my imaginary ulcer could be kicking up because of the other person . . . and delivered the same line with the same anger suggested by the writer, but also with the experience of "*being done to*" by the mere fact of the other's continued presence.

It has served as a quick way to illustrate the vast difference in the degrees of effectiveness between the two approaches---*"being done to"* as compared to the "doing to" concept. There would be no question as to which character would rivet the audience member's or viewer's attention. In the latter version of the moment it's the character *being done to* who's doing the sending out of the office and yet it's that character who's being caused the most upsetting experience.

Through emphasizing the *"being done to"* aspects in most moments of roles the actor easily and excitingly finds those experiences that are both *anger and crying* at the same time, *resentment that's also self-loathing* in the same moment, and many, many other combinations of the outer-directed and inner emotional responses in single moments. The approach makes potentially one-dimensional moments take on more excitement and more complete life for both the actor and the viewer.

The script's writer has always provided the "single dimension" moment. The writer is progressing a story. And the actor who *takes action* primarily is simply *doubling what the writer has already provided.* That actor should remember that his or her character *doesn't know* the next pages of the script; *doesn't know* that this moment won't go away for some time. That *not knowing* can be best served if in the present moments, one after another, the character is continually experiencing some manner of "being done to".

And the difference in the actor's own personal experiencing of moments is astonishing! The amount of true relating to other characters is greatly enhanced, because those other characters are the source of whatever is being done to our own character.

How difficult it's been sometimes to persuade the previously *action and intention*-trained actor of the value of becoming the baseball instead of the bat! . . . the punching bag instead of the fist! . . . the pincushion instead of the pin! Actors who couldn't at least consider the change of approach weren't accepted.

I'm reminded that Stella Adler, even though first and foremost an advocate of *action and intention,* has often taught actors to some of the time imagine someone *sticking a pin in their eyes.* That's an example of *being done to.* We're saying the same thing.

■ **None of us would argue about this next item . . .**

Body Participation

It Often Requires Some Retraining!

Leonardo DaVinci said *"The soul desires to dwell with the body because without the members of the body it can neither act nor feel."*

If you're told to *"Forget your body . . . it'll do what it needs to do if your mind's in the right place,"* ignore the advice. It may have forgotten how.

Clarity to the eyes of an observer can't be based simply on dialogue delivery or even on an actor's truthful experiencing of moments . . . without the body's being attracted and moved into participation. We spend so much of our real life thinking and feeling about different subject matters without conveying them to those around us, often even concealing our thoughts. It's possible for the actor to do the same in roles unintentionally. When that happens there's nothing that can be clearly perceived by the observer.

For those planning lives as actors it can be one of the most stimulating studies, commencing at the earliest possible moment, to continually observe the interrelationship between thoughts and feelings and the body.

For those who look back after many years to childhood years when they'd already decided to pursue acting, it's amusing---albeit a little embarrassing too---to remember those performances on back porches and patios with other neighbor children when "acting" was so simple, when each role embodied so many surface observations so easily exaggerated and overacted but still reflected the child's interest in role-playing . . . usually to the hilt.

A tough policeman, a worried mother, a stern father, a bully or whatever other stereotype the actor-to-be child wanted to portray could so easily be overacted for the fun of appearing in those "dress-up-in-older-clothes" back porch shows.

Another observation the actor might make later in life is that, although those performances were embarrassingly overdrawn, each of those characters was instinctively played by the young body without too much thinking about those moments of strutting, bellowing or whimpering. Purely through association, they came automatically. In that sense at least, the young body involved was already tuned to thoughts and feelings!

The Usual Source Of Problems

Unfortunately, there come the teenage years when the vast majority of us undergo the socializing processes and learn that for our survival and upward mobility we must take all of those exaggerated thoughts and feelings into a hiding place within us and be careful to have little of them showing for others to see.

It's precisely when that socializing process sets in that a would-be actor should attempt to resist the overwhelming demands of social environment and attempt to stay in touch with the combined processes of his mind and body.

A talent for acting---contrary to the common belief that the word *talent* is difficult to define in certain terms---can be the savior, and in anyone destined for acting success it will usually be just that.

It's during those teenage years, as the would-be actor goes through the worries, self doubts and confusions that impinge on any developing personality during that period, that he should try to focus attention on the *experiencing* of each negative or positive event and its step by step progression, whatever course that progression may take. Focusing on the *experiencing* at all times will prompt the body into the habit of fully participating in all thought and feeling moments.

The important discovery an actor should make early on is that his body should be expertly tuned to each passing thought and feeling, even if on occasion he risks nakedly exposing those inner clarities that may offend or anger someone.

The Problem

There are few roles which remain so one-dimensional throughout their courses of created life that they encounter no changes along the way---moments in which they abandon their adopted images, drop their masks for a moment, expose the other aspects that comprise a complete human being.

The otherwise one-dimensional tough or threatening character almost always (at least in good writing) has its moments of fear, doubt, anxiety, exultation, triumph, desperation and despair. The actor who can't see the necessity of experiencing those variations with *both mind and body* will fall far short of professional clarity.

53

The body won't necessarily respond automatically to quiet thought or generalized feeling moments. The actor should develop the art of stimulating the body into participation with clear, definite thoughts that include meaningful attitudes and feelings.

For example, the process described by Stanislavski in his writings as the *Inner Dialogue* and *Inner Monologue*, if the actor enjoys using one or both, can be used---the planning of specific "talking to oneself" dialogue and using it in moments when the character isn't actually speaking aloud. Of course this too could be used with such secrecy and incompleteness that any surface clarity would be absent. It shouldn't be.

No clarity might occur unless the actor utilizes his powers of invention and in both the wording and use of these Stanislavski approaches brings *interesting and creative, body-attracting wording choices that prompt the body to joyfully participate.*

Inner Monologue / Dialogue Thoughts Can Easily Move The Body

For example, an action descriptive might indicate that an old lady in a rocking chair hears her cat meow nearby and, recognizing that the cat's hungry, realizes it's time to feed it.

The sequence might be done simply and uninterestingly by one actress while another, recognizing the importance of the mind and body working together and seeking to create an interesting mind / body experience in each moment, might activate the body via the inner thoughts by constructing the following *Inner Monologue*:

"Was that Tabby?" (Her body would surely crane the neck and ear, and the eyes might search the room through the old lady's bifocals.)

"Oh, dear, it must be milk time." (She might consult the old clock on the wall briefly and sigh, resigning herself to once more playing waitress and nurse.)

"Now, where's that dratted cane?" (Looking for her cane, she might discover it's fallen to the floor while she was dozing.)

"You bad, bad boy!" (She'd be prompted to spank the cane for hiding from her.)

"Now, hold still, you!" (She'd grip the arm of the rocking chair with one hand and start to rise very carefully after first speaking to the rocking chair silently and demanding that it not make her lose her balance.)

"Whew! I made it!" (She'd smile with pleasure that her back didn't go out on her again as she got up, and might straighten to her full height to enjoy the fact.)

54

"Aim myself in the right direction." (A self-cautioning moment, as she moves her cane and turns her feet one after the other toward the cat's saucer) . . . and so on.

It's easy to see how much more interesting this actress's performance of the moment would be, with her body tuned to her *Inner Dialogue and Monologue* thoughts because they're inventive and provocative through involving thoughts of her body condition, the humanizing of props, and making the simple turning of her body toward the cat's saucer a small challenge.

Brief Physical Objectives Move the Body Too

Another Stanislavski device for this tuning of the body to thoughts and feelings for the sake of clarity of moments was labeled by him in the book *"Creating A Role"* as *Physical Objectives.* They're tiny, quite brief *surface actions* that need not distract from the primary involvement of the character.

The latter device, too, is directed toward making worded choices for a sequence of brief involvements which, together in sequence, make up a moment of longer duration. Again, it, like the *Inner Monologue* and *Inner Dialogue* approaches, is aimed at inspiring the body through imaginative, creative suggestions to participate in an interesting manner. (*Physical Objectives* are discussed more lengthily in the chapter with that title.)

Both of these manners of prompting the body's continuous participation in moments can be highly productive, although it must be the actor in the end who must be able to seduce the body into enjoying those separate moments as adventures through *the manner of wording the inner thoughts* ahead of time.

These manners of training the mind and body to participate equally in the interest of utter clarity of moments are of course applicable in the main to only moments. The clarity required of good actors goes far beyond such brief moments, with the dominating clarity (that's required from the first moment a character appears on the scene to the final exit) being *personality* clarity!

The Body-Involving Value of Emotionally Charged Objects

To create a vivid character---a recognizable, pulsating organism, the single tool that Stanislavski recommended for use as its core---the *Super Objective*---isn't deemed by some of us to be specific enough by itself.

A character built with a Super Objective (which is really a *"life action"*) like *"Make them respect me!"* is still a theatrically conceived character with only outgoing action to afford it full clarity. The same character, with the addition of its dominant

55

causal source, perhaps in the form of an *Object*---in this case we'd call it a *Life Object*---like *"This gutter smell I can't get rid of!"* is a complete, easily recognizable *personality*.

Since *Objects* are discussed lengthily in so many other sections of this book, this example is given at this point simply to point out that the actor involved with a simple *Super Objective* or *Life Action* of trying to make people respect him (the character) has just one dimension and the *personality source* of that dimension may not be clear at all.

But the actor who's more focused on something like the suggested *Life Object* ---in this example the "gutter smell" his character will always carry in its conditioned mind---will bring shadings and dimensions which offer so many clarities for the viewer and so many experiential values for the body of the actor playing the character that any viewer's attention will remain riveted to his far more interesting performance.

And in any lengthy sequence of a role there are the moments of whatever length, one after another, that require their individual clarities. Actors trained in the use of a method, or system---whether Stanislavski's, an outgrowth of Stanislavski's or some other---generally realize that those separate small sections of lengthier scenes (called *Beats* in this book) should be broken down and be given their unique involvements.

Those separate small sections of lengthier scenes, one after another throughout the role, should be used to focus the character's attention and meaningful involvement first on one experience, then on another, later another, and so on.

While there's controversy among the different schools of systematic preparation approaches as to precisely what should be the content of the separate beats---which tools to use and how they should be prepared, the fact remains that this manner of deciding when a certain concern or thought and feeling focus begins and ends and is immediately replaced by another is the best manner for clarifying, for both the viewer and the actor, what the most important aspect of each individual moment of the character's life shall be. Whatever tool the actor uses in those moments should be clear and generating for the *body* as well as the mind. The body is attracted by clarity.

A final point to be repeated here as to the bringing of *personality* clarity through generating natural body responses---because it can't be repeated too often---is that while events around the character impact it to whatever degree, and the people around it demand attention as they form those events, the actor who focuses the character's attention too exclusively upon the events or characters around it will be laying aside unused the most important concern of any character---its own *personal experience* . . . and *the body responds more organically to personal experience.*

Actors should always seek out the *self*-experience aspects of their characters first and foremost, regardless of the external urgencies, threats, demands or other scenic situations in which their characters find themselves.

The frustrations, the blind rages, the defeats, the anguishes, the joys and ecstasies . . . they're all there . . . in *the character's own personal experience.*. The body understands and responds to those experiences more than to any others.

In a moment of peak anger at someone or something, rather than focusing on the other person who is causing the anger, the actor can more experientially focus on *"This bust something feeling!"* (his character's own experience) or *"Something to calm me down!"* (again, the character's own experience) or perhaps *"My goddam ulcer!"*

Remember, you're not trying to create a feeling in such use. You're still really concentrating on *what's happening to your character that's causing* the feeling that troubles you.

Similarly, in a moment of ecstatic joy upon achieving a big goal, instead of focusing the content of the then current Beat of the role on someone or something else within the situation, or even on the attaining of the goal itself, the actor can achieve far more personal experience and result---and in the process generate more body participation---by focusing on an Object such as *"How long I've waited !"* or *"The sweet smell of success!"* or *"The king of the mountain!"*

Such self-experiencing *Objects* would far exceed in value the kinds of objects that would with so much less effectiveness be focused on externals of any kind, including other people in the scene or event, even though the other people or the event may be the cause for the character's supreme anger or ecstasy.

Ironically, the word *action* suggests some specific movement of the body that's involved in the process of taking it. But the actor wanting to generate more body participation in every kind of feeling moment should test *Objects* and observe the difference in terms of the body's expanded circuit of response.

■ **Most teachers devote some teaching to one or more of the highly creative approaches. Many create their own from some of the widely recognized ingredients for achieving the *more theatrical realities* adocated by Vakhtangov.   What's involved with these approaches is the *strictly creative version* of the character's otherwise simple reality.   Here's one of my own such approaches:**

Creative Psychological Objective

A Special Tool For Special Occasions

After determining the *Beats*---their beginnings and their endings, the actor's at the point where most coaches who teach specific methodologies start disagreeing with each other. Similarly, their students clash over terminologies and creative approaches, running the gamut from ridiculous absurdities to profoundly beautiful theories and back again to absurdities. (The arguments pro and con the many different *purely creative* approaches will probably never end.)

No matter what any *strictly creative* approach involves, no matter how it sounds, no matter how you translate it in order to learn and use it . . . it also has to work when called upon; it has to work well; and it has to work for all moments of all roles where it's used. If it doesn't, it's time to look elsewhere.

If it doesn't work for *you*---even though it appears to for others, you should keep searching until you find one that does. Some of the strictly *creative* tools work more effectively for some people and not well or at all for others, no matter how effective the tools themselves may be, since there are *cerebral actors, emotional actors and simply physical actors.*

The unique and individual processes of different actors' individual personalities and the parameters within which they can experience imaginary stimuli vary so universally from actor to actor that what works ideally for one may not for all.

Each should find his own, because simple reality doesn't always satisfy. Most actors can bring "adequate" involvement, concentration and imagination to most roles. If they can't bring those things they shouldn't be actors. It's the actor who can bring *much more* who's destined for attention and respect

Here, after those preliminary comments, is what I consider to be an exciting tool for the actor seeking a more total *mind / body / feeling* manner of experiencing (by the actor) and perceiving (by the viewer) of a character's inner processes in moments. But it's also a tool that requires judgment as to when and how, as well as whether, it should be used.

Here, we're discussing an approach that takes simple reality beyond the ordinary. The actor who desires a heightened *"theatrical realism"* in moments of a role might consider this exciting approach. I think he'd be surprised at what can happen.

58

It's a *strictly creative* tool that's uniquely ideal for the theatre actor who must project the character's combined inner thought and feeling processes from a distant proscenium to the last member of a large audience. When formed and used ideally in theatre it's without a peer in my estimation.

I'd caution against its use in film or television performance except in moments of heightened intensity, or in calmer moments where the actor longs to create a more visibly apparent inner reality, and perhaps in those moments of roles where characters' experiences are continually free of any social consciousness or behavioral obligation. The tool is *so creative, so vivid* and *so totally body involving* that film actors know it would appear extreme unless used ideally and with consummate judgment.

Stanislavski sought such a tool to combine the psycho-physical processes toward a *more creative and expressive* version of a moment without forfeiting the inner truth of the character and the actor. Vakhtangov sought the same heightened expressiveness that could insure the same psycho-physical process being implemented in the preparing of moments but could also achieve a *more theatrical* realism.

Stanislavski's progression from the *"as if"* to the *"magic if"* was directed to that end, but failed to achieve his goal ideally. Vakhtangov came nearer (through the limitless possibilities of *Objects*), as the personally affective wordings of his recommended *Objects* achieved more access to the right brain experience, and as his *Motive (Imaginary) Center* produced an amazing interaction between the body and affective memory.

In more recent decades, Poland's Jerzy Grotowski joined the search---especially in his work with the body's *Resonators* (paralleling the *Motive Center* and the *Imaginary Center*) and his *Negation* exercises, fully crediting much of his inspiration to Vakhtangov's search for *theatrical realism with complete psychological truth.*

In *"Creating A Role"*, the last of the Stanislavski trilogy to reach print, on pages 51 through 56, there's discussion of what these *more creative* objectives could do in terms of involving the feelings and moving the body more excitingly.

Those who advocate the use of the Vakhtangovian *Objects* and who feel that for some moments (perhaps entire beats) of roles the *Object* should be used, after finding the Object might consider using it as a stepping stone toward the forming of this tool---the *Creative Psychological Objective.*

As will be discussed in the upcoming paragraphs, it comprises *a composite Inner Object* and a two-word *action verb* aimed at doing something to the resulting *Inner Object.*

59

An *Inner Object* of the type being considered here is most often and most easily found by a process I call *"body-searching"* (a manner of obtaining the body's help in reevoking important memories from the right brain's affective memory files, which process will be described shortly. The right brain is full of such affective memories. The body can readily access those right brain files, and those *Inner Objects* brought forth from the right brain are much more evocative than the words simply describing an emotional experience could be for the actor.

A printed interview with Rod Steiger which appeared in *"Playboy"* magazine some years ago quoted that actor (in one of his very rare moments of talking about his approach to acting) as relating that in a scene from the film version of *"The Big Knife"* (in which he portrayed a movie mogul as a closeted homosexual), seeing a woman entering a conference in his office he thought of her as *a garbage can that hadn't been cleaned in ages*. That's an example of an *Inner Object*, even though it's quite a few words.

In Robert Lewis's excellent book *"Method----Or Madness"* there's a fine example of two different actors' interpretations of a moment from Tolstoi's *"The Human Corpse"* in which the character stands before a mirror preparing to shoot himself.

One actor used the early Stanislavski "as if", trying to imagine what he himself would feel like in such a moment, while the other, the gifted Jacob Ben Ami, used the *Sense Memory*---an *Inner Object*---of stepping into a cold shower. One can imagine how effective that experience of anticipating those *"ice needles"* of cold water (here turned into a two word *Inner Object*) was.

This example, by adding an *action verb* to such a two word *Inner Object*, would constitute the ingredients of what's called the *Creative Psychological Objective*.

"The CPO" (the shorter title I've given it to save words in my own classes) can make the Beat Object on which it's based (and from which it's formed) a more vivid, more physically exciting experience for the *body* whenever the actor decides it's desirable to use it.

No matter what form it may be presented in, or what it may be called, this is one of the Stanislavski / Vakhtagov-*inspired* tools (not found during their searching but based on those searches) which can add astonishly vivid and visually impressive colors to actors' work. It can turn what could be less exciting moments of roles into highly creative ones for both the actor's inner experience and for the observer's clear perception; and can convey to the observer, more detectably than most other similar tools can (via the sensory qualities of the composite *action / object* experience) the specific inner experience of the character.

It involves the body more creatively in the actor's performance, through physical and psycho-physical memory processes, and persuades the body out of orginary, potentially uninteresting behavior and movement habits, into creative and always more interesting and more meaningful accompaniment to the reality thoughts and feelings of characters.

It has the unique capacity to reach into our associative memory bin and extract for use *a composite rather than a single sense memory source.* This is one of those tools which can replace the cumbersome, ritualistic *Affective Memory exercise* of some teachers. The body, in this process, finds *both the unconscious and conscious sense memories and affective memories!* And it does it so quickly and easily!

Its intensity is more variable from moment to moment (as true life subtext is) than the culminating experience hopefully (not always) produced by the Strasberg exercise. It affords an unbelievably wide and varied spectrum of experience through the double truth---the reality and the *sensory, affective parallels* included in its final form . . . and it's exciting to observe!

Forming A Creative Psychological Objective

After wording the *Thought Object* into a form which evokes definite feelings within you, the next step is to find out what that *Object* suggests to the body in its own sense memory and affective memory terms.

To do this, first close your eyes (to shut out the visible realities around you), then think and feel the *Object* in an intensified degree and encourage the body to respond continually during an improvised movement experience of its own as specifically prompted by the intensified feeling of the *Object.*

For the actor who prefers an *Action or Intention* the adaptation for one of those tools' setting out toward a CPO is probably easiest if the actor concentrates more upon the object toward which any intention should be aimed (as Bobby Lewis advises) than upon the intention itself.

Once this *body-improvising* is in progress you should "zoom in" on one of the first strange impressions---things, sounds, colors, smells, textures and body sensations---which will begin appearing from the body's memory bank of associations of all kinds. It takes only a moment for these to begin appearing, even though hazily. They're the right brain's *Inner Objects!*

One could continue this process for a long time and most of the impressions could be allowed to remain dim if we don't force ourself to "zoom in" on one of the earliest impressions even be-

61

fore we know what it is. By "zooming in", we can almost immediately bring it into bright clarity for ourself.

For some this "zooming in" is a fairly automatic process resulting from remaining very sensitive to impression. For others it may require a disciplined thrust of determinedly bringing an impression into clearer focus.

(This process may require some practice for any contemporary actors whose senses have long ago been allowed to atrophy in our eye-oriented culture and mind-only survival structures. However, the lost art of *"listening to the body"*---as Isadora Duncan and Rudolf Steiner dubbed it long ago---can be easily cultivated through practice.)

The phenomenon that many actors may not readily accept is that the body-improvising prompted by the feelings of the *Object* (when sufficiently intensified) can *almost immediately* produce what are perhaps the most important associative memories of sensory parallels upon beginning its participation. It has instant access to the exact file drawer in the right brain, and can produce a mosaic of related impressions---*memory keys*---immediately!

As you maintain the intensified feeling, don't bypass that immediately emerging impression which seems a total non sequitur seeming to have absolutely nothing to do with the Object's experiencing. A one or two word label of what it is will occur almost simultaneously as you "zoom in" on it and bring it to clarity. Don't fail to label whatever's produced. Bypassing that earliest impression may make you miss out on one of the most potent associative memories that can occur during this finding process.

Label it immediately! Without your having any basis for accepting it as being potentially productive, the body has determined that it's something off one of the right brain's filecards of interrelated sense memories and emotional memories stored among your probably long forgotten experiences.

Perhaps a living thing, a color or a sound will come first--- even though, like those that follow, it will be only dimly recognizable and you won't know what it is if you don't "zoom in" and bring it into clarity. When an impression of whatever kind or form comes, force yourself to "zoom in" on it till it's recognizable.

Perhaps you'll sense a sound, or a glob of color or texture, or a particular scent. The important thing is, something is coming and it should be quickly brought to clarity because, without your understanding why, it's important and will assuredly be productive.

It's a memory key stored away by the body, by the senses and by the *experiential and emotional memory combined* in some long ago moment.

If you vaguely at first see blood, or feel satin, or smell perfume, or see ocean waves, and are tempted by the skeptical left brain to pass the impression by, *don't! Trust it!* It can be used by your body in its own way because it's already in that moment being associated by the body with what it's experiencing from your maintaining of the intense Object feeling. What's coming *means something to both the body and the right brain.*

Now, once you have the first *Inner Object* and have labeled it, set it aside. You won't need to write it down because it can be remembered vividly, perhaps because it's *so puzzling.*

Now, return to intensified thinking and feeling with the original *Object* wording---*not the Inner Object just found!* Repeat the words of the Object to yourself. Experience it turned up to pitch level. With your eyes again closed, repeat the same process of bringing out of the darkness another impression, then bringing it to sharp clarity. Again you're looking for an *Inner Object.* Again "zoom in" immediately as a dim impression comes, bring it into focus, know what it is, label it.

When you have your second one, the two should be combined. Ignore the suspicion that neither makes any sense at all. To your conscious mind----especially to your skeptical left brain file clerks---the two reevoked objects probably won't. Don't think you've failed if they sound improbable and rather ridiculous, even totally illogical. *Combine them!*

You may find you now have either a "bloody rainbow" or "rainbow blood" (if in testing the experiencing of the strange combination you prefer one juxtaposition over the other, as you surely will), because, strange as it still seems to you, the combination you prefer will definitely be more potent for you. One word will be more powerfully affecting for you because it was more affecting in the earlier life moment when it was engraved indelibly in your right brain and file-carded by the body.

You may now have "lilac albatross" or "albatross lilac". It could be a "waving bonfire" or a "bonfire wave", a "highchair stop sign" or a "stop sign highchair" if after testing you find one combination moving the body and feeling experience more than the other.

You see, *you probably won't consciously remember,* for example, that once in early childhood you saw the blood around your little dog's body after it had been run over by a car and your body formed a *revulsion-reactive behavior pattern* during a long moment of that experience, or that you once saw a rainbow reflected in a little stream in a gutter as you watched your treasured little paper sailboat swallowed up in the gutter's whirlpool, and the body formed a *loss-reactive behavior pattern* in that moment.

Similarly, *you don't have to remember consciously at all---and probably can't*---that, for another example, your fat aunt's lilac perfume made you sick at your stomach as she leaned down to kiss you once, and the body formed a *stomach-wrenching-reactive behavior pattern*, or that once when you got bawled out in school and so acutely embarassed by a teacher it was over your poor reading aloud from *"The Albatross"* and your body formed another *reactive behavior pattern* which *it hasn't forgotten* and still associates with many similar moments.

It was some years ago when I observed that actors using only one reevoked *Inner Object*, through whatever process they might employ in the finding of it, tended to then search into that single memory consciously and exhaustively for some connection---but with only their limited conscious minds. Even those single keys proved evocative because they were recognizable to the body as being attached to their physical sensations in like moments, but actors too often felt they needed to understand where those single associative memories came from.

I also discovered that the addition of a second *Inner Object* t tied to the first involved a larger amount of the appropriate sensory parallels stored away in the right brain and even more surely connected with long forgotten affective memories which caused their filing there in the first place in similar moments. The second object key brings more than using just one does, because together they bring out an *entire filefolder* of similar experiences.

Don't waste time trying to remember where those associations of the body originated. It's usually impossible, although on occasion it might be obvious immediately. Whether any source for the association comes to mind or not, the effect is the same.

Perhaps Jacob Ben Ami had discovered or at least sensed the same thing when he used the equivalent of the "ice needles" of that cold shower in the moment of planning to shoot himself in front of the mirror. At any rate, the body of the actor is even more enriched and even more stimulated as to its parallel experiencing in creative terms by the *two word Inner Object* approach, similar to the result that would certainly be gained from combining "ice" and "needles".

The next step, again with the eyes closed, is to feel yourself *surrounded on all sides* by the *composite, two word Inner Object* formed from those two items.

Feel the combined object tight against all your pores! With it encasing every part of you in your imagination, like an either very pleasant or very unpleasant cocoon, begin observing *the body's inner reaction* to being wrapped tightly in the cocoon of the two word *Inner Object* that's either pleasant or unpleasant.

Feel all the inner muscles of your body moving reactively to try to *do something to* it. Whether it's pleasant or unpleasant, the body will be trying to do something to it with the *total of the inner muscles!*

Observe what those inner muscles are trying to do. Observe their contraction, expansion, their directed energy. They're trying in their own *inner muscles* manner to bring it closer (because it's desirable) or get rid of it (because it's undesirable).

Also observe the *direction* (in, out, away, up, down, off, etc.) in which they're straining to accomplish it.

Note---because it's important---that at this point we're not saying do *about* it or *because* of it. Now we're saying *doing to it directly.* There's a vast difference in the result of the use of the CPO later between those reactions.

Observe that the chest, the stomach, the armpits, the neck glands, in fact all the inner body muscles, are trying to perhaps *"pull in"*, or *"squeeze out"*, or *"push off"* or *"caress up"* or possibly *"knock away"* whatever is encasing your body.

This moment is when the recognition of this tool's effectiveness begins to really impress you. You'll recognize that *you've had similar mind / will / feeling body experiences before!* You don't need to remember when or where. At those earlier times in your life, going through similar moments, you weren't conscious that, in body language, you were trying to *"Squeeze out the bloody rainbow"* or *"Shiver off the lilac albatross".*

Now you would have---after those steps which may appear so complicated until you've practiced them just a few times---a very dynamic creative tool for any Beat in which you feel both *acute right brain personalization* and the addition of *creative physicalization* are desirable.

Some actors appreciate the extra excitements of *highly creative physicalization* to such a degree that they use a tool like the CPO (or some other creative approach) in many more Beats of roles than others would. There are many actors who simply prefer to work with *reality*-thought Objects in the main, and only occasionally if ever prepare a tool such as the CPO which may seem too labored and complex in preparation for their tastes.

Again I want to mention that this tool is ideal for theatre---where the inner processes of the character must be projected to the last seat in the top balcony, but it's probably best reserved for only a few moments, perhaps mostly climactic ones, in a film performance, where the camera and its wide selection of lenses (closeup, wide angle, etc.) can't be accurately judged by the actor working before it. Geraldine Page, for instance, never let herself be concerned about such things, but most actors should beware.

65

The following examples may lend more graphic clarification:

Object	Inner Object	Action Verb	The CPO
How much she hates me!	Screaming Whirlpool!	Squeeze off!	Squeeze off the Screaming Whirlpool!
How stupid I've been!	Bloody Maggots!	Scrape off!	Scrape off the Bloody Maggots!

Also, a few things should be pointed out to help your understanding and to encourage ideal use of the CPO:

(1) Don't use only the mind, without letting the body enjoy the tool it helped you find. Perhaps the body will use it subtly much of the time (only slightly creating any discernible body movement), then at appropriate moments cause it to explode or surge up inside you to the level which causes the body to join in much broader participation. The body will vary its own intensity of use with the varying intensity of the character's thoughts.

In any event, regardless of the intensity of the moment or its physical manifestation, if your toes feel like curling, let them curl. If your shoulders want to hunch up, don't stop them. If your hands feel like clenching or simply hanging limp at your sides, let them do as they wish. The body knows what it's doing!

(2) Don't let the hands do the work, as they're so accustomed to doing in contemporary cultures. The hands mustn't be a single member trying to do the total of what should be *kept inside the body and experienced by all the inner muscles.*

After all, your hands need to be free to carry things, touch things, handle things, etc., while simply adapting in their own manner because of the CPO into particular muscle-system-directed movement patterns they wouldn't otherwise reflect. *"Rub away..."*, for instance, would appear idiotic, repetitive and senseless if the hands are literally rubbing away at everything rather than the *total inner body* experiencing the very different results of the same Action Verb, without the hands rubbing at all.

The chest, the shoulders, the stomach, the toes, the armpits, the elbows, the neck glands, the eyes and even the teeth---in other words, all parts of the body---have their individual manners of employing *"Rub away..."*, just as they did when you were finding the CPO originally, and as they did in those moments of your prior personal experiences when you were experiencing the same feelings that affected you so.

(3) Explore how the total CPO experience of the body handles props, dictates the way you walk, stand, sit and adjust to all its physical tasks and the manners of their execution. Trust the CPO more than the logic of Academy-trained theatrical movement which doesn't even apply for all characters and in fact obscures the different living moments of most particularized characters.

The CPO will make all movement meaningful in terms of the character's experience itself, keeping the psycho-physical inner life ever present for sensing even when it's barely visible.

(4) After the CPO has been used during the studying of lines--- during which it will have become habit automatically attached to and maintained by the Beat's dialogue and actions later . . . *throw it away!* That's right. Stop using it consciously.

Revert back to *thinking the character's real thoughts and experiencing its true feelings!* This tool is so effective that, once the creative habits of it have been formed during line study, the body will continue experiencing the CPO's body and movement patterns after your mind has returned to *truly living the character's moment.*

I'm aware of the kinds of questions which may occur in the reader's mind about the different processes discussed here. Some of them have come up before from actors and actresses who've attended seminars I've conducted over my thirty years of teaching in Hollywood and elsewhere before people not in my classes.

There was a fairly stiff, visibly inhibited film and television actress in one audience. She felt that the thing she'd always noticed about actors and actresses using such creative tools was the amount of "unnecessary" movement.

She especially pointed out Geraldine Page. She felt that Miss Page's thoughts too often made her "twitch, wiggle, squirm around and appear undisciplined and awkward". (Those were her words.)

She questioned what she called the physical "overacting" she felt Miss Page's creative approaches led to and felt the adding of anything like the CPO would make that "overacting" (again her words) still more exaggerated.

The actress speaking was a bit player in film. Aware of the limitations imposed on bit role players by film cameras---realizing that bit players aren't expected to attract any attention from the leading players and encouraged to keep their work simple, I could understand where her statement came from.

I was familiar with her work in quite small film and television roles. I'd observed that sometimes it was evident that *her body wanted to move* but wasn't allowed to; that her mind was getting in the way and deciding that a certain position was too nice and tidy to be messed up.

Having worked with Katherine Cornell in the Italian and French tours of *"The Barretts Of Wimpole Street"* and having watched her husband, director Guthrie McClintic, directing her body use in even the most minute details moment after moment to achieve body participation (which didn't come naturally to Miss Cornell), I could almost hear the actress who was raising the question saying to herself in those dull moments of her performances, *"Now I must sit down carefully, like Katherine Cornell, with my hands lying in my lap just so."* Like Miss Cornell, she certainly couldn't ever have been accused of "twitching or squirming around" too much!

I offered my opinion that if she kept up the habit of self-constraining and self-inhibiting in all her performances for the rest of her career she certainly wouldn't ever be given any roles where "twitching or squirming" would be appropriate, so she needn't worry about those items.

I'd seen her play several secretaries, an airline reservation clerk, a cousin or something in a scene at a wedding, and things of that sort; never the frustrated boss of the secretary, or the nervously agitated passenger at the airline reservation desk, or in a wedding scene any kind of important member of the wedding.

I told her that she always appeared to me to be stiff and contained to the point that neither I nor even the camera could perceive the slightest hint of what was really going on inside her.

About "Twitching And Squirming"

I mentioned Geraldine Page and the "twitching and squirming" Miss Page first brought to the production of Tennessee Williams' *"Summer And Smoke"* (at the urging of director José Quintero) which brought her instant recognition and prominence in the New York theatre; also the "twitching and squirming" she then brought as important facets of her other characters as the wife of Louis Jourdain in Andre Gide's *"The Immoralist"* and as Alexandra del Lago in Tennessee Williams' *"Sweet Bird Of Youth"*.

Observed to be a little stiff and socially contained herself in earlier years---once commenting to me privately that she saw herself as a big cow, Miss Page had learned that she must overcome that stiffness to afford her body more freedom of experiencing in roles. Her work became stunningly brilliant!

68

Having singled out Katherine Cornell in the previous paragraphs, and after the questioning actress made the statement that
*"No earlier stars ever did all that unnecessary twitching and
squirming,"* I mentioned several contemporaries of Miss Cornell
whose "twitchings and squirmings" were uniquely important
facets of what brought them to stardom and kept them there.
(The actress questioning was old enough to rememer them.) And I
made the point that none of Ms. Cornell's contemporaries I mentioned were method-trained actresses.

Tallulah Bankhead, whether entertaining parties of friends
nude in her New York apartment or visiting beside the pool at her
"Windows" home upstate, usually nude there too (because she simply enjoyed nudity, and all around her accepted it comfortably),
was always squirming!

Ruth Gordon, another Cornell contemporary, was particularly noted for hers. Gloria Swanson, whether sitting with one of
her beloved champagne cocktails or having an ego tantrum on occasion, did more twitching and squirming than most remember.
And the former French film star of just a few years later, Corinne
Calvet, with whom I worked for a time in the nineteen-seventies,
was a twitcher and squirmer as part of her great appeal. Helen
Hayes, still another contemporary who wasn't noted for such
body manifestations in her carefully choreographed performances, still employed such body agitation very consciously
when it was to her liking for characters.

I also mentioned some of the actresses of subsequent years
who have done and still do more twitching and squirming than is
immediately evident in watching them: The wonderful Maggi
Smith knows its value for many characters (of course not all).
Angela Lansbury knows it's part of her "J. B. Fletcher" charm in
"Murder, She Wrote". Crazy, marvelously zany Margaret
Rutherford and her frequent costar Alistair Sim were forever
twitching and squirming. And even Dame Judith Anderson, her
tiny body controllable when she desired, was quite fidgety in conversation and some of it is clearly there in a number of her wonderful film performances. These folks---all from England, a
country where twitching and squirming is far from the national
image---have employed it sensationally.

Soap opera addicts of the current period might watch more
closely the performances of those soap opera stars so loved by
their audiences. There's what the actress called twitching and
squirming every moment as those poor people go through hell.

In another of my seminars, an actor hit upon a very big word
in criticizing essentially the same item---the amount of *"agitation"* (he called it) evident in so many highly creative performances.

About The Absence of Agitation

He was a film actor also, concerned with the demands of the camera for a certain amount of simplicity. He'd appeared in top roles in two or three fairly low-budget motion pictures and I'd seen his work in two of them. I remembered that both were motion pictures in which he got the girl (Yvette Mimieux) in the end and everything worked out very nicely for his character.

However, I'd had the feeling all the time that his character wasn't doing any of the working out of things for itself; that the writer had done it all ahead of time. The actor had appeared to be just coasting through the entirety of the film on good looks, confidence and intelligent line readings. I couldn't feel anything for his character, because he didn't seem to even realize the problems his character was facing from one scene to another. His performance had been, to put it bluntly, dull and boring.

There seemed no survival energy of any kind. The big thing I'd sensed to be missing was any *inner problem agitation* having been planned for his character to experience. After a period of similar starring roles---mostly because he was a handsome devil in the period when handsome mattered---he had faded away.

In working with him later, I found him quickly responsive to this tool, the *Creative Psychological Objective.* His finding of *Inner and Thought Objects* became easy and his experiencing of their wonderful product was ideal. Their effect on his inner neural muscle system evoked natural degrees of the *agitation* he'd been missing. Today, that actor is playing fairly top supporting roles in more important films because his performances now have the *agitation of their inner lives* that they lacked before.

In Behalf of Inner Agitation

Stanislavski himself advocated intense inner agitation. Those of us who've come later also recognize its importance in the use of *any* acting approach.

One of the attributes of the CPO, in fact, is that it *agitates the body.* So does an Object (from which the CPO is generated). So can an Action, an Intention or an Objective. Without the varying degrees of inner agitation in different moments of roles a planned approach item of any kind whatsoever would be meaningless for the actor.

Our inner processes don't stop just because a surface must cover them for a time. It's the same with characters. At least a certain amount of agitation should be continuing behind the surface at most times.

The CPO, involving the body to the extent it does, is an excellent manner of keeping that inner life apparent for the spectator, even if almost subliminally, since its use involves a continuous agitation of the body's *inner muscle system* once it's been practiced during line study. That agitation remains in the performance after the actor returns to thinking the *reality* thoughts of the character and its situation.

Then, there are those other moments of roles when characters can let out their inner feelings totally without any regard for other characters around them. The CPO's use can make those moments devastating in drama or hilarious in comedy.

Of course those role moments allow far more expansive use with tools such as the CPO. The CPO can make them doubly exciting for both the actor and the spectator.

The CPO's value as an acting tool in preparing roles is equalled only by its value as an acting class means of nurturing the imagination, conditioning the actor's body and right brain to work together ideally, and fostering in the actor the desire to seek creative alternatives for moments in roles where they can involve more of the actor's unique resources.

■ **Although some of us don't teach the following item, some teachers recommend it and some actors feel it's productive . . .**

History Of The Character

A Biography of The Character's Imagined Past Life

I'll preface my own comments about this approach that some coaches recommend with the suggestion that the reader interested in testing it might study the manner in which Uta Hagen, who recommends it, details it ideally and fully in Chapter 22 of her book *"Respect For Acting"*. She feels it's a contributive item, and has persuasively explained *why* and *how* in her book.

If the actor handles this *History of the Character* (its imaginary life up to the time of the beginning of the written role) in the manner she recommends, and finds value in it, fine. There may well be value in its exploring for some.

However, some of us feel that it serves best *only* those actors who use *Actions* and *Intentions* as their primary tools. We feel those who use *Objects* don't need these attempts to find parallels out of their private lives to enhance belief in the past of their characters. It's our firm belief that *Objects* kindle those.

Some coaches present this *"history of the character"* as a *shortcut alternative* to the actual listing and appraising of the facts of the author. It falls far short. And that's certainly not how Ms. Hagen recommends it be considered.

The pitfall most often observed is that many actors, in constructing that fictional pre-script life, find themselves trying to experience the hundreds of later facts of the author---many of which are so different from each other---with some core feeling which would justify each and every one of those individual later moments of the character---the *many* simple, individual actions, for the most part, rather than looking for the *emotional conditioning and the resulting behavior patterns* that would define them more ideally. Individual actions themselves are of so little significance without the dominating experience that particularizes them!

Many of us consider this approach in the hands of too many actors to be wheel-spinning and a futile waste of time---this creating of detail after detail out of an imaginary past to justify each in turn of all those individual later actions.

We feel it *confuses* the actor, obfuscates any already at least skeletally formed concept of the inner life of the character, and serves neither the actor nor the character in the end.

There's the tendency of some *"history of the character"* actors to extend such attempts at personalizing and finding of hopefully causative events into *late teens and early adult life, sometimes continuing right up to the moment of the beginning of the role*. . . long after childhood trauma moments would have created the character's conditioned response structure in a far more specific manner.

Pencil and paper before them, some actors who try to gain result with "history of the character" are in the end working from a *left brain library of logic and reasoning.* What some of us see as the fallacy of this whole activity is that the character---if it has any foundation in truth of experience---should be operating throughout its life from *a base of impaired reasoning,* not left brain logic.

A Far More Powerful Alternative

Conditioned responses aren't created by *histories* . . . they're formed in specific *neurosis provoking moments* in childhood when the child's psychology isn't sufficiently developed to cope---in *a final, single traumatic moment!*---with what society throws at it. What's true for psychologists and therapists should be true for actors and the characters they construct as well.

It's my personal conviction that the actor who wants to construct a *"history of the character"* that can truly justify the character's many hundreds of different kinds of actions in the script might better consider constructing a "history" that occurred in the time-span of perhaps *five seconds!*

Even if as the culmination or final "breaking" moment of several or many similar experiences that similarly assaulted the child's undeveloped psychology (as is true in most cases), the mind sciences agree that in *a single, unbearable moment* the psychology became impaired for all time. In that single *neurosis provoking moment in the formative years* the child's concept of itself, its society and its coming life experiences became fixated.

This is precisely what Stanislavski and Vakhtangov primarily were struggling with at the time of Vakhtangov's untimely death in 1922 and still at the time of Stanislavski's in 1938. . . the emerging theories about *conditioned response produced by childhood traumas* that were becoming recognized as valid in that period.

The search for the *truly psycholical* source for our characters' realities . . . the differences between theatrical concepts for characters and truly psychological realities for them . . . should lead to *that single traumatic moment* in early life.

And it was one of the first things that attracted my dear friend Miriam Goldina (who studied with Vakhtangov and Stanislavski and later translated and adapted the two books *"Stanislavski Directs"* and *"Stanislavski's Brilliant Heir: Vakhtangov"*) to my own work . . . the observation that I was proceeding beyond Stanislavski's and Vakhtangov's nascent perception (in the final years of their lives) of *childhood traumas* as the dynamic sources for the conditioning of all later life actions.

They were influenced by the news of Charcot's, Ribot's and Freud's findings, and were striving to adapt those findings to the use of actors. However, neither defined an approach that later appeared in their writings.

The "tool" which Miriam observed me teaching has been called by me the *Neurosis Provoking Moment.*

My recommended manner of creating the *Neurosis Provoking Moment*---after the actor's analysis of the writer's facts, and after the forming of at least a *vague, temporary or rough Super Objective* (Stanislavski's and Vakhtangov's term) for the character---was labeled that.

The manner of constructing imagined *Neurosis Provoking Moments* for characters is written about lengthily in my earlier book *"Since Stanislavski And Vakhtangov"*.

Briefly, here, it involves a first step for the actor of (1) *thinking and feeling to a heightened degree the two (vague or temporary) top tools thus far planned for the character---the Life Object and the Vague Super Objective---and . . .*

(2) *while maintaining that feeling in an intensified level, very swiftly (too swiftly for intellectual control), improvising aloud an imaginary childhood of cumulative relationships and events that assaulted the child's vulnerable psychology and led up to the culminating moment (still in childhood or very early teens) when . . .*

(3) *there was a "snapping", a final thwarting moment when the trauma formed the single defense structure for the whole life.*

The "tool" being sought---the *final Super Objective* that emerges from that *single, final "snapping' moment* of the Neurosis Provoking Moment (that moment when a specific, urgent action is envisioned in order to cope but *is not taken and is suppressed violently*) is unbelievably potent!

This is accomplished because, as the actor swiftly improvises the cumulative details, one after another, the intense feelings of those two top tools (held at pitch throughout) create a crescendo of impacting experiences in those imagined, important formative years that led up to the final breaking point---the *Neurosis Provoking Moment.* And, because it's inevitable that through the requisite swiftness of imagining, any similar moments of the actor's own personal childhood experience, whether recognized or not, will be touched on briefly in passing, creating a *Super Objective of a more evocative form* as a living force for that actor.

After my initially conceiving of the *"NPM"* and introducing it in classes, a member of my class came to me and said that her psychotherapist, the noted Dr. Richard Renneker, the then head of the Ford Foundation Psychotherapy Group, would like to come and observe its forming and use. I was happy to receive his input. He marvelled afterward that it had been discovered in an acting class. Some time later I received from him a copy of an article he had written about it in the *Journal of Psychiatry.*

My dear friend Miriam Goldina called me excitedly from New York while appearing in *"Sunrise At Campobello"* on Broadway. *"Larry! I used your neurosis proving moment to prepare my character! It is wonderful! Thank you, thank you, thank you!"* She later, in a visit to Moscow, lectured on it before the faculty and student body at the Vakhtangov Theatre.

Agreeing with psychologists, I hold to the firm belief that a personality is most surely fixated early in life by *one single traumatic moment,* and that such single, personality-fixating NPM's can be ideally imagined for actors' characters.

Returning to the approach being discussed---the preparing of a *History Of The Character*, or as some call it *Biography Of The Character*, if you're interested in using it I'd recommend that you get Uta Hagen's book and read that Chapter 22. Like many other approach items, its use may be to your liking.

■ **Michael Chekhov taught the following approach for finding Ideas for the embodiment of characters . . .**

Human Images

as Sources For External/Internal Characterization Inspirations

Chekhov postulated that actors could seek inspirations for *external* characterizations by observing other humans and copying their characteristics and mannerisms. However, in the 1955 tapings of his own personal discussion of his many approaches, he's personally recorded as commenting, *"But . . . once inside the body of that other human being . . . you don't know what to do."*

In using *Human Images* to personify a character most actors, unlike Chekhov, aren't as often these days also seeking the inner life of the character, as he did, for a reference point. *Human Image*, when used as a tool by the contemporary actor, is most often viewed as an external characterization approach. The actor may or may not have already analyzed the personality of the character provided by the writer. The wiser actors want to do that first, then perhaps think of a person they know whose external behavior suggests that kind of personality.

Others who use this approach like to visualize the kind of person their intuitive judgment tells them the character emerging from the writer's descriptions and actions might look like and how that person might talk, move, etc. Then that particular actor in all probability searches his mind for someone who fits those specifics.

In both cases, it's best if it's someone the actor knows, works with or at least sees frequently, so the opportunities can be created to observe the person more fully.

Laurence Olivier said that his portrayal of *"Richard III"* was based on the American producer Jed Harris, whom he had worked for and heartily disliked. Other leading actors have come upon inspiring *Human Images* quite by accident and suddenly thought to use the manners and certain visual characteristics of those other persons as being appropriate for the characters they're working on.

Whether seeking an appropriate human image intentionally or coming upon one by accident and deciding to use it, it's one way to find ideas for a character that won't come to mind by simply looking in a mirror.

While for film and television there are makeup specialists to provide the externals, most theatre actors spend hours sitting in front of their mirrors trying to imagine the ideal makeup and hairstyles, physical manners and other surface embodiments for characters already planned as to their emotional lives but which remain to be adorned with external highlights. Theatre actors are often expected to suggest those items for themselves!

If you're one who's been through this experience (as most theatre actors certainly have), you'll recall that after coming up with some interesting ideas you've partially or totally tailored those ideas back out of existence because, looking at yourself in the mirror, you felt they wouldn't work with your particular face, nose, head shape, neck, body or some other aspect of your own appearance. Actors have spent many futile hours of such searching and then, as an alternative, found Chekhov's *Human Image* to be helpful.

■ **There's a very handy alternative that can bypass many hours of those dressing room struggles and *Human Image* searchings:**

Imaginary Characters
that Offer Unlimited Numbers of Inspirations

In my own working with a cast preparing the odd assortment of derelicts in one play, I found it helpful to suggest to the cast members that they imagine two or three characters of the general social strata involved but each in a different place and even of a different generic type.

They were to be imagined in stationary moments, so the actors wouldn't become involved with a developing story and distract themselves from imagining those characters' externals strictly from close scrutinies of imagined characteristics of their physical appearance.

Some examples that were found included (1) a bum who slept in roadside caves and parks at night, (2) a wino on Skid Row sleeping beside a trashcan, (3) an itinerant field worker standing in line for a job of artichoke-picking, (4) a Skid Row missionary minister supervising a bread-and-soup kitchen, and (5) a ragged hermit in his junkyard hovel on the edge of town.

Imagining each individual character singly, the actors were told to ask themselves *"What's wrong with...?"*---his nose, his hands, his shirt, his left shoe, his hair, his eyebrows, his mouth, his hat or cap, his pants, his socks, his belt and as many other details as they liked, until they had a big list containing many small ideas to afford their characters' externals move vivid life.

Another question that provides productive inspirations in such an exercise/search is *"What's unusual about...?"* applied to the same kind of imagined characters list. Still more idea-gathering possibilities: *"What's in each of his pockets?"*, *"What are those things he's carrying?"* and other similar questions, each set of questions bringing more inspirations.

Of course all the ideas brought out won't be used, but the actor will have a rich gardenful of new ideas from which to choose.

For characters on higher social levels, the questions might be changed, in order to provide ideas more appropriate for those upper class or middle class characters, to *"What's unusual about...?"* or *"What's special about...?"* or *"What's impressive about...?"*---applied to all those same separate items.

Even a member of the other gender can often be productive. Characteristics found in an imagined female character for a man's role, or in an imagined man for a woman's role, can be adapted to the other sex. (Don't scoff at this till you've tried it.)

Whatever manner may be employed for creating the physical embodiment of a character, after its choice is made the actor can certainly profit from also exploring it in improvisations involving physical tasks and activities, to discover the unique manners in which the imagined character would move and behave.

■ **The next upcoming approach is one that can't be too highly praised. If there's one teacher who doesn't teach it, there certainly shouldn't be!**

Imaginary Centers
for "Instant Characters"

One of Michael Chekhov's teaching approaches at the Moscow Art Theatre was based on what he himself labeled the *"Imaginary Center"*. His approach was first designed to help actors attain classic form for their stance and movement.

In Chekhov's first conceived form, it involved the imagining of a string lifting the top center of the actor's chest up and forward.   It produced graceful movement for the bodies of actors who had no graceful movement otherwise.

With the top center of the chest being lifted in the actor's imagination, the neural muscle system would cause the total body to flow gracefully at all times with the resulting coordination supplied by that one single point on the body.

That original concept of the *Imaginary Center* created the same beauty and grace of movement that is taught by balletmasters.   It created the *dancing*-acting for which Michael Chekhov was noted.   Students of Chekhov and others who've read of or been taught and have appreciated this approach---as well as many dancers already accustomed to such "centering"---did then and still do enjoy that manner of working.

But his longtime roommate, Vakhtangov, observed the limitation of Chekhov's approach--- the resulting grace of movement that was out of place for so many characters, and saw the "imaginary center" in a very different light.

Through experimentation, Vakhtangov and Chekhov discovered that by moving an *imaginary center* to many different locations on or in the body it was possible to create quite different, total body results for the many, many characters that should not move so gracefully.

It was their adaptation of Chekhov's approach, and Vakhtangov's occasional relabeling it *"Motive Center"*, which has enhanced its potential use for so many varied characters.

In the Vakhtangov-suggested manner, the *"Motive Center"* can bring rather miraculous results and authentic movement patterns for so many different purposes.

The *Motive Center* as I'm describing it here is an imaginary spot or object on or in the body at some point, through whch all feelings, thoughts, sensations and experiences such as seeing, hearing, smelling, even speaking, are channeled creatively, both incoming and outgoing, for the sake of creating certain characters more organically by (in effect) relocating *the entire neural muscle system center*, through the actor's imagination and to the extent that the imagination can convincingly accomplish this.

When such a tool is used, not only are the larger movements affected---as in standing, sitting, walking, etc., but also we discover through the *Motive Center* the exciting little adjustments and movements which it would not be possible to conceptualize intellectually or find with equal authenticity and effective result in any other manner.

Some coaches, myself included, have found that---as Jerzy Grotowski taught in Poland, later in America---the *voice re-*

sonators are the most important parts of the actor's body in the search for an ideal *Motive Center*. It's the actor or actress who can experience the sensation of actually *talking through different parts of the body* at different times who can obtain the best results from a Motive Center. Ridiculous as this may appear to the less imaginative, it's indeed possible and it's in fact rather necessary for the actor to have the ability to imagine doing this in order to fully utilize this tool and reap all its possible benefits.

You might, at this point, before even reading on, set the book aside and try first to talk out of the side of the mouth softly, then out of the middle, then the other side. That much is easy, of course, since you'll be talking out of the mouth itself.

Next, however, try talking out of these spots, convincing yourself along the way that you're actually sending your voice out through them: the right nostril. the tip of the nose, the top of the bottom palate, the middle of the right cheek, the bottom of the chin. the front of the teeth, the tip of the tongue. Doing those, you've already observed the "instant characters" such use of the *Motive Center* has created. Next, try these more difficult ones:

For the previously discussed truck driver home from the road (in the *Animate Images* chapter), instead of the bear image, explore what talking through a large "beer bellybutton" produces for the entire instrument. For the role of Helen Keller in *"The Miracle Worker"* at that early age---denied sight, hearing and speech, explore what happens throughout your entire being when trying to make non-talking sounds through an empty cave in the middle of the head with a small roller bearing rolling around on its floor through which all sensation must be channeled.

For Cliff Robertson's Award-winning role of *"Charly"* in the television picture of that name some years ago, see what a spot under the right jaw about three inches back from the chin (to bring the retardation of that fascinating character, flowing to all parts of the body) can bring into speech and body movement, wardrobe and other inspirations.

And for "Stanley Kowalski" in *"A Streetcar Named Desire"*, try an imaginary iron bar stretching across the back of the character's neck from shoulder to shoulder---and discover that one of your arms will hang limply at your side in that gesture which became a "Marlon Brando mimicing" position in the years just subsequent to his portrayal of that character in the Broadway and film versions of Tennessee Williams' work.

As the truck driver (with the beer bellybutton), you'll have experienced the heaviness and deep voice of the man, the different way that the beer can would be held, the difficulty in getting up from the chair, the slumped position in sitting, etc.

79

As Helen Keller, you'll have experienced the strange sensation of wanting to hear through that small roller bearing, the effort required to make first sounds through it, the sensation of touching something not with the fingertips but with the roller bearing, etc., as well as the implosive experience of channeling the fury of Helen's deprivation problem through the same spot as it made your body twist and turn in frustration.

As "Charly", you found your body slanted, the right jaw drooping and uncontrollable, the slurred and difficult speaking, the feeling that your wardrobe should hang to the right, also the unique manner of using your arms and hands. If you were to try running down a hallway as "Charly" did in the story at one point, the *Motive Center* would amaze you with the distorted running down the long hallway it would produce.

Whether you use the *Imaginary or Motive Center* consciously *only* to discover the forms of movement and the total experience and continue to use it in practice, then discard the conscious use of it later (since the body will remember to use it in the practiced manner in actual performance)---or choose to still use it consciously in actual performance (as Tom Hanks appears to have used it in *"Forrest Gump"*). . . it works marvellously either way.

While the relocating of the neural muscle system center--- which you're essentially doing when you use a *Motive Center*--- creates a so complete experience for the actor *inside* those externals, it's also the result in *external appearance, movements, speech and other inspirations* which come in profusion from *Imaginary or Motive Center* use for which this tool is created to primarily serve. The character who seems to be warped a little in an interesting way because of its personality via a chosen *Center* usually has its hair parted to fall a certain way or straight backward or forward, for example. The actor can simply *feel through the Center* the way that will be right. The wardrobe of the character will want to be a little askew in a certain way, and will *feel through the Center* to somehow be wrong in any other way.

If the head tends to lean in some direction, the hat or cap will want to be adjusted a little as well. Props will want to be held in one way and no other, because the hands and arms are formed in a certain way by the Center's effect on the total neural muscle system. A successfully created *Imaginary or Motive Center* character very clearly makes all these decisions for you!

Visualize (or try for yourself), for instance, a *"chrysanthe-mum-at-the-shoulder"* clubwoman who in effect *"chrysanthe-mums"* everything she does . . . simpering through it, gossiping covertly through it, walking with its selfconscious one-sided erectness, sitting with its left-side uplift apparent as she presents her importance before her peers, listening through it to the guest

80

speaker at the Thursday tea, sniffing sideways through it to find out what perfume her neighbor is wearing, and speaking with the slight breathiness which the relocated *Center* causes.

The actress using this Motive Center would observe that her lips would be pursed a little, her chin would want to rise to the left a little, her hands clasped politely in her lap would want to be a little to the right or left. Such things are automatic results and are easily observed in first experiencings with this tool.

We needn't go down the entire list of fairly obvious real life *Imaginary Center* characters around us, but we're sure to know at least one front-of-the-bottom-teeth bully, a few upper or lower palate gullible folks, some corner-of-the-mouth cynics, one or two top-of-the-shoulder movie starlets, some kidney-pain older people, one or two top-of-the-tight-behind people pleasers, etc.

In a group of people, look around at one after another. Try to imagine where one's *center* is located and what its form. When you decide, try it on your own body. It's a remarkably effective tool for the actor. The characters it can produce are limitless. And then allow the *Center* itself to determine wardrobe and how it's worn, hair style, all kinds of movements and manners of handling props, etc. The entire process of applying this tool in characterization is a fantastic trip!

Many contemporay actors use this marvelous tool, and do so often, after learning what it can produce for external characterization.

■ **I regret that in discussing the following item, which I consider to be so important in actors' training and in their later professional lives as well, I feel honor bound to also state my personal views about certain other kinds of acting classes that are conducted by many teachers who are friends and acquaintances of mine and who will probably find some of my comments about the manners in which they work offensive . . .**

Improvisation

vs. Scene Study

The two most often encountered kinds of acting classes are *"Scene (And Monologue) Study"* and *"Improvisation"* classes. One or the other is offered by teachers for all levels---*Beginning, Intermediate, Advanced and Professional*---sometimes without concern for individual actors' specific needs, rather because one or the other is simply the chosen specialization of the coach.

Improvisation has its unique values. Scene Study has its. But the thing for actors to consider when selecting one or the other kind of acting class is the manner in which either of the two serves the next development steps the actor's seeking.

The answer should be obvious, for many reasons. Unfortunately, some people disagree.

Scene And Monologue Classes

For a new, beginning actor, Scene Study is too often a quantum leap ahead of what the actor needs in development terms. Too often the preparing of scenes and monologues at a too early point in the actor's development becomes an exercise in simply taking directions and suggestions offered by the coach in critiques. Too often the typical scene and monologue study class or workshop devotes almost no class time to the study of technique.

The actor may be learning little or nothing that contributes to developing his imagination, sensitizing his instrument, preparing characters, achieving coordinated use of his mind and body . . . because of simply not being ready in some or all of those respects to experience character-based belief in a prepared fiction as if it were truth.

For the highly advanced actor, on the other hand, a Scene Study class offers opportunities to try new areas of characterization, expand his horizons of inspiration, or deepen his experience through attempts and failures with new insight, contributive critique and suggestions from the coach.

As an example, Lee Strasberg, when working solely with already top professional actors at the Actors Studio, mustly conducted scene and monologue work with those accomplished talents, because those actors wanted to (or were goaded by Lee to) try new areas, deal with still existing problems in their work, etc. For them, such scene and monologue work was ideal for those explorations of new areas.

In his private classes for less advanced actors, Lee generally postponed actual scene work until the actors were ready.

Even for the professional, a Scene Study class too often means simply preparing a selected scene or monologue, presenting it as "work in progress" time and again, receiving directorial suggestions, and sometimes spending even months working on the same single character and same single kind of moments, left on his own as to how to remedy problems.

I realize it will offend some scene study conductors that I believe, in the final analysis, scene study and monologue work is at best *a series of rehearsals* in which the person conducting such work is essentially *a director*, in too many cases critiquing the work and simply offering *directorial comments* and perhaps one or two suggestions to be tried. Strasberg's scene work was different. *Ideally contributive suggestions* were one of Strasberg's very strong points. But the actor can't expect those everywhere.

Those *supervised rehearsals* (that's really all they sometimes are) are usually just once a week, extending over long periods, and are even less frequently presented by their participants if partners haven't been available or willing to rehearse and actors must simply watch other actors' work in many sessions between their own showings. The scene or monologue chosen may or may not even offer the actor any real development of the kind that's hoped to take place in any class the actor's paying to attend. A lot of the actor's time can be wasted in such workshops.

The actor who's ideally ready for scene study and monologue work, and who seeks a place to involve with it, can judge for himself whether he's getting what he's hoping to get.

But for the new, *beginning* and even what's commonly called an *intermediate* level actor, there are worse drawbacks in exclusively scene study and monologue work:

Each scene or monologue involves *just one personality type in just one kind of situation.* That's not what a still developing actor needs! And repeating the same piece over and over---even if there's gradual improvement each time, over the same long period of *supervised rehearsals* mentioned before---can extend the actor's learning phase into infinity.

In limiting himself to exclusively scene and monologue work, the still developing actor is usually not learning any new technique items; is experiencing only one personality type for that long period; isn't continually expanding his spectrum of emotional experiences into new areas in class session after class session; and is seldom involved with specific areas of development that need attention. What he's getting is often strictly director suggestions and, to the extent such class time allows, coaching in preparing a single kind of role.

Improvisations offer so much more! Robert Lewis and others of us conduct many, many improvisations in classes for training purposes (in his case with *Intentions* involved, in my own with *Objects* instead), so actors are constantly preparing approach items that affect them via evocative wordings, practicing the executing and controlling of their preparation and concentration, and being *obliged* to do all those things class after class because no writer has supplied any dialogue or outline.

There's the added advantage---for those who've involved extensively with improvisation before entering the professional mainstream---that no matter what happens unexpectedly and without rehearsal, whether it be on stage or on a film set, the ability to deal with the occurrence spontaneously and with a sense of truth is ready.

My own first introduction to improvisation on any professional level was when, as a young GI stationed in Rome during World War II, managing the theatre in the *Foro Mussolini* (later called *Foro d'Italia* for obvious reasons), I managed to be cast for a tiny role (as an American GI) in Roberto Rossellini's film *"La Vita Ricominciata"*.

Rossellini had the beautiful French star Danielle Darrieux and me briefly improvise an imaginary scene, then our scripted scene without dialogue, then had us add our lines and finally play the scene for the camera.

Ms. Darrieux was a very busy actress at the time, and she was insecure with her dialogue when actual filming of our scene came. At one point she simply forgot her next line and stared at me. I expected Rossellini to stop the shot. He didn't. I looked back at her numbly for what seemed forever, then probably out of nervousness (and expecting the shot to be stopped) we both smiled. She finally remembered her line and Rossellini was ecstatic! The long silence and the smiles were left in the film and through the magic of the camera and music and some of the largest two heads closeups I've ever had, the long silent interval worked!

Dustin Hoffman considers improvising of film sequences a wonderful manner of finding additional moments for the scenes' participants. He speaks warmly of the improvisations of scenes for *"Kramer vs. Kramer"*, *"The Graduate"* and other films. He's also pointed out one scene in *"Midnight Cowboy"* when, as Ratso, he was walking across the street in traffic, during a take, and a car almost hit him. His pounding the hood of the car and yelling at the driver *"I'm walking here!"* wasn't in the script. But it was kept in because it added a nice, typically Ratso moment.

Gerry Page told Lorrie Hull she *"adored improvisation in actual performance; that if we just say the lines as written we often have to leap from mountain crag to mountain crag in our thinking, but in improvising, stretching the fabric, poking around in it, we find the links that aren't immediately observable."*

Actors' ability to improvise has saved many moments in theatre productions! It allowed me to overcome the obstacles Gloria Swanson threw at me in my first performance with her, as mentioned in the *"Attention and Concentration"* chapter later.

And I recall another summer theatre experience: The following week's play, *"Murder Without Crime"*, had been rehearsing all week until Saturday of the previous week, when the director,

84

Larry Dobkin, realized that the leading man playing Steven couldn't possibly be ready with his role for the Monday opening.

It was my Actors Equity "rest week", but Larry persuaded me to stay up all night Saturday studying the role, be ready for dress rehearsal Sunday night and open in the role Monday night! (My character, Stephen, was on stage every moment of the play!)

There was a fight scene involving a large knife. There was barely time to even stage it. On Monday night, with the knife in my hand, I accidentally nicked the actor playing Matthew as he wrested it from me, and he accidentally knocked me out just before the second act curtain. He began bleeding heavily and was rushed to the doctor during intermission, and I was revived. As the third act curtain rose on him standing over me in the second act closing position he improvised, *"I hope you don't mind, Stephen. I borrowed one of your bandaids while you were out."*

Many film directors like to call together their cast members before filmings begin, especially if they haven't worked together before, and have them improvise imaginary scenes not in the scripts, to help them as well as himself become acquainted with how each works and form the foundation for their scripted relationships. Among them, Elia Kazan has been one of the most quoted about these improvisations' values.

New York acting teacher Michael Schulman cites the importance of improvisation in all acting training: He points out that the actor learns through improvisation to rely on the realities of the moment---what he sees, hears, smells, touches and tastes, and on the private, internal realities of what he thinks and feels.

Acting teachers who work as I myself do (primarily teaching approach items actors can rely upon in most roles and situations) especially value improvisations and devote most of our classes to their use as the means of practicing those items that are new to the class members.

In an *improvisation* class, there's time for a teacher to teach new approaches and time for the actors to practice them. There's the opportunity for the actor to learn at least one new approach item and its use in each class attended and, in the same class, practice the approach toward forming its habits. There's time in an improvisation class for each actor to work at least twice, perhaps several times, depending on what's being practiced.

I believe an ideal kind of improvisation class is one where the actors use whatever approach they're being taught for preparing characters and prior to improvising are given a period for choosing and preparing one or perhaps two different personalities to be brought into their one or two improvisations. In that manner they're practicing the preparation of characters, with

85

whatever tools, and then experiencing the subtexts of those personalities during their improvising. In addition, they may try personality types they know they need to work on.

In such a class *the actor's development needs* are more strikingly observable to the teacher and those needs can be dealt with on the spot, having nothing to do with the limited parameters of a written character.

In my own classes, I've generally assigned couples (less often three or four people) to work together and provided them, prior to "preparation time", with slips detailing their situations.

The slip given each person details only what they should personally know of the situation details, nothing of what personality the other person will bring.

Since I've always taught manners of preparing characters, they've then been afforded preparation time to prepare the characterizations that are needed to justify their actions.

In this manner I've been able to assign work most needed by the individual; the individual then practices in an area needed, and is also practicing the preparing and experiencing of specific personality types, usually other than his or her own.

Consider carefully in making your choice as to which kind of class will best serve your needs. There's a world of difference between the two kinds!

■ **The next item is certainly of importance for actors who use** *Actions* **or** *Intentions* **primarily. For those actors it's one of the most necessary additional approach items . . .**

Justification

It's What Motivates the Character's Actions

This is an approach item taught primarily---maybe exclusively---by those who follow Stanislavski's outline of the preparation process religiously. They're the teachers who teach *Actions* and *Intentions*. Those who teach *Objects,* following Vakhtangov in the preparation areas involved, find them simply repetitive time-takers. They're already part of the *given facts* of the writer, and if they're character / personality based the personality "tools" will already have been prepared, providing all of those elements. In the teaching of those who advocate the use of *Objects,* the *Justification* is a step the actor is grateful to be able to eliminate.

Stanislavski created the term *"Justification"* to identify the inner motivation of the character---firmly rooted in the character's personality, its *Super Objective* and its large and small goals as the scripted events are experienced throughout its role. Those who teach in the manner I do are following his work outline except in the bypassing of *Justifications.*

Vakhtangov---while loyally teaching *Justifications* to adhere to Stanislavski's System---realized, as do many of us who have come later, that were the actor to employ *Objects* in the manner Vakhtangov suggested (rather than one of the *"action"* tools), such *Justifications*, like some of the other items designed to particularize the action items, would have been superfluous.

Objects aren't *actions.* They're the subject of whatever nature the character's attention is focused upon. They most often *include the justifications themselves* for whatever actions the character might find necessary or desirable to take. Further, if the actor is using *actions* instead of *objects*, then for characters who by reason of their personality structures are *unable* to take the desired actions yet another approach item---it's called the *Obstacle*---is demanded! For the latter characters *something* has to stand in the way, determining that the *action* can't be taken.

One character who, consistent with its personality, is fully able to actually take a desired action (without the slightest doubt of its logic or possible danger) might be guided by the actor's choice to *"make them stop obstructing me!"* or perhaps *"get past their damn roadblocks!."* There's nothing wrong with either of those actions if the character is ideally capable. A *Justification* isn't all that necessary, since the very choice by the actor of one of those wordings implies that the character who would think in that language has few if any deterring concerns.

Still considering the actor who uses *Actions* out of preference but now considering the actor who uses some of those imprecise and colorless *Action* wordings like *"to persevere"*, or *"to win"* (or some other wording that contains none of the sentiment and thought-wording form of the character) . . . certainly something like a *Justification* (a *"because of"*, in other words) is needed to lend meaningful substance to such an imprecise choice.

And later, such a *Justification* or *"because of"* would need to be *kept in the consciousness of the actor, in fact, in addition to the Action*, throughout whatever duration of time is spent in that particular Beat!

The same determined character, if not as capable, and if the actor uses an *Object* for that Beat instead of an *Action*, would need no item like a *Justification* because that actor would know to choose the problem of the obstructions, the roadblocks, and in the sentiment and language of such a character would be using some wording like *"How impossible this is!"* or *"How weak I am!"* It's obvious that nothing like a *Justification* needs to be added. The personality is inherent in the wording, as it can always be in the *Object* approach.

■ **Next . . . something many actors haven't been prompted by teachers to explore and encourage into their work. If you haven't been urged to try the following, try on your own. It's something you'll fall in love with because of the many ways in which it enhances belief and enriches your work with many more human colors that wouldn't be there otherwise. . .**

The Living Sounds
of The Animal Within

Be ready for the director who might innocently ask why you're making a certain *sound* at some point in dialogue or action when it isn't called for in the script!

Present day actors (and that director) have been reared in a world where the *conscious* use of sounds has gradually diminished before the onslaught of civilization and language, with the latter having become inadequate substitutes for the experience and communication sounds which have been the natural heritage of man since the primates.

Nowadays we make sounds unconsciously for the most part and more in private---usually because of the socialization of our cultures on everything but *The Animal Within,* which is the only part of us that's managed to avoid this socialization by remaining hidden most of the time.

Sounds illuminate our inner processes. They're generally involuntary, often unconscious in our private lives, but for the actor they need to be used consciously and recognized for the added degee of experiencing their use creates, for the inspirations they can bring moment after moment and for the spontaneity and the freedom they provide in acting roles.

Sounds are made by us in real life much more often than we realize. Many of our *thoughts* produce sounds. Our *moods* produce sounds. Our *feelings* and certainly our *emotions* produce sounds. Our *body conditions* produce sounds. Many simple *actions* involving any amount of exertion produce sounds. *Reactions* produce sounds, whether we notice them or not. Yet many actors leave sounds out of their acting experience!

Sounds produce *the next moment's truth* more fully, because the body responds to them. They *communicate more fully than mere words* could possibly communicate. They add *emotional flavor, more interesting colors and more truth* to all moments.

They bypass the intelligence and the conditioned cautions of self-consciousness. They go directly to, and come more than words can come from, *the viscera . . . the gut!*

They're "feeling blobs" more often than formed thoughts. They're *experiences . . .* and most of them, by reason of their sources, are *private and personal,* even when with others.

After a number of years of treading water in low-budget films, Jack Nicholson's career exploded suddenly into stardom in the first moments of *"Easy Rider"* with those waking up sounds with a terrible hangover in his jail cell. Oscar winners like Geraldine Page, Cher, Shirley MacLaine, Sally Field, William Hurt, Meryl Streep, Dustin Hoffman, Jessica Lange . . . and even English stars Anthony Hopkins, Peter O'Toole, Glenda Jackson, Maggi Smith and Angela Lansbury use them quite consciously all the time, which is remarkable, considering the English actor's emphasis on dialogue.

Watch more closely. Notice that most top stars use them, whether consciously or unconsciously, many of them appreciating the added human colors and true moments they produce.

That almost *no complete experience* is without its living sounds is indisputable. That living sounds *enhance most experiences' truths* for actors is equally beyond question. That they automatically *involve the body organically* is one bonus; that they *help create next moments* naturally and more fully is another; *how good they feel* to the actor using them, *how totally relaxing they are* to the body, and *how completely they're shared by viewers . . .* all those should be the ultimate persuasions for actors to use them forever!

Lee Strasberg insisted on his class members making *sounds* during relaxation exercises as a very important part of achieving the desired relaxed states. Try relaxing without the throaty exhalation that goes with it. Sounds help actors in that way also.

If you haven't already been adding sounds to your dialogue and other types of experiences, and haven't consciously explored *"The Living Sounds"* in a class, right now try some. First, set the book aside to leave your body free to note how *most living sounds experiences move the body as well as relax it.* Try these, one at a time. You'll see what wonderfully complete experiences the sounds create in simple living moments:

A boring Sunday at home. A frustrating problem. Trying to get to sleep on a hot night. Cuddling with someone on a sofa.

Getting into a hot jacuzzi. An unbearably cold room. A speaker whom you can't stand is delivering a lecture. You have a terrible sunburn. Reading a ridiculous love letter. Your niece is murdering an etude on the piano. You're checking your role in the upcoming script. Getting into, taking, and getting out of a cold shower.

If you're in a class working on *The Living Sounds*, with some of the foregoing exercises being asked of class members, notice in your own work that the demand to produce many sounds, moment after moment, makes you discover so many little inspirations that come from your imaginary situation that you'd otherwise overlook. And notice that *no sound fails to move the body in some manner.*

In observing the work of others, notice the same things. And don't fail to observe how *organically and truthfully* the body is automatically involved by each and every sound.

There are a couple of other sound experiences I've conducted for many years in my classes:

The first is a group experience. I call it *"Dial Switching."* I have a group of people, supposedly family members or roommates, sit around comfortably staring at an imaginary television set. There's no dialogue. I call out perhaps *"Claudette has to watch her soap opera,"* and even while Claudette is on her way to the imaginary television set the sound reactions begin.

All kinds of reactions, all strictly in sound only, come from the others watching an enjoyable or hated or ridiculed soap opera. After a few moments I might call out *"Harry wants to watch President Clinton's speech,"* and he rises to switch to it. Again sounds come from others' reactions and his own.

Then, after some moments, I call out to someone else to switch, saying what's being switched to so everyody knows. It's a group exercise that definitely promotes the practicing with and enjoyment of making sounds of all kinds. Throughout the group of *Dial Switching* television programs it's impossible for observers to not notice how much natural movement of all the bodies results from the adding of sounds to the moments.

Another exercise I use to really excite actors with what sounds can mean in dialogue moments of their work is a *"Going Someplace Before Responding"*.

Individual class members, one at a time, sit up front before the class ready to respond to all questions. The assignment is to react first with a sound, any kind of sound, that the question from a class member prompts, then retain the feeling of the sound that precedes the words as the response is verbalized. The manner of speaking maintains the sound that precedes the words.

If a question elicits a big guffaw from the respondent, then in a sentence or two following that guffaw, the words are to come out as almost guffaws also. If a depressed sound comes before the response, then the sentence or two of response following that depressed sound is to have the same tone.

In real life we're usually unconscious of those brief reaction sounds that so often come before a reply is worded. The sound response is a natural reaction that simply hasn't been put into words so quickly.

When the noted playwright Ben Hecht and I were working together, in reminiscing about Michael Chekhov's performance in Ben's film *"The Spectre Of The Rose"*, he commented that making apparently involuntary sounds before many of his speeches was apparently one of Chekhov's secrets. He told Ben that he and Vakhtangov, when they were roommates for a time at the Moscow Art Theatre, would play *"sounds"* games together frequently and those moments of spontaneous, unworded, feeling responses took him comfortably into his characters' responses.

Once when Dr. Dick Renneker and I were sitting in his office discussing the *Neurosis Provoking Moment*, we somehow got onto a discussion of *Living Sounds*. He scribbled just one word on a piece of paper, *"Fine,"* pulled out a tape recording from one of his therapy sessions with a patient, cued it up and played it.

Renneker: *"Well, how'd your week go?"*

Patient: A depressed laugh *("What a stupid question!")* . . . A long drawn out groan *("Christ, where do I start?")* . . . A cynical half chuckle *("You want the whole shitpot?")* . . . A giant exhalation of irritation *("Aw, what's the use?")* . . . A helpless little half-laugh *("Same as always, pretty shitty!")* . . . Another groan *("What the hell am I doing here?")*, etc., etc., for what must have been a whole minute before any word, each sound clearly representing its own unspoken inner experience . . . then finally, the single word *"Fine."*

Dr. Renneker told me that the Ford Foundation Psychotherapy Group members listen to those tapes and analyze sounds.

Next time you're working on a role, try mixing *the living sounds* into many of your character's moments during the studying of your lines. You'll be thrilled with the result!

If you're not sold on adding living sounds to your work at all times after the foregoing experiments---forming their use as habit and enjoying what they produce, you'll be the loser.

Form the habit of bringing them into your work regularly and enjoyably. You'll find even the dullest dialogue of your character brought to life for you.

■ Now, at the risk of being accused of heresy, I must state that some of Stanislavski's writings really do need reexamining in the light of more recent behavioral science findings. Many of us now feel the most productive results of analyzing characters' personalities must derive from the determining of the character's . . .

Negative Conditioning
that Lies Behind Even "Positive Goal" Personalities

For an actor who's easily satisfied with only a modicum of his own experiential feeling reservoir in performance, there can always be the most obvious choice available---the *Positive Goal*. How can it be wrong, when Stanislavski himself suggested such goals---*Peace, Love, A Better World To Live In* and some other similar, certainly *positive* goals for the cores of characters' personalities?

Those are in his notes as his earliest recommendations . . . those notes made before he had considered Ribot's, Charcot's and finally Freud's theories. Unfortunately, actors who read his early ideas in his books read his recommendations of *Positive Goals*.

Such a choice---a *positive goal*---seems at first to spring obviously into bright and temporarily attractive clarity from first readings of a role. What the character seems to want is fairly apparent through the writer's progression of the story, and the gratifying denouement would seem to provide enough satisfaction deriving from the achieving of a very apparent goal.

Some actors, so easily satisfied, simply aren't aware of what they're missing, and what Stanislavski later realized he too was missing. They'll prepare a positive goal character and as a result will in the later performance determinedly bring as convincingly as they can what's only a half-life. The character they create may of course be a well oiled machine functioning properly and effectively. Regrettably, though, the spectator will probably not be watching such a character or feeling anything for it.

How much more exciting it can be for both the actor and the spectator if the tender underbelly of a *negative-driven* character is prepared from the outset to go through the experiences the writer demands of it.

I recall an answer Tennessee Williams once gave an interiewer when asked what he thought was the secret of his playwriting success. I don't recall his exact words, but in essence he replied *"I turn over rocks and show what's underneath."*

92

A character experiencing its own pressures, its own ungratified needs and its own survival drives emanating from a powerful *negative problem* core is a far more engrossing character, as well as offering a far deeper and more emotionally conditioned characterization for the actor to experience throughout all its many moments. There's always more interesting life under a rock than on its sunwashed surface.

The "positive goal" character that wants *peace*, for example, can be somewhat frustrated in its outreaching search, but it won't lend itself to experiencing the cacophony of noisy intruders, the cage-claustrophobia of close relationships, or the empty wastelands of aloneness when they're (if ever) produced by the very peace the character seeks. Without the opposite---the *negative*---there's little experience!

The *negative-driven* character, more focused on the intrusions, the claustrophobia and the environment of the cage, will experience all of those and many more beautifully negative moments; will find the more human agonies and anguishes and frustrations throughout the role; will still serve the author's requirement that peace be something devoutly desired, but will justify that goal far more surely because for the *negative-driven* character *peace* can never be found.

The "positive goal" character who obviously wants *love* will seldom experience the pain of always imminent and always expected rejection, the despair of the thing which causes love to be denied or the hopelessness of attempting to relate more fully with other characters.

Instead of seeking love, the agony of the lack of it is so much more potent for the actor and much more illuminating and involving for the spectator.

The "positive goal" character who wants *a better world to live in*---this, like the others, being one of Stanislavski's own (unfortunately, also written about) early ideas for possible life goals---will sorely miss the depth experiences which the *escapee from a slums neighbohood childhood* could feel throughout the same role---the disgust at conditions still evident around it, whether they're real or only imagined; the fanaticism of the Messianic revoltist firing its blood and its senses with the religious fervor which will create prairie fires of determination to drive its fixated lifelong struggle against conditions surrounding it, even if they've changed substantially without the change being noticed or appreciated by the character itself at later life points in such a role.

An electrician would scoff at anyone who tries to attach a positive to a positive and achieve any power until the *negative* is attached. Similarly, the knowing actor would scoff at anyone seeking depth of experiencing out of a "positive goal" character when its experiencing is limited to only positive attempts to achieve its goals.

Actors who've read those early books prepared from Stanislavski's notes---"*An Actor Prepares*", "*Building A Character*" and "*Creating A Role*"---have read and perhaps accepted as final the suggestions that positive goals should be planned for characters. All those examples in the previous paragraphs are still there and still being read in college drama departments, libraries and some acting classes.

What hasn't been sufficiently documented is that, with his exposure to Pavlov's *conditioned response* discoveries and his own resulting adaptations of his own earlier theories, Stanislavski's own appreciation of the value of *negative causal fixations behind all desired actions* increased dynamically. Those three books mentioned---all published so far behind time in English (and recently found to be incorrectly edited in some details) don't sufficiently reflect any realization of the values of *internal objects and other approaches of a more negative nature.*

Someone who doesn't have to struggle against any negative experienced in childhood---if there be any such person at all in real life---would be inclined to experience the attempts to attain positive goals less deeply, less emotionally and less interestingly, and to take attainment of them more for granted.

On the other hand, someone who has since childhood had to fight for everything he gets with gritted teeth and clenched fists of determination will experience more fully the fanaticism and emotional stresses produced by that fanaticism along the way. That *negative-driven* person will experience with more complete gratification the fruits of the hard efforts in the moments of picking the harvest.

A positive goal is like a tiny, bright light shining at the far distant end of a dark tunnel, with the actor's attention so steadfastly and exclusively focused on that tiny spot up ahead that it can't experience or perhaps even notice the many, many small problem moments and experiences along the way.

But the *negative-experiencing* character is constantly assaulted by its own negatives (both real and imagined) and the necessity of coping with them every step along the way through that same dark tunnel. Its feelings are constantly agitated, bringing myriad impulses which lend added life energy and interestingness to the work of the actor playing the role. It finds so many and so deeply emotional opportunities which the "positive goal" character couldn't possibly experience.

94

In addition, the exploring of *negative-focused* characters will bring to the actor's work---through the formation of habit as well as through single roles' exciting results---active involvement of those parts of his own mind and body which lie dormant and closed away by habit for so long in daily life.

In real life we don't willingly sink into moodiness or dejection. We never send ourselves voluntarily into despair for the sake of reexperiencing it. We attempt to contain our angers--- often to the point that we can't later experience anger consciously until a psychotherapist forces our bringing it to the surface for catharsis. We deny our negative processes in real life for as long as we're able to do so. Denying them, though, does't mean they go away for us, and they shouldn't go away for characters we play.

If we don't find and use the *negative* avenues for these experiences which are available to the actor if he seeks them out, they won't be automatically available on call for truthful and deep experiencing in moments of roles.

The dramatic character requires so many of these negative moments of experience, whether for only brief periods or for the entirety of a role. If they're not practiced, ready on call without fail and emotionally grounded, the attempts to touch their responses---after allowing them to lie fallow for so long---will assuredly fail when they're most sorely needed.

Today's Leading Roles Are Different

In the 1930's and 1940's roles began changing as the scientific understanding of human psychology advanced, and since that time have continued to gravitate toward *negative-driven* characters. Now---and continually moreso---*anti-heroes* have replaced heroes in most literature. Problem characters now abound in created works just as they do in life. They're more interesting.

And, more important for the actor to recognize, the leading roles which are designed to gain our sympathy now have their own interesting personal torments, their own feelings of inadequacy and their own built-in (often self-created) problems working against the probable achievement of their goals.

Playwrights and screenwriters have long since discovered that leading characters are far more engrossing to watch and easier for the viewer to empathize with if they have always present insecuries, self-doubts, fears, guilts and other negative aspects built into their psychologies.

In other words, most of our current-day idols have feet of clay, and the contemporary actor who wants to succeed in the professional mainstream needs to practice the experience of having

95

his charaters' feet planted in the mud and forcing his characters to *flounder in the muck of their problems* if he's going to be considered for the more important roles of today.

Negatives are driving forces, more often than not creating very positive results from very positive goals which are simply brought into sharper focus and heightened emotional urgency primarily by those negative forces which make them necessary.

Eleanor Roosevelt once said that she devoted her life to charitable causes primarily out of feelings of guilt about her own so abundantly privileged childhood. Helen Keller said all her accomplishments could be credited to her functional deprivations.

What the actor should seek to find in early readings of roles are the *parallel behavior patterns* which suggest some *negative* inner experience at work behind all those patterns, in fact creating them. Such patterns will certainly be there and available to be recognized in any respectably important role.

It's terribly important that the actor look past all those surface actions and manifestations for their cause. It has a nice title: *Conditioned response!* Just as in real life, *without some degree of neurosis in a prepared characterization there can be little or no conditioned response.*

Intellectualized, "positive goal" decisions don't satisfy the spirit of the knowing actor or actress in today's roles. Such tepid truths are only half experiences based on guessing, choice-making, many questionmarks as to their appropriateness, and frustrations which result from the sense of incompleteness suffered by the actor in attempting to breathe life into them.

It's an accepted fact that a neurotic personality in real life isn't generally able to make intellectual calculations as to its responses. It's conditioned from an early childhood period to rely instead on one single basic response structure in moments provoking reaction or demanding action.

Denied the use of logic in most moments, the neurotic personality sees its own *conditioned* truth and is ignorant of the fact that its truth is a distortion which turns most simple life events into the inevitable pressings, over and over, of its most vulnerable danger button.

The writers of today generally provide those "danger buttons" early in roles, to lie there (like the writer's suspense-creating device of the revolver hidden in the drawer) ready to cause their characters problems of their own creation in addition to the scenic problems which they encounter and must cope with.

This is the kind of inner life conditioning that Eugene Vakhtangov urged upon Stanislavski toward achieving *a more theatrical realism*, but Stanislavski couldn't easily adapt it into his System that was already so firmly based upon *action directed at a positive goal*.

That *negative conditioning* is the kind of inner life conditioning which some other teachers and I recommend for actors---the kind that more clearly identifies the personality of the character for the spectator and that causes anticipation that experience after experience of that personality will provoke a *conditioned response* which will probably cause it even more difficulty.

(A tragic but also somewhat amusing example of the latter is the personality that some psychologists and therapists call *"the Injustice Collector".* That personality type, if encountering anything akin to even the slightest injustice, will through his or her responsive action do something that will cause an even worse responsive action from the other person, in order to create an even worse yet injustice for the "injustice collector" himself to suffer.)

Should I observe an actor failing to find the inner torments of overwhelming struggle in a role, I know that actor either doesn't understand the value of a *negative-generated* character base or is simply too disinterested in the preparation of an acting experience to search it out.

Give me instead the actor who turns unhappiness into pain, doubts or confusions into self-torture or self-loathing, happiness into an unbearable ecstasy, shame into suicidal self-abasement, anger into murderous hate and resentment into the rumbling of an earthquake. These experiencings are possible only with a *negatively conditioned response* base.

That's another reason for at least this author's preference for *Objects* in place of *Actions, Intentions or Objectives*, as so often stated throughout this book. An *Action* is to me the positive goal pursuit that results from a decision about something, even if caused by a problem that's negative-based.

Like the other acting teacher, Eric Morris, quoted earlier about (in that quote) *Objectives*, I feel too many forms of Actions, Intentions and Objectives are *after the fact.*

When Robert Lewis advises that all *Intentions should be aimed at some objects*, he's certainly implying that what's being aimed at would need to be already there.

The bottom line with respect to *Negative-Conditioning* and *Negatives* in general is that they supply so much more urgency to justify the desire to take action. They're more immediately tangible. The need to do something about them---if doing something about them is even possible---is greater. And they remain more potent in the experience for as long as they last before some form of action can be decided that succeeds in driving them away.

97

■ And here comes the item many teachers still resist, just as Stanislavski did when Vakhtangov urged its more important use in the System. Those who teach it, teach it in many ways. There aren't many yet who present its use in the following manner...

Objects

as Logical Alternatives To Actions and Intentions!

Have you ever heard the phrase *"Attention to an Action"* or *"Concentration on an Intention?"* Of course not! But---sprinkled throughout the writings of Stanislavski, on page after page of most of the books on acting, heard time after time in lectures by celebrated teachers of the Stanislavski and Vakhtangov Systems and Strasberg's Method when dealing with attention and concentration, and discussed repeatedly in acting classes where methodology is taught---haven't you often heard the phrases *"Attention to an Object"* and *"Concentration on an Object?"*

Ask any teacher who advocates the use of *Actions and Intentions* what the actor's mind should always be on. The answer will most often be something like *"The Object of Attention,"* If the answer from some is *"On the Action (or Intention),"* ask why. *"Because of the Object of Attention"* or something similar should be the answer!

The whole philosophy and methodology of the use of *Objects* instead of or even with *Actions* (or *Intentions* or *Objectives*) in Beats is still new to so many actors, perhaps always will be.

Some actors really have no idea who Eugene Vakhtangov was. His suggestion of a vastly increased *Objects of Attention* emphasis in the System received only token credit by Stanislavski for its tremendous contribution to the working of the rest of the System.

Ironically, Stanislavski himself had used the phrase *Object of Attention* before Vakhtangov began working with him. But the use of *Objects* as recommended by Vakhtangov became, and remain today, one of the *most important keys* to the excitements of the entire Stanislavski System. Here are Vakhtangov's words:

"Every moment an actor is onstage, he must have an Object of Attention. Objects of attention on stage naturally engage the actor's awareness as they would in life. ... Although a performer can use many different kinds of Objects of Attention in a single scene, only one can be the subject at any given moment. "

What isn't widely enough known is that Vakhtangov often advocated the use of *Thought Objects* over longer moments!

Since the *Inner Object's* teaching by Uta Hagen (which she combines with Actions), Bobby Lewis's stressing of *Intentions* being aimed at Objects, and the Object's use by others of us (in several variations) has been less publicized in written descriptions of acting techniques, it warrants some lengthy disussion here.

Lee Strasberg, who taught *Objects* in *Physical Object* terms for practice, also taught *Inner Objects* (imagined) and *Thought Objects* (about events, problems, etc.) as valuable in role moments. Among actual role preparation items, he favored *Objects* as one of the important ones. In Lorrie Hull's book, she reports him as saying *"The object and the concentration that results from attention to the object are the basic building blocks from which the actor works. The objects on which the actor concentrates produce a sense of belief and of faith and involvement in what he's doing, and this in turn leads to unconscious experience and behavior."*

Morris Carnovsky, one of the Group Theatre's most brilliant character actors and dubbed "the Dean" of the acting company, in one of his important articles about his own roles, wrote:

"Action may be thought of as an expression of the energy which is set up between the self and the Object." In another section of the same article: *"Actors weave a continuous tissue of these Objects, these "lies like truth," amusing fictions, coruscating images, grim deeds and memories. They are on intimate terms with them, unbidden as they frequently are when they come. In return they "give" him something, as we say---a focus of concentration."* He was obviously talking about *Objects* that stayed in the mind for longer moments.

Objects' main functions are the focusing of actors' attention on primary concerns---thoughts of situations and problems, other characters, the personal experience, and they provide the truthful, actor feeling-involving specifics for the mind and body, both as long-range *total life or larger units'* focuses for thought and feeling conditioning bases, behavior patterns, psychological appropriateness, etc., and as *individual moments'* focuses *(as Beat Objects)* for the purpose of experiencing more meaningfully the changes of shorter subtext experiences supplied by the writer.

Objects are not simply ideas for use to briefly punctuate the continuing chain of living moments of a role. In any level, as *Life, Unit* or *Beat Objects*, they can be the character's continuous underlying experiences throughout whatever lengths of the role to which they apply.

Unlike the *Actions and Intentions*, they are the *sources and particularizers* of all those experiences!

They lend themselves to being so easily held in the conscious-ness, fixed and pulsating within both the character and the actor for their duration, providing *incoming stimuli* and causing myri-ad *impulses to take some action* while still, for the desired length of time of their use, creating the *inability to cope meaningfully* or else *cope more urgently* with whatever problem is imbedded in the concentration by their wordings.

It's not the *taking of any action* or the *pursuing of any in-tention* which distinguishes the actor's moments in a role. It's where the mind of the character and the actor is focused, the feel-ings and emotions kindled by what's focused upon, and the total experience that can be produced by an *Object* worded by the actor to give it importance, feeling impact and the resulting impulses and behavioral moments *behind and between the lines* of dia-logue and any attempts there may be at taking action.

An actor may be quite "adequate", yet simply be serving as a functionary, an interpreter of what the writer's already been paid for. A different actor may be brilliant---with insight, nuance, inner dynamics and creatively interesting facets throughout his work---through focusing upon and involving the conditioned per-sonality responses of the character and allowing them to involve and inspire his own deepest feelings and his own creative art. *Inner Objects and Thought Objects* make all that possible!

Acting, in the end, is more often *not acting*. It's essentially *believing and being.* Actors who can freely take action at all times usually forget to truly *be.* Their human counterparts, more often floundering in the muck of their problems, aren't so able.

Acting is its most brilliant and most affecting for the viewer when it's sharing its experience---allowing its character to be seen to suffer, to try without success to overcome what's over-whelming it; to experience sometimes elongated moments of in-adequacy, confusion and indecision; to exhibit all the human frailties with which its viewer can more totally identify than would be possible with a totally capable, action-taking effigy of competence and logic.

It's the unique opportunity of the actor---and one seldom ac-corded to real life experience---to have the luxury of sharing and baring, moment after moment, those rich inner sources of feeling and emotion which are the reasons why paying theatregoers and filmgoers flock to watch them and enjoy the catharsis of vicari-ous experience through being allowed to look in their windows and see the most private of events occurring in their characters' subtexts.

Objects make *being*, in its most truthfully experienced form, possible, and further, through the actor's devising of colorful and deep choices, they can turn *simply being* into a creative and affecting experience.

The feeling use of an *Inner Object* or *Thought Object* affects the body moment after moment in manners not dictated by the situation in which the character finds itself but by its *feelings about* the situation and what those feelings send cascading through the actor's instrument to its farthest extremities, enhancing the expressive performance of the actor.

The *Object* also affects the voice and speech, affecting the ability to communicate and enriching the actor's dialogue with emotional timbre and mood color.

A special advantage of *Object* is its versatility and its varying levels of available intensity. It can explode in a moment in any or all directions. It can abate in the next moment to a brooding, soft-edged experience when not agitated by some circumstance. It simply *is . . .* without any manipulation or self-directing by the actor (such as an *Action* requires) as to how to use it in different moments.

It sustains, because it hangs in the mind and feelings so easily and so potently. As opposed to an *Action,* it frees the actor, even in its most agitated and intensified state or level, from concern with *how* to do something. Its many varied impulses come from it being less like the directed arrow of the *"action-playing archer"*---constantly aimed so singly in one direction and forsaking all other experience content---and more like a *porcupine,* for example, with its quills ready, tensed, and available to throw in many directions at once.

Stanislavski almost always added the word *"desired"* when discussing actions. He didn't often use the word *"decided".* Not being limited to a decided *action,* but rather being the source focus that makes action desirable but perhaps impossible for the moment, the Object includes in its use all the myriad experiences which are potential in any important moment for a character. It creates---and includes in its experiencing---those frustrations, irritations, angers, feelings of inadequacy and helplessness in appropriate moments and in precisely appropriate forms for the particular personality.

The so long established technique of employing *actions, intentions* and *objectives* within Beats of roles being still today the approach most generally known to actors, perhaps the following *object vs. action / intention* approach variations may help clarify exactly what's involved.

Here are some examples of how *Objects* can illuminate characters' moments and imbue simple dialogue and action with more specific colors and experiential values than other tools might:

A company employee, in a meeting with his boss and coworkers as his boss decides who's to receive a prize assignment, can be far more interesting for the viewer and himself if an *Object* such as *"All that responsibility!"* makes his detail-discussing hesitant and slightly frightened because of his personality---even though the assignment would mean more money for him---than if he uses an *action* or *intention* or *objective* such as *"Get the assignment!"* No matter what other particularizing tools may be added---*Circumstances, Atmosphere, Obstacle, Justification* or whatever else, there's no comparison!

A housewife, tired of marriage, children, housework and spousal neglect, would plan a tenth wedding anniversary party with her husband in a far more interesting manner ---in spite of the detail-involving dialogue---if using an *Object* such as *"Ten miserable lifetimes!"* because of her personality and circumstances, than if she were simply using an *action* or *intention* or *objective* such as *"Make sure everything's planned right"* (again, regardless of any other particularizing tools that might and probably would have to be added in order to make the action ideally applicable).

A young street gang member, obliged to report to his gang friends about a knifing by a rival gang's member and suggesting the need for retaliatory violence of some kind on his gang's part because it's expected of him, would be far more interesting to the viewer---in spite of his violent sounding dialogue urging to action---if he were using an *Object* such as *"Another stupid f---ing bloodbath!"* rather than an *action* or *intention* such as *"Get back at the bastards!"*, then having to add several other particularizing items in the attempt (which might never succeed) to bring more meaningful life to the action or intention. The mixture of angry outburst on the outside and the crying inside of such an *Object* would be devastating.

A corporation board chairman, sitting in a crucial meeting where the dialogue is dull and simply detail-involved, would be infinitely more interesting to the viewer---even while detail-explaining with apparently total interest, if using an *Object* such as *"These mealy-mouth hypocrites!"* (because of his awareness of the eager upcomers' one-upsmanships against him and his character's conditioned guardedness against all such attempts)---than any simple *action* or *intention* such as *"Straighten this mess out!"*

In other words, if the character is acutely self-doubting, *that self doubt* is the employee's situation more than getting the coveted assignment. The fact that the author indicates in dialogue and any action that he does ask for the assignment would require so many of the above suggested *qualifiers and particularizers of ac-*

tion to get to the conditioned personality base. The *Object* can so easily and quickly *include* all those qualifying circumstances as it goes straight to the core of both personality and situation!

If the character is conditioned to feeling mistreated all her life, *those ten years of mistreatment* ---whether they're true or figments of her conditioned imagination---are her situation more than planning the wedding anniversary details. Although the author indicates that that's what she's doing physically at the moment, and that's what she will do, again so many steps of particularizing that task will be needed to finally get to her conditioned feeling base . . . each particularization as it's considered separately twisting the actor first this way and then another.

Again it should be acknowledged that the author of each of these examples will have previously determined that certain actions will be taken by the characters involved. Those actions are in the script. They will be taken. The important thing is the *how* in which they're taken by specifically conditioned characters.

Situations simply *intrude upon* characters and their personalities. They come and go. They may be different in form and substance, but they should be dealt with, first and foremost, through the manner in which a given character will deal with them as a result of its unique conditioning and behavior patterns.

The bottom line is that when an actor and his character are so involved in the taking of an *action*---especially with five or six particularizing tools having to be attached and each demanding its own particular self-directing by the actor, the actor's mind will be so busy with the action and the qualifying circumstances and conditions that the underlying feelings and emotional experiences (which should be present to so easily provide all that's needed to cause the action to be taken in a cerain manner) will have little opportunity to come into conscious awareness!

Preparing Objects

Webster's definition of an *Object* is "a thing". The *Object* is literally a *"thing" to be focused upon* which, in an ideally worded form, not only provides meaningful concentration for the mind of the actor but also provides in its wording sufficient feeling content to provide more inner experience of feeling nature than will be called into use in many of the moments of the role. Therefore, the manners of wording the tool for optimum results are important:

A *question* wording wouldn't be an *Object, a thing.* If it were, it would focus the actor not on *this moment's experiencing* but on seeking a solution or answer, rendering itself totally useless by taking the actor into the *next moment.*

Full sentences that state facts, no matter how brief or pithy, would feel like the repeating of broken records in use, limiting the spectrum of experiencing that the *Object* can provide in more ideal forms.

Wordings that don't contain the appropriate feeling vocabulary and sentiment of the character would confuse and obfuscate the ongoing personality and behavior patterns as well as inner involvements that are consistent with the personality.

Most of us who teach the *Object* have observed that, to hang in the mind easily and generate feeling experience most effectively, *Objects* should feel like just what their title implies----*Things* . . . most often *phrases that in their composite wordings constitute Nouns*---like objects are generally described in school grammar texts, but with some apt adjectives added to generate more specific attitudes about those nouns. The only notable exceptions are in wordings that, if more closely examined, are more truly *adjective* or *adverb* phrases which *feel like* nouns.

Here are some examples of different forms of *Objects*. Whether composite nouns with their adjectives or adjective / adverb phrases, they can be taken into the mind, can be easily held there, and can bring unique truth of experiencing and exciting colors to the moments in which they're used.   Note that they're divided into groups whose wordings have the same beginning words, to help the actor more quickly establish in his mind the forms of wordings that can be most effective:

Noun Type Objects

The way they all treat me! . . *The* last (cussword) straw! . . . . *The* usual runaround gobbledygook! . . . . *The* happiest day of my life! . . . *The* stupidity I have to deal with! . . . . *The* hole I've dug for my-self! . . .

This impossible situation! . . . *This* (adjective) rat race! . . . . *This* endless waiting! . . . *This* weird turnaround! . . . *This* crazy world! . . . *Those* snotnose bastards! . . . *Those* phony smiles! . . . *Those* crazy yesterdays! . . . *Those* (adjective) footdraggers! . . . *Those* (adjective) snoopers! . . .

These painful last hours! . . . *These* (adjective) obligations! . . . *These* stupid parlor game nights! . . . *These* (adjective) rituals! . . .

More (adjective) obstacles! . . . *More* delaying tactics! . . . *More* lonely nights . . . *More* (adjective) clumsiness! . . .

My last chance! . . . *My* screwed up brain! . . . *My* shattered dreams . . . *My* (adjective) secret . . .

His stupid ideas! . . . *Her* never-ending carping! . . . *His* holier than thou attitude! . . . . *Our* only hope! . . . . *Our* last night together!

104

... *Our* garbage can lives! ... *Their* (adjective) insinuations! ...
Another grin-and-bear-it Sunday night ... *Another* useless try! .
.. *Another* mountain to climb! ... *Another* silly-ass game! ...

Some Other Noun Types

Somebody to hold me! ... *A* hole to crawl into! ... *So many* (adjective) don'ts! ... *Aspirin! Tylenol! Anything!* ... *Prison bars and handcuffs again!* ... *What* imbeciles we've been! ...

Adjective and Verb-Type Objects

How wired I am today! ... *How crazy* this is! ... *How ignored* I am! ... *How long* I've waited for this! ... *How messy* it's getting! ... *How slow* it's going !. ... *How* (adjective) they are! ...

The (adjective) notations above are included to suggest that individual actors and also their characters have their own vocabularies of strong-feeling adjectives which are associated with intense experiences and attitudes of all kinds. Some of these are perhaps four-letter-word adjectives which are habit with the actor as well as expressive of the sentiments of their characters. (Any language that's inappropriate for the charater is obviously wrong.) Others are simply cusswords or, failing that, perfect Webster's Dictionary words that are just as appropriate for other characters, and just as feeling-intensifying for other actors.

The point here is that a good adjective can bring a deeper feeling experience---with the acompanying physical agitation---to whatever it's applied to. And it belongs, almost always and carefully chosen for its power, in a good *Object*. The actor who adds a good, descriptive adjective always profits from the more interesting colors it'll bring. (A *problem* is only a problem until *"stupid", or "silly", or "gigantic", or a cussword, or even an adjectival profanity* is added to lend it some particular, feeling-evoking substance. A *situation* is still vague until *"gowawful"* or *a cussword, or an adjectival profanity* is added to do the same.

Lee Strasberg, who didn't teach in quite the same worded forms for *Objects* as I do, granted on at least one occasion that an actor may also use as *objects*---either as experienced by the actor or as imagined by him----*"specific thoughts, situations or events, emotions, characters,"* etc.

Objects and Actions Are At Least Related

In spite of the vast differences between them, *Objects* and *Actions (also Intentions and Objectives)* are at least cousins. Each is used to focus the actor's attention and concentration.

Actions and Intentions are aimed at *Objects* for their stimulus. Either can serve the actor in a Beat, in a Unit or even for the entire life of a character. And look closely at the *Justifications, Personalizations, Circumstances, Motivations, Atmospheres* and other items that so many teachers recommend as the next steps (after choosing an Action of Intention). Even though there's a tendency to word those particularizing items in short sentence form, as facts, they're all implicitly *Objects*.

By placing the choice of the *Action or Intention* first in sequence, then (not earlier) adding item upon item, the actor will usually wind up with the equivalent of a composite *Object.*

Recognizing that the two different approaches---an *action* tool and an *object*---are related, at least cousins, some of us prefer to think of *Objects* as simply the richer of the two cousins.

■ **Even for the *Action*-oriented actor, the *Object* has a function. As Robert Lewis states (while others often fail to point out), "An Intention should be aimed at an object." For actors who don't understand that simple truth, and who prepare with *actions* or *intentions* or *objectives* as their primary concerns, the *objects* are sometimes accidentally come upon in the form of . . .**

Obstacles

The Action-Oriented Actor Often Needs Them

Some teachers who emphasize the use of *Action* (or *Intention or Objective*) as the primary tool for use also teach this tool---*Obstacle*---for use in either a Beat or a Unit if what the author has written makes one appropriate because (1) what the character must do (for some reason) requires behavior varying substantively from its basic patterns, or (2) its desired and attempted action, while consistent with its behavior patterns, is affected by some deterring circumstance or thought that it must consider because it literally *stands in the way.*

This is sometimes evident in a sort of in-and-out or on-and-off set of circumstances.

This tool can serve especially where the character is forced by some circumstance beyond its control to go against its basic grain for the duration of an entire Unit or an entire Beat in order to cope with external conditions, surroundings or other influences requiring the character to hold itself back from manifesting its own feelings in order to get, keep or avoid something important to it for the duration of its use.

106

Webster's definition of an *Obstacle* is exactly right for the *Action*-oriented actor: *Something which stands in the way; an obstruction.* That's what the *Obstacle* is for the character and the actor ---some circumstance which stands in the way; an obstruction.

This tool is mentioned many times in Stanislavski's works, sprinkled throughout his writings, occasionally given the title as an actual "tool".

The refining of it into a "tool" has afforded *Action and Intention* actors a manner of incorporating *a second reality* (over and above the action tool) which most often has nothing to do with the true emotional life. (The *Object* actor doesn't need an *Obstacle*, because what would be an *Obstacle* can be and usually is easily implied in the wording of the *Object.*)

The concern with the character's problem, whatever label it may be given, and its manner of trying to cope in action terms, contribute a continuing focus consonant with the personality of the character. The addition of an *Obstacle*---usually in no way related to the *action*---helps the actor achieve more interestingly varied moments as at times the character is overwhelmed by the deterring thought (the *Obstacle*) and at other times must exert strong determination to overcome that deterring thought to do what has to be done or simply suffocate the character's own desire to take action for the prolonged moment.

The *Obstacle* can be best used as a thought brought back time and time again, to overwhelm, overcome, subdue or even totally stop for a moment the character's desired *Outer Action*-taking as that thought demands temporary recognition and produces its moments of entirely different feeling experience.

Certainly those actors of *Action* orientation---preferring to concentrate on action-taking rather than the *Object* which prompts the desire to action---might wisely employ something similar to the *Obstacle*, even if only to bring some added dimension in terms of the personal experience of the character behind the sometimes one-dimensional action. In other words, here is one more of those "tools" which are sometimes needed to particularize a simple action.

The Obstacle serves best---and obstructs most interestingly, in those moments when it intrudes upon and impedes action---if it's worded as *a simple fact* which provides *a definite feeling moment of its own kind* which is different from the feelings of the *Action.*

As previously mentioned, very obvious Obstacles are sometimes stated or implied by the author at different moments of a role. Sometimes, though, they need to be added by the actor to justify the experiencing of any apparent non sequiturs in the original writing. They should probably be caused by the character's personality or some conflicting thought.

There are *Internal* Obstacles (something about the character and its own experience that stands in the way of desired action) and *External* Obstacles (something about other people, things, God, laws, nature, time of day, etc., that stand in the way of desired action).

Following are some examples as they might be chosen to obstruct *totally unrelated Actions* or provide an *alternate focus of attention for Objects*, thereby bringing additional dimension to prolonged moments by nagging at the character's concentration from time to time or continually:

Harassed by someone pestering her for attention, she might be wanting to *"Make him leave me alone!"* but might in Obstacle terms be pulled at by the thought that *"He looks so pitiful."*   In another situation, he might be desperately trying to *"Show her I need her!"* but some of the time have the deterring thought that *"She's a dyed-in-the-wool Republican."*   A roommate might be trying to *"Make him move out!"* but be constantly stopped by the thought that *"The rent's due Tuesday."*   A frazzled wife, overwhelmed by bills due and other seemingly insurmountable problems, might be desiring to *"Get the hell out of this mess!"* but be conscious that *"The kids need me."*   A landlady, having waited as long as possible to collect his rent, in kicking him out might be determined to *"Get him out by tonight,"* but be haunted throughout by the fact that *"He reminds me so much of my Henry."*

If used as a *secret of the character*, to obstruct and at least partially overcome the main concentration and desired coping action of the character (for whatever time-span may be determined by the actor) it will automatically be shared with the spectator to the degree that it's used with its feeling either continually or sporadically by the actor.

While the *Obstacle* can be a productive *second reality* tool for the dramatic actor, it's a really handy little item for a comedy player as well!

In a comedy role requiring that the character must attempt to maintain a false exterior with some difficulty, an *Obstacle* can provide the comic *problem* behind the pretense, clearly revealing for the viewer the effort to keep the *secret* which must be hidden with Herculean effort. The fact that the audience or viewer is allowed to share the secret behind the pretense beforehand creates what Bob Orben, the writer of all those books about comedy, calls *"The Dynamic Secret"*. The audience, fully aware of the secret, watches the attempts to present a false front amd enjoys it.

It's really such a simple and basic tool that it doesn't need a lot of describing. If and when the actor feels something like the *Obstacle* is desirable, because there's some thought or some circumstance that *stands in the way of* whatever it is that the character wants to do, the actor needs only to have that specific thought affect his ability to do what he wants to do for however long the *Obstacle* seems to apply.

■ **This next item is something too many actors are hesitant to use because of fear of offending their directors. They don't realize that most directors who aren't insecure and therefore sometimes defensive are normally pleased if their cast members offer some suggestions for their own. . .**

Organic Blocking

The Actor's Directorial Contributions

Are you a follower? . . . someone who likes to leave everything to your director? Forget *Organic Blocking*. It's for actors who want to contribute . . . not only to their character's use of itself in scenic terms but also to the effectiveness of the whole production.

Organic Blocking is what can occur when an actor is allowed by a director to contribute his or her own ideas of many kinds, based on the actor's prior use of the *Six Questions* (or whatever other means) to gain inspiration and inspire research---ideas for wardrobe, props, movements, activities, etc., that the writer hasn't provided and the director might not think of.

Some directors even recognize the value of scheduling special *pre-rehearsal meetings* with their casts at which they encourage their cast members to bring their own ideas about such items for their individual characters or even for the over all productions.

New York director Ellis Rabb, preparing to direct a revival of the comedy *"You Can't Take It With You,"* had Rosemary Harris and other members of the cast go through the "Six Questions" exercise (described in the *"Subtext, The Analytical Phase"* chapter) and bring from home all their ideas. The hundreds of suggestions of enriching ideas for not only their own characters but also for the setting, props, etc., were almost all used!

The *"blocking"* part of this fairly common phrase refers to the interjecting of suggested activities not thought of by the writer at ideal spots in the actor's anticipated performance, rather than the director simply throughout the "blocking" of the actor's ac-

109

tion laying it out in "Move down center," "Take one step toward camera and look off to your left" and "Go to the window and look out anxiously" terms.

The actor's performance is in the end judged on its own merits. Critics and audiences tend to not realize that an actor's less than exciting performance may be because of oversight and perhaps even confusing direction of the actor by a busy director more concerned with the over-all scenic progression of individual scenes and total productions.

So many character-and-authenticity-enriching items, as well as even ideas concerning set dressing and props, can be suggested by the actors---especially if they've used the *Six Questions* or some other manner of finding inspirations for them!

If the director fails to suggest a pre-rehearsal meeting for the purpose of receiving the cast members' suggestions (so all or at least some of them can be integrated from the start of rehearsals), an actor can certainly ask to meet with the director to offer those suggestions.

In such a pre-rehearsal meeting I once held with the two cast members of one of my own one-act plays, which I scheduled a week before beginning rehearsals for the two cast members' bringing of their suggestions, an extraordinarily talented and creative actress who had used the *Six Questions* contributed the following many items to her own performance as a factory worker's wife and to the play itself:

Her *Who* (the first of the *Six Questions* inspirations) included the following, and each item was grabbed up eagerly:

Embroidery she'd return to twice during the play---because she couldn't afford to buy pretty things . . . Supermarket grocery ads open on the coffee table (to save money) . . . A darned sock hanging out of a paper sack sewing bag (because she couldn't afford a nice etui). . . Her shoes off, because she knew they couldn't afford to go out . . . The front door open, because they couldn't afford air-conditioning . . . Dusting off her going-out shoes before leaving alone to go to the party across the street---because she seldom had occasion to wear them . . .

Her *What* inspirations: Standing in the open doorway listening to the party gaiety across the street, her frustrations with her husband continually intensified by her jealousy and feelings of isolation . . . Returning to the door occasionally to pointedly express her dissatisfaction . . . Rehearsing of feminine wiles in front of the mirror before going to the party, because she knew her husband's boss (at the party across the street) was a womanizer . . . Closing the door before raising her voice to rail at her husband's islationism. . .and many more valuable "blocking suggestions.

When---*(after dinner, hot summer night):* TV dinners beside both her and her husband (because it could never be known what time he'd get off work) . . . Shutting off the Evening News telecast to talk turkey to her husband . . . Opening the front window further to let the party sounds in more loudly. . . and more.

Where brought more. But it was the *Why* searching and its result of which she was most proud:

To jusfify her even staying married to her husband, she suggested a probable Catholic upbringing, which suggested a crucifix around her neck and a Madonna on a wall sconce . . . Taking off the crucifix at the mirror before going out, knowing what she'd have to do at the party . . .

How suggested irritation with the needle and stitches of her embroidering while angry . . . Sitting position more appropriate for the life she was denied than for the factory worker wife she found herself compromised into being. . . Not looking at her husband much, since he reminded her of what she'd settled for . . . and more that I've forgotten.

Small touches, yes. But those are the kinds of things busy directors overlook sometimes. And those are the kinds of things which, although critics in their reviews may suppose are in the authors' scripts, cause actors to be praised for details.

In the same pre-reheasal meeting held for the purpose of receiving their contributions, the actor playing her isolationist factory worker husband brought the following valuable items:

The *Who* items of the *Factory Worker* suggested keeping on his factory worker clothes . . . One workboot off and the foot being flexed and rubbed from time to time because of job footache . . .A beer can beside his chair . . .

The *Who* of *a man unable to relate to people* suggested a pipe, as an excuse for endless silence . . . A pile of sports pages under his chair, his lunch pail, his pipe stand and ashtray, his beer cans and his work things clustered close around him like an island of refuge because of his personality . . .The sports pages of the day's paper held as a wall to hide behind . . . His lunch pail set beside his big chair, because his character would seek the refuge of his chair immediately upon coming home . . . Going out to the kitchen occasionally for a fresh beer, to avoid his wife's prodding . . . For the outburst later in the play, standing in the center of the room, away from his wife but also away from furniture and any connection with his surroundings . . .

The *Who* of *a husband in his wife's living room* suggested dumping his pipe ashes very carefully---to avoid another complaint by her . . . Moving his stockinged foot farther under his chair when she came closer because of its sweaty odor . . .

111

A number of the *What* and *When* items he brought duplicated those brought by his wife, which happens often in these meetings, since in the main they're provided or hinted by the writer.

The *Why in his case, being almost exclusively psychological,* suggested the book *"Man Alone"* on his chairside stand with inserted markers to indicate the importance he attributed to its content. . . His work shirt buttoned up, because of his personality . . . Fairly thick glasses, as further protection from seeing and relating with others . . . His work shirt wrinkled and sweaty, because of no concern with social neatness . . .

As the playwright and director, I was pleased with reviewers' comments about my *"attention to so many small and illuminating details."* But my actors and I knew how much they'd individually contributed to the partially undeserved credit given the director (through the use of *Organic Blocking*).

Even for film, director Lawrence Dobkin, among others, always invites his actors to *"Bring something from home"* to these first meetings, and a Russian-American director we know invites them to *"Make from yourself some things you should do before you kyum."*

The foregoing *Six Questions* suggestions list from one of my own casts is just one example. Never hesitate, if the director doesn't suggest this kind of contribution by you for your own character and for the production itself. Ask if some suggestions ahead of time would be welcomed.

Stars are often encouraged to offer their ideas. Your own---even if not a star---may be welcome also, and if they prove helpful the director should be and probably will be gratedul.

■ **I suspect that anyone who teaches preparation approaches for *inner characterization* suggests the following as one of the first steps in the analyzing of characters provided by writers. If there's any better way, most of us haven't found it yet.**

Parallel Behavior Patterns
The Keys To The Character's Personality

Although these important "highway signs" along the road of analyzing a character presented by a writer are dealt with less expansively in *"The Subtext, Analytical"* pages of this book, under the heading *"Listing The Facts . . . Appraising Them"*, they're so important in the actor's process of arriving at a character's personality that they're being elaborated on here.

Don't let anyone convince you that, once you have a fairly clear idea of your character's personality, its conditioning and its behavioral stimuli, that's all the analyzing you need to do!

In one or two readings of a role there should in all probability be one or two or perhaps at most three behavior patterns and response categories which are most frequently observed as they recur time after time in detectably similar form.

After a moment of recalling those fairly similar behavior patterns most frequently observed, it's easy to divide the two or three into general, first-impression categories. This first step of categorizing them into separate columns affords a more accelerated perception of the dominating patterns as one column of facts will grow swiftly while one or more of the other columns will grow more slowly.

To illustrate more clearly how this "several columns" listing process can clarify and speed the zeroing in on the source personality, following is an example of a three-categoried list of entries of *Parallel Behavior Patterns* which might become evident as an actor culls through the facts presented by a writer:

Feels Caged, Needs Freedom

Often leafs through travel magazines... Often leans against the window looking out... Grabs the telephone as soon as it rings... Tells his mother he hates home cooking... Tells Sara their affair means less to him than to her... Refuses to discuss marriage with her... His mother says he drives too fast... Tells his mother he can't come see her on Sunday because he's too busy when he really isn't...

Sara says he's always a bundle of nerves, can't settle anywhere... He sometimes stays out, walking around all night without coming back to the apartment... After Sara tells him she's pregnant he stays away two days... Hates the shirt Sara bought him; says it makes him look like a "family man"...

His mother says he stole a car when he was sixteen, went joyriding... He tried LSD and other drugs; still smokes pot... Ran away from home, Mom says, when he was twelve, again when he was seventeen... Avoids family get-togethers, finds some excuse to stay away from them time after time...

(That first column's list of facts might continue, perhaps gathering the most items because the actor saw it originally as the dominant personality and relates most actions to that apparently dominant personality category.)

Status-Starved

He's jealous of his boss and other employees... Buys the convertible instead of the Volkswagen bargain... Always overdrawn at the bank because of overspending for expensive clothes... Carries the briefcase, even when there's nothing in it... The car he stole as a boy belonged to rich Lonnie...

Loses his job at the ad agency because of irritating one-upsmanship ploys reported by his coworkers... Tries to get the bank loan to start his own agency immediately after being fired... Doesn't like to visit Mom in the old family home in the low cost housing district...

(That column might have fewer facts, but it's still evident as an at least somewhat different behavior pattern and needs to be listed separately because of those detectable differences.)

Puts Other People Down

Is sarcastic about Sara's friends and their husbands... Refuses to visit her friends with her... Says his brother Don is a nobody and Don's wife is a baby factory... Sarcastic about the people at the agency party... Tells his mother she dresses like somebody's maid... Always puts his long dead Dad down with apparent hatred...

(That category might have fewer or more than the middle column, but it indicates yet another recurring behavior pattern.)

Having completed the listing of the facts supplied by the writer, the actor will perhaps have found the largest number of facts involve a *"caged"* feeling and a desire for freedom. The actor might feel that the longer list indicates that the *"caged"* feeling appears the single, obviously dominating experience of the character. He might stop there and prepare a character based on just that one facet---*"caged"*, or *"suffocated"* or *"adventure starved"*.

But the wiser actor will know that the facts in the other two columns, shorter lists though they may be, shouldn't be ignored. They exist in the writer's text. They need to be considered to find their relativity within the character's neurotic framework. The actor who knows they matter is smart.

Immediately upon checking and analyzing one after another of the second column's facts the actor would begin to see how important *"status"* is to him. Everything in that column, rather than pointing to *freedom* or being *caged*, points more to *recognition of status and identity in other people's eyes.* Those facts have to be considered.

The originally difficult to relate jealousy of his boss points to status *jealousy.* The convertible, being overdrawn at the bank and buying expensive things indicates a need for possessions that are special and status *projecting* more than a need for freedom. Carrying an empty briefcase indicates status *costuming* for a desired role. Constant one-upsmanship ploys at the agency leaves little doubt that he would step on anyone and everyone to advance himself. Not liking to visit his childhood home stands as a reminder of his low beginnings and his habit of putting down anything that isn't withinin the frame of upward mobility.

The second column suggests that *"status driven"* or *"status frenzy"* is a part of the character as much as *"caged"*.

"Puts other people down" remains to be dealt with. Sarcasm about Sara's friends and their husbands suggests dissatisfacion with their current primary circle. Refusing to visit them with her shows a lack of concern for either her feelings or for maintaining any social life that's currently available. Calling his brother Don a nobody and his wife a baby factory suggests disgust with all nobodies and all obstacles like having children. Sarcasm about the people at the office could suggest that he'll never be satisfied with people currently around him. Telling Mom she dresses like somebody's maid suggests possible embarassment at the low social milieu of his beginnings. Putting his father down with apparent hatred could indicate hatred for where he came from and the deprived childhood he suffered because of his father's brown collar lifestyle.

At this point the actor has perhaps three possibles---maybe just two, since columns two and three can be combined . The last step of combining the major aspects and patterns into one personality type label is easier than the actor might think.

A *positive* goal choice (of the type Stanislavski first recognized) could be made, but how much life will the actor find in simply *Freedom* or *Status*? Not much. Go for the *negative* first, always. It's where the character comes to life!

Combining the different facets, what might come to the mind could be *"Slum-suffocated!"* . . . *"Gutter Smelling"* . . . *"Thompson Street"* (a mostly tenement, cold water flat area in lower Manhattan). . . The imagination of the actor can easily evoke the most urgent and aggravated core feelings for the character if the thinking is allowed to wander through the *negative* environment already recognized as affecting the character throughout the role and fixating its personality and behavior.

What's important is that any one of those labels the actor might decide to use has been based on *all of the facts provided by the writer*. They've all been gathered together through the interrelating of *all* of them into one single, central, several-dimensioned *conditioned response core*.

Zeroing in on character personality in this careful, painstaking and thorough manner makes it improbable that any director will later have to point out to the actor something important about the character which may have been overlooked and will then have to be reconsidered as the actor goes back to square one and starts fresh in the preparing of the character's personality---when it's too late to do it effectively!

Zeroing in in this manner not only creates a reliable insurance policy against proceeding headling into preparing a personality type that later has to be changed. At the same time it can create new excitement about the character in the imagination of the actor. Each of those composite, item-gathering lists has contributed to a more colorful and more interesting whole.

The actor who works in this manner will be freshly excited as the next steps are taken.

■ **And there are all kinds of "next steps" to be taken. For the taking of those steps, whatever their nature, size or individual importance, actors may of course use whatever approach or methodology they prefer in laying out for themselves the *steps* of the major items of their script breakdowns. But there's an approach that many actors use to bring tiny moments to life, called . . .**

Physical Objectives

for Bringing the Surroundings to Life

Here's one form of *action* with which this author heartily agrees.

There's an excellent discussion of these little, briefly used *Physical Objectives* in Stanislavski's own words in "Creating A Role", detailing the work with them by Stanislavski himself in preparing the role of "Chatski" in Griboyedov's *"Woe From Too Much Wit"*.

It gives a very clear idea of what the tiny *Physical Objectives* are and what they're for. They're often the product of impulses experienced during rehearsals, but they can be thought of and planned for use even earlier. They should be considered as to their value for use later simply because they can bring added reality or interesting, truthful moments to a situation.

Physical Objectives, as discussed here at least, are tiny actions of only momentary life which bring the emotional charac-

116

ter into direct contact with the physical realities around it. They provide the little justifications for simple action as the character moves from Point A to Point B in an extended moment. And they bring exciting little human recognition moments for viewers.

For instance, when the author says merely "He sits" or "She paces" the actor can find little *Physical Objectives* which give the sitting or the pacing some purpose. Perhaps the character should "sit" in order to *"rest my tired bones", "show them I mean business", "control my temper"*, or perhaps *"show them I've stopped listening."* Perhaps the character "paces" to *"get my head staightened out", "stop his yelling"* or *"show them I'm ready to start".*

Since Physical Objectives are for the purpose of involving both the mind and the body (not simply thought alone) with the physical surroundings, they provide interesting moments of illumination throughout their brief lifespans.

By the way, during a single beat there may be a bunch of little *Physical Objectives* which flow naturally out of the beat's involvement tool. The manner in which they establish strong contact between the character and its physical surroundings is up to the actor.

As an example of the use of *Physical Objectives* in a dramatic scene, there's a dramatic play entitled *"The Andersonville Trial"*. In the play, Chipman, as prosecutor, is to bring into the last day of the trial the witness who he feels is his only hope of finally winning a conviction against Wirz, the former Commandant responsible for the inhuman treatment of enemy prisoners at the Andersonville prison camp.

Before the witness is brought into the courtroom for a second appearance, and leading up to the start of his questioning of the young soldier, Chipman must go through certain hurried, last-minute preparations. Here are some possible *Physical Objectives* which might be used in the beat before the questioning is commenced:

Get that key question in mind! (He picks up the previous testimony transcript, searches for the sentence and finds it.)

Find out what he was about to say! (He squints toward the horizon, remembering the nervous faltering of that prior moment.)

Memorize the details! (His eyes shut and his head bobs as he plans the words that may key the rest of the damning details.)

(At this point Davidson is led in and Chipman turns to inspect his condition.)

See if he's up to it! (He appraises the condition of the emaciated, frightened soldier.)

Give him my strength! (He goes to meet Davidson and leads him gently to the witness chair, pats him softly and sympathetically to reassure the lad prior to another grilling testifying.)

Make sure the judges notice his condition! (He looks intently at the judges one after another as he stands to one side to give all a good view of the boy's condition.)

Show Wirz he's done for! (A flick of a half-threatening, half triumphant look at the defendant.)

Keep him from freaking out again! (He leans semi-casually on the witness chair arm and briefly smiles encouragingly down at Davidson.)

Get it over with quickly! (He fills his lungs quickly and adopts a strong starting position.)

While *Physical Objectives* add the tiny, moment to moment details for dramatic acting, they're also a marvelous boon to comedians and comedy playing.

Imagine, for instance, a drunk arriving at his own door in the early morning hours who, not wanting to awaken his wife as he sneaks groggily into the house, begins this sequence of Physical Objectives the French comedian Raimu might have used:

Make it stop moving around! (He tries to locate the doorknob.)

Thank it for holding still! (He pats the doorknob gratefully for letting him find it.)

Make sure it doesn't squeak this time! (He turns the doorknob ever so carefully; opens the door with the same precaution in mind; shuts it after going through it, still with the same thought.)

Get these tattletales off! (Looks down at his shoes and the bit of noise they're making; leans down and takes them off and spanks each in turn gently; decides to carry them.)

Aim myself in the right direction! (Squints to find the bedroom; laboriously plants his feet in that direction; starts to take a step.)

Show it it's not going to get me this time! (Looks at a floorboard, shakes his finger at it craftily, steps around it.)

Make sure she's asleep! He stops and cocks an ear toward the bedroom door.)

(A car might honk loudly outside at this point and continue honking for a moment.)

Kill the bastard! (After checking for any sound from within, he grimaces toward the window, shakes his fist at the car horn.)

For comedy especially, *Physical Objectives* are a nice way in which to bring inanimate objects to very funny life---treating them as if they were human, whether friends or enemies.

For effective use of them, *Physical Objectives* depend upon the imagination and inventiveness of their creator. With most who find they enjoy using them, a bit of practice brings their finding and use to vivid life in figuratively "embroidering" the tiny moments of individual beats where there is progressing of story.

■ **Have you sat through endless hours of class time watching a few class members go through silent activities, hesitating at times to think of next moments and when they find them appearing to gain little from what they're doing? That can happen, and does in some classes. But many teachers conduct . . .**

Private Moment Exercises

There Are Some Values To Be Derived, But . . .

Here's a handy little class timetaker for a teacher, and I've come to suspect that it's brought into class after class by some teachers who are busy professionally and simply don't have the time or energy to plan some other class exercises. It has value, but it can be overused. And even when there's some result it's not as effective toward its prime goal as *The Living Sounds,* as will be explained in this discussion.

It can without question benefit the actor or actress who does too much "in general" work and who needs to have it pointed out that in simple human and private moments there are many more little human things that occur---momentary tasks, peripheral activities, ways of doing things, closer attention to small details involved---of which the actor is often unconscious.

But there have been and still are some coaches who devote periods of classes to having actors (often just one person at a time) explore *Private Moments*---taking a shower, getting dressed to go to a party, etc.---while others are obligated to watch or perhaps go to sleep (as Geraldine Page said she did sometimes at the Actors Studio when watching some newer actors going through the exercise, even tho' she loved Mr. Strasberg and was a Board Member, because she'd sat through so many *Private Moments* and most often didn't find them interesting or all that productive).

If an actor or actress needs this kind of expanding of imagination, I and a few others I know of recommend an alternative--- the exercising of the *Living Sounds* with approximately the same awareness-expanding activity. In any kind of private mment---if the *living sounds* are required to be added---the obligation to *keep interjecting sounds* forces the actor to discover so many more little moments of the kind being desired for the actor. Exercising with getting ready to go to a party, for instance---and seeking out the little moments the *living sounds* automatically prompt---can be much more productive.

Different coaches employ different manners of promoting the development of self-awareness. I guarantee that no class member would go to sleep watching someone explore a private moment if the *living sounds* are included in the exercise those many sounds would be if the moment were truly private.

There are two marvelous examples of the *Private Moment with Living Sounds* in use by the gifted Marlon Brando in the film *"Reflections In A Golden Eye"*: At one point, in the hall downstairs, preparing to go upstairs to his wife, he stopped before the mirror and preened in a manner that was amusing albeit a bit embarassing to observe because of its fragments of pure privacy, with their *living sounds* of the kinds that are seldom brought into actors' performances. His apparently unconscious (but with Brando very conscious) muttered sounds, of the type many of us make in such moments, added stunning reality to that moment.

In another scene of the same film, in his bedroom when young Williams is heard entering the house and Brando's character thinks Williams is coming to him instead of his wife, Brando's preparing himself, again with those apparently unconscious but magic *living sounds* accompanying his preparations, struck recognition chords of the actor's genius.

■ **Only a few teachers are sufficiently grounded in the teaching of the next item. Even the students of its creator at the Moscow Art Theatre, generally failed to realize desired results with it . . .**

Psychological Gesture

Michael Chekhov's "Instant Character" Tool

This item is included among the other approach items described simply because Michael Chekhov himself called it a *"shortcut to characterization"* and it's taught by a few advocates of his approaches with that claim. It must work for some.

It was one of the major departures of Chekhov from the teachings of Stanislavski, and he personally taught it to his classes at the Moscow Art Theatre. Although it was at first repre-

120

sented by him to be related to Stanislavski's System, it's very obviously in direct conflict with those teachings and, after
Chekhov's assertion that *"If Stanislavski's system is high
school, my system is college"* was learned of by Stanislavski it
caused a schism between the two that lasted for several years.

Having more faith in Stanislavski's analytical approach
than in this theory which was represented by Chekhov as rendering much of Stanislavski's System of characterization analysis
unnecessary, I've never taught it. However, in case it can truly accomplish for some actors what Chekhov believed it could, it
should at least be mentioned in this list.

Those curious about the possible value of this approach toward forming the psychology and *Life Objective* of a character
will find it defined briefly by Mala Powers, Executor of the
Chekhov Estate, in the Preface to the Mel Gordon edited book
"Michael Chekhov On The Technique Of Acting" as a manner of
using the actor's entire body, executing certain steps with intensity to visualize the embodiment of the character and also find the
moods suggested by the writer.

And in his own book *"The Stanislavsky Technique: Russia"*
Mr. Gordon explains this approach similarly, describing it as essentially a physical movement that the actor can use as a key to
the hidden features of his character's psychology. He explains
that it may be large or small, something abstract or something
more real for the actor, that is found through observing the character's actions and the apparent feeling experiences that define
them. He states that there may only be one Psychological Gesture
for the character, and that the actor's internal experiencing of the
character's feelings can be enhanced by thinking of the gesture.

Chekhov himself, in his book *"Michael Chekhov On The
Technique Of Acting"* opined that there is one Psychological
Gesture to be found in the inner experience of any character; that
every character has its most deeply felt desires and goals; that
these are manifested in its behavior, its manner of relating with
other characters and the feeling experiences of the character that
can become evident in some physical form as the actor continues
to observe the character in its most meaningful moments .

He maintained that, as one reviews the moods and actions of
a scripted character throughout its role, by continuing to imagine
the character's form, manner, what it does and how it does it---vi-
sualizing it, it presents a living performance for the actor. Fixing
the actor's attention on moments that seem the most significant
or expressive, the actor should try to "see" what the character is
aiming at, what is its wish, its desire, and seek to penetrate as
clearly and vividly as possible into the character's mind.

As soon as you begin to guess *what* the character is doing physically and psychologically from the images before your mind's eye, try to find the most simple *Psychological Gesture* for what the character is doing. Do it physically, all the while observing your own image as well as the imagined one.

It was his theory that the *Psychological Gesture* will appear before the mind's eye and, after being practiced, will always remain with the actor as a kind of inspiration while acting.

His suggested exercises toward discovering the *Psychological Gesture* include one, perhaps the most directly productive---of choosing a play, even one the actor doesn't know well, and imagining the performance of the character, concentrating on the most expressive moments; asking the character to act before the actor, to help the actor discover his goals and desires. Watching how the character performs, and from its action only, the actor could intuit its *Psychological Gesture* and then perform it physically himself.

Chekhov himself was a marvelously sensitized actor. His many performances of completely dissimilar characters were highly praised not only in Russia but throughout many other theatre capitols of the world. That the *Psychological Gesture* worked for him is apparently beyond question. That it has been equally understood and rendered productive for other actors is less widely confirmed.

In other than expert hands, it has been observed by some to limit the physicality of actors to single physical behaviors and images throughout their total performances.

In any event, it's the feeling of this author that it's an approach for only the very daring, the possessor of exquisite taste and judgment, and, in the end, the actor who is *more visually and physically* oriented.

Chekhov himself was deeply affected by Rudolf Steiner's *Eurythmics,* and the fertile grounds for the *Psychological Gesture* were apparently nurtured by his eurythmics experience and his own natural grace of movement. His own *neural muscle system center* experience was responsive to Steiner's teachings. And his own exploring of the *Imaginary Center* for which he's credited is easily traceable to the Steiner concepts of the natural flow of the body from one part to another in movement.

In his writings about the *Gesture,* Chekhov suggests that the actor, having found the *Psychological Gesture* for a character, experiment with small adjustments at other points in the body (i.e., tilting the head to one side) to experience the slight change such an adjustment would affect to the *Gesture.* In that way, he certainly related the *Gesture* to the *Imaginary Center.*

122

One of his own most celebrated uses of the approach involved the imaginary *"reaching into the heart"* of other characters.

As mentioned earlier, Playwright Ben Hecht reminisced once in a work session with me about Michael Chekhov's performance in Hecht's film *"The Spectre Of The Rose"*. He said Chekhov's performance was like *"a nervous butterfly desperate to fly."*

There are apparently not too many present day acting teachers who conduct training devoted to this approach. Those of us who question its importance for actors base our lack of enthusiasm for it on its utilizing *primarily visualization based on physical impression* of characters with, we feel, much less concern for and involvement with any extensive analysis of their *psychologies* in other manners.

One of the leading teachers of all of Chekhov's techniques---including his *Psychological Gesture*---is George Shdanoff, teaching in Los Angeles, a longtime close associate of Chekhov. The 1942 version of Chekhov's *"On The Technique of Acting"*, entitled simply *"To The Actor"*, is dedicated to George Shdanoff.

■ **There's no question that the next item is important in actors' work. But the manners of teaching it vary from class to class, and in the end each actor must find his or her own preferences and balances as to how much attention they personally focus on other characters, on situations, or on their characters' personal experience. I believe the latter is the far more important, but here are some things the actor might consider about the two kinds of *Concentration on Objects* (that's what relating is) that imply focusing strictly on *externals*. First ...**

Relating

To Other Characters

Out front, this author wants to go on record, as I do elsewhere in the book, as saying that relating with other characters on the *interpersonal* level is highly overrated in the first place! There's more to life---our characters' lives as well as our own---than *relating to others!*

Hamlet's larger struggle was with himself. Macbeth's also. Joan of Arc's as well. Hedda Gabler, Nora in *"A Doll's House"*, Willy Loman in *"Death Of A Salesman"*, to point to a few more that are more focused on their own experience.

But these are only a few. Think of any really enduring dramatic characters ever created by master playwrights or outstanding screenwriters. If you look beneath their surface conflicts with other characters with whom they're scenically involved you'll find the *acutely personal experiences* that molded their destinies and guided their steps along the way. Few were simply event participants dependent upon their relating with other characters for the progressing of their dramatic experiences.

Granted, in most of the strictly violent action dramas that dot network television schedules and draw violent action-relishing teenagers to motion picture boxoffices in the nineties there are all those characters trying to *get something from* or *do something to* each other from first moment to last. Their struggles are certainly *interpersonal!*

But even in that arena of the actor's professional world there's also increasing attention to the psychological conflicts and *personal experience* struggles of the leading characters that humanize even those primarily *action* stories.

But . . . to the subject at hand---manners of *relating with other characters* to the extent that they serve the ongoing stories of our writers as our characters relate and attempt to cope with those other characters:

Communicating by leading characters with other characters is no longer afforded the importance that it once was.

Increasingly, important characters in all but those "action" stories spend *less time* communicating, have *less willingness* to communicate, and have *more difficulty* communicating, because of the more human and more interesting psychologies that people today's dramas.

In most of today's performance art, dialogue with other characters is included only to the extent necessary and usually used to the extent necessary to progress simple story action. It's almost never the primary story progression element for the character itself. Most contemporary drama focuses on the characters' minds---their *personal experiences* behind the masks they present and *behind their words*---as they enter stories with one basic attitude about life and even they usually experience growth to a more enlightened one along the way toward the end of their story.

Contemporary dialogue between characters----communication--- is seldom as direct, clear and concise as it used to be when it was the main story progressing element!

Watch some of the films of the 30's and 40's. Notice how clear and concise every speech was. Notice how those films' actors always *"picked up their cues"*, knew exactly what they wanted to say, said it, then listened attentively to the other character as the other character spoke in the same easy, capital-letter-to-period manner.

Notice how little time was devoted to the characters' *private, undialogued experiences.* There was continuous interpersonal *action.* There was a lot of dialogue communication. There was a lot of that kind of *relating with other characters* . . . and not always much else when there were more than one person in the same place at the same time.

The viewer or audience member was *told in dialogue exchange* what the character was going through, what it was struggling with, how it felt about the other character in a scene, what it was planning to do and even how it was planning to do it, etc. No wonder the early 30's films were called *"talkies!"*

It's easy to understand why, in those days, *action* tools were often sufficient, even most appropriate, for actors' use. Still today, pure *action* tools are sufficient (still not ideal, but sufficient) for some roles---stock heavies whose story functions are simply *doing things to others* and no more; bit roles that have *only brief functions* in stories; and any other *unimportant event participants that we aren't supposed to feel anything about or for.*

Another thing about most contemporary roles that suggests more use of *Objects* than of *Action or Intention*: "*Giving up on changing*" other characters is an important key now in relating to them---especially in characters that have known each other for any period of time---business associates, friends, or even those who've heard enough about each other before meeting to be able to predict the others' behavior.

Except in the "action" genre, so many contemporary roles know each other, have been involved with each other over periods of time, know each other's faults and shortcomings and have come to accept them. It always appears ridiculous if a character in a long standing relationship chooses this one present moment ---even if the author's dialogue seems to suggest it---to attempt some *action that hopes to change* the other person.

Giving up on changing that other person---having to accept their irritating faults and shortcomings---offers the actor so much more in terms of *reactions* in all encounters with them!

Simply adopting the point of view for your character that the other person *won't ever change*---no matter how hard you might try to teach them and bring them out of their misapprehensions, mend their ways or whatever (because the writer's scripted exchanges seem to indicate the attempt)---produces the continuous opportunity to experience disgust, irritation, futility, exasperation and many other *personal experiences* throughout all of our characters' moments when in their presence.

Adopting the viewpoint that they're not just *being* impossible, silly, offensive, self pitying, stupid or prejudiced in this single present moment, but instead *are* impossible or whatever else, *always,* certainly suggests to any perceptive actor that any *action* approach in dealing with them in the present moment is destined to be less productive. The total discarding of any thought of *trying to change, teach, correct, enlighten or meaningfully affect that other person in any way,* even when surface dialogue may suggest it, will vividly identify the relationship for the spectator as one that has extended over a long period of time.

For any long standing relationship, when the dialogue suggests an attempt to change or teach the other character, simply tell yourself that what they're doing they've done forever. You'll find a rich, fertile field for *reactions!* There's a vast difference for the actor in observing somebody's behavior for the first time and observing it as if *again, for the hundredth time.*

The mother who cautions her daughter to come home by curfew time must surely have attempted the same cautioning a hundred times before, even if the writer doesn't say so. The mother-daughter relationship will appear far more authentic and lifelike for both actresses and will produce much more *personal experience* for both if it's related to as if for *the hundredth time.*

The moment of reacting to a character's comment or the observing of behavior in real life often causes a reflexive reaction on our part---especially if it's for *the one hundredth time*---of what could be called *"Going someplace before responding'"* (mentioned earlier in the *"Living Sounds"* discussion)... not skipping that involuntary, reflexive reaction that produces a much more productive relating experience!

In life we almost always "go someplace"---to a *reflexive reaction* rather than a worded thought---when somebody asks us something or says something we either agree or disagree with. We are literally "sent someplace" . . . often to a *spontaneous reaction that produces a sound* . . . before we respond with words, actually before the words occur to us. This is not only a phenomenon of normal human dialogue exchange but it's also part---and certainly an important part---of the "illusion of the first time" that all acting should present.

The biggest value of this *"going someplace before responding"* is the truth, the easy naturalness and the feeling-rich response that occurs before the words come and usually remains while they're spoken.

Actors who jump to dialogue response without these *"going someplace"* thresholds before the words commence miss important opportunities for their own expressiveness. Feelings should

126

always dominate dialogue. Any meaningful character should always *be having an experience* while talking, rather than just talking.

"Going someplace before responding" instantly catapaults an actor into a *responsive feeling* of some kind. Retaining that feeling as the dialogue response is delivered enriches it, gives it added truth. It's so easy and so fulfilling to be sent instantly to a free, open and full feeling before the worded response flows out of that feeling. *Don't end* the "going someplace" to begin the words! Let the *feeling* talk!

■ **In the same context, the manner in which an actor determines that the character is to relate to** *situations* **around it can create a pedestrian, situation-playing performance that barely if at all holds any interest for the spectator, or it can distinguish the actor as one who is engrossing to observe. There are important things to keep in mind in . . .**

Relating

to Situations

Now, compare those heavily dialogued sequences out of the past with the films of today. In today's performance writing the leading characters and other protagonists intended by the writers to evoke any sympathy or empathy on the part of the viewer are more *"being done to"* than *"doing to"*. (See the chapter entitled *"Being Done To"*.)

Modern day film, for the actor, is more *personal experience* than interpersonal *action.* Actions finally taken are preceded by lengthier periods of *inner struggle,* more *"wallowing in the muck"* of problems, salt-and-peppering of more moments with what psychotherapists and analysts have come to call simply *"feeling blobs"*---tiny, brief moments of inchoate, unformed, fragments of totally disoriented, agitated *problem experiencing* instead of solution-planning in *action* terms. Those *"feeling blob"* moments abound in situation-focused moments of characters' experiences. The actor need only observe them.

Some writers, both in action descriptives and any dialogue, very clearly indicate that the character's attention should remain on the *problem experiencing* , the *floundering,* the *apparent hopelessness* at such times. When the writer leaves those times to the actor's own choice for the character, the same choice should be made.

The always popular *"Indiana Jones"*, even when taking action, is desperate and frightened rather than efficient and confident . . . and most of the time even he is *"being done to"* much more than "doing to", and experiencing problems with little hope of solutions. It's what people flock to *"Indiana Jones"* films for. The *"Die Hard"* series is another example. And those are even in the "violent action" category!

We may cheer with relief in moments when a jeopardy situation is finally overcome, but those moments aren't what we paid at the boxoffice to experience. We looked forward to the awesome problem situations that were more central to the story. And we enjoyed being suspended on the front of our seats for the duration of all those interminable periods when it appeared to the character---and to us---that there would be no solution!

What was keeping us on the edge of our seats? Of course it was the *thing*---the *Object*---creating the jeopardy and peril!

That's one of the most cogent arguments for today's actors to focus their attention and planned involvement on the situation more than on other characters or even on situations' solutions until those solutions are found and provided by the writer!

It's not that revolutionary or heretical to state that---in order to best serve today's more advanced concepts of *human experience* as it appears in today's performance dramas---the actor should either discard and forget or at least hold off for longer moments a lot of those *action* approaches.

An actor *planning* action isn't that interesting to observe as he or she typically squints into the distance---into the *next moment!*---to find a solution and plan a strategy. An actor *taking* action is often simply an event. In the first place, the *situation and problem* still exist, and they're far more fertile objects of concentration for the actor. In such moments, concentrate on the situation!

Although it's perfectly logical that in problem moments one would perhaps in real life be searching a way out of the problem, if the writer hasn't yet in the scene indicated that a solution is forming in the mind, don't waste those moments looking for it. The finding of it is all the more evocative for you, and for your character as well, if just as the author sends your character into a decided responsive action---a solution---in that same moment, not before, it's found by your character!

■ **The next item is important for all actors. It's something every actor must learn to deal with!**

Relaxation

Tensions Result From So Many Different Causes!

The dictionary defines tension as the result of stretching or straining, tightness, mental strain, nervous anxiety. Although the sources for most actors' tensions are mental processes, those tightening thoughts---or worse, mental strains that make thinking impossible---flow through the neural system, tighten the muscles in many parts of the actor's body and cripple him, create self-consciousness, impair his ability to function comfortably.

Strasberg called tension *"the occupational disease of the actor."* And Stanislavski pointed to relaxation as an actual professional activity of actors. He stressed relaxation as the essential first stage in all acting.

The actor's main source of such tensions is perhaps the fear of failure, of not being good enough, of being judged. Regrettably, it's the nature of acting that the actor is led to believe that he must *perform for others.* So much *ego tension* would be felt to drain away if the actor could find the joy of working for *himself.* That's a state not too many actors achieve. So tension remains one of the primary concerns with which the actor must deal.

There are so many recommended manners for the relaxing of the instrument by actors! Some work; some don't. An actor doesn't have to be neurasthenic, or psychasthenic, or psychogenic or anything else to suffer bodily tensions that affect his work. The simplest feelings of insecurity for whatever reason or constant social role playing in private life can produce tensions, and those tensions can be continuous, day in, day out, also in the actor's performance of roles, all the actor's life.

The manners in which actors can be helped to relax their instruments' tensions and free their instruments for the flowing of sensations and feelings are a major concern for any teacher. One of the most immediately effective manners of relaxing as much as possible of the total instrument was found by Michael Chekhov:

Chekhov discovered that if he told an actor to *"relax"* (as Stanislavski often did) the actor immediately became more tense and made an effort to relax that totally defeated its own attempt. He discovered a nice, simple phrase to use with his actors which many of us have later found to be effective . . . "Stand or sit with . . . *a feeling of ease."* Actors can do that. And the result is immediately visible. It's so simple, one of the simplest remedies, and it works remarkably well for many actors!

In passing, I hope the actor won't fail to note that Stanislavski's admonition to *"relax"* demanded an *action.* Chekhov's suggestion of settling into *"a feeling of ease"*, is essentially an *object.* And Chekhov's simple advice works for many actors. But there are many other suggestions forwarded by other teachers.

Some coaches recommend leaning down and toe-touching. Some recommend batting the air in a circular motion. Some recommend letting everything droop. One coach recommends that actors imagine themselves lying in a hammock that's floating in a void. At least it feels good. Whether it reduces any tensions that are deeprooted is questionable.

Another teacher, Don Richardson, recommends something that I've observed works for some people:

First, shaking of the hands as though the hands and wrists are rubber. This supposedly relaxes your arms, shoulders and hands. Closing your eyes and thinking of jet-black water, nothing else, can relax and clear your mind, and if continued for a time can relax much of the whole body.

Another recommendation of Don Richardson is dropping your head forward and letting it roll slowly clockwise, by its own weight, completely around to where you began. You can hear little cracklings in your neck as the tension goes away at least temporarily. Doing the same counterclockwise will relax your neck, your vocal cords and shoulders---again, at least temporarily.

Most of these are purely physical appoaches (some are mental) for the achieving of relaxation for a few moments. If they work at all for the actor, they probably work only occasionally. Nervous tension doesn't come from the body; it's the result of where the mind is. Relaxing the mind is relatively easy for some, not ever completely accomplishable for others.

However, here's one approach that I'd recommend actors try at least once to discover whether it works for them or not. It truly involves the mind, from whence real tensions come. There are many coaches who recommend this one: Whatever position you're in---sitting (the most desirable and the most productive), standing, lying down, walking or whatever . . .

(1) Consciously relax the highest areas on both sides of the forehead (the temples), where the blue nerves are located that connect with the brain and where stress causes some people to experience migraine headaches. Let relaxation flow downward from the scalp and into the temples . . .

(2) Consciously flow the relaxation across the eyebrows very slowly to the the spot between the eyebrows at the top of the nose (where worry and self-doubt can tense us). Don't hurry the relaxing of this important area. Many areas of our face are more in-

volved with observation of and relating with others, but this spot at the top of the bridge of the nose is where our foreheads wrinkle in concern (most often self concern, by the way). Give this area time to achieve a feeling of total ease . . .

Then (3) flow the relaxation slowly down the sides of the nose to the bottoms of both the outer sides of your nostrils. Experience the draining of tenseness from the checks as this downward relaxation route progresses and connects with them (where our "mask" cheeks have become tense from continuous presentation of image). Note the feeling that your whole face feels as if it's becoming longer from your eyes to your jaw as this area achieves relaxation . . .

(4) Continue the flow of relaxation (of the "mask", in this area) downward along the folds that run from the nostrils to the outside corners of the mouth. Those folds can often become definite lines from the same tensions of the continuing "mask" effort of presenting our desired personal image. Feel the entire cheeks becoming soft, losing all the nerve end tenseness that you may well live with all the time without noticing it. . .

Then, finally, (5) relax the corners of the mouth (those tattletales that we know reveal so much of our thought and feeling attitudes). We know instinctively that they convey much of our inner thought and attitude process and we try to control them much of the time. Very consciously flow the relaxation to those mouth corners and feel the jaw relaxing with them.

An advantage of this latter relaxation exercise is that it can be used anywhere, anytime---in the company of others, in moments of a role, wherever---without an observer (or audience member) being the least bit aware.

A gifted English actor who always appears totally at ease has confided that when he finds himself experiencing any tension he simply takes a moment to "go out of himself" to an "out of body" experience of communing with some distant non-human sound. It might be the ticking of a distant clock, traffic sounds outside or something else of non-human source.

Those who can easily read the body signs of tension emanating from the mind have called attention especially to one telltale item. It's mentioned in *Body Communication* books studied by Personnel Managers toward reading the signs of psychologies evidenced by the bodies of applicants in interviews for employment.

Do you sometimes observe yourself with your thumbs folded under the fingers of your hand? This, they tell us, is invariably a sign of tight, insecure, perhaps even troubled mind processes. It's a visual signal of the person who in interpersonal relationships *"knuckles under"* involuntarily.

131

Now, take a moment and lay both hands on your legs, fold both your thumbs under all fingers with your fingers folded down tightly over them. It's a familiar position for some.   Now---still with your hands lying comfortably on your legs, open your thumbs and lay them outside the rest of your hand, *curled outward*. You should experience a feeling of ease that flows beyond your hands into much of your being!

But---repeating the suggestion in the earlier chapter *"Off Center"*, one of the quickest ways to relax is, if there's a wall handy, to lean against it in some off-center position. If there's a chair handy, loll in it instead of sitting upright. You'll experience what Chekhov's simple but very effective suggestion posited: What will come is *"a feeling of ease"*. That's relaxation.

■ **I hope that my constant repetition of certain suggestions I make throughout the book (as in the previous paragraph, again recommending *off center* experiencing) won't be too annoying.**

"Repetition" is, in fact, one of the exercises for which one of our leading American teachers is most noted. He long ago conceived of an exercise which he employs repeatedly with all his class members.   It even bears that title . . .

Repetition

The Sanford Meisner Exercise

The highly respected New York acting teacher Sanford Meisner invented this excellent exercise devised to foster the development of response, spontaneity, invention and exploitation of the actor's ability to go fully from one experience and attitude to another.

New York veteran teacher William Esper, who studied with Mr. Meisner and has since 1965 had his own studio, describes this Meisner exercise which he uses in his first year classes as one wherein actors are taught to listen to each other and then respond truthfuly from their own point of view. Because they have to repeat everything, they have to listen to each other in order to do the exercise.

One actor may say *"It's a beautiful day."*   The other actor must repeat the same words, but with a different feeling of his or her own. Perhaps the first means it; is enjoying the pleasantness of it. The other actor, quickly seeking to make it otherwise, might appear ready to regurgitate as s/he responds *"It's a beautiful day"* sarcastically, making fun of the first speaker's stupidity.

The first, spontaneously seeking another feeling, might appear affronted by the contradiction and defensively repeat *"It's a beautiful day!"* with force and finality, as if the argument is finished. The other might quickly appear tired of arguing and resignedly say *"It's a beautiful day"* in a manner that suggests it's useless to argue with a stupid person. The first, happy that s/he's apparently won the argument and overlooking the implied comment, might smile broadly and exult *"It's a beautiful day,"* happy in triumph.

Now the other is really teed off! *"It's a beautiful day!"* s/he growls, maybe adding a groan of disgust. *"It's a beautiful day,"* the first responds, crooning the words musically to further upset the other. The other looks heavenward and responds *"It's a beautiful day"* as if the first is really crazy. The first . . . etc., etc. The exchange could go on forever, with each response saying something other than the mere words.

It's an exercise in dexterity and snapping to new attitudes quickly and confidently. Spontaneity is the natural result. And as the exercise continues, at some point one of them feels the impulse to change the dialogue, and the process begins anew.

Another benefit of the exercise is the *listening behind the words.* One senses the actor doesn't mean what he or she is saying, and responds to the behavior rather than just the words.

The Meisner Technique uses the *Repetition* exercise at an early point in class members' training, and continues into the adding of *Independent Activities*---urgent tasks to be completed while the Repetition exercise resumes its progress, then to endowing the urgent Independent Actitivities with *Justifications, Emotional Circumstances,* etc.

The Repetition basis of Meisner's teaching is one this author certainly approves of, since it stems from Meisner's so often stated principle that *"What a character does doesn't depend on him or her, but on what one or more other characters are doing to him or her."* Meisner believes and has often stated that this is the foundation from which all acting training should begin.

The same philosophy is discussed in this book's chapter *"Being Done To . . . Instead of Doing To".*

■ **Some classwork with the following perfectly valid item feels absolutely kindergartenish, but its purpose in even time-taking** *Communion With An Object exercises* **is basically honorable.**

Many of us feel that using it consciously in performance in substitution for characters' realities, as some recommend it be used, is not constructive. But it's an important item!

Sense memories

The Body's Treasure Troves

This is an item that's unfortunately controversial, but only with respect to those who teach its use in *actual performance of roles in place of the character's own reality.*

Sense Memory of one type or another is involved in *almost all aspects of any acting methodology!* It's merely taught differently by different coaches when broken down to be worked on by itself.

It's available to be used in the finding of most involvement tools through the body's *associative memory* processes, and it's perhaps the main key toward reaching into the right brain's rich storehouse of *affective* memories. It's one of the most productive resources of an actor's talent, because it's the closet from which all remembered and even subconscious experience flows forth!

A *Sense Memory* is what the body has caused the right brain's storehouse of associative memory to store away and retain forever after we've experienced something physically through one or more of the senses or perhaps through most of the senses combined in a single experience.

There's the *Tactile Sense* (of touch), the *Olfactory Sense* (of smell), the *Gustatory Sense* (of taste), the *Visual Sense* (of sight) and the *Auditory Sense* (of hearing).

In addition to its simple contribution to our experiencing of the natures of physical objects, a *Sense Memory* often involves the body with some experience of its own which it associates with a definite thought or feeling or both. This is why some coaches, myself included, recommend the *body-searching* process for discovering affective words for preparation tools, so that the complete instrument of the actor can be brought into play, rather than simply a feeling or thought basis for an experience which may or may not later attract the body's important participation.

As a simple class exercise in some teaching to stimulate the imagination, it often involves examining, for instance, the imaginary contents of an old trunk in an attic and exploring each item with a sensory experiencing of its characteristics. In addition to imagining its form, its texture, its smell, its weight, etc., the actor is often encouraged to imagine where it might have come from, what it reminds him of, how it makes him feel, etc. Strasberg employed this manner of sense memory exporation in many of his private classes.

Other class exercises with *Sense Memory* might involve, for example, simply lying in the sand on a sunny beach on a hot day.

The actor would be encouraged to experience the heat of the sun on already hot skin; the rubbing of suntan oil and its soothing softness; the little tinkly sounds wafted from far across the sand; the caress of the sun-filtered breezes; the smell of the surf; etc.---storing or reviving sense memories which might serve the actor by suggesting body involvements in some peacefully relaxed moment of a role at a future time.

These kinds of class exercisings with *Sense Memory* are more generally simple developmental exercises to increase the actor's appreciation of the body-involving aspects of any good sense memory.

One of the benefits of these class exercisings with *Sense Memory* is that the actor can't fail to note the involvement of the body which any *Sense Memory* promotes.

Some teachers who recommend the use of single *Sense Memories* in separate, prolonged moments of *actual performance of roles* (as I don't) also recommend the following manner of finding an appropriate one for use in a particular role moment:

Instead of trying to find an appropriate and highly productive *Sense Memory* via a simple result word like "hate" or "love" or "confusion" the actor can, rather, think about what such a single word *most feels like to him or her personally* . . . nothing sensory yet; at least nothing planned to feel or sound sensory yet in its wording.

One actor's right brain / body combination might see "hate" as *"wanting to bust something"*, while another might in his mind redefine the same single word as *"not able to think clearly"*. Such differences do exist among different personalities' experiencing of identical words. The different manners of experiencing of course stem from actors' different psychologies' defense systems and their unique filtering and coping structures.

It's important that you find *your own uniquely personal* redefinitions, in strictly mental terms, for the feelings for which *Sense Memories* are to be sought. The single words describing feelings are too general. Then and not before, try to remember a moment not when you felt "hate" but when you "wanted to bust something" or when you were "not able to think clearly". There's a vast difference. The best sense memories come easily that way.

The remarkable thing that happens when this redefining approach is employed is that, by summoning the body's help in the redefining of *"What does it feel like to you?"* a sense memory will come which is much more appropriate for you personally than one found through the simple one-word approach.

135

It should be mentioned that if you're one to whom a simple *Sense Memory* appeals for use in actual performance, there's the danger of violating or overlooking the over-all personality (the emotional identity) of your character. When the experiencing of a *Sense Memory* is held foremost in the mind, without the psychological conditioning of the character, it's possible that the reality of the character---which must always be there---will be lost.

■ **Not often included in teachers' work is this next item, but it might help actors to know about it, know what it is and how to use it, because there are often moments in roles that call for its use. Actors who know how to handle it can easily incorporate its second dimension in preparation, while actors for whom it's a first time experience sometimes require directors patient enough to teach them in rehearsal. Careful balancing of two different involvements is involved in using . . .**

The Social Mask

For Use When The Surface Must Attempt To Deceive

Few roles exist where the character can show all its feelings openly all the time and still be able to *get, keep or avoid* something important to it. Those are the keys in determining situations which suggest or require the use of a *Social Mask* as a "cover-up" tool. It should be noted that a *Social Mask* works ideally with either an *Action* or an *Object.* But it's most often appropriate when there's some need to *get, keep or avoid* something--- in otherwords, when it's needed for use with an *Action.*

No matter what the true inner feelings of a character may be, there are moments and often entire sequences in roles when the character must cover those feelings (actually, *attempt* to cover them) in order to *get* something (perhaps a raise, a sale, a contract, some respect), or *keep* something (perhaps a marriage, a job, some peace, an inheritance, an upper hand) or *avoid* something (being fired, being discovered, causing a fight, committing a social *faux pas* or spoiling a group's fun). Each of those occasions might suggest an *Action* or *Intention* at work.

In real life we probably have friends or associates who may not really like us at all, but who treat us in perhaps one of these manners: *friendly, loving, interested, helpful, cooperative or indulgent.* Underneath those facades we may not even detect that there's *jealousy, loathing, prejudice, sexual calculation, resentment* or something else.

136

Perhaps on the other hand we may know that they like us very much but, to protect themselves from becoming too involved, they pretend *disinterest, casual acceptance, critical distance, too busy* or something else.

The *Social Mask* is a flat-out lie. In acting terms, just as in everyday life, it's a *pretense.* It's a "represented" feeling, a "role-playing" designed to cover whatever true feelings lie behind it.

When actors attempt to "play simple results" such as adjectives they tend to theatricalize their efforts because they aren't really experiencing those feelings in any inner manner. It's the same with a *Social Mask*, and in using this nice tool in a role the actor should do precisely the opposite of what he must do for true experiencing . . . he must *"represent", "play simple result"* and *"role-play"* on the surface for as long as the *Social Mask* is necessary in order to get, keep or avoid something.

This use of a *Social Mask* for the character in sometimes long moments of roles is like visiting an old friend in real life. The process is so very familiar for all of us. For the actor who decides to use one, it's one of the most natural and easiest processes of all. The *Social Mask* itself feels like the back porch "play-acting" from childhood days. It's important that it *not be ideally real.* But it's a gas to "perform". A "performance" is all it is.

Since the true inner character behind the *Social Mask* is still there, and should be apparent in its true inner experience for the viewer ---while the character is attempting to get away with a surface lie to other characters around it, the actor should employ the most obviously called for approach, forming a *Social Mask* for those moments when the character needs one. Therefore, there's nothing more sure to work than those self-same *adjectives* and *role labels* which, alone, usually create *transparently untruthful acting.*

In that manner ---just as in life, the viewer will still be able to detect the *inner truths* of the character hiding behind the surface "representation" and "result-playing" effort of the character as it attempts to mislead other characters.

The audience member, seeing through the sham, can hurt because he knows that while attempting to be brave or courageous on the surface the character is suffering deeply inside.

On the other hand, wonderful comedy can result, and the viewer will laugh as he shares the dynamic secret of a character's true inner thought while the pretense on the surface is allowed to be ridiculously transparent and false.

The *Social Mask,* in its most appropriate use, is for the man who's dependent on his wife but can't stand her, and the wife who can't stand her husband one more day but needs him, who, together---as they entertain the husband's superior at a sit-down din-ner---pretend *"The world's most loving couple"*. The boss him-self, sitting across from them and smiling---although he can't stand his employee and loathes the man's wife---may be pretend-ing *"Jovial benefactor"* or something else on the surface.

For comedy, it's also for the frightened virgin, out with a man who's known to have a wild reputation, who perhaps pre-tends to be *"A foxy doxie"*, while the roué across from her, anx-ious to finish the evening with the desired event, pretends to be a *"Harmless puppy dog"*.

It's for the friend who can't wait to leave your party because she's unbelievably bored, who pretends *"Having a ball"* because her husband works for you.

Remember that simple adjectives or adjectival phrases aren't the only forms of *Social Mask*. They work ideally for this purpose, but many actors enjoy more those catchy *labels or stereotype titles* such as are spoken of in the preceding para-graphs. Either way works. The choice is up to the actor who plans to use this tool in a scene where the surface must be a lie.

■ **Uta Hagen pioneered the following item, gave it its title in her teaching. Sometimes misunderstood (from its title) to be similar to Strasberg's approach of *substituting actors' past experiences for character's realities in performance moments*, it's quite dif-ferent, and can be immensely effective for actors.**

Substitutions

The Actor's Memory Bin as an Acting Tool

Uta Haven describes this item in Chapter 3 of her book *"Respect For Acting"* as a manner of finding the character within ourself, through forming a continuing and overlapping series of *Substitutions* out of our own life's experiences and remem-brances, using imaginative extension of realities of those experi-ences, and putting them in the place of the character's fictions in moments of the play *after first adapting them into the character.*

She specifically advocates that the *Substitutions* should be found and then *transferred and adapted into the character's own moments.* She strongly recommends against the approach being still worked on by the actor for its experiencing during the perfor-mance of a role through stepping outside the character's reality into the actor's personal past.

Ms. Hagen recommends that *Substitutions* can serve the actor not only in *some* moments of the role (when the material provided by the writer fails to stimulate sufficiently) but also in *every moment* of the role to aid the actor in believing the *time,* the *place,* the *surroundings,* the *conditioning forces,* the *character itself* and the *character's relationship to other characters.*

She gives examples of how to use this approach that is some-what similar to the use of many individual *Affective Memories,* but without a lengthy procedure in the *finding* process, and then, rather than actually reliving those moments in the performance (substituting the actor's personal memory moment), using what they've produced in personalizing such moments for ourself *after adapting that product* to make it part of *the character's experience. The adapting of it into the character's reality* is important enough to warrant this reiteration.

She recommends that the process of finding *Substitutions* should remain private, not shared with the director or other cast members. Those people haven't been a part of the actor's own life experience.

She, like Stella Adler and others, sticks to the *Action* as the main approach item and, like Ms. Adler, proceeds to add *Substitutions, Memories of Emotion* (not in the Strasberg manner of finding or use), *Sense Memories, Circumstances, Objectives* and *Obstacles* to each *Action* to give it total life.

Ms. Hagen's *Substitutions* are an excellent approach when used as she suggests---especially since she doesn't recommend that actors depart from their characters' experiences and substitute their own past moments during actual performance; instead, finding them out of their past lives, obtaining the desired personalization of experience from what they evoke, then transferring and adapting them into the character's own experience.

■ **Any teacher who doesn't include in classwork some approaches that are at least equivalent to the following two major phases of preparing the *inner life* of characters shouldn't lay claim to being of Stanislavski System persuasion.**

Before the approaches for the realizing of the character's continuing experience are laid out step by step, there are the first obligations of the actor toward creating *the inner and outer character* presented by the writer . . . the *Analytical Subtext* (the personality and life drives of the character) and the *Directed Subtext* (the actor's decisions as to the manner in which the character shall fulfill the author's intentions throughout the role from beginning to end). The planning of those two Subtexts, more than anything else, determines the quality of the actor's performance!

For these two important preparation phases this author prefers to describe their details in the manner, and with the approach items, in which he most believes. They essentially follow the approaches recommended by Stanislavski and Vakhtangov, with only minor adaptations.

Subtext

The Analytical Phase

The following manner of first analyzing the role is my own preference, as it was Stanislavski's and Vakhtangov's. Although some coaches approach the first analyzing of the role in relation to the play or film differently, the following manner parallels that of Stanislavski and Vakhtangov quite faithfully, and I've found it to be more thorough, in my estimation, than others of which I'm aware.

In my opinion, it also leads more surely to producing immediate (and earliest) impressions of the psychology of the character through the process of *Listing The Facts* (not overlooking any), and seeking to determine the *reasons, stemming from psychological fixations and conditioned response yet to be determined, for the character's behavior in all moments of the role.*

When an actor first reads the role it's important to remain alert for the bits and pieces of cumulative information and facts provided by the author.

A dedicated actor ---keenly tuned to the observing of *parallel behavior patterns* and the twistings and turnings of the character's interpersonal relationships and their conflicts as they're created by those *parallel behavior patterns* moment after moment throughout the role---can find great pleasure in noting those patterns as they continually recur throughout the role.

These *parallel behavior patterns* can't be too emphatically stressed. They're signposts to the character's inner goals or problems, its manner of experiencing different circumstances and events, its positive or negative mindset and its *personal experiencing* of its moments as they differ from how other types of characters would experience the same things.

They're the *golden keys to the inner life of the character!* The actor *must* observe them and analyze them for their significances, then incorporate their analysis into the creating of the appropriate personality type for the role. Whatever other procedure might be used, those "signposts" are certainly what must be looked for.

The very first reading will usually arouse many feelings and emotional responses in the actor. That those responses diminish and have less impact in subsequent readings is inevitable, since those subsequent rereadings are for the purpose of gaining keener insight and familiarity with the character. In those subsequent rereadings the *work* has begun, replacing the initial *audience* responses.

In later readings some behavior patterns are observed to recur more frequently than have initially been perceived.

Psychologists, analysts and psychotherapists go over the same ground time and time again in attempting to study their patients. Actors should do no less with their characters. Except for small or hurriedly prepared film roles, there's normally time for this analysis-in-depth process and it's neglectful of the actor, sometimes later disastrous, to dismiss it as "tiresome work" which he has no inclination to do, hoping the director will later supply all the illumination needed.

The dedication with which the actor examines and analyzes these *recurring behavior patterns* of the character will most often be *the scale on which the entire preparation and performance of the role will later be weighed!*

Analysis, following observation, is the key! There are so many, many personalities which lie behind the simple shells of behavior which can be missed by actors who don't look for them or, having even found them, later don't prepare their characterizations with those *recurring behavior patterns* and insighted analysis of them held in mind.

It can't be too strongly stated that *a clearly defined personality is the first and most important consideration in the actor's preparation of a role.*

Listing The Facts; Appraising Them

Pages 12 through 18 of the 1989 Routledge/Theatre Arts Books paperback edition of *"Creating A Role"* (the third and last of Stanislavski's three book trilogy) offer a thorough discussion of what Stanislavski normally called *Listing The Facts* under the title *Putting Life Into The External Circumstances,* and commencing on page 18 is the same kind of discussion of the next step, *Appraising The Facts.* There's even a list of facts from one role offered as an illustration of the process.

Prior to this next step, it's possible to make too hasty judgment of the *recurring behavior patterns* mentioned. What the author presents as facts may suggest snap judgments and assumptions too easily drawn from those facts.

Facts run the gamut of descriptions---events that take place, circumstances that exist, characters' behavior patterns and actions which are taken because of those patterns and their own and others' statements.

Sometimes the author's facts are even presented a little sneakily by the writer in brief parenthetical words or phrases such as *(shyly)* or *(grudgingly)* or *(shaken)*. Those tiny one word parenthetical hints should be studied also (even if, as most coaches recommend, they're struck out of the script by the actor because in actual performance they suggest a limited type of feeling or emotion or manner of doing, leading to momentary detours from the character's and the actor's truthfulness).

The only way to avoid the missing of individually important facts, and I think the best way to successfully glean their nuances as to the character's personality, is to first...

List The Facts, One After Another . . .

. . . down a page (or probably several pages, since there'll be so many facts). Put off all asumption and all appraisal of the separate facts listed until the simple job of listing them is completed.

Then and only then, go back and give close scrutiny to fact after fact, squeezing every drop of nuance and suggestion and justification from each in turn.

In first readings there will have been one or two or perhaps at most three behavior patterns and response categories which have been most frequently observed. You may want to separate those two or three easily observed kinds of behavior patterns into two or three separate columns on your page, as suggested earlier in this book.

One column of listed facts may grow swiftly because of the many times the same general behavior occurs, while one or more of the other columns may grow more slowly and in the end have fewer entries. The larger list of facts in the longer column will command the greater emphasis, but the shorter columns' entries should be considered too. Those shorter columns, with fewer notings of certain occurrings of their items, are important too.

As you go back to appraise and analyze each fact as to its *raison d'etre*, you may find that certain entries in one column seem simple result actions or reactions and they may actually belong in another of the few columns. Often the shorter columns' entries will one after another be transferred to the longer column as their at first overlooked relationships to it are detected.

For the actor willing to go through this deep and searching scrutiny of all the facts provided, it's a tougher self-imposed task.

It takes time and thought. Persuade yourself that the confidence in the result is worth the effort. It is.

What you should hope to wind up with is a personality descriptive phrase that can send you with security into the next preparation phase. But *listing the facts* is the first step.

The separate columns may be labeled *"caged"*, *"status-driven"* and *"primary circle critical"*, as described in the earlier chapter. By seeking the most dominant of the three but still seeking to involve the behavior colors of the others you might wind up with a personality label such as *"slum suffocated"* or *"gutter-smelling"* or *"Thompson Street Jailbird"* (again referring to the combined personality label from the earlier example).

What's important at this point is that your choice of a label for the personality be finally turned into one central core label.

Once the most exciting and personally meaningful label possible is found, some actors---having thus far only a label for the character's personality---might at this point decide to proceed immediately into the preparing of the "tools" of the *Directed Subtext*. Others might find their brain tired from the "analyzing" and welcome a respite, but that's not the main reason for (at this exact point) going to this seeming "side trip" that could be but may definitely not be unrelated to the emotional core:

The Six Questions. . .

One reason for considering going to this step next (although it was never recommended by Stanislavski in print) is that on occasion it produces sentiments, social milieux, dominant societal and cultural influences or other modifying conditions which should be blended into the character's *inner experience* through slight adaptations because of environment, location, social role or other important consideration, before proceeding further.

Journalism students certainly know the *"Six Questions"* --- the *Who, What, When, Where, How* and *Why* that are requisites in the first paragraph of any news item's detailing. Actors may not know them, not realize how they can be used in role preparing, and may miss out on so much of the excitement available through their use.

So, for those who'll take the time to find this exciting side trip's benefits, they need to be explained.

Who, What, When, Where, How and Why? . . .

. . . apply to acting in two different ways---as an omnibus description of a role's entirety, much as its brief story might be written up in a first paragraph of a news story, as prescribed in Journalism I classes and publicity courses: *Who* (the character) does *What* (the over-all scripted event), *When* (in what period of history, at what time of year, month, day and hour), *Where* (in what country, state or province, region, town, physical location where scenes are to be played), *How* (the manner of doing) and *Why* (the apparent reasons for doing what is done).

For actors, the questions are important as *inspiration triggerers, research reminders, authenticity enrichers and reality gatherers.* The many role-enriching inspirations that can be found through using the *"Six Questions"* at this particular point in the preparation are absolutely staggering!

Commencing with the *Who (the character),* jot down the inspirations which come to mind regarding appropriate props, wardrobe, makeup, hairstyle, activities not mentioned by the writer, etc. Every *Who* has several "roles" that can be examined, one after another, for that purpose. *Age, psychology, family role, profession, interests, nationality, religion,* etc. Each of these can produce many, many inspirations.

The character might be a *father,* a *president of the school board,* a *farmer,* a *football or basketball enthusiast,* but still, throughout the script's timeframe be a *tourist on vacation* for sightseeing in New York. Think of all the things which can be thought of and explored for integrating into the role if each of those separate "roles" is studied separately on its own merits!

Similarly, the role of a doctor---even though the emotional life of this doctor will have been fairly well thought out earlier---still requires researching of the kinds of *activities, props, schedules, commonly used terms, practical wardrobe, preoccupations, daily "automatic role behavior" items,* etc.

Once you've completed this kind of application for just this first question, the *Who,* you'll feel excitement beginning to build. Your character is starting to take more tangible physical shape!

In listing the *What* (what the character does in the script), there's the one main thing that the character does most throughout the script, but there are also separate parts of the script in which the character does other things along the progressions of the story line.

If the character is one who grovels for food out of trashcans, sleeps in alleyways, spends meaningless daytimes walking the slum district streets, etc., there are so many tiny details involved which can inspire ideas to enrich and excite the preparation of the role as well as trigger any needed or desirable research. If the character does something with which you're not familiar, *research it!*

When can really bring excitement.   Considering timeframe, first: Is the character really of the same time and place with which the overall work is concerned, or is it maybe living in the past and holding onto an earlier era's lifestyle, like an old spin-ster aunt, a grandparent, a hermit?

When suggests first of all researching anything not known about a specific period in history . . . costumes, interesting hand props, customs, social manners, dominant religious beliefs, hair styles, etc., etc.

The *specific year* can pinpoint wardrobe more specifically, suggest the earlier kind of props used in daily life---fans, spats, pocket watches, rapiers and other easily overlooked items of wardrobe, props, etc.

Don't overlook the *month or season*. Winter, spring, summer and fall suggest substantive differences in wardrobe and props, activities the author may have overlooked, etc. Of course the di-rector and set designer and costume designer will have supplied the major details, but the ingenuity of the actor, after this kind of research, can supply so many fascinating smaller touches which make the standard wardrobe, props and activities spring to life more dynamically. Many will have been overlooked by the writ-er but certainly belong in the finished performance.

The *week of the month* might be of little importance, but the *day of the week* will suggest many, many items. If the script doesn't specify the day of the week, consult the director for deci-sion. So many small inspirations can come from the day of the week. Standard work weekdays, if the character works, often suggest many activity details not in the script. Friday suggests its own, as do Satuday and Sunday.

In listing the *Where* items, consider *country*. It may require researching of language, dialect, social influence, government and how individual lives are affected by it, its customs, its unique dress, dominating hairstyles and usual props.

Also, in any country there are *regional* variations of lan-guage, climate, politics, customs, dress, dialects, family life, props, etc.

Next, don't overlook the differences among *urban, suburban, village, farm or ranch* existences and lifestyles. Each has its dis-tinctive habits and activities, also wardrobe, etc., which will probably have been overlooked by the author preoccupied with the unfolding of a story. There may be a common life pace or rhythm, an education level, accepted norms, etc.

Even the *exact locations* in which scenes occur can affect wardrobe, props, atmosphere and manner, etc. The kitchen or bedroom has its atmosphere. The densely quiet Yale Club has its.

The country club lounge does also. The barnyard is not the twenty-third floor executive office.

The last two questions are more or less wrap-up items. For *Why*, even if your character's psychology is the main *Why*, consider whether influences like religion, societally imposed lifestyle, etc., contribute, as they do in Arthur Miller's *"The Crucible"*. That play's many unique requirements certainly belong in the early planning of its characters' lives.

For the *How*, consider not only the personality behavior but also how things to be done would be done by such a character in that time and place.

Do as much of the *Six Questions* research and inspiration-seeking at this point in your preparation as you have time or the will to do. You'll be amazed at how much more excitingly the role will have already sprung to life for you as you're about to get back to the preparing of the character's inner life.

The *Six Questions* contribute mightily To *"Organic Blocking"* later! As discussed earlier under that heading, some directors encourage their cast members to bring their own ideas for their own characters to rehearsals and perhaps even contribute inspirations for setting refinements, wardrobe, props, activities to be integrated, etc. *"Organic Blocking"* is the moment when all the research and inspiration searching suggested here has its big opportunity to contribute.

What has now been completed---by the preliminary steps of *Listing The Facts, Appraising Them, forming a Personality Label for the Character, then using The Six Questions to enrich and inspire*---is the *Analytic Subtext* for the character.

■ **The actor is now ready to *choose the "tools"* (or whatever the actor calls his preferred approach items) for . . .**

Subtext

The Directed Phase

Those of us who call this next step *"The Directed Phase"* do so because it's no longer subtext analyzed from what the author has presented, but instead is the actor, beginning now, *directing his own preparation.*

Everything the actor has hopefully done toward the deciding and early preparing of the personality type for the role is basically *text.* Much of it has been contributed by the writer. The actor has simply added what assumptions about the character's personality could be gleaned from close scrutiny to the writer's details, analyzed them, and enriched them through the actor's own research and inspirations.

The *text*, what is thus far on paper or at least in the mind, will be the basis for these next steps . . . the planning of the definite *approach items*---of whatever kind the actor knows---to use in *creating and "self-directing" the emotional and other experiences of the character's Subtext throughout the life of the role!*.

We're at the challenging point of finally "getting into the character" and "getting the character into us". This is the point where most of us part ways of proceeding.

The *"I never do anything consciously"* people leave everything from here on up to instinctual inspiration. I believe the majority of us would consider that too chancey and a little stupid in its egoistic assumption of its own genius.

Another utterly ridiculous version of the *Directed Subtext* might be for an actor or actress to prepare in the manner that a beautiful but modestly talented film star used in preparing her first and only Broadway role---after coming to me for help, then deciding the help suggested was *"too much work."*

Before coming to me, R. W. had broken the script down by deciding to be *"Happy from here to here"*, *"Frightened from here to here"*, *"Sorry from here to here"*, *"Vengeful from here to here"!* If that actress should read this, she'll surely recognize herself, and she'll recall that when questioned about how she intended to bring the *personality* of the character she replied, *"It's just me. That's why they want me. I don't need to prepare anything to be me."* I politely cut our meeting short and have never seen her again.

One critic's opening night review included this sentence: *"Her greatest accomplishment in the role was that she didn't trip leaving the stage in her final exit."* (The only worse review I can remember ever reading was this one: *"Tallulah Bankhead sailed down the Nile last night as Cleopatra . . . and sank."*)

The replacement in a Broadway leading role, taking over a role from another player who originated the role, has little choice as to *The Directed Subtext*, since it's already been directed---unless it's someone like Uta Hagen replacing Jessica Tandy in the original *"A Streetcar Named Desire"*, who was so respected by Elia Kazan, the director, that she was trusted to bring her own brilliant concept of Blanche.

Most incoming replacements (especially in smaller supporting roles), unlike the freedom and respect afforded Ms. Hagen by Kazan, will often be required to essentially duplicate in every detail the performances of the ones who originated the roles. Laying out their own version of the *Directed Subtext* is futile if working with a director of the *"This is how I want it done"* school of directing. But the actor never knows he won't be directed (even as a replacement) by someone who'll encourage the actor's own new version of the character.

The hurried film actor, hired over the weekend to unexpetedly replace another actor at a distant filming location site and hustled onto a plane for line study enroute to the location, hasn't much time for elaborate preparation of the character's *Directed Subtext* and must at such a time rely pretty much on his or her instinct, natural talent and quickly formed approach items of whatever kind for bringing the separate moments of the first few days' filming sequences to life. Even in such a situation, though, the actor owes it to his own best interests to prepare what he can.

Others---with time and the opportunity to prepare more fully, in whatever many different manners and with whatever many different approaches---should at this point proceed to form some kind of "tools" to create the focal *motivations* and *manners of experiencing the moments of the role* for the total *life* of the character, from the moment of first appearance to the last moment.

They probably then at least note and form a manner of interpreting the *larger individual sections* of the role (widely called *Units*) where circumstances remain the same over periods of time. Then, if really thorough in their preparation, they break down the separate *units* into *separate moments* of varying duration (*Beats*) in which the character's attention and feeling experiences for the duration of each of those individual moments need to be focused on something appropriate for the character and evocative for the actor's interpretation.

Stanislavski's proposal, in the final section of *"Creating A Role"*, in his notes about the improvisations on *"Othello"*---without laying out any proposed and labeled "tools", hypothesized that the right course of creativeness operates *from the text to the mind* (those first readings of the role and the absorbing of what the author presents); *from the mind to the proposed circumstances* (the gleaning of the facts and, through appraising them, discerning what they imply to us about the character); and *from the proposed circumstances to the subtext.*

That's where we are at this point---at the door to the next subtext---the one that continues throughout the role. . . *The Directed Subtext.* To proceed, he recommended continuing *from the subtext to feeling (emotions), from emotions to the objective (desire, will) and from the desire to action.* (Those of us who teach Vakhtangov's version of *Objects* have noted that the second step---Stanislavski calls it *objective (desire, will)*---implies *action* and actually duplicates the last step, *action.* An alternate ---based more on Vakhtangov's theories---appears in upcoming paragraphs.)

Not many of us would argue with that over-all recommendation. Most of us who teach the many different preparation approaches that exist today still accept that neat package---some accepting every word.

But some of us, more disposed to value Vakhtangov's "object" contribution, would simply change the very last word to *"Object."* It's our conviction, as it was Vakhtangov's, that an "Object" includes *implied action* but also includes the focus of concentration and the feeling thought that *prompts* action, affording it more complete truth and enhanced *experience* without the adding of many qualifiers and particularizers.

Two Tools for Creating The Character's Personality . . .

The first tool that should be worded----no matter the wording---should embody the "thing" that lies at the core of the personality, the thing that causes it, gives it its particular life. In Stanislavski's early codifications of such a "thing" he recommended a *positive goal*, as mentioned in previous chapters--*a "thing"* strongly desired by the character throughout its life. Examples he suggested included *love, power, peace, acceptance, fulfillment, a better world to live in, etc.*

But the decades since---with the increasing knowledge of human psychology and the different conditioned responses resulting from different childhood traumas, and with actors and teachers coming to recognize the far more potentially vitalizing power of *negative experience*---have made most coaches conscious that the choosing of *negative* "things" (instead of positive ones) to direct characters' personalities is more ideal, more clinically true, and much more specific than those single word positive goals that could apply to many different personalities in so many different ways.

Consider, for the *love*-desiring character the alternative *negative* urgency of always feeling *rejected, ignored, isolated, shut out, thrown away!* For the *power*-hungry character, consider the *negative* frenzy of always feeling *roadblocked, dominated, controlled, looked down on,* etc.

For the *peace*-desiring character, the *negative*, never ceasing experiencing of *all that violence, these constant conflicts, this crazy rat race, etc.* For the *acceptance*-beggar, a negative such as *all those closed doors!, how inferior they think I am, how cold everybody is, etc.*

149

Think those negative thoughts for a moment. You'll see why an increasing number of present day coaches prefer and recommend the negative alternatives to Stanislavski's positive goals. In each negative thought's experiencing, didn't you experience some form of inner agitation? And didn't you feel the *desire and will to take action* without spelling out a single kind of action and thereby limiting your sphere of action?

With this *thing* now chosen---the first *tool of whatever type* you might choose to focus and enliven the motive source forming the character's personality---there needs to be now, not first before choosing that *thing,* a decision of *the character's manner of attempting throughout its life to cope with the negative experience.* Almost all teachers would agree that the *desire and perhaps the continuous attempt to take action* is still---just as Stanislavski intuited---an important part of the core of personality.

After choosing the first thought-focusing negative tool of the actor's choice that lies behind and causes its behavior patterns, the next tool---because it needs to be fairly specific in its manner of directing the character's lifelong manner of struggling against the negative throughout all the circumstances and events provided by the writer---best serves if it's worded as an *action!*

If the character always feels shut out or ignored, what might it *try all its life to do* because of that feeling? If the character always feels dominated or controlled, what might it *try all its life to do*---but never succeed at accomplishing?

Word it as you like; use it as you like---but at least with a never disappearing urgency inside. Call it, if you like, a *Life Action,* a *Super Objective* or *Spine* or *Through Line of Action* (for the whole role), whatever. Stanislavski himself often called the same tools by different titles in his notes---at least in Mrs. Hapgood's translations of his notes, which are all we thus far have for referring to.

Stanislavski taught both the *Super Objective* and the *Through Line of Action* as the *desired action* (in Mrs. Hapgood's translations) which the character feels it must attempt to take throughout all its life as a result of its life problem or goal.

The actor should remember, with regard to this *action* tool for the whole life of the character, that it should remain *impossible to ever be accompished,* at least to the desired degree. In that manner of using this first *action* tool (for the whole life) those two thus far found "top tools"---whatever you decide to label them in terminology---work together with an astounding emotional clarity and effect for the actor. *Never achieved,* they remain simmering and smouldering inside the character!

You might try a couple of examples: The first tool might be something like *"How ignored I am!"* and the second tool resulting from that particular psychological problem might be *"Show them I'm somebody too!"* You can see how those would work together and feed each other's experiencing.

Or another combination, *"How stupid I am!"* and *"Show them I'm really trying!"* Or still another couple, *"All those closed doors!"* and *"Make them let me in!"*

Actors who can achieve ideal inner emotional agitation for their characters' experiences and their own feeling sources can effectively bring the same approach (a combination of these two involvement tools) to planning the concentration focus and any resulting actions they want to use within . . .

The Separate Units Of The Role

In any role there are certain major turning points---new and changed circumstances met with and obliged to be experienced, endured or coped with by the character for a period of time. In most teaching these larger divisions of a role, lacking a more ideal label, are broadly called *"Units"*, as Stanislavski taught they could productively be called.

While the character always has its life problem and its effort to cope with it (those two tools described above) at the core of its experience throughout the role, centralizing its experience and particularizing its behavior, there are distinctly "good and bad periods" which exist along the way for varying timespans of the character's scripted life.

It would be confusing and lead to vagueness if an entire role were to be prepared without dividing it up into its easy and hard times, its obstacle-fighting times, its setbacks and its few successful, easy-flowing periods.

In our own lives there are lawsuits, divorces, family tragedies, accidents and other things that affect and to a degree change our life patterns for periods of time. There are also some good times which have the same patterns-changing effect on us for a time.

Since the over-all character---directed by those two first "top tools" or other similar approach items---determines *how* such changing circumstances will affect the character, I suggest to my people that each *Unit* of the role (sometimes three, four or five for leading roles) be determined---and the exact point at which the previous one ends and the new one begins---before considering each unit's content (its *Unit Object* or *Object of Attention* or, if the actor prefers, its *Action, Intention or Objective*).

151

Each *Unit,* once its duration (from Point A to Point B) is decided, needs to be assigned its focus. With the basic emotional feeling of the character itself continually dictated throughout the role by those first too tools (for the whole life) described above, each *Unit* needs the clear core of involvement (perhaps a *Unit Object* or a *Unit Objective*) which is to be its main concern throughout the *Unit.*

And, a related *action attempt* caused by that concern should also be planned to lay out the attempted action desired to be taken throughout the *Unit* because of the *Unit Object.*

Let's say the *Object* (or whatever tool of the actor's choice) for a Unit is something like *"What they're doing to me!"* . . . the attempt to cope might be an *action attempt* such as *"Make them stop suffocating me!"* Or, when a marriage is floundering for the duration of a Unit, perhaps a problem wording like *"This godawful mess!"* as the *Unit Object* and a *Through Line of Action* such as *"Get out of this snake pit!"* or perhaps *"Show her I can't take this crap!"*

In dividing the role up into these major parts (its *Units*) the actor's able to more easily refine the separate contents of those parts and create more separately distinctive involvements for each than would be possible if the *Units* weren't broken down.

In this manner also, the character's experience and its conditioned behavior can be skillfully and continually maintained through all the changing circumstances it encounters along the way during the role. If the actor doesn't employ the *Unit Breakdown* process there's the possibility that the core personality might be taken astray by the shifting conditions it encounters, resulting in simple *situation-playing* throughout.

When the two *Unit tools* have been decided, some actors and teachers recommend the consideration at that point of using an *"Obstacle"*. Some of us feel it's basically an unneeded duplication if the Unit's two other tools, just described, are right. At any rate, *"Obstacle"* is described under its own heading in the book, so it won't be detailed here.

This chapter and the last preceding chapter outline a highly recommendable manner of exploring, researching and deciding *"The Analytical Subtext"* and then forming *"The Directed Subtext"* for bringing of the whole life of the character . . . figuratively "designing the house" and then "constructing the house." The foregoing essentially follows the course recommended by Stanislavski and Vakhtangov.

From the point where this much of the preparation is completed it would be ridiculous under these or similar headings to describe where the many different role preparation approaches go off to in their different directions for searching the best *furniture and decor* for furnishing the house that's now built and ready for occupancy. There are so many different approaches!

The rest of the conscious preparation---laying out the smaller moments, one after another, within the separate Units---is normally called *"The Creative Subtext"* . . . but the multitudes of recommended manners taught by the multitudes of acting teachers for laying out *the creative interpretation of the role's moments* are so many and so diverse that each is dealt with under its separate term or label elsewhere in the book.

■   **There have always been different understandings of Stanislaski's terms *Super Objectives*, *Through Lines of Action* and *Spine*, since he himself used the three terms interchangeably at times, or perhaps Mrs. Hapgood did in her translating. But two of those items especially warrant some reexamination. As mentioned in the next chapter, reconsideration should be given both the *Through Line Of Action* and . . .**

Super Objectives

As Stanislavski Formed Them...and Some Later Thoughts

Stanislavski proposed the idea of a *Super Objective* which would articulate a character's motivation from first entrance to final exit. As mentioned earlier, the term was originally coined by Nemirovich-Danchenko, the literary head of the Moscow Art Theatre. Stanislavski immediately recognized its worth for actors and incorporated it into his System terms.

In applying the *Super Objective* to his evolving system, as described in *"An Actor Prepares"*, in *"Building A Character"* and in *"Creating A Role"*, Stanislavski saw the *Super Objective* as the innermost center, the core of the role, where all the objectives of the score converge, into one *"super objective, the concentration of the entire score of the role, of all of its major and minor units."*

He saw the *Super Objective* as being in harmony with the intentions of the playwright and at the same time arousing a response in the soul of the actor. He advocated searching for it not only in the role but in the actor himself.

In his *"Creating A Role"* description he points to Dostoyevski's novel *"The Brothers Karamazov"* and opines that the *Super objective* is the author's search for God and Devil in the soul of man, and to Shakespeare's *"Hamlet"* as having the *Super objective* of comprehending the secrets of being. He suggests that for Chekhov's *"The Three Sisters"* it's the aspiration for a better life, and for Leo Tolstoy's plays it was Tolstoy's unending search for self-perfection.

He saw the *Super Objective* as creating and manifesting the thousands of separate small objectives that occur on the external plane of a part, as the main foundation of a character's life and part, and saw all the minor objectives as corollary to it as the inevitable consequence and reflection of the basic one.

My own earlier work with the *Super Objective* and *Through Line Of Action*---both of which Stanislavski envisioned as the continuing cores of a character's striving to attain---brought the eventual appraisal that, both of those items so often in his descriptions being action-oriented, they at least peripherally duplicated each other. Each is certainly important. It simply occurred to me that the *Super Objective* belongs as the continuing manner of the character's striving to attain a strongly desired end *throughout an entire role*---and that a *Through Line Of Action* could ideally be applied as the same centralizing item for each of the separate *Units* of the role. That's how I've taught the two so similar tools productively over the years.

My reasoning (which led to this variation of my own from the original use of these two items by Stanislavski) was, and still is, that while the *Super Objective* lies behind all moments of a role---indeed as motivation behind all *Units* of the role as well, the given circumstances change very tangibly and sometimes drastically at different points of the role and continue to affect the character (but in particular manners, because of changing circumstances) for the duration of their existence. I felt the *Units*, too, needed some definite approach item to center their concentration and justify their desired actions.

Applying a new *Through Line Of Action* for each new *Unit*, based on its changed circumstance, provides a manner of focusing the actor's attention more particularly on that period's special and unique experiencing while still relating it to the *Super Objective* as the determinant of the character's primary (lifelong) concerns.

I've found it productive to combine Stanislavski's *Through Line Of Action* with my own manner of teaching the use of Vakhtangov's *Inner Objects* and *Thought Objects*---which I honestly believe Stanislavski was also arriving at in his late years (1935-1938) of evidencing more respect for Vakhtangov's *Objects*.

For example, imagine a female character with a (Vakhtangov-type) *Life Object* such as *How inadequate I feel!* and a (Stanislavski-type) *Super Objective* of *"Show them I'm trying!"*

154

In one *Unit*--- wherein for a period her husband is having an affair with another woman but the writer indicates that she must silently endure it, she might have for that period a (Vakhtangov-type) *Unit Object* like *"How humiliating this is!"* and, denied any real action response by the writer during that period, a (Parke-type) *Through Line Of Action* of *"Keep it from killing me!"*

Then, when her husband's affair is discovered by the children one night, and the author finally allows her to assert herself (to the extent that her "inadequate" psychology allows any assertive action), her (Vakhtangov-type) *Unit Object* might change, in the new given circumstances, to *"How frightening divorce is!"* and her (Parke-type) *Through Line Of Action* might change to *"Face what I have to do!"*

Her life's *Super Objective* ideally determines the degree to which action is ever possible for her, also the manner in which action is limited and particularized by that *Super Objective*. In this manner---applying uniquely applicable*Through Lines Of Action* to the two separate *Units* ---and enhancing each of them with the specific *Unit* problems of Vakhtangov's *Objects*, a more complete and fulfilling experience can be created for the actor.

■ **And now, with the clearly separate definitions of the *Super Objectives* and the *Through Lines Of Action*, actors might give some reconsideration to the separate and unique function of the latter in the carrying forward throughout the role of the character's personality and conditionings as formed by the *Super Objective*...**

Through Lines Of Action
Can Offer Their Own Opportunities for Creative Actors

It's in the choosing of a *Through Line of Action* for a Unit where some actors emerge as far more interesting than others in their choices. While one actor might for a Unit choose something as simplistic as *"Get away"*, another might choose something like *"Make him stop suffocating me!"*

Here are some examples of *Unit Objects* with their possible *Through Lines of Action*, for the purpose of clarifying the manner in which they can take the core personality of the character through the shifting tides of changing circumstances, in this example involving a marriage failure, dissolution and eventual reconciliation---without losing the core personality of (as an example) an obviously pretty mixed up, conflict-enjoying character:

155

UNIT OBJECT	THROUGH LINE OF ACTION

When the marriage is obviously failing....

"This ----ed up mess!"   *"Get out of this snake pit!"*

In the divorce-details hassling and divorce hearing...

"Her ----ing greediness!" or   *"Hang onto everything I can!"* or

"Her shyster lawyer!"   *"Show 'em I can threaten too!"*

Living alone after divorce, miserable with no one to fight with...

"How ----ing dull life is!"   *"Get some yelling back into my*

or *"Nobody to fight with!"*   *life!"*

Finally calling her, meeting, up to the final reconciliation...

"The only ----ing solution!",   *"Make her take me back!"* or

"The begging I have to do!"   *"Show her I need her yelling!"*

or *"That snapping turtle*   or *"Make her start yelling at me*

sound!"   *again!"*

It should be evident that in dividing the role into these major parts (its *Units*) the actor will be able to more easily refine the separate and unique circumstances of those parts and create more interesting involvements for each than would be possible if the Units weren't broken down.

It should also be noted that a character who apparently can't feel much love except when it includes continuing hassles (as this one apparently can't) can be kept within its own personality parameters and its complex spectrum of experiencing in this manner, whereas if the actor doesn't employ the Unit breakdown procedure there's the possibility that the core personality might be lured astray by the shifting conditions, resulting in simple *"situation-playing"* throughout.

Through the kind of breaking down of Units offered in this example the behavior patterns of the character prior to the divorce decision can be conditioned by the core personality (not the simple conflict) . . . the divorce hassling period can be just the kind of experience this crazy character loves (not hates) . . .

. . . the living alone period faithfully retains the character's need for conflict (instead of suggesting some standard version of loneliness or loss) . . . and the eventual calling, meeting and seeking reconciliation, which could without the Unit breakdown process suggest a standard cliché of a simple love-needing type, instead (as in the above example) can maintain the character's need for conflict.

The *Units* (for dividing with clarity as situations change), with a *Unit Object* for each (establishing the point of concentration) and a *Through Line of Action* for each (to establish the objective action generated by the Object) make it possible to maintain the above sample character's unique personality and conflict-inspired language as it adapts in its own warped, conditioned manner to the changing circumstnces without becoming lost in a sea of standardized generalities.

■ **A final item belongs in this Section of the book: The similarities---and similar sources for those similarities---among different teachers' approach items.**

Many similaritiers are there if the actor looks closely. As approach items, they're usually called by different label words of the different teachers' preferences, but their *raisons d'etre* as being important in the actor's portfolio of techniques are really similar in quite a few respects. To at least some degree they even follow similar outlines in the manners of their use.

The teachers' individual searches for their best use have simply taken different routes, and along the way new labels have come into their vocabularies in teaching.

It should be encouraging for actors that those similarities do exist in spite of their different approach labels. It must surely be evidence that *most* if not *all* acting teaching---at least insofar as the processes for preparing roles is concerned---eventually includes most of what the actor needs.

Similar Approaches / Just Different Labels

Even Some Manners of Teaching Them Are Similar

Most teachers who teach characterization must and do inevitably arrive at fairly similar manners of analyzing the characters provided by the writers. They simply have different labels for Stanislavski's and Vakhtangov's *Super Objectives,Through Lines of Action, Units, Beats, Actions and Intentions, Objectives, Objects*, etc.

Boleslavsky's and Strasberg's emphasis on *Affective Memory* (evoking of a past life moment that affected the actor, then in a role performance moment reliving that moment instead of remaining in the character's own reality) can easily be related to Uta Hagen's *Substitutions* (which in a simpler manner consciously recalls past life moments that help the actor identify more personally with script moments). The salient difference is that Strasberg's approach proposed secretly *dropping out of character* for a moment during actual performance to relive the *affective memory* moment exclusively as the actor, while Ms. Hagen's *Substitutions* are recalled, then *adapted into the character itself*, with no interruption of the character's reality during performance.

Hollywood teacher Eric Morris's exercises involve many of the same *past life* moments (his *"You Never Gave Me..."* and other similar explorations), even though some of his exercises cover longer timespans and evoke many, many more of those past moments in single explorations of remembered experiences.

Robert Lewis, in recommending *Intentions*, clearly believes as Vakhtangov did, and many others of us do, that any worthy *Intention* must always be aimed at an *Object*. Stella Adler's teaching simply teaches what some of us call *Objects* via her *Justifications, Given Circumstances, Atmospheres* and several other approach items in the list of particularizers to be applied to *Actions*. (The processes of finding are simply reversed.)

New York teacher Michael Schulman, a practicing psychologist himself, in teaching actors to recognize and exploit *Behavioral Stimuli*, is discussing what in this book I label *Being Done To*---whether by another character's action or word or by an unexpected occurrence, and what in Sandy Meisner's approach is described by him as *What Other Characters Are Doing To Us*, etc. Strasberg advocated the imagining of the person or occurrence as something or someone else (from private life) that evoked a vivid response, somewhat similar to Uta Hagen's *Substitution*.

Most teachers include *Sense Memory* work in their programs in some form. They're the stairsteps toward a Strasberg *Affective Memory*, they're the easily seen stepping stones toward the finding of Ms. Hagen's *Substitutions*; they're the body's associated *Inner and Thought Objects* in my own and others' teaching during the *Body Searching* process. They're used in classroom exercises by most teachers (although not with the same frequency) to sensitize the actor's communion with objects and to develop attention and concentration.

Teachers who seek to add more *strictly creative, more stunningly theatrical realism*-achieving to the simple reality base for their actors almost all, eventually, turn in one manner or another to *Action Verbs*---for the more interesting and clear body participation they bring to feeling moments of the character (perhaps *Curl up*, instead of *Enjoy*; maybe *Smash out*, instead of

158

Put an end to or something as equally generalized as *Stop*). For the same enhanced body participation, most recommend that appropriate *Sense Memories* be somehow involved with them.

Strasberg's often employed *Private Moment* exercise is quite similar to this author's *Living Sounds* explorations, both serving to bring a fuller, more human experiencing to moments.   Most teachers have their own exercises, if not some form of these, for accomplishing the same end.

Even Stanislavski and Vakhtangov recommended *the eradication of clichés* --- that far in the distant past. Today, to keep very ordinary functions, movements and manners of behavior from being *too* uninteresting, most coaches recommend their own versions of *Finding A Different Way* or something similar to remind actors of the desirability of doing simple things more interestingly (like Telly Savalas's unusual cigarette-holding, which as a chain smoker in real life he consciously developed as a trademark).   Sandy Meisner and others of us recommend *Activities* and *Where I've Just Come From, What I'm Doing Here, What I'm Going To Do Next.* Almost all coaches with few exceptions advocate (in their own manners) the lifting of common actions out of the ordinary in some physically distinctive manner.

Although in recent years an increasing number of teachers teach the use of *Objects*, Uta Hagen recommends *Inner Objects* (imagined) primarily as very brief, quickly passed thoughts that occur to the character during moments when there is an *Action* in progress. Bobby Lewis advocates an ever present awareness of *Objects* (of whatever kinds) as the focus of intentions. Strasberg, agreeing, further dignified *Objects* of several kinds with the phrase *"the basic building blocks from which the actor works".* In this book and in my own teaching specifically *Thought Objects* (of whatever kinds, like Bobby Lewis and Strasberg often used them) are continually recommended, with examples, but my own are in the form of *worded thoughts that can actually replace actions and intentions over periods of longer duration.*

And almost all teachers offer manners of preparing roles--- also teaching manners in which actors can achieve optimum personal experiencing of their characters' moments---believing that performing roles is the primary function of the actor.

That Strasberg included fewer *specifically labeled* role preparation items than some others (except for *affective memory, sense memory, objects* and a few others) is probably the source of the impression some have had that he didn't teach role preparation. The stars he surrounded himself with at the Actors Studio all had their own already developed approaches (which they'd learned from others) and didn't need study of role preparation in the *standard labeled* terms, and that's not what they were seek-

159

ing at the Studio. But the new actors he worked with in his private classes were taught some items for role preparation. The *Objects* of Vakhtangov were certainly important. His teaching simply differed from the others (who teach so many role preparation items with *labels to identify them as clear steps*) primarily in the fact that he preferred to *discuss those same items lengthily* and not often apply any standard labels to them.

In my early years, my own experience in Lee's private classes sometimes left me a little puzzled as to exactly what steps were being so lengthily discussed. Sometimes experiencing the same lack of understanding that Reuven Adiv (now teaching in London) says he did at the time---spending a lot of time trying to figure out what it all meant, I must confess that I too missed a more extensive use of specific labels to identify what Lee was talking about.

I now believe, looking back to the 1940's, there'd probably have been fewer comments that Lee *"didn't teach specific role preparation approaches"* if he'd simply used more of those *labels*, like so many others did, and hadn't preferred his sometimes very lengthy discursive manner of dealing with them.

In Lorrie Hull's book *"Strasberg's Method As Taught By Lorrie Hull"*, mentioned several times in this book, the majority of those approach items to which others apply *standard labels* are described as being included in Lee's work to some extent.

The point is, all of us who teach may teach differently, but we're often teaching the same things, just in different manners and using different vocabularies.

Acting Studies
Often Neglected By Actors
And Not Included in
Most Teaching Programs

■ **It's not true that you can't learn Comedy. It's not even true that a Comic Sense can't be developed!**

Comedy

It's Simpler Than You May Think!

Of course it's true that *Comedy* is most often the result of talent and an innate comic sense than a technique to be mastered. And it's true that there are people who simply have a wonderful *comic sense* and the ability to turn any ordinary subject or situation into a comic experience.

But there are others who understand at least the basic requirements of comedy whose comedy performances---more technically produced though they may be---rival those of "natural comedians".

And some basics of comedy performance can be practiced for developing even if they don't come naturally to the actor.

Current television is salted and peppered with *Situation Comedies*, wherein there are certain basic comedy-playing requirements for all characters, such as *"takes"* . . . comfort with *facing the audience or the camera lens* while delivering lines to other characters or while reacting with *takes* about them . . . *exaggerated attitudes*, so that the comic collisions can occur continually between characters . . . and *timing*.

Beyond these basics, little more is required of *situation* comedy performers except, to begin with, a personality that *can be* amusing at will if the writers supply the right material with which it can be amusing. *Situation Comedy* generally depends upon comic situations more than the actors, as the title implies.

Then there's *Character Comedy,* wherein the character must be so amusingly prepared and brought---by itself and independent of any script---that even if it should just walk into a room, without any lines, it's going to be amusing. There are usually one or two fine "character comedy" performers in each television "sitcom". They help sustain the series when the comedy writers falter, and they're usually the reason why viewers return week after week to enjoy them.

Naturally, the character comedy player must also know *takes, facing the audience or camera, exaggerated reactions and attitudes* and *timing*. But, over and above these requirements, the character comedy player also has to be able to *build the comic character*. Only occasionally can he simply clown his way through on his own unique comic talents to such a degree that he doesn't need anything else.

There's also *Farce*. Again, all the elements of the other "sit-com" approaches apply in this type of comedy. However, in addition, for ideal playing of farce the farce player must understand which end of the farcical situation he's on.

It's the nature of *farce*---as it's distinguished from other comedy forms---that there must always be *one or more characters in an impossible situation and other characters complicating the situation further* at all times.

The farce player must recognize which category his character falls into of the aforementioned two, then employ all the usually oversize experiencing of that character's moments which are ideal for the one or the other. This *"one side of the fence or the other"* aspect is the prime characteristic of farce. The dilemmas and outrageous complications that are heaped upon the one in the impossible situation are what create the comedy for the spectator.

In addition to these styles of comedy most often seen in films, television and theatre, there's of course the *Standup Comedy* style also. There's little definition possible for this, except that whatever the comedian or comedienne does amusingly determines his or her own style, and probably no one else could duplicate its unique presentation.

If good, though, the *Standup Comic* could well be a role model for all comedy players working in the first three categories named. The "Standup" *faces front* with most of his or her lines; s/he does *"takes"* constantly; s/he develops impeccable *timing*; and the success of his or her material usually depends on a *definite attitude being clearly exaggerated.*

The basic requirements of the *Sitcom Player, the Character Comedy Player and the Farceur* must all be perfected by the *Standup*, because there's no one with him or her, and no writer's situation to carry the comic continuity in any moment if s/he falters.

Lucille Ball, in a private rap session about comedy some years ago at one of Chico Marx's parties I attended and (I was told) also later in a talk before an acting class, stated that *"Comedy is something that if you ain't got you ain't gonna get."*

While it's true that the comic sense is difficult to teach, still some of the ingredients can certainly be extrapolated from the whole and worked on for possible development in classes.

"Takes" can be practiced if the primarily dramatic actor or actress isn't too embarassed to "mug" with exaggerated facial reactions, which is what any good "take" of the garden variety en-

163

tails. There are the other "takes", even simpler and closer to home and a bit less exaggerated, which are those such as comedians Jack Benny, Bob Hope, Johnny Carson and Bob Newhart have been famous for. Those are the almost expressionless "takes" in moments when some bigger reaction is expected by the viewer and instead the comic simply looks at the audience or camera with the barest hint of a reaction.

It behooves any actor who would like some comic role opportunities to become accustomed to feeling a little silly and ridiculous and enjoying every minute of it, in order to learn to do those oversize "takes" easily and effectively.

The *"facing front with lines, with thinking moments and reactions"* item---also required when good film, theatre and television comedy performance is involved---is the hardest item for essentially dramatic actors to practice with any comfort, even harder for them to remember to use when reading for comic roles or performing them.

The feeling of essentially *announcing* their thoughts or lines in the presence of other characters, which this process requires, is usually quite foreign to them, and they may resist it until that day when a director forces them to do it and they discover then, under duress, the silly pleasure sensation it brings via making their character more ridiculous.

Some coaches, myself included, have employed plain old *Comic Melodrama* style work to sneak the facing front into skeptical dramatic players' development toward doing comedy.

In that style---usually comic to us in the present time but taken so seriously when it was popular, there are so many *"aside"* moments directed toward the audience when the character is truly itself and is free to honestly show and share its true colors, its thoughts, its explaining of what it's going through, etc.

I point out to my people that the *other* moments in such melodrama---when the character is working directly with other characters---are generally the false ones! It usually works, and helps some dramatic actors overcome their fears of the *"facing front"* item. They can consider this melodrama requisite to be only a *style* (which it is) while they think and fear that all aspects of comedy are more a *gift* which they're sure they don't possess.

The *exaggerated attitudes* of comedy can either be brought by deciding them and "playing" them ridiculously (without any character preparation tools of any sort), or in other cases the same attitudes in exaggerated levels can be achieved by the player who has some comic sense to begin with that enables him to form the tools of characterization into somewhat "petty" or in any event fairly extreme versions, so they'll appear ridiculous.

If any preparation "tools" are to be used in preparation, then that same ridiculousness, that same pettiness, that same outrageousness and silliness should be built into all the preparation items from the top down.

The actor who wants to develop comedy should explore and find which approach works best for him---preparing with or without preparation tools.

Comedy timing is perhaps an unfortunate title for that other requisite for good comedy, since it implies some secret art or gift that one either does or doesn't possess. It's really quite simple, and anyone can learn it.

Comedy timing will occur all by itself if the actor continually does *"takes" about other characters' statements or about what the other characters have just done*, instead of popping right back with dialogue or outgoing action of some kind.

In fact, timing isn't often the domain of the person who's speaking at the moment. It's the result of the *the other person's stopping to do a "take"* which tells the viewer that the other who has just said or done something is crazy, absurd, disgusting, stupid, shocking or something else. It's honestly that simple!

When actors can accept this easy relief from the responsibility implied by that word *"timing"* there's much less hesitation to take the moments to do "takes" on the other characters and, via those "take" moments, easily create perfect comedy timing!

The sum total of all the basic ingredients of good comedy mentioned in these paragraphs is that *an exaggerated attitude* will insure the comic collision with other equally definite attitudes. Even in advance, the audience is allowed to share the dynamic secret that those collisions are assuredly going to occur *because of those exaggerated attitudes*.

The many "takes" any good, ridiculously exaggerated attitude will produce all by itself will make not only the actor's own character amusing because of its outrageously offendable sensibilities; they'll also make the other character's last prior moment more amusing as well---whether it was all that amusing or not by itself, simply because it causes a "take" on the part of another character.

And the *"facing front"* as much of the time as possible can point up your character's own ridiculousness and what's behind it that the audience enjoys sharing. It'll also put your body in a position (facing front) to become the secret butt of other character's "takes" behind your back, and those takes will again make you even more comic because of the unspoken comments being made about you behind your back.

It's really a neat package---the result of combining these three main aspects of good comedy playing, and one which'll enable you to do comedy whether you think you're a natural comedian or not. Work on these separate items sufficiently and you may well surprise yourself with the discovery of a comic "gift" you didn't think you had.

The *Character Comedy Player* might profit from some suggested items on a *Comic Character Checklist* given to me by Chico Marx, of the famous Marx Brothers, when we were together in a production of *"The Fifth Season"* for a summer theatre tour years ago.

Thinking it over later, I realized that the Marx Brothers must have indeed used most of these listed items to construct those zany characterizations which made them, and kept them for so long, one of the most famous comedy groups in the entertainment world's history.

I'm happy to pass the list along to readers in case part or all of the list appeals to them:

A Comic Character Checklist

1. *A ridiculously exaggerated attitude* . . .

2. *A special walk*---either ridiculously right for the character or ridiculously out of place . . .

3. *A special speech or dialect.* Try an exaggerated version of the one that's most appropriate, but don't overlook the comic possibilities of one that's totally out of place . . .

4. *A special hairstyle* . . .

5. *One piece of special wardrobe.* Again, either to make your character more obvious or to be ridiculously out of place . . .

6. *One recurring body mannerism or habit* . . . to constitute an available "running gag", perhaps a total non sequitur, as it recurs suddenly and without warning from time to time . . .

7. *One special hand prop*, if not more than one. Make sure it doesn't get in the way of or complicate moments that would be funnier without it or them . . .

If the aficionados of those old Marx Brothers films stop to consider each of those crazy characters, they'll observe that this list may very well have been the source for all the ridiculous items that made each of the Marxes so hilariously funny.

In addition to using the Marx Brothers checklist often in my Theatre Today's *"The Agenda"* comic improvisational group, I've used it many times in my private classes to help otherwise exclusively dramatic actors cross the bridge of fear into *at least trying* comic characters with some hope of desirable result. I recall one class vividly:

Even though all class members had been warned that the next session would be *Character Comedy*, and although all class members had been provided with the above checklist, many did little preparation at home, hoping the checklist would in class at the last moment bring them all the inspirations they'd need.

One fellow who later starred in the *"Emergency"* series on television, and who's always been a fine dramatic actor but who had always been afraid to try comedy, did his homework . . . and it paid off for him.

He'd used the checklist, item by item. He brought from home a pocketful of sunglasses and glasses, two different changes of clothes from what he wore to class, a number of other things which I've forgotten, and then arrived early for class to scout up two wigs, a broom and some other odds and ends, later kept the rest of the class in stitches three times during the evening by having a complete plan for each of his three characters and providing all the *Comic Character Checklist* inspirations---obviously well practiced ahead of time and ready---along with very close to professional quality "routines" for each!

He hadn't known whether it would all work, he said afterward, but he was so overjoyed with his success and the other class members' responses during the evening that he remained in the studio for some time after the class ended, just sitting in a dazed state and numbly reexperiencing the moments of his first triumph over the demon comedy.

He wasn't sure he hadn't "cheated" by using the Comic Character Checklist because he'd been afraid of failing in an area he hadn't thought could ever work for him. I reminded him that that had been why I gave out the Checklist ahead of time. I imagine he's used it since, because he began to be cast in comedy roles occasionally, as well as his still predominately dramatic ones, after the series ended its television run.

Do a little "cheating" yourself with the Checklist, and see the remarkably comic results!

Some Class Exercises That Make Comedy Easier

There are some comedy exercises that I like to spring on classes unexpectedly because, after the loud moans and groans that come from many class members immediately upon hearing the announcement of the demon *Comedy*, they reassure even the self-doubting skeptics that comedy is easier than they think:

Standup Routines

One actor at a time is sent to the front and, without any preparation or any idea of what he or she is to deliver a *"Standup Comic Routine"* about, is abruptly thrown a start-up phrase--- just a short lead-in phrase, to make any planning impossible. Then the actor has to pick up immediately and finish the sentence, and continue at a fairly rapid pace, having no idea what he'll say next but having to simply keep going.

The teacher might throw one of the following lead-ins: *"I'm conducting this nose survey. We're trying to find out..."* . . . *"Certainly turtles have sex. You see, every time..."* . . . *"My new inventions for automobiles include..."* . . . *"My dalmatian wants to be an actor. This morning he..."* . . . *"All my wives were really weird. The first one..."* . . . *"We're working on some new designs for the human body. For instance...",* etc.

Under the stress of having to continue without stopping to think ahead, the actor is amazed at how easily crazy, ridiculous ideas can be produced without planning. Even the most frightened when they're called up for the exercise find they have comic abilities as laughter comes non-stop from other class members!

Juxtaposition Of The Incongruous

Bob Orben, who's written all those books about the ingredients of comedy, suggested this one:

Juxtaposition Of The Incongruous being one of the ideal sources for sure and constant comedy, especially in situations involving people meeting for the first time, actors are paired off and told to prepare some location where two people might meet---a dentist's or psychiatrist's outer office, a bus or railroad station waiting room, an airport waiting area, etc.

They're told to plan *two very opposite personalities* for their improvisation, each actor's planning to include manner, speech, wardrobe, any props, etc., that will make his or her character as obvious as possible and each told to practice the manner, speech, etc., of his or her character ahead of time.

Examples might include *a religious fanatic and a vulgar sex maniac, a snobbish intellectual and a know-it-all dumdum, a bar stool queen and a homophobic macho, a prude and a four-letter-worder, a first day policeman and a long rap sheet hood, a girl from the slums meeting for the first time the snobbish mother of her rich fiancée, a pretentious, narcissistic psychotherapist meeting a dypsomaniacal new patient, a rock star meeting a celebrated classical composer, a romantic idealist and an earthy cynic,* etc.

The justaposition of the incongruous combination is a never-fail manner of producing comedy, even when neither participant believes there's an ounce of comedy in him or her.

But although the actor may come to understand and even enjoy using the basic ingredients of comedy, the key to the highest form of comedy is still *the character itself.* Use the *Comic Character Checklist* described here. It works!

■ **This next is another of those most often neglected areas in actors' development. Not many actors are willing to devote much time, if any, to the study of the many different dialects they'll possibly need in many different roles throughout their careers.**

Dialects and Languages

Most Actors Need One Or Both Sooner or Later!

During any extensive professional career, an actor could conceivably be called upon unexpectedly to play a German professor, an Irish school monitor, a Muslim terrorist, a Massachusetts senator, a New Orleans City Councilperson, a Nebraska farmer or farmwife, a French physicist and a Cajun flood victim. All those roles have either entirely different languages or at least very different dialects.

In *"The Grapes Of Wrath"*, Ivy said *"Everybody says words different. Arkansas folks says 'em different, and Oklahomy folks says 'em different. And we seen a lady from Massachusetts, an' she said 'em differentest of all. Couldn't hardly make out what she was sayin'."* . . . And that quote applies for just America!

For foreign roles it's even more of a challenge, because most foreign roles involve not only unique languages but in the speaking of those different languages there are often unique formations of the mouth, lene or aspirated word endings, unique speech rhythms, dropping or elevated inflections, and consonant and vowel sounds that are foreign to the American ear and tongue.

A single Italian vowel often arcs from a middle C upward to a middle G then back down to a bass F in the space of a second. The a in an Irishwo/man's *"father"* winds up somewhere between *rather* and *druther.* A German *"ach"* should be spelled *ack-kkhhh,* but it isn't. A Russian v has a w attached to it and the n has a y behind it. The French r needs a soft uvular *"gr"* pronunciation, and some of the French n's are often not even audible in spoken words. Also for an authentic-sounding French dialect the last consonant of the previous word becomes the first sound of the following word instead of the last of the previous. The English customarily aspirate their consonants like t's, d's, p's, b's, etc. A complete Brazilian sentence takes about half a second.

The American mouth, tongue, teeth and throat must even be formed differently for many of those foreign languages, and the dialects based on those languages' American actor versions of them, to sound authentic, usually require the same unique formations of the mouth.

And, although easier to fake with varying levels of success, our American regional dialects aren't much simpler, and Oxford English, spoken by an American with an accent, can be excruciatingly funny as well.   Once when I attended a university performance of *"Romeo And Juliet"* in Alabama, I heard *"Rohm-yoh, Rohm-yoh, wheah-fo' aht thay-oh?"*

For an episode of the old *"Route 66"* television series, I was called in to play a German immigrant father now living in Vermont, and was asked to combine the German accent (which they knew I'd taught) with the Downeasterner dialect (which I'd use later as the mailman Perkins in the *"Real McCoys"* series).

I worked overnight on combining the two, found it impossible, then it dawned on me that no self-respecting German would ever lose his native sound just because he was now in Vermont. I persuaded the producer and director of that fact.

In 1947, in New York, I studied at home Lewis and Marguerite Hermans' excellent *"American Dialects"* book in preparing for the role of Tobin (from Texas) in *"The Great Big Doorstep"*, and dug into their book *"Foreign Dialects"* later that same year before playing Torvald Helmer in Ibsen's *"A Doll's House"*, and I give that book some of the credit for the Vernon Rice (early Off Broadway) Award the role won me.

Within months, early in 1948, I went back to the same book for a Scotch dialect as Lachie in Margalo Gillmore's production of *"The Hasty Heart"* and for an authentic Russian dialect for George Freedley's production of *"A Game Of Chess"*.   The same book helped when I went into the *"Mama"* television series in its last season as Papa's Norwegian Office Manager in 1955.   And back I went to their book *"American Dialects"* in 1956 for the series role of Downeasterner Luke in the *"Harbourmaster"* series, because all the Rockport fishermen around me would be local, authentic Downeasterners and I knew I'd have to match their *"Ay-uh"* sounds to even say *"yes."*

To employ a Dialects Coach, either in Hollywood or New York at the last minute for a role, is very, very expensive. Robert

Easton (in Hollywood) is the very best, but expensive. Or actors could buy at Samuel French and other actors' bookstores (at least in New York or Hollywood) one of David Alan Stern's fairly inexpensive dialect tapes.

If the actor doesn't have time or the wherewithal to take lessons in either the dialects of the many different nationalities or the regional dialects of our own country, I strongly recommend those two books of the Hermans' mentioned above---"*American Dialects*" (Theatre Arts Books, 1947) and *"Foreign Dialects"* (Theate Arts Books, 1943). Have them handy for quick study.

■ **Once you've mastered the basics of Comedy you're already ahead of the game for this next item, because it relies more on the kind of comedy that appears in all television "sitcoms" ---comedy already on the paper from the writer ...**

Farce

Comedy . . . Usually at Breakneck Speed!

Described briefly in the previous chapter, *Farce* is the kind of comedy that makes children of us all as we either observe it as a spectator or appear as participants in farcical performances.

As mentioned before, the main requirements of farce are (1) one character (usually a bit ridiculous in its exaggerated personality to begin with), placed in an impossible situation, with (2) one or more other characters further complicating its situation moment after moment.

The actor approaching a role in a farce of any kind is obliged to determine, first of all, which s/he is . . . *"the one in the impossible situation" or "a complicator"*.

Then, to enjoy farce more fully, and to provide the optimum high comedy experience for the audience, whatever character trait, attitude, manner and degree of experiencing is provided by the writer should be exaggerated in every possible manner, both in its over-all personality and in its manner of experiencing all of its moments.

But farce thrives even more on *character comedy*. To best serve farcical work, the actor should conceive of the character as ridiculous from the start, then continue its construction with anything that will make it still more ridiculous.

The perspective of the character should be unique, quirky, offbeat in some respect, then simply stretched to an extreme.

A stuffy character should be painfully stuffy. A clumsy oaf should be outrageously clumsy. A hypochondriac should be absolutely manic. These are just a couple of examples of the exaggeration of characters upon which farce thrives.

All actions taken should be definite. Most actions should be exaggerated. Reactions, too, should be comic *"takes"*.

There's one other item that distinguishes farce from other kinds of comedy: *Pace.* Farce is often less ideal without an accelerated pace---of action, dialogue, takes and other reactions.

A general rule of thumb is one that I heard the late Robert Q. Lewis quote to another comic when we were touring summer theatres in the out-of-town tryout of the revue *"What's The Rush"* (which didn't make it to Broadway in spite of some great Adams & Strouse music which later became popular in their Broadway production *"All American Girl"*):

"Start, complete, finish!" was the rule-of-thumb Bob quoted. In other words, in any moment of action or dialogue in farce, including *takes, "start clean, make it completely clear, finish quickly"* to get to the next moment without delay.

Farce often includes what comedy book author Bob Orben calls the *Dynamic Secret . . .* a secret shared by the audience such as the man hidden in the closet when the husband comes home to his wife unexpectedly; a copy of *"Safe Sex"* the audience has seen stuffed under a pillow by the minister and known to be hidden there when the Bishop is visiting and several times starts to pick up the pillow to stress a point; some of the traps arranged ahead of time by the young boy in the movie *"Home Alone"* for deviling the two expected burglars; etc.

One more item to make sure your farcical character should have---it should be *sympathetic,* even in its extreme perspective. In all probability the writer will have given the character some *flaw* it's unable to overcome which is connected with its perspective but that makes it *basically likable in spite of its faults* so you can share some of its misfortunes and missteps throughout its story with some sympathy even as you laugh at them..

But, again, just as in any other kind of comedy, it's the skillfully created *Comic Character* prepared by the actor ahead of time that will produce the framework for all the farcical elements written for it by the writer. And the keyword to never forget is *Exaggeration!*

The ability to *exaggerate* is of the essence in any kind of comedy, and is especially necessary in farce. Some dramatic actors simply can't exaggerate. They're the only ones who probably will never enjoy any kind of comedy. But there are often some *comic relief* moments in even dramatic roles. Learn comedy!

172

■ Many of today's male actors (especially of the "scratch and mumble" school of acting) resist this next item like the plague---the study of graceful form, plasticity of movement and any and all concepts of theatrical composition and focus. They have that right, but the time may come suddenly when their gym and bar-room swaggers may not be enough, when they need to know...

Form, Movement and Composition
Another of the Actor's Arts Often Neglected

A certain amount of feeling for form and movement can't be taught. It lies like the fluid of truth itself at the bottom of the well when all the water of technique has been drained from it. It flavors, refines, distills, and is what makes an actor a true artist just as it would another practitioner in any visual medium---whether it be painting, architecture, dance, landscaping or graphic design.

The aesthetically aware actor saves an immeasurable amount of time for directors during the preparation of any kind of production, whether it be theatre or film. For some of the classics it's a given, but form, movement and composition are often demanded by directors for contemporary street scenes and other sequences as well. Of course if they have to, directors will take valuable time to show the actor just how to stand or sit, but they really can't afford that time and are seldomwilling to do it twice.

Even the highly involved actor or actress, if not aesthetically and scenically aware, runs the risk of being extremely limited in many directors' estimation.

Any true art requires some *composition*, and any meaningful art requires *focus*. How often we see one inept actor or actress unconsciously distort some carefully formed composition and as a result find ourselves watching an entire scene suffer because of an inadvertent shifting of focus or the destroying of a certain beauty of form.

The ability to *help create beauty* or *help present a composite truth theatrically*---without letting it take away from the inner concentration, which it needn't---must exist in the actor who aspires to be an artist.

Stanislavski taught form. Vakhtangov taught it. Chekhov taught it. Yet today few of the teachers of the Stanislavski Sysem(s) or the "Strasberg Method" teach it at all. The most famed teachers down through the history of the theatre and film arts have taught it.

Vsevolod Meyerhold's *bio-mechanics* approach was exclusively form and movement. Bertolt Brecht's entire Epic Theatre was based substantively on its use. The latter's *"A Formation"* made it possible for him to focus entire audiences on propaganda and the over-all ideas he wanted to communicate in his works.

The German director Reinhardt's success was based in part on his feeling for huge spectacle and on his constant and brilliant employing of focus, form and movement. The busy stages of Shakespeare, Marlowe and others would be impossibly cluttered and unclear, and the beauties of their works would be lost completely, without consummate attention to form and composition.

Some excellent manners of developing the actor's feeling for these aesthetics of human body form and movement have been contributed by Michael Chekhov in his book *"On The Technique Of Acting"* or its smaller, earlier version *"To The Actor"*. Actors find his *Moulding The Air, Radiating, Imaginary Center* and *Floating* exercises very helpful.

However, class exercises with Brecht's *"A Formation"*, Reinhardt's *"Composite Focus"* approaches and Vakhtangov's *"Triangle of Attention"* (as seen in his production of *"The Dybbuk"* at the Habimah Theatre) haven't been all that effectively outlined elsewhere, so I'll describe the kinds of classwork which might ideally instill those concepts:

Exercising With Brecht's "A Formation"

Over and above the over-all triangulation of actors' positions---so arranged in order to rivet attention on one person who is meant to be the focal point at a given moment, the forming of the actors' individual bodies, as well, can assist mightily in the achieving of the desired result.

This exercise can provide those actors and actresses whose senses of aesthetics aren't sufficiently developed with a much enhanced understanding of the ways in which they can assist in focusing the viewer's attention on a single player when desired.

One actor is designated to *"Take focus!"* It's understood by the others in the group that until someone else is designated to *take focus* they're all to *"assist focus"*.

The *"Take Focus"* actor seeks the strongest, most visually dominant place at which to situate himself; at the same time attempts to enhance and strengthen his domination of the scene in body positions which may not have occurred to him before.

As he adopts one position and remains in that position until others around him have all formed themselves into *focus-assisting* positions, he gains valuable recognition of what is and what

174

isn't a strong, dominating position in relating to others around him.

It's an exhilarating experience for the one *maintaining focus* as he observes his own body wanting to lean or slant or stretch to the sky to more strongly focus on something real or imagined and physically dominate by doing so.

Meanwhile, the *focus-assisting* players develop (under the coach's guidance if necessary at first) positions and forms which help focus attention on the one chosen to dominate. Their focus-assisting roles illustrate for them (again under the coach's guidance if required) how their bodies can be formed to assist in composition of an over-all spectacle involving groups of participants.

They learn to consider the extensions of their own extremities as they aim themselves totally toward or extend backward away from the focal center of the scene. They also learn how their own bodies can relate to other bodies beside, before or behind them in creating smaller, individual attention-focused groupings involving two or more focus-assisting observers.

They quickly realize that the players closest to the focal player can adopt positions which are higher off the floor in some way than those positions into which the farther away players must form for best effect. Those at the farthest points from the focal player find they need to extend their bodies more and lie or half-lie in almost prone positions as they strain forward.

That's the manner in which Brecht, Reinhardt and others managed their individual versions of what to Brecht was his "A Formation".

Jerzy Grotowsky, in Poland, utilized the same approach often. And an amusing story is told by the American director-teacher Robert Lewis: In staging a scene in *"The Teahouse Of The August Moon"* on Broadway, he tells how one actor at the outer rim of the circle listening to David Wayne couldn't understand why he should need to lie prone on one elbow, one leg extended in a curve behind him as Mr. Lewis directed. Out of desperation, Bobby told him *"Because you're a dancer in private life."* Then the actor found the position justifiable and comfortable.

The "Iago" Attack

This is an exercise I thought I had created, but I've since learned that in approximately the same form was taught by Jerzy Grotowski in Poland and perhaps by others elsewhere.

It's a three player formation that can further the actor's awareness of the dynamics of the *aiming force* aspect involved in assisting with focus in smaller, three or four player groups.

One player is supposedly being attacked verbally or perhaps threatened physically by another. The latter is being *violently aimed and urged on* by a third player, much in the manner of a typical moment in which someone might be siccing a dog at someone or something, or a moment when Iago is urging Othello to avenge himself against Desdemona. The same effect is involved. This exercise, for its optimum result as a form experience, should be done with most (not all) of the body low on the floor.

The player *under attack* stretches his entire body away from an imaginary attacker (who isn't yet in an attacking position). The *under attack* player must remain rooted to one spot and stretch back to get away but be unable to do so.

Then the *attacker* experiments for the position (probably on one hand and knee) which affords him the strongest feeling of attacking and threatening---with a finger stretched forward like a gun toward the one under attack and the other hand supporting his forward-thrust body, supplying the most possible force itself, and with one of his legs extended back of him, his total body seeking the most effective position for thrusting forward his attack.

When the *attacker* has settled into his most forceful position choice, the third player, the *aimer or instigator at his side*, experiments to find his own most forceful-feeling position for aiming and urging on the atacker, trying at the same time to infuse his own attacking spirit and force into the attacker's spirit through finding a position which feels most like it's fusing the two attackers' bodies and strengths into one.

An actor who isn't experienced with classic staging forms and their focus-assisting may take additional time to discover either the attacking position or the aiming position. The longer it takes that actor to consciously find the best ways to arrange the parts of his body, the more effective the learning process going on, simply because this kind of work is new to him and requires more conscious adapting of each of his body parts into a total form which for some may be experienced for the first time.

Even if inexperienced, both the attacker and aimer will generally recognize the strongest body positions when they're finally found and---at least in the case of actors who aren't also dance trained and whose muscles may not be tuned---it's wise to *end this exercise as soon as that final position of the three actors is ideally formed*, since the dynamics of so much force and strain of attacking thrust or retreating contraction or extension could otherwise cause muscle cramps. (Grotowsky's actors experienced those cramps often---it's been said even in performances, and had to relax out of those carefully formed and rehearsed positions as inconspicuously as possible.)

176

A Focal Leader Exercise

There's another exercise---of my own devising---that I call *"Focal Leader"*. I've found it, like *"The Iago Attack"*, ideal for training actors for the kinds of *elongated classical movement and form* needed for some early Greek tragedies and other epic dramas---like Dame Judith Anderson's beautiful floor-groveling in her critically acclaimed *"Medea"*.

It won't be new to any dancers or dance-trained people in the group, since it comprises the same extensions, contractions and expansions in much the same manner as does ballet, modern and jazz dance.

The inspiration for this development exercise must be credited to my longtime friend, balletmaster Vincenzo Celli, who years ago taught and conducted regular workout sessions for some of the greatest ballet dancers of the century in his modest upstairs studio on Broadway.

Observing some of Vincenzo's classes composed of Alexandra Danilova, Toumanova, Moira Shearer, Anton Dolin and others of the American Ballet Theatre, I watched Vincenzo snap his wand against the back of some of those stars' knees when it appeared to him that their entire bodies weren't involved in a single muscle-flow position, however brief.

I watched him attack those and other stars in emotional frenzies when their movements didn't result from the natural muscle system flow but rather from simple progression to re-membered next positions. I observed the incalculable difference when he got what he was demanding. And an adaptation for im-plementing this phenomenon for training actors' bodies formed in my mind.

I use this exercise to assure actors that, even without dance training, their bodies can assume ideally graceful positions at will and maintain graceful movement over periods of time as po-sitions are required to be changed. Of course this is an *exercise* when desired to be used as one, but it's also a *tool* whenever it can serve in a role.

I formed and first actually used this exercise some years ago when a production required the ultimate in classical form for one of my actresses and, while otherwise brilliantly qualified for the role, she wasn't a movement-trained player.

The methodology involved here is that the muscle systems of our bodies are capable of flowing one into another behind an ex-tended part of the body. If that *focal leader* is for one moment of a role ideal to be a pointed finger, and that pointed finger is stretched forth to its emotional extreme as well as its physical limit, the combination of the emotional urgency and the efforts

177

of the body to assist what that urgent pointing is generating, will result in the rest of the entire body's forming itself into a completely graceful extension of all parts falling into their muscle-system-created extensions all the way back to the pointed toe at the farthest point from that pointed finger (the *focal leader*) as it seems to be pulling in the opposite direction. It's the same as what occurs with a dancer's body in a moment of "extension".

When *different focal leaders* are used in sequence, one after another with changing of them when required to move, the body adjusts to each *focal leader* via the same muscle system flow and becomes in each new focal leader position or movement a perfectly formed, graceful organism.

The same can apply if the actor is constructing a stationary pose for some purpose. By employing the *Focal Leader* which best creates the pose desired, the natural flow of extension, contraction and expansion of the muscle system takes place and the actor, even though untrained in form and movement, can in this manner easily create beauty of form.

Even changing of positions can easily be accomplished, each momentary position having its complete form before the change to another position. After any progressive movement from one spot to another with a first *focal leader*, the actor can easily find a new *focal leader* (another part of the body) to take the body in some new direction. S/he could perhaps change from an elbow to a knee to lead the body in one direction, from a pointed finger to a shoulder to flow the body in a different direction. At the extreme limit of stretching one *focal leader* in the direction desired, simply delegate some other part of the body to continue the body's progress forward or in any desired new direction.

If a videotape camera is handy, or even an instant-print camera, it can document for the players' viewing later the constant beauty, composition and form which their bodies flowing from such focal points can create through their own magical muscle system coordinations!

You might try some of Michael Chekhov's exercises too---his *"Molding The Air"*, *"Radiating"*, *"Floating"* and some of the other exercises written about in his two books *"To The Actor"* and *"Michael Chekhov On The Technique Of Acting"*. Chekhov was an actor of consummate grace. Even his twisted, deformed, psychotic characters had their own particular grace, form and movement.

Or play Satie's *"Gymnopedies"* and feel it waft your body into flowing movement. Observe the body's flowing naturally from whatever part begins a movement. Then you won't feel that form and movement are something you simply don't have.

■ Of course you have your own "style"---your manner of doing what you do, but how much do you know about other styles, even those of people you pass on street corners? Sooner or later, every actor needs some knowledge of...

Styles

There are Production, Period, even Many Contemporary Styles!

The study of *Acting Styles*---which many actors don't realize Stanislavski considered important, and regularly taught---is one of the never ending studies of actors, also one of the most arduous and time-taking. As a result, it's one of the most neglected by actors until they're suddenly confronted with a particular style's being necessary in the obtaining of a role.

Style is defined by Webster's Dictionary as *"a characteristic manner of expression in any art, period, etc."* The problem with so many solely intuitive actors and actresses as they approach roles requiring specific styles is that they've mostly worked in *only their own style*, and their own *characteristic manners of expression* sometimes aren't all that elastic that they can bend toward any different styles with inner conviction.

Further, even in their own specialized work, what they bring over and above (or under or behind) the surface is sometimes negligible at best, except for perhaps a charismatic personality, if they aren't also employing some methodology for the creating of characters with personalities dissimilar to their own.

It would be unthinkable to even attempt to play Shakespeare without training in movement, speech, fencing, the positions and movements suggested by and required for movement in those earlier periods' costumes and other physical requirements of most of Shakespeare's roles. The Elizabethan style included tights and ruffs. It's difficult to bend your neck in a ruff. There are rapiers and bodkins. Sitting down, an actor must arrange room for and poise the rapier deliberately.

As for the language of Shakespeare, present day actors worry about sounding unnatural, thereore often omit all emphasis in delivering those eloquently phrased lines, and as a result really do sound unnatural because Shakespeare's characters are all intelligent, make brilliant arguments and describe their feelings brilliantly. The actor must bring the kind of character that has that degree of brilliance and intelligence, must comprehend what's being said, must imbue the dialogue and the thoughts that produce those words with conviction, and manage to make that character's brilliance and intelligence his own.

179

Many present day actors are also prone to simply caricature Noel Coward's scintillating characters, and proceed to overdo those qualities with obvious effort. The best Noel Coward performances are comfortable and effortless.

As to the styles of *particular periods of history*, none of the basic methodologies of acting even pretend to teach how people moved in 1860 or 1900 or any other year, how costumes and props should be handled, the sentiments of the time, the characteristic pastimes, the modes of speech, etc. The researching of those periods of history is left to the actor who's conscientious and dedicated enough to do it--- outside of normal acting technique classes.

Imagine the young actor who comes to costume fittings for an Edwardian role and attempts to sit without first lifting the knees of his trousers to allow room inside for his knees to bend into the larger enclosure tailored for the calves in that period. Or imagine the young actress who's never worn a hoop skirt deciding to sit down and sending the whole hoop skirt flying back over her head!

The actor should recognize that any role-preparation system is an approach to building the *inner life and cerain externals* of roles which must be used *side by side with a knowledge of periods, costumes, customs, characteristic movements and prop handling, wigs, makeup, social demeanor and the sentiments of the languages* prevalent in periods different from his own.

Some systems for preparing roles don't even include recommended steps to remind the actor of *the necessity of researching* the many elements of style in the earlier phase of breaking down roles. The *"Six Questions"* step described in this book and others that include mention of it---embodying research and inspiration reminders as it does---should point the actor preparing a "style" role in the right direction and take him even more deeply into such research through its thoroughness than he might be able to go without those evocative questions to lead him.

In any event, the study of different periods---their different peoples, different countries and their customs, different religions and their dogmas, different modes of dress, etc.---can never be considered complete. It should be continuous, in addition to the manners of preparing roles and their personality cores.

Since acting study isn't possible twenty-four hours a day, every day, not much classwork time is devoted to the study of style, periods., etc., except of course in those classes specifically devoted to the study of Shakespeare and other classics. In some classes, such as Robert Lewis's in New York, paintings, music and other art forms are someimes used as examples of different styles, to expand class members' aesthetic awareness of composition and form and the acting, dance and other movement styles they clearly suggest: Perhaps the peaceful serenity of Degas, the slow undulating of Satie's *"Gymnopedies"*, the abandon of Ravel's *"Bolero"*, the languor of Reubens' paintings of reclining nudes, the stoic quiet of Rembrandt's masterpieces, etc.

The styles of different eras of history are especially desirable for actors to research. Those styles can't be found for observing except in old paintings, illustrations in books, early photos, etc. To dig them out of library shelves and absorb what they offer from those long ago times is work. But it's work that the most conscientious actors know they should do . . . whether they ultimately do it or not.

Those exceptionally dedicated actors who continue gathering private reference files of style research have probably foreseen the benefit of having them at those future moments when such research is needed and may be expected of them on a moment's notice. When such a moment comes unexpectedly there probably wouldn't be enough time for a sufficient amount of "cramming" research.

There are two excellent books every actor who can afford them should have on the library shelf. One is *"Everyday Life Through The Ages"*, edited by Michael Worth Davison and Consulting Editor Asa Briggs, published by The Readers Digest Association Limited, London. The people, also the costumes, jewelry, props of the periods, etc., are pictured and described in full detail from the earliest days of humankind down to the present. It's a wonderful reference book for actors, directors, designers, writers and others.

The other, for researching and correlating every period's History and Politics, Literature and Theatre, Religion, Philosophy and Learning, Visual Arts, Music, Science and Technology Growth, even Daily Life---from the first exactly dated year in history up through 1978---is *"The Timetables Of History"*, by Bernard Grum, a Touchstone Book published by Simon & Schuster in 1979. By turning to a particular year's Timetable the reader can find, across two facing pages, the significant events and developments and everything else imaginable that apply for that year.

Style isn't only involved in Moliere farce, Greek tragedy, Noel Coward, John Steinbeck, Henrik Ibsen or Shakespeare. There is *style* involved in the role of a present day Social Registerite, a nun, a ballerina, a bricklayer, a Nebraska farmer and many other contemporary callings, professions or lifestyles.

Regrettably, studies of even some of those more contemporary styles are too often taken for granted and prepared sketchily.

For example, for the *Nebraska Farmer:*

Speech is slow, in simple comments with no wasted words. What's said is thought out, formed to be said right, then uttered. Since much of farm life is solitary and silent, farm people often tend to nod their heads slowly when speaking, as if pumping up thoughts and how to express them with cautious effort. There are many silences between farmers and farmwives, as each continues the business and responsibilities of the particular time of day even when together. In the play *"Ned McCobb's Daughter"* there is this line about a farmer: *"He don't talk much, but what he says is awful pithy."* And Arthur Miller captured this faithfully in *"The Crucible"* in those long, loaded pauses between John and Elizabeth Proctor at the table.

Walking, because of hard and tiring work days, is an unwelcome necessity. Carrying and lifting heavy objects creates constant fatigue and back problems. Sitting down is looked forward to. Longer strides, to save the double effort of shorter ones.

Relationships contain little demonstration of affection. Farming is a business. The man has his duties; the woman has hers. Children too become employees, staff members with assigned duties at early ages and new assignments as they grow. The farmer is the CEO of the business. His wife is usually an obedient, accepting vice president, but sometimes the manager instead of the husband. When there's a family talk it's essentially a business conference with almost no small talk.

Behavior and Manner: Too busy with farming, and most of the time away from any social or public life, manners are often self-conscious and elaborately careful in public. Women and men both often carefully form their bodies in "correct" positions when sitting, even when with close neighbors, still moreso at any public gatherings like church or PTA meetings, etc. Body movements are often slower, because quick movements scare horses and to other farm family members could suggest insecurity.

Men separate from women in public, to talk their topics, far across rooms from the women. *Women separate from men* to talk their topics. This is not only because of mutual interests, but also because both the men and the women, serious about their unique roles and responsibilities, are always anxious to exchange and gain knowledge about their separate functions.

Activities: Actors seeking to contribute small realities and activities toward "organic blocking" suggestions to busy directors that may have been overlooked by writers should note that when home the farmer is more concerned with television weather reports, today's newspaper to be caught up with at the end of the day, relaxing and his back problems, than with socializing.

182

With her family at night, the farm wife is more concerned wih dinner preparing, dishwashing, keeping the place clean, protecting the furniture, repairing garments, perhaps reading the "wish book" from Sears or Montgomery Ward, than with fawning over either her husband or her children.

Each member of the family has his or her treadworn path to an acknowledged spot. The big chair is Dad's. The comfortable chair or the end of the sofa with the sewing box beside it is Mom's. The young learn to adopt their own special spaces, head for them automatically, and seldom leave them except to go to dinner, school, outdoor chores or bed.

If a writer overlooks some facts, the actor who has done research knows that no farmer comes into the house without washing his hands and perhaps his face, maybe taking off muddy boots, then going directly to the table or the newspaper or the television for the next day's weather predictions.

Another example of contemporary *styles*---the *Social Register (Blue Book) Style:*

This style presents many contemporary actors of middle class, blue or brown collar backgrounds with unique problems because they haven't learned the "correct" and "incorrect" manners of doing everything in Vassar, Bryn Mawr or Smith College educations (for young women) or terms at Phillips Exeter or another exclusive academy (for young men).

The correct manners of social conduct are written in stone. Ladies don't cross their legs when in the company of men. Men don't sit spraddle-legged in the company of women. The rule of thumb regarding sitting and standing positions is that *neither hands nor arms nor legs should distract.* The resulting norm is for legs and feet to be under the body when sitting and hands and arms to be quiet, composed and (in effect) hidden. No one ever fidgets. No one slouches.

Everyone is taught to look directly at the person with whom they're speaking and continue looking directly at them when listening to them. Anything else is impolite.

Women often keep their hats on indoors in social groups. Men eschew current fads like the plague and dress conservatively, often wear "school stripe" ties identifying their universities.

There's an unspoken "pecking order" always observed in gatherings. One doesn't move to sit close to a host or hostess, visiting royalty, a grande dame, family matriarch or patriarch, unless invited. Also, one doesn't remain too long in isolated conversation with just one other person. In any gathering the only polite thing to do is to make yourself simply "one of the group". If you don't, either out of preference or ignorance, you'll shortly be drawn into the group politely but quite pointedly by the host or hostess.

Men should never offer their hands to women until the women offer theirs. Standing, men's hands should be clasped either in front of them or behind their backs. Women's hands belong clasped in front. Hands in pockets is a no-no.

Speech volume should be easy for all to hear. Softer or louder is annoying. Under no condition talk with your hands. Never talk your profession or business unless asked by someone who doesn't know better, then only briefly out of politeness. Talk things that everyone is expected to be knowledgeable about.

Men shouldn't light up either cigars or cigarettes until the women have adjourned to the library leaving the men at the dinner table for the traditional after-dinner conversation. No raucous laughter at any time. Mostly just polite chuckles.

Most personalities and uniquenesses that might be expressed freely elsewhere are usually suffocated into the correct social mold in gatherings. Even when talk is less than interesting, interest should be feigned out of politeness. Once a topic is introduced, each person present must at least feign interest.

It's not acceptable to talk endlessly, ramble on. Conversation must be two-sided or open group. Brief comments or questions, followed by periods of listening avidly, will bring second invitations later. Monopolizing of a group conversation through excess rambling means no future invitation.

Display of affection in public is frowned upon. Private problems with any unhappy or conflict aspects are not acceptable in conversation. Even husbands and wives refrain from any amount of body touching, hand holding or closeness, so they'll be felt to be more open as individual presences to all others present.

Even at home with a spouse, forget slouchy behavior or over demonstrativeness. Habits of social demeanor remain so fixed, and custom so secure, that even home life---no matter how basically affectionate---often appears polite, cool and sterile to the uninformed.

One of the few actors or actresses allowed to be listed continually in the Social Register is said to have once described the Social Register acting style as *"imagining you're sitting for a formal family portrait."* And Gloria Venderbilt, of the Blue Book Vanderbilts---who herself took what she reportedly called a *"fun fling"* at acting, reportedly chuckled and told some other fellow members of the cast of a Broadway play she was in, *"Imagine yourself wearing a crown with your royal ermine draped around your feet."*

All these and many more social etiquette precepts are spelled out in recipe books for proper social demeanor available at most public libraries. In their times, Emily Post and Amy Vanderbilt edited a number of those books. They're still on library and bookstore shelves. They make fascinating reading and can be quick study sources when suddenly needed.

As a young actor in New York years ago, I met and married the daughter of a Social Register family. Although at the time (as an actor) fairly well versed in some cultures, I was still a former Nebraska farm boy suddenly exposed to all those Social Register laws of behavior that I hadn't needed to know before.

After the first meeting with the parents of my wife to be, her mother remarked to her that I was *"a little rough-edged."* I spent some time with Emily Post and Amy Vanderbilt and was astounded at how much there was to learn. Reading those books, I realized how much more I should have known before playing the old Baron in *"Death Takes A Holiday"* and some other characters earlier in Off Broadway and summer theatre productions.

Still another example of style, and the one most often appearing in today's performance writing, is the *Slums and (some) Blue Collar* style. Actually, doing research into these two style areas can inspire many actiities and manners that fit just as easily into *Middle Class* characters' currently more relaxed body experiences. Study of even these styles (with which so many actors feel they're surely sufficiently familiar) can produce many items that would be overlooked otherwise.

Often living like caged animals, there's never any escape in sight for these folks and almost everything makes them basically unhappy, depressed and constantly complaining. Forced to live under cramped, crowded conditions, slum families form the habit of talking loudly to be heard. They sound like they're arguing or fighting, even when they're not. Hard work and disappointments all day make them tired and irritable.

Many don't know any good manners; usually don't use them with anyone but the mother even if they know them, often not even with her. A slums mother is sometimes the only member of the family who wants and tries to maintain any family decorum, good behavior and religious consciousness.

Family members often share bedrooms and bathrooms all their lives, so they think nothing of walking around apartments half-clothed. There's little reason to dress because nobody has anyplace to go. And it's practical to save any dressup clothes for their next wearings.

Beer cans, cheap wine. Women darning or ironing or reading "uptown romance" paperbacks. More good-natured handling

185

and cuffing of other family members. Work clothes and dinner pails simply dropped and left where they fall. Nearest chairs flopped into. Nobody sits up straight except a mother trying to set an example. Sore feet after work. Personal hygiene often handled in the living room---toenail clipping, hair being set in curlers, etc. Backs rubbed against doorframes. Dandruff-flaked head-itching.

Writers will usually have supplied a constant stream of four letter words. The "slums" dictionary usually has about four or five words in it of the graphic and explicit kind that are heard more often than any others. Noses are picked. Ears are cleaned with fingernails. Itches are scratched with impunity. Belches aren't stifled; they're enjoyed. The many kinds of "living sounds" are more frequent and louder. Anything that elsewhere might be considered bad manners, vulgar, crude or gross is so common in many such cramped apartments that it's not even noticed.

Space is at a premium. Once claimed for a moment a chair or sofa space is jealously guarded. Distractions evoke pushing, yells and temper. There are never enough chairs or sofa spaces for all. There's abrupt elbowing of others who crowd someone.

The foregoing are just a few examples of *styles* that the contemporary actor might tend to take for granted but shouldn't. One never knows when an unexpected opportunity may come and there may not be sufficient time then to do all the desirable research. This can happen in the actor's or director's private life, too, as occurred in my first meeting with my first wife's parents.

Any respectable acting methology can and does work with all styles, but the actor must realize that the building of a character's internal life is one preparation; the external life often involves a particular *style* dictated by the outer ircumstances. The *style* elements need to be researched as well and incorporated into the final performance.

Some additional study areas are discussed in the next chapter.

There Are So Many
Other Types Of
Acting Study Programs

Some Actors Never Studied At All

There was no "method" in the acting of Greta Garbo's, Bar-bara Stanwyck's or Bette Davis's acting except their own.   John Forsythe, who did observe some of the Actors Studio work for a time in response to one of Mr. Strasberg's invitations, probably wouldn't be called a Method actor. George C. Scott, referring to Strasberg (who once refused him entry into the Studio) calls him "Lee you-should-excuse-the-expression Strasberg."

Walter Huston ridiculed the emerging Method approach at every opportunity.   John Barrymore hadn't heard of the Stanislavski System until he and his sister Ethel---already es-tablished stars---attended a matinee of The Moscow Art Theatre during its American appearances.

Alfred Lunt and Lynn Fontanne, Helen Hayes, Edward G. Robinson, Paul Muni, Spencer Tracy, James Cagney, Joan Craw-ford and many others developed their own manners of working without coaching.

It's amusing, and an indication of Mr. Strasberg's basic philosophies about acting, that in a Sunday article for *The New York Times*, published Sept. 2, 1956, Strasberg mentioned Gary Cooper, John Wayne and Spencer Tracy---three stars who never studied acting!--- as examples of Method actors because those ac-tors tried to *be themselves* rather than to act, pointing out that they refused to say or do anything they felt to not be consonant with their own characters.

Sylvia Sidney (with no study background) was an impressive actress before she came to the Group Theatre from an established Hollywood starring career. She didn't come to the Group to work with Mr. Strasberg and resisted doing so, but rather was drawn to the Group because the philosophy of the Group attracted her.

It's not generally known that Marilyn Monroe studied for a time in her beginning years with Hollywood coach Raikin Ben-Ari (who was directed by Vakhtangov at the Habimah Theatre in Russia and later taught several leading players in Hollywood), but she never succeeded in persuading Hollywood to let her use her talents---that were actually there naturally and also were deve-

188

loped far beyond what film audiences ever knew. Hollywood simply wanted the image they created for her and limited her to it.

After seeking Mr. Strasberg's help later in her career---intent upon at last becoming recognized as the actress she knew she could have been all along, she's said to have lost the inner confidence that she possessed those unused talents and also found it emotionally impossible to simply return to exploiting those qualities that had brought her stardom. Working in her last film, *"The Misfits"* (with Paula Strasberg, the first Mrs. Lee Strasberg, by her side as coach), she was observed to have become manically depressed and more difficult to work with than she had been out of simple frustration before.

Her own statement about turning to the Actors Studio and Mr. Strasberg while still at the peak of her starring career was: *"To put it bluntly, I seem to be a whole superstructure with no foundation. But I'm working on the foundation."*

In her eagerly anticipated first scene presentation at the Actors Studio before Mr. Strasberg and fellow class members, she displayed an actress's talent that surprised everyone in the audience and that indicated what she might have become if, after the early developing of her talent in Hollywood under the coaching of Raikin Ben-Ari, she'd been strong enough to avoid the stereotyping that made her a different kind of star. She could never persuade the Hollywood studios that she could be an actress.

Jason Robards' classic comment was once *"Method? Shit! Just tell me what button you want me to push."*

Even those acting teachers who in the past exploited the apparent advantages of paying lip service to more celebrated teachers' names (and who may have even included some of those teachers' formulae in their teachings) have often come to the realization that they must devise *new methods of their own,* in order to distance themselves from the clichés and the controversies surrounding some of those early approaches at this later time.

What actors should search out is simply a supportive atmosphere where the items pioneered by Stanislavski and Vakhtangov, Strasberg or some other master teachers---and probably developed further by others who've come later---are taught, hopefully with the needs of the actor in today's swift-paced acting mediums in mind.

Whether the actor opts to investigate the teaching of one or more of the most generally respected teachers mentioned in one of the early chapters, the following are other types of study comprising a fairly complete list of programs and approaches available to today's actor---not in any order of importance or recommendation by this author:

■ The "No Technique" Approach

The approach most often questioned by other teachers is this *"No Technique"* technique advocated by one Hollywood teacher who originated it and by a few alumni of his classes who are now themselves teaching what he teaches.

He and those others who offer his approach explain it as the eschewing of all technique---essentially advocating the actor's *"getting out of his or her own way "* (some even call it *"getting out of his or her mind"*) to free the use of his or her own unique art---abjuring any and all technique, which this kind of teaching claims perverts the actor's own most exciting processes.

But it appears to offer *its own version of technique*, in that it advocates the actors' experiencing of responses based exclusively on what is received from other actors, but with neither actor being concerned with preparing characterizations, planning sub-texts of any kind, etc.

In the previous paragraph's description it might seem that there is some similarity to the *"Repetition"* exercise of Sanford Meisner, but Mr. Meisner uses this basic exercising to lead actors developmentally, step by step, into the use of a number of the traditional approach items. And even in the early steps of Mr. Meisner's exercise the actor is urged to make spontaneous changes to responses other than those simply suggested by the tenor of the other actor's comment.

This "no technique" technique has produced the comment from some who have experienced it that---with each actor trying to work only with what is received from the other---little is brought by either.

It could certainly be satisfying and reassuring to the ego to be assured that all the actor needs is already within himself. Perhaps that's what appeals to those who seek out this type of coaching and indulge themselves with it for any length of time.

■ Improvisation Without Any Approach Items

Bearing some similarity to the previously described type of study are some programs describing themselves as *"Improvisational Workshops"* that are in a sense comparable to simple freeform aerobic exercise sessions, in that no technique is taught or advocated and actors are simply involved with improvising situations with no prepared characterizations or direction. Not much should be expected to happen.

In some such workshops, the actors are at least given simple situations and tasks to accomplish with or in spite of other actors in the situations with them.

With no particular character or personality to guide them, in many such workshops one will often observe little more than *protracted shouting matches, much direct eye-to-eye and perhaps even nose-to-nose confrontation, much hand-flailing because of trying to "do something to" or "get something from" other characters, and a continuous whirlwind of outgoing action and assault*, more than any inner experience of the kind that would be generated by a particular personality.

With respect to this kind of "workshop activity"---which should not be (but often is) called teaching, one might bear in mind Lajos Egri's advice in his book *"The Art Of Dramatic Writing"*, that *"It is the dramatic character who creates the dramatic situation, not the other way around."*

There are habits nurtured by this kind of simple *situation-playing* which would need to be eradicated or vastly modified later, certainly prior to professional work of any importance in either film or theatre.

The actor can expect to leave this kind of simple "workshopping" experience with exactly (and only) what he brought when he came. Most of us feel it's a shameful, exploitative waste of time.

■ "Being" and Other Basically Therapy Programs

This kind of program can usually be accurately predicted as conducting *self-acceptance, self-expanding and self-realization* experiences in most if not all sessions, with perhaps some *psychodrama and confrontation* and other experiences designed by their presenters to promote the optimum involving of theretofore unused assets which have lain inaccessible in the actor. Such a program should ideally be offered by someone with at least a Ph. D. in psychology or by someone fully accredited and fully qualified in some other manner, but there are a few brilliant exceptions who are totally self-taught.

Some actors emerge from such programs with magnificent personal growth results, but there are also those who have come away with psychological problems they didn't have before.

This kind of program may well cure inhibition and shyness, possibly eliminate much self doubt and self-hiding, and replace these with more self assertion and agressive behavior, since those are the areas that this experience assaults most assiduously, quickly and dynamically.

There is often no formatted or single system-oriented role preparation or work of any kind on acting roles in this type of program except, in some cases, the use of one or more of the class exercises for creating more involvement of self in moments or throughout the whole of a role. It's almost exclusively work on self, the freeing of instrumental blocks and accessing of the actor's inner resources.

■ Academies, Conservatories, Institutes

There are a number of the large Academy, Conservatory and Institute facilities in both New York and Hollywood, and they proliferate in London, offering curriculae that include, along with many different acting technique items, *term and semester courses of I, II and III levels of whatever acting technique, also Voice, Speech, Diction, Directing, Dance, Comedy, Musical Comedy, Singing, Theatre History and Research, Career Guidance, Physicality and Movement, Fencing, Shakespeare, Film Acting, Music Theory, Commercial Acting, Modeling, Voice Over, Theatre Games, even perhaps Polish Mime Theatre.*

Primarily attracting beginning actors, these facilities are more like postsecondary education in school atmospheres. Although particular subjects may be elected by enrollees, there are often many more subjects that may not be desired by the acting student but are required along with those personal choices.

The teaching staffs of such facilities are often of predominately academic backgrounds rather than professional. Someone interested in such a facility should consider the backgrounds of the teaching staff members.

If a prospective enrollee's interests are purely "study" of the acting art, its history, etc., a teaching staff comprising class conductors of primarily academic backgrounds (perhaps with little or no professional acting backgrounds) might even be superior to a staff of working professionals who might not possess as much formal education. Such classes can normally be expected to specialize in simple postsecondary education of a post-graduate type.

But if one is interested in entering the professional acting world as promptly and as fully prepared as possible it would seem far more desirable to seek a facility with more experienced working professionals conducting its courses. They could certainly offer more experienced advice and guidance with respect to the professional world's practices.

Some large, many departmented faciliies insert advertisements in national magazines that display photos of a few stars who assertedly studied with them, usually long ago. Such promotion should be viewed with a grain of salt, since whatever stars may have studied there may have done so fresh out of college or high school and gained little that might help them later as they entered the professional milieu, or their names may appear on old class rosters from only brief and disappointed attendance.

Two prominent, heavily advertised facilities each regularly display advertisements featuring a photo of the celebrated teacher whose name the Conservatory or Institute bears, totally omitting any mention that the celebrated teacher whose name the Institute bears passed away some years before.

Also, it's important to consider the desirability for the individual of the long term commitments (often at least two and sometimes three years) that these organizations usually require.

■ Comedy Workshops

The majority of these workshops are excellent, simply because the heading of such a workshop is often more of a compulsion (to remain active in comedy in some manner every hour of the day) than it is designed as a moneymaking enterprise.

These workshops are usually headed by someone who is himself or herself well known in comedy circles, sometimes even well known to the general public.

Their offerings usually include *Standup Comedy, Joke and Routine Writing, Comedy Improvisation,* with some also offering *Private Coaching in Developing Standup and other Club Acts.*

If headed by a known comic talent these workshops often allow and encourage industry visitors to come and observe. It's not uncommon to see casting people, agents, television sitcom producers and writers, etc., sitting in, scouting either performers or writing ideas.

Some of the best comedy workshops are fairly exclusive, especially in Hollywood, where comedy training is exceptional because of the celebrated talents involved in the best of such groups, and because top comedians often come there to work out with others of their own professional level.

It's a good idea to find out all you can about the comedy background and public recognition of the workshop head---if you don't already know it---prior to applying for admittance.

■ Commercial Workshops

Although many other acting study facilities and programs advertise the teaching of *Commercial Acting,* the best workshops in which to study this unique kind of acting are those workshops devoted exclusively to the subject.

Expect to learn *Commercial Auditioning, Storyboards, Cue Cards (Copy Boards), what Commercial Agencies' A and B Lists are, the Different Kinds of Commercials, Holding Fee and Conflict details, the differences between Commercial Principals and*

Extras, etc., in addition to the *Commercial Acting Styles.*

In such workshops---especially in the longest established (there are four or five), the would-be commerial actor not only learns the acting styles, procedures and demands of commercials and works in most sessions, but also is often scouted in class sessions by visiting and observing commercial casting directors, commercial agents and commercial producers and directors.

Those folks are always scouting for new, unfamiliar faces and regularly visit the top commercial workshop sessions to do so. It's not uncommon for many new actors to get their first acting employments and their Screen Actors Guild membership cards through such workshop exposures.

■ Musical Theatre Workshops

Of course these workshops offer *Singing, Dance and Movement For The Stage, Audition Material Selection and Coaching, Scene Work including Musical Numbers*, probably *Voice Production* and *Individual Music Styles.*

The more experienced the head of such a workshop is in terms of their own actual musical theatre background (especially if it includes Broadway), the more likely that the training is going to be ideally productive.

The personal background of the teacher is the most important consideration for someone seeking this training.

■ Private Coaching

Although private coaching is ideal for many performance arts such as singing, dance, musical instruments, voice, speech, diction and dialects, for example, this author feels that---except for the preparing of actual roles or important auditions (for which private coaching is ideal)---private coaching is less effective, slower and possibly more bad-habit-forming than an acting class experience of working with other actors would be.

I feel that an acting class where the actor continually works with other actors---observes others' examples of success and failure, gains cumulative experience in acting in participation with others (which is what most acting roles involve)---is far more productive in rapid and firm progress for the actor.

As a manner of developing the actor's talents and technique, private coaching is too often limited by that privacy to simply preparing monologues one after another, presenting them for critique and suggestions in session after session and, with no partners for either scene work or improvisation work, must lack the important aspect of developing the ability to work with and use what the actor receives from others in most role performances.

■ Theatre Games

Viola Spolin, whose book *"Improvisation For The Theatre"* records her pioneering of this type of development work, has produced a number of later teachers who now specialize in this area. Some excellent *Theatre Games* classes exist in both New York and Hollywood.

This kind of workshop offers improvisations in movement (and some verbal) exercises of many kinds for freeing the actors' instruments and expanding their acquaintance with many types of characterizations.

Mrs. Spolin's theories, as originally described by her in the book *"Improvisation For The Theatre"* mentioned above, have been the springboard of inspiration for many teachers throughout the world and have been important in many talents' careers.

■ Voice, Speech and Diction Coaching

These types of coaching are most often left to trained specialists, as they should be. They are of necessity conducted privately, in the main, in one-on-one sessions.

To deepen or enrich the voice, a *Voice Coach*. To improve speech, a *Speech or Diction Coach* (usually one and the same). Either of the latter two is normally qualified to also help actors eliminate unwanted national or regional accents. However, to learn and practice *Dialects* of any kind, whether national or regional, it's wisest to seek out a good *Dialects Coach.*

However, unless the actor senses or has been told that there is some speech problem, such coaching may be not only unnecessary but also detrimental in removing some distinct and unique quality of speech that can in fact bring professional employments more quickly than long and assiduously studied, perfect Noel Cowardian speech. Except in classical works, there's much less demand for perfect speech these days, especially for those aspiring to film careers, because in industry circles there's a preference for what's called *"Middle American"*---speech not identifiable as being Texan or Southern drawl, New Yorkese or Bostonian or Downesterner.

■ Voice Over Training

This training is for the actor or actress who's interested in going into the field of providing many different voices for animation characters and cartoons, voice over work in providing off-camera messages for both television and radio commercials, narration for industrial and training films, voice work in music videos, etc. There's a vast market for these talents.

If the actor enjoys producing "trick voices"--- babies' cooings, dog barks, race cars zooming past, foghorns, lion roars, etc., there's a busy market for those talents too.

Make sure it's an experienced (probably still regularly working) voice over expert who'll teach you. Those folks, recognizing the importance of the actor having a *"demo tape"* to help obtain an agent and help the agent obtain employments, usually offer to help the actor prepare one of those during the term of study.

■ Film Acting Classes

Of course these abound in Hollywood. Most offer *on-camera experience via videotape equipment.* Some teach the basics of *Movement for The Camera, Matching, Hitting Marks, Angles, Film Set Terminology, Best Manners of Acting For The Camera* and other demands of film and television.

Some of the better ones hand out scenes, have the actors learn them at home, afford them the normal brief rehearsals before takes, with blocking by directors that's specifically designed for the camera, then videotape the work and later play it back for expert critique and points for producing better work in future tapings. This is certainly the ideal circumstance.

But there are others who simply have actors learn and rehearse scenes outside of class time and bring their work in for taping *without any direction for the camera.* Such taping as is done is sometimes characterized by *clumsy zoom-ins as the only closeups, actors misusing their heads, hands and bodies* (from camera standpoint), *constantly poor focus* (because of lack of direction to accommodate focal depths) and many more bad-habit-forming and ignorance-perpetuating results for naive actors who may be so fascinated with simply watching themselves on tape that they fail to note that they're not really learning anything about the processes of working before the camera.

If *Acting For The Camera* is what the actor feels he or she needs, rather than acting study itself, then the best suggestion we can offer is to investigate the leading, longest established *Film Workshops.* Observe their work, their equipment, their handling of actors in scenes, their concepts and their finished results and comments in critiques. (Most of these permit one-time audits.)

Since these workshops focus on *Acting For The Camera* almost exclusively, it's probably wise to consider this training as exactly what it says it is, not expecting the development of basic acting talents, and proceed to develop the over-all use of your talents in other classes of your choice, perhaps at the same time. The emphasis in these (mostly excellent) workshops is on training the actor in all phases of *acting for the camera*.

■ Cold Reading and Auditioning Classes

Cold Reading and Auditioning Coaching is everywhere these days. It ranges the whole gamut from good to bad, of helpful to harmful and simply exploitative.

There are even more and more of the popular "classes"---or more aptly entitled "casting showcases"---conducted by some casting directors, where the casting director may or may not be last year's casting secretary, may not know anything about how actors achieve desirable results in reading interviews and may not be qualified as a teacher even if he or she does in fact know what's needed. There are only a few of the current casting directors who have any acting background themselves.

Attendance at such a "class" conducted by a casting director should be considered by only those actors who know beyond a shadow of doubt that they're ideally ready to have their talents judged. These should really be called "paid auditions", because that's precisely what they are. The actors who attend are quite calculatedly paying for the opportunity to be "auditioned" by a casting person.

There are the classes (to quickly avoid) that recommend so much and so elaborate preparation in the outer office before a reading that the actor has little time to come to *comfortably believe* that he or she is simply the character and that the situation in the script is actually happening around him or her during the reading. That actor will be so tense and so involved with trying to remember planned line readings and ideas, etc., that the reading will be a shambles and the actor will be added to the "Never Call Back" list of the casting person involved.

A good *Cold Reading and Auditioning Class* should teach that there is one style of reading to obtain "bit" roles when the actor needs them and a very different reading style for obtaining swift promotion into top role categories.

If coaching for reading and auditioning is of the *eye-to-eye every second* variety---which results in readings that suggest the actor as being ideal for only tiny one-line roles, it should be shunned, because the human characteristics of the kind of experiencing that film cameras seek in leading players are missing or are overwhelmed and rendered impossible by so much emphasis on *communication and line readings*.

Some coaches have actors practice cold reading by reading opposite other actors in front of class groups. There are others who more closely duplicate the conditions of actual reading interviews by having the actors prepare in an outer office, probably with other class members preparing other or the same roles beside them (as occurs at actual casting interviews), then having the individual actors come in singly to a private office to read and receive the more individualized coaching they may profit from in that manner of the conducting of a class.

■ "Talent Showcasing" Workshops

These are seldom worth the actor's time and attendance fees. They're sometimes in fact out and out ripoffs. The fact that a workshop advertises prominently in its ads that there's showcasing doesn't mean that it's often or even occasionally attended by any industry people when offered.

There are many workshops of this kind that recognize and exploit the actor's desire to be "showcased" and that can actually damage the future prospects of the actors they present. They may direct the actors ineptly if at all, often presenting them in embarassing work, while they build their personal bank accounts on the foolish hopes of naive actors.

The credentials of the people who are to direct and help prepare the offerings of such a workshop are of prime importance. Make sure they're experienced directors. Check out in whatever manner possible their boasts and claims, which may well be a pack of lies.

If you decide to work with one of these, make sure they contribute excitement to what you're working on. Make sure, first of all in fact, by asking around, that casting and agency people respect the work done by the workshop enough to regularly or at least sometimes attend. If all these items aren't convincingly established, look for another "showcasing" opportunity if you feel you must. There's one around every corner these days.

■ Acting Teachers

Just as there are many kinds of acting study programs, there are as many kinds of teachers offering them. And there are many levels of competency among those many teachers.

Here, we're discussing the teachers themselves rather than the many approaches and study programs mentioned previously. There are many teachers who conduct private classes, most usually on a continuing, monthly attendance fee basis and usually with entry at any time following acceptance in an interview.

198

New actors usually have little awareness of what particular areas of first or later development may be needed. After some amount of professional experience an actor can usually gain awareness of certain problems or feelings of inadequacy in certain areas and seek an appropriate "doctor" to help deal with them, but too often what's actually needed to correct a problem isn't known.

Most coaches and teachers who conduct private classes specialize. Some teach approaches more suitable to theatre; others specialize in teaching approaches needed by film actors. As regards acting development, most have long ago opted to teach a single approach which comprises what they feel are all the necessary development steps and facets or have opted to concentrate their teaching almost exclusively upon a single facet of development of the instrument and resources of those with whom they choose to work.

Attending a coach's teaching session, the experienced actor can probably judge whether he or she is apt to learn something new which has value, but the would-be actor with little or no experience and little or no knowledge of acting beforehand often can't accurately judge whether he or she is really learning anything at all that's going to be of value toward the furthering of a meaningful acting career.

Those seeking acting study programs in either New York or Hollywood have a veritable supermarket of offerings in each of those two centers from which they may choose.

The Acting World Books periodical *"The Hollywood Acting Coaches And Teachers Directory"*, updated each quarter, regularly lists no less than two hundred and sometimes closer to three hundred coaches and teachers, acting academies and workshops located in or near Hollywood and Greater Los Angeles. Similar directories in New York duplicate that number, with more actors becoming teachers all the time on both coasts, qualified or not.

On both coasts, the huge lists of teachers run the gamut from long established and highly respected teachers to the actors and actresses who---feeling the pinch of unemployment periods and having spent lengthy periods themselves in learning the approaches of their own teachers---decide to offer their own programs for supportive income. Professional background of the teacher should be the first consideration. Some have little.

In recent years even some film and television casting directors have become teachers, mostly of cold reading, auditioning and acting for commercials but not exclusively. Some of the latter, egregiously unqualified but opportunistic and desperate during their own periods of unemployment, also "teach acting".

■ All Those Confusing Ads!

Whether in New York or Hollywood, there are those hundreds of ads for study programs in every issue of actor publications. In New York they're in *Backstage* and other weekly, monthly and some standard shelfstock yearly publications (the latter usually being woefully out of date). Teachers move around often. In Hollywood their ads fill the pages of *Drama-Logue* ---the leading and most dependable "actors' newspaper"--- every week.

Without the actor's knowing in advance the reputation and specialization areas of a teacher's perhaps even well known name, most ads in actor publications offer little hint of what they offer because display adverising space costs discourage the lengthy descriptions required to explicitly describe them.

The words *Studio, Academy, Institute, Professional Classes* and *Workshop* could mean anything---*Theatre Technique (only), Film Technique (only), Commercial Acting, The Stanislavski System, the Strasberg Method, Shakespeare and The Classics, Scene Study, Improvisation, Script Analysis, Theatre Games, Cold Reading and Auditioning, Psychotherapy* or whatever!

And there are other considerations: Some less than highly principled study programs' ads offer a few highly praising quotes---without any names credited---which should be summarily set aside as pure advertising hype. Some offer "industry showcases" as an enticement. (Even a few of the top teachers sometimes---though rarely---do showcase their more deserving students for the industry, but those who continually advertise showcasing in nice big, bold print might well be suspect as cynical exploiters.)

Some ads display the photo and name of the organization founder, as mentioned in a previous paragraph, not mentioning that that celebrated founder has passed away, or the photo and name of another celebrated teacher whose name the Academy, Conservatory or Institute bears but who never comes west of the Hudson more than once a year, and then only briefly.

Some list stars they've "taught or worked with", being careful to include the phrase "or worked with" because that (maybe even in a tiny supporting role) may have been the extent of any association. Sometimes in such listings appear the names of now recognizable people who may have attended one class and beat a hasty exit.

Don't fall for the ploy if a teacher promises to obtain employment or even important contacts for you (in return for your class attendance tuition). The obtaining of acting roles requires a talent agent license from the State and a franchise from the Screen Actors Guild, or AFTRA (American Federation of Television and Radio Artists) or Actors Equity, or all three if the agent operates in all of those unions' purviews as most respected agencies do. That's what this kind of "promiser" is implying he or she is, and it's obviously untrue.

Similarly, the promise of obtaining important industry contacts for you implies a position of prominence in the industry that only a top coach or teacher possesses. No reputable teacher would make or even imply such a promise to an actor who comes to his office as a stranger and whose talents aren't yet known.

The best advice one can give the serious newcomer starting to shop for a study venue in either New York or Hollywood is to go to a leading actor bookstore and obtain a directory of the type that lists and describes the teachers and their programs and (disregarding the "hype" ads that can be found in profusion in *Drama-Logue* in Hollywood and in *Backstage* in New York), first try for the best, the most respected and the longest established.

There's a fine (although selective and far from complete) book, *"The New Generation Of Acting Teachers"*, by Eva Mekler, published by Penguin Books in 1987, listing an arbitrary selection of more than twenty of today's respected teachers on both the East and West Coasts, with lengthy, in-depth interviews with each about their teaching approaches and their own backgrounds.

And at least in Hollywood, the current quarterly issue of *"The Hollywood Acting Coaches And Teachers Directory"*, available at Samuel French Theatre Bookshops, lists approximately forty coaches and teachers with over twenty years of respected teaching and in the neighborhood of fifty others with close to that many years of top work with actors. In addition, this directory describes the teaching approaches and personal backgrounds of as many as possible of those listed.

Again, try for the best. There are always others.

■ Auditing Acting Classes

It's easy to understand why actors considering a teacher's classes would like to audit (observe) that teacher's work as well as the quality of the current class members before deciding to join. But it's also easy to understand the reasons offered by teachers who don't permit it.

An acting class should be a protected environment where those present are there to learn and grow. Too often an acting class which permits auditing turns into something else. It's obvious that any observers present are there to check out the teacher, the technique taught or other work conducted, and the professional level and quality of class members working in the class.

201

If the class members appreciate what they're learning, they may tend to *demonstrate its value* for the visitor. Instead of themselves growing in the session, they *perform* for the observer, and the session is wasted for them.

Even if they don't consciously work to demonstrate the effectiveness of the technique, they're distracted by the observers' presence into doing their own best (safest, most secure) work to avoid public embarassment before the outsiders, neglecting any possible growth opportunity presented by the session's work.

In addition, many teachers' techniques are of forms which must be taught item by item in different sessions. If one certain item is being worked on by all class members in a session when a visitor is observing, it's possible that the visitor will come away thinking that that one item is the total of the teacher's technique.

Teachers know these things, and those who permit auditing may---probably will---schedule *demonstration* work of a type that isn't in any way developmental for the current class members. The teachers too are playing it safe, wasting their own and their class members' time.

There's certainly no harm, when interviewing a teacher toward the possibility of enrolling in a class, in asking whether the teacher permits auditing. If you're permitted to audit prior to possibly enrolling it may be fine for you. But if you were already enrolled in the same class would you want people coming to audit, watching you perhaps fall on your face when you're brave enough to be trying something that's new to you?

A teacher who permits auditing is, after all, himself or herself *auditioning* for the observer, in all probability hoping for approval and the addition of another attendance fee payer to the class roster.

Lee Strasberg is reported as telling applicants for auditing privilege *"If you want to observe the actors, see them in the lobby between ten-thirty and eleven o'clock. At eleven o'clock the doors shut and it's just us."* That makes sense.

■ Choosing an Acting Technique Based on Career Goals

The first decision the actor should make is his or her early and later career goals . . . Broadway, film, television . . . or a career that ranges among all three of those mediums. That should, in some respects, determine whether to head for New York or Hollywood first. There are many excellent---and some less than excellent---teachers in both locations who can prepare actors for *all* acting development and just as many who specifically emphasize either *theatre* or the *two filmed arts*.

202

There are several things today's actor might consider before opting for a specific kind of study program, whether it be in New York or Hollywood or wherever:

What's still needed---*in addition to acting talent and any previous training*---for the optimum chance to actually work as an actor?

■ Voice and Speech

If the goal is theatre first, be prepared to face the fact that good speech will unquestionably be requisite. Voice placement and production, if not already studied and advanced, may be needed for projection and intelligibility on large stages. A shallow, metallic or nasal voice with little or no resonance must be deepened and must acquire timbre. Enunciation and articulation must be already developed or will need quick doctoring.

A regional accent is limiting. Even those in the "character actor" categories need either good natural or trained voices and speech for Broadway or any other large stages, and for any hope of major theatre success in *leading* roles the voice and speech must be pleasing to the ear and easily projected. This applies for both males and females.

Film and television don't place as stringent requirements on voice and speech, because there are boom mikes that make projection less important. Still, for *leading* roles of any kind---leading man, leading woman, juvenile, ingenue, character actor or comedian/comedienne (in other words, all categories and types that nowadays play leading roles)---the voice and speech of whatever kind the actor may have must be produced without effort even for film and television.

Given, an actor who recognizes his or her physical appearance as suggesting more *character* role opportunities (because of unique facial characteristics, size or shape of body or some other obvious consideration) may have *almost any kind of voice and speech whatever*, as long as it can be projected for theatre stages or be easily recorded for film.

Bottom line: If the actor has a weak, undeveloped voice, that needs to be dealt with before anything else. There are Voice and Speech Specialists in both New York and Hollywood. This phase of the actor's work on the instrument isn't the main determinant as to which center is chosen for early study---rather, is perhaps of first consideration for both.

Dialogue delivery isn't the most important aspect of acting in any of the arts nowadays, but it's certainly a big consideration that has to be dealt with.

■ **There are Theatre, Film and Television on Both Coasts---and Teachers on Both Coasts Who Specialize in One or The Other of those Careers' Approaches...**

Although there's much more film and television produced in (or at least headquartered in) Southern California than in New York and in other East Coast locations, there's more theatre (at least of the paying kind) in New York.

The actor who hopes to seek some early roles in one or the other might consider which location will most likely offer the best hope for any early exposure toward actual paid employment.

There are fewer acting studios and conservatories in New York that offer much training for film and television, just as there are fewer programs in Hollywood devoted exclusively to training for theatre. Training programs are essentially suburbs of their particular entertainment industry production centers.

But for the actor who prefers one city over the other for the early period of acting study, for whatever reason, there are a number of excellent programs in both cities for both theatre and film study (singly) as well as training for total development of the actor in all respects. Some top Hollywood teachers teach for certain periods of each year in New York, and vice versa.

In this step of the actor's decision-making we're talking only about the most hopeful location for combining acting study of whatever duration with an early start of paid employment. All things considered, the nod must go to Hollywood at this time.

With the stringent requirements of any meaningful legitimate theatre venue, it has to be assumed that Hollywood offers the best chance for the less trained actor with exciting talent to be earlier exposed for casting opportunities.

In New York, to work in even the farthest Off Off Broadway theatre requires some voice projection, clarity of speech, some amount of stage presence, perhaps some movement training, often more awareness of different styles (of periods, theatre literature and classic dramaturgy, national characteristics, etc.), and survival in New York, where costs of living decently are higher, requires searching out one of the much harder to find workweek jobs, to pay rent and eat while also studying.

In Hollywood, while studying, the actor finds part-time or full time employments more plentiful. And there are plenty of small, 99-seat theatres for gaining theatre experience (sometimes side by side with stars of theatre, film and television appearing in new productions as favors to friends whose plays are being tried out). And rents of fairly decent living quarters are cheaper.

In some of the smaller Los Angeles Area theatres of the "99 seat" category, sanctioned by Actors Equity for appearance in productions' casts by both Equity and non-union actors, the actor's talents are being showcased, sometimes magnificently, before invited audiences of casting, agency and production people who are scouting new talents.

In New York's current theatre scene---with Broadway's inconceivably costly production budget problems and therefore an amount of apathy toward chance-taking with new and untried talents, there's considerably less scouting in the Off Off Broadway venues for Broadway theatre employment, still less scouting for film and television casting. The actor's chances of any early visibility toward paid employment are fewer there as a result.

■ Acting Study Choices Can Be Based On Goals

A carpenter knows he needs a hammer, several kinds of saws, all kinds of nails and screws, a bit and auger, a screwdriver, pliers, a miter box, a ladder and several other things. But most of all, he needs *wood.* For actors, the wood is his *talent . . .* but it probably won't mean much unless the right "tools" are at hand for what's being constructed.

A writer needs a computer, wordprocessor or typewriter, reference books, dictionaries, thesauruses, a desk and a chair. But most of all, he needs *material.* The actor's material is, again, his *talent . . .*and the "tools" he chooses for his toolbox can determine what happens with that material.

An actor should be concerned with obtaining the most appropriate tools and the best instructions as to their use for *the particular career goal* to which he aspires. Granted, good acting talent can move from stage to film and television and back again, in fact in an ongoing career is called upon to do that regularly . . .

But, like a carpenter who has the wrong kinds of hammers and saws, the wrong types and sizes of nails and screws, the wrong screwdriver and other tools that can't help him on the kinds of jobs most likely to come up unexpectedly because of location, the actor may have a tool chest full of tools that he'll find of little use when a professional opportunity comes without warning.

The theatre actor has time . . . to make complicated, intricate diagrams, study them, make scads of decisions as to what's needed, lay out and organize all the tools in his toolbox, be supplied with more tools by his director and practice the use of all those tools while building the structure for his character.

He can do all that because he has time. Granted, not as much time as Stanislavski customarily took in *building a character---*

often many months or several years---but time to fit hundreds of little pieces together, start construction, then if necessary tear the whole thing down at the insistence of his job boss (the director), start again from scratch and in most cases still meet the deadline for completing the construction.

Actors whose careers either begin or simply evolve rapidly into film and television---whether those careers have also included legitimate theatre or not---don't have all that time.

Roles come suddenly and unexpectedly for all except top stars, often for them as well. Preparation has to be accelerated in the brief timespans between being cast in roles and their performances before cameras. For all but top stars (who usually have the scripts far in advance of filming), there's no time for making mistakes and little time for tiny details. Film and television actors' final performances are essentially what have been constructed by the actors themselves . . . without any supervision or help before they arrive before the cameras.

What actors in today's multi-media performance arts might consider from the start is that---even if their professional careers begin in theatre, as so many do, and in that career phase they have the luxury of time on their side, if their work excels there will come times when they suddenly find themselves robbed of that luxury. Film and television opportunities come suddenly and unexpectedly, and do just that.

If they lack a framework and system that can work expertly under the pressure of "minutes on film" limitations---soundstage distractions, the absence of directorial guidance ahead of time, explicit matching of actions in the several repeats (for different angles of the same sequences)---and a system that can produce complex characterization and instant feeling depth at the push of a button . . . they will fail.

The choices among different approaches and the tools they comprise exist for the actor's making. And the making of the choice can be crucial. Ask any actor or actress who plays important or even meaningful supporting roles in film and television.

There are the hundreds of the original Stanislavski and Stanislavski-derivative approaches taught by leading teachers, studied and practiced over and over in beginners' acting classes, intermediate acting classes and advanced acting classes. They often require lengthy study before the actor is ready to work.

It should be apparent that, while a large number of those approaches' items are for classroom development of the instrument of the actor, *a still large number of them are taught as being needed, item by item, for the preparing of roles.* That's a lot of "item by item" work and it takes a lot of time!

206

It should also be apparent that with so large a number of them recommended as being productive in the preparing of roles there's nowhere in creation they can serve the actor so ideally (as *composite role preparation* techniques) as in the theatre.

The learning and practicing of most of them is a stimulating imagination-developing, consciousness-expanding, approach item-file-carding experience. Your instrument will be sensitized and developed. Your talent resources and access to them will be expanded. But there probably won't be enough time in either today's theatre rehearsal periods or in film and television's accelerated processes to use all of them at once.

Prepare with them in classes if you like, for as many years as you like. You'll still have to eventually select those items that work ideally for you and those you'll have time for on individual occasions, whether for theatre, film or television.

There are other approaches that are used by actors because they find they provide exciting role preparation methods and can be used to prepare with equal effectiveness in a fraction of the time.

An alternative is usually the actor's own adaptation and selection from the large list of items that are taught in the approaches requiring lengthy study which after some experience emerge as the more important and singly most effective items. The actor is, in making such selections, devising his own personal System. And Stanislavski would have applauded that.

Few television series stars, for example, have time to read and reread their upcoming scripts, then effectively plot the courses of their characters' involvements throughout the complete scripts, and still study their lines over the few weekend hours between episodes' filmings.

Working with a number of such series stars---who were usually filming one episode Monday through Friday in one week week, and on Monday of the next week were to begin filming of the next episode, with insufficient time between for any complex preparation, the quicker *Objects*-oriented techniques of my teaching have made it possible for me to receive from the productions' front offices copies of the next scripts, make suggestions and break down the moments of the roles with *Thought Object* ideas, meet with the actors to discuss the suggested plans, and help them make their own desired, more personalized changes quite quickly, so they could get to line study.

And director-teacher Don Richardson's small but idea-rich book *"Acting Without Agony"* (one of the books discussed in the later *"Actor's Library"* section of this book) offers an alternative for all actors, not just film and television actors. His postula-

207

tions work, and they work excellently and quickly. He too recommends the use of *Objectives, Analyzing the Character* and manners of involving *Emotional Truth*, but he simplifies the processes of *Consulting the Body for What it Remembers and involving it in Characterization*, and proposes *Creating Character And Actor Truth of Experiencing* in a far less complex manner.

Except for those actors who like the total of Don Richardson's technique---perhaps being already backgrounded in the finding and use of *Objectives* of the kind he recommends, who will find the adjustment into his technique quick and satisfying, I'd still suggest a simpler and I think far superior technique than any *action* tool for more quickly forming the character's and the actor's experience in *all steps of the preparation . . . Objects!* Not *Actions*, not *Intentions* or *Objectives. . . Objects!*

■ Still More on Objects . . . Because They're Easily Found and So Effective!. . .

Geraldine Page, mentioned often in this book, was a stunning example of what can be achieved by the use of *Thought Objects* of the types described throughout these pages. They were one of the secrets of her brilliance.

In the *New York Times* article announcing her death, published June 15th, 1987, Jose Quintero, who directed her in the production of *"Summer And Smoke"* at the Circle In The Square that brought her instant stardom, said when interviewed:

"The Objects she planned and brought into her 'inner landscaping' gave her the remarkable ability to communicate, with her own deepest experiencing of them, joys, unhappinesses, longings and all those undefinable and by no means ordinary mysteries hidden in all of our lives."

And Gerry's own comments about *Objects*, as advice to actors in a *New Yorker* magazine interview:

"The main thing is the ability to control your instrument, which in the actor is yourself. You need to look the way you want the character to look and sound the way you want the character to sound, yes, but to train the instrument you still need to plan the Objects that that particular character would be feeling something about deeply for all its moments. Then your instrument takes care of itself."

The *Object*---described in great detail in this book's chapter devoted to it, and constantly referred to so often throughout the book because I feel it needs to be---uses the *Concentration Point, the Language, the Attitudes and Personality of the Character;* is based upon and focused upon *the Problem;* combines *the Outer* and Inner Ojectives and Motivations; and involves the Body and its Easy Access to The Actor's Right Brain Files of Sense Memories and Emotional Memories. The point in rementioning it here is that it accomplishes all of those desirables in a tenth of the time required by some *Action and Intention* approaches.

In theatre, *Objects* sustain your character's and your own feeling experiences more effectively; expand your body's manifestation of thoughts and feelings through the body/right brain relationship; and avoid the continuous self-directing that the use of an *Action, Intention or Objective* would involve.

In film and television roles, *Objects* will speed your preparation; will hang in the mind more easily and more totally under filming's sometimes hectic conditions; will bring instant feeling when the director yells "Action!"; will provide the clarity the camera seeks behind your eyes in closeups as well as the body involvements it seeks in long shots; and will enable you to "match" ideally for the editor when the exterior shots have ben filmed on location in Ann Arbor, Michigan, and the very next (continuing) scenes of entering interiors are shot weeks later on a soundstage on the Paramount lot.

So many actors have sweated in their dressing room trailers trying to remember exactly what was in their mind in those earlier moments, and they've often been unable to remember unless they've marked their ideas in their scripts. And some of those actors may have been using *Actions* or *Intentions* that at the earlier time seemed excellent but in the time period between the two shots of the scene may have become vague.

They'll even quicken your line study and make the remembering of your lines later in front of the camera more secure, because your characters' inner experiences will be more surely imbedded in your right brain (where they belong), leaving your left brain to cope with the intrusive and distracting location or soundstage surroundings. By the way, they do the same for line study and later forgetting of the audience in theatre!

■ **Whatever You Choose, Go Forward With It And Improve It!**

As mentioned earlier, in fact throughout this book, whatever technique or approach one chooses for studying, for adopting as customary practice, for adapting to different kinds of circumstances as professional acting employments may demand, and for perhaps someday teaching it to others, the constant quest for improvements should never cease.

When the noted director Gordon Craig was in Moscow to direct *"Hamlet"* at Stanislavski's invitation, Stanislavski discussed with him the differences between the Russian and Western cultures and advised him *"Don't use my system. Create your own."*

After whatever time an actor spends studying one or more approaches handed down by others, that's what he will eventually realize he must do.

Straight Talk...
About Some of The Myths,
Myth-Understandings,
Mystiques and Mistakes
In The Actor's World

■ There's probably not a single actor who's serious about acting who doesn't know of the Actors Studio. But there aren't too many who know any great amount of the details and history of...

The Actors Studio and Lee Strasberg

The Emerging of the American Method

For the most complete history of the Actors Studio and the approaches developed by Lee Strasberg, plus a clear cross-referencing of his teaching concepts to the approaches recommended by Stanislavski and Vakhtangov (which no amount of Strasberg's own writings or recorded discussions provide so clearly), get Lorrie Hull's book *"Strasberg's Method As Taught by Lorrie Hull"*. (It's discussed in *"The Actor's Library"* chapter.)

The Actors Studio, which is recognized as *"the home of the American (Strasberg) Method"*, opened on October 5th, 1947, under the direction of Elia Kazan, Cheryl Crawford and Robert Lewis. Its purpose, according to Kazan, was to carry on the tradition of The Group Theatre and promote a common language so that directors could direct actors rather than have to teach them; so there could be a common vocabulary between directors and actors to facilitate the preparation of theatre and film works.

Kazan initially taught the beginners' class. Robert (affectionately "Bobby") Lewis taught the advanced. Miss Crawford was the administrator, handling the Studio's business affairs.

When Bobby Lewis withdrew in 1948, Kazan taught most of the classes briefly, then Daniel Mann and Sandy Meisner came in briefly to keep the classes going. Finally, Kazan and Miss Crawford looked around for another teacher to reduce Kazan's classroom load. It was against Kazan's better judgment that they finally decided to bring in Mr. Strasberg to conduct the sessions, but there appeared no alternative.

Strasberg had not been brought in as an initial founder of the Studio because of the difficulty Group Theare members had experienced in working with him---the volatile, suddenly erupting temper and chastising fury, his tyranny over actors, and his dogged control of every situation.

But when Bobby Lewis left the Studio there seemed nobody else. So Miss Crawford and Kazan brought Strasberg from his teaching at The American Theatre Wing and his private classes to conduct the acting sessions at the Studio.

With his unique manner of working with actors, by the early 1950's Strasberg had completely taken over Kazan's position and was by then conducting all sessions.

What isn't generally realized about the Actors Studio is that it seldom taught beginning actors who came without at least some study background. Many professional actors---most already stars or well established and developed to brilliance by other teachers---came, first, to work with Kazan and Robert Lewis, later upon invitations from Strasberg to observe and sometimes participate, while less established actors (also already well trained by other teachers) were allowed to audition before the Board and then, if approved by the Board, were allowed to audition before Strasberg, and if approved by him were permitted to join, where they could *work with other professionals, paying no attendance fee.* Those were two very persuasive drawing cards! The *absence of any membership charge* was a special magnet.

What an opportunity the Studio offered!---a place to work with other actors daily, work on scenes, mix with top directors and playwrights . . . and not have to pay a cent!

A special drawing card for the more experienced, established talents was the presence of a number of the *creme de la creme* directors and writers at sessions---they too having begun participation at the Studio upon personal invitation, observing, critiquing and becoming more intimately acquainted with all the members' further potentials. What those top professionals' attendance represented for many was visibility, regular auditioning and possible casting opportunities through those daily associations!

Strasberg was not often the original teacher of the Actors Studio members. Even most of the newer people who came, auditioned and were accepted in that manner were most often previously taught. They came primarily for those same reasons mentioned---to work with other good actors in a controlled environment, under Strasberg's clinical eye, to continue their growth through those associations, to constantly audition before directors in attendance, and for the reason that actor Ron Liebman summed up nicely . . . *"It was free!"*

The Studio---with its ever increasing galaxy of invited celebrities, the daily camaraderie among leading industry peers, plus its free membership---attracted a flurry of attention! Strasberg basked in that attention and his reputation was enhanced by the position into which he had fallen and which he quickly entrenched, and by the volumes of publicity continually generated for the Studio because of its star-studded membership.

What some of those already starring actors who came to continue their development in a protected environment gained were the mechanics for refining some approaches they'd perhaps been using instinctively but which in watching other actors with similar problems and through Strasberg's lengthy, incisive discussions of those problems became more conscious for them.

One of the celebrated members of the Studio referred to Strasberg as being less a teacher and more *"a clinical diagnostician, uniquely able to detect those problems that even stars and top players still worried about, and offer ways for them to explore toward clearing up those real or imagined problems."* He added, chuckling, *"When Lee didn't have an answer he could fake one so convincingly, so quickly, that it sounded completely logical."* Then, sobering, he added, *"I have to admit, most of the time it was."*

Strasberg became a self-appointed guru; according to Maureen Stapleton *"a rabbi"*; to some a priest. Even the Studio venue (a former church) and Strasberg's usual garb (vaguely resembling a man of the cloth) helped create an aura of some kind of sacrosanct seminary for the Studio. But over the years he was also criticized by many.

Marlon Brando, in his autogiography *"Brando: Songs My Mother Taught Me"*, put him down soundly, accusing him of trying to take credit for Brando's acting success. *"He never taught me anything,"* Brando wrote. *"He would have claimed credit for the sun and the moon. He was an ambitious, selfish man who exploited the people who attended the Actors Studio. And he tried to project himself as an acting oracle and guru."*

Mr. Brando's comment parallels a few others' comments made in strict privacy, only occasionally in public print, by those who deeply resented what they viewed as the continuous exploitation of their sometimes only peripheral associations with the Actors Studio.

Sandy Meisner put in print in his book what many professionals already knew and accepted. His recorded comments in one of his classes summed up what had been mostly insider information about Strasberg and the Actors Studio: *"Strasberg would see a talented actor and invite him to join the Studio---one of those already famous, talented people---and then say later, 'He was my student!'"* But they *were* also Lee's students; *did* work with him. Strasberg was justified in making the claim.

Sandy pointed to many top starring actors for whom Strasberg took credit who had studied with Sandy and others before Strasberg, giving their reasons for Studio participation: *"They went to the Studio to work on themselves, not to learn to act. It was a place where there were other actors. That was the merit of the Actors Studio."* That was probably true for many.

214

In another moment he said *"In the back of the Neighorhood Playhouse there's a list of the graduates. If you want to amuse yourself in a sickening kind of way, go through that list and see how many people he invited to the Studio and then later said 'He was my student.' It's amazing."* Some of us who read those comments were aware of the long-standing love-hate relationship between Sandy and Lee and were aware that many starring actors who attended the Studio did so for some of the aforementioned reasons. But their being there helped build the Studio.

From its beginning---with the celebrities drawn to work with Kazan and Bobby Lewis, then with more and more top stars, top directors and top playwrights joining the earlier arrivals, either at their own request or in response to Strasberg's invitations, the Studio grew to become the most awe-inspiring assemblage of notables ever seen anywhere except at the Academy Awards.

In spite of the body of important theatre and film production that the Studio spawned---with most of its playwrights, screenwriters, directors and casts all Studio members, the Studio was to be abandoned by some top actors who perhaps failed to find what they had joined for. Others stayed and are still members today.

Many have said (some in print) that it became more and more apparent to them over varying periods of time that Lee's emphasis was more on *conditioning actors' instruments and helping them clear up any personal acting problems they might have* --- which they said were the main focus of his contributions---than on teaching them any new methods for preparing roles that they didn't already know.

Herbert Berghof left in the early 1950's---soon after Strasberg's arrival---to open his own now well-known HB Acting Studio where he and Uta Hagen (Mrs. Berghof) taught side by side until his death and where Ms. Hagen teaches today. He preferred a closer adherence to Stanislavski's approaches and more attention to the preparing of roles that he felt Lee didn't offer.

Allan Miller, in recent years himself a leading and highly respected teacher and coach in hollywood, says he left the Studio because it was his observation that Strasberg never worked on character, only on the actor's problems. True or not, that criticism has been echoed by many others who left the Studio summarily or simply drifted away for similar reasons.

Kazan, who was to eventually fall away from the Studio he helped create, opined that Lee's *Affective Memory* and *Sense Memory* approaches were false when used in performances as Srasberg recommended; that actors were *"playing with something in themselves rather than being in a scene; were somewhere else instead of in the scene as the character."*

Lee's son, John Strasberg, who for a time taught for his father at the Strasberg Institute, rebelled and left in the sixties to form and teach at his own studio in New York. While acknowledging that his father had worked out a system of well-thought-out exercises for helping actors come into contact with their feelings, he reports that he came to the conclusion that actors should come into contact with emotions through the circumstances of the play, rather than use incidents from their own lives as his father taught.

Strasberg's first involvement with acting came in his late teens, when a friend invited him to join the Students of Art and Drama at the Chrystie Street Settlement in New York. As a purely social activity, he started playing small parts there. Then Philip Loeb, casting director for the Theatre Guild, coming to see a friend perform, later invited Strasberg to look him up, which invitation Strasberg accepted some years later, resulting in his first step into the professional world.

Earlier, after seeing Stanislavski and the company of the Moscow Art Theatre, he decided to pursue acting and theatre as a career. He enrolled in the Clare Tree Major School of the Theatre (where there was nothing taught that even remotely approximated what had so impressed him in the Russian company's work) and attended there for three months, disillusioned and frustrated. Then a friend suggested he look into the American Actors Lab, headed by Richard Boleslavsky and Maria Ouspenskaya. He studied there in 1924 and 1925. The Lab, and his first professional opportunity, were the turning points.

Finallly in 1924 accepting the invitation of Philip Loeb, he began rehearsing a role and assistant stage managing for the Theatre Guild. The acquaintance and close associations with Harold Clurman, Cheryl Crawford and others began there and led to his being installed as teacher with the Group Theatre when it was formed, starting his own private classes when he left the Group, and, years later, being brought in to conduct sessions at and later becoming head of the Actors Studio training.

The Actors Studio grew, partially because of the publicity generated by its many starring attendees, to attract a number of top directors and playwrights, who accepted Lee's invitations because of the stars and top players who had also become members at Strasberg's invitation. In 1957-'58 a Playwrights Unit was established, and in 1960 the Directors Unit was added.

It's been well documented that Strasberg's memory was formidable. He remembered, often literally, everything he had ever read or seen or heard about celebrated actors and critical comments and essays about their art and craft.

That memory, and the ability to quote celebrated actors' comments about acting and critical comments about their perfor-mances impressed all who were present to observe his phenome-nal capacity for recall. And he never forgot his challengers or questioners. This author had two demonstrations of that:

In Lee's classes at The American Theatre Wing in the 1940's I constantly raised my hand to question a statement. Like Michael Schulman, now a leading New York coach (also a practicing psy-chologist), I felt even at that early point in my own development, that some of the things Lee said seemed not all that applicable. (Michael though some were "downright silly".) And Reuven Adiv, who is currently the Head of Acting at the Drama Centre in London (another former student of Lee), has said that he person-ally spent a lot of time trying to figure out what it all meant.

Having been constantly questioned and criticized by Harold Clurman at the Group Theatre and later, Lee began responding to my often raised hand with a look similar to that seen when a busy mother is asked a silly quesion by a child, usually growling "Yes, Clurman, what is it?"

What characteristically followed any questioning or chal-lenging comment by a class member ---and I'm told this never changed during his Actors Studio years---was a much more effec-tive and illuminating elaboration on the point by Lee under such prodding. Years later I understood why he called me "Clurman."

And still later (1958), when The Theatre Group at The Mark Taper Forum of The Music Center in Los Angeles was forming, many of us from New York and Los Angeles met in conference at Lake Arrowhead to help celebrate and define its formation. Lee was one who came from New York. I was honored to be in the Los Angeles contingent.

Lee and I passed each other in the hallway the first day. I did-n't say hello, figuring he'd surely have forgotten me from that long ago time and not wanting to embarass myself. But Lee's eyes narrowed as we met. "Hello, Clurman," he muttered with a half smile.

And it was a still bigger shock to me when in 1963, teaching in Hollywood, I received a call from the French singing star Chantal, saying Lee had recommended she come to me for help in preparing the dramatic segments of her two musical numbers and her participations in short sketches for her upoming guest ap-pearance side by side with Jack Benny on The Ed Sullivan Show. I knew then that Lee must have forgiven me for those annoying questionings years earlier. (I was coaching the star on November 22nd, 1963, when my muted television began showing the scene of President Kennedy's assassination in Dallas.)

The Actors Studio still thrives on both Coasts. Leading actors, top writers and directors are permanent members. Work-in-progress scenes are presented for an appointed leader's and other peers' critiques, reading performances of new works are presented for development, and members fraternize and carry on the Studio traditions in their continuing quests for further personal development.

And there are now the Lee Strasberg Institutes in both New York and Hollywood, to which new actors are attracted by the *Method* approaches taught in both locations by mostly former students carrying on his teaching tradition.

Mr. Strasberg has passed on, leaving behind a celebrated and unique legacy. But in spite of that celebrity which is deservedly accorded him in the annals of an American acting style's development, and in spite of his making the name Stanislavski practically a household word, because he attributed his Method so wholly to Stanislavski and Vakhtangov, then focused so much of his work on some exercises of his own that have been viewed by many as controversial---he also created a number of questionmarks through association about some of the approaches of Stanislavski and Vakhtangov as well.

■ **Were you the star in a lot of Drama Department productions in college? Are you singled out in production reviews as being "always entertaining"? Do you have many little tricks that set you apart as an actor? Read on.**

Actorisms

Why Some Actors are Dismissed as "Hams"

Actorisms are most often for bad or extremely limited actors. Those who have and regularly use them usually don't realize how evident they are. You might check right now to observe whether you have any of these in your work:

Actorisms include gesticulating and illustrating with arms and hands to emphasize almost every word of every speech uttered. They include amateurishly calculated body positions---leaning forward uncomfortably (calculated to represent attention, thinking and anger); looking down at the floor (to convey tiredness, unhappiness, shame, despair); contracting into a little ball (to epitomize fear, worry, withdrawal); and positions to indicate anything and everything else the actor feels must be *demonstrated with a physical cliché* for the viewer.

They include loud volume, excessive energy, flailing about in some moments (to indicate upset states), and the opposite, settling into polite silence and bodily repose when other characters are speaking (to avoid distraction from another's "moment")!

Some *actorisms* may have been developed accidentally in single moments of past rehearsals when a director may have told the actor to do or not do something---simply for that single moment---and the actor thereafter assumed that if that instruction was a precept of even that one director it must therefore be an important precept of all other directors as well.   Many of what would be called *"actorisms"* are often that foolishly born.

Actorisms are almost always misconceptions of the actor's own or misunderstanding of a too respected director's admonition in a single moment in the past that the actors misconstrued as a rule of thumb for all acting.

I'm reminded of an example of such a possible misconception of a director's comment in one of those single moments.

I once had the joyful experience of directing my dear friend, Miriam Goldina---the Habimah actress-teacher, former wife of that organization's founder Nahum Zemach, who had herself studied with Stanislavski and Vakhtangov and many years later translated and adapted books about Vakhtangov for their English versions---in a production of *"Rosmersholm"*.   Miriam was certainly not a *"ham"* in any sense of the word, and had blessedly few recognizable "actorisms".   But my beloved friend apparently had one.   One moment in that production's rehearsals comes to mind:

Asked by me to continue doing what she was doing without interruption while the actor opposite her was talking, her eyes widened and she responded in a voice that clearly implied I was uttering heresy, *"Larry!   the Master* (She always called both Stanislavski and Vakhtangov that) *would never approve of that."*

Of course we were working on a play from a period when actors of that era might certainly have paused and remained silent (and a bit stiff in keeping with much of the acting style of the period) in such a moment.   We discussed that.   But, judging from all of Stanislavski's writings, I would guess she was thinking back to a single and particular kind of moment out of the volume of her work with him.   There are too many recorded moments from both his and Vakhtangov's rehearsals stating quite the contrary.

The point of the example is that it seems unnatural for a character---especially in this later time---to stop doing something (that really isn't that distracting and needs to be done) simply because another character is speaking.

Actorisms often include the same classic enunciation and careful inflection of words and phrases for all characters the actor plays without regard for what a unique and individual personality and its inner experience can and should contribute in terms of affecting its speech and its manner of delivery. The latter *actorism* often results from too much speech and diction, perhaps even Shakespearean scansion, so assiduously studied and perfected in college and university Drama Department courses, then perhaps being retained as a part of the actor's "portfolio" into early professional life.

Equally qualifying to be called an *Actorism* is the maintaining of so much concentration on voice placement and voice production that a viewer will be constantly reminded that it's an actor, not a human character, that's being observed.

They include every visible result of the actor's seeing characters in their most common and cliché embodiments . . . picture-posing of characters to make sure the characters' personalities are continuously apparent and crystal clear for the viewer.

Seeded in children's back porch role-playing melodramatics, further developed and often praised in college and university Drama Departments, highly praised by small town drama critics as being *"fun to watch"* . . . such actorisms often delude would-be actors that they possess some special "things" which must be brought to all characters they play.

Regrettably, all those carefully nurtured but often very bad acting habits must be painstakingly chipped away, one after another, leaving temporary disorientation and acute embarassment in their wake, when the actor first encounters the demands of professionalism under the eye of a perceptive director.

Long ago such "acting" was praised in even some professional venues, but actors who pose, strut, bellow and tear passions to tatters don't work very often now. Theatre audiences and film and television viewers find them laughable now and appreciate them only in comedy. That's probably where a "ham actor" should and probably will end up.

■ **There's no single item in all of acting that has produced more controversy and more division among leaders and others in the teaching profession, as well as among directors, producers, theatre and film critics and actors in heated discussions over late night coffees, than this next item.**

Stanislavski tested it, later deeply regretted it. Learning of it through his friend and associate Leopold Sulerzhitski, he explored it for use by actors. It proved to be a Pandora's box!

Affective Memory

A Right Brain Asset Actors Can and Assuredly Must Access . . .
But Its Worth As a Dependable Acting Tool in Substituion for
the Character's Reality is Widely Questioned

This is the approach advocated and continually taught by Lee Strasberg which has evoked more scathingly critical comments about his work than has any of his other theories.   There have been raging prairie fires of condemnation of *Affective Memory* as an "in performance" approach.   That was the way he recommended that it be used.

Those two simple words have over the recent decades become synonymous with the name Lee Strasberg.   His never-flagging determination to continue its promotion have evoked more comment about it and him than any other aspect of his work.

What is it? I'll keep it brief and simple. To evoke a specific emotion you can take yourself back to a past moment when you felt that way and, remembering as many sensory details as possible that led up to that moment, hope to arrive at the emotion.   We know from psychology that emotions have conditioning factors. *Affective memory* involves the reconstructing of a chain of conditioning factors in order to arouse certain emotional results.

The arguments for and against this approach as an acting technique for actors' use in actual performance moments has been raging for many, many years.   It's well known that Strasberg considered it *"the cornerstone of the modern method of training the actor."* He often called it that.

There's no doubt that *affective memory* is a wonderful thing; that it's something every actor should already have in abundance. But the battles about employing specific affective memories as *a manner of experiencing moments of roles during performance* have been fought from the early period of Stanislavski (who tried it and abandoned it) up to the present.

The *affective memory* was introduced in 1896 by the French psychologist Theodule Ribot, and was later developed as described in his *"Problémes de Psychologie Affective (1910)"*.   It was he who gave it its title *"Affective Memory"*.   He taught it to Charcot, who taught it to Freud.

Stanislavski came upon it through his associate Sulerzhitski and for a time investigated its use as a viable approach for actors' use. He explored its use in his actors' classes for a time, but soon totally discarded it. Before discarding it, however, he had recommended it in some of his writings and through those recommendations had set off a chain of events he later wished he could reverse, but it was too late.

It's defined in *"Stanislavski And The Method"*, by Charles Marowitz, who opined that *"the most popular of the Method exercises"* at the time of the writing of his book was without doubt the Emotional Memory or Emotional Recall (Affective Memory). He described the exercise aptly as *"an attempt by the actor to reconstruct a moment out of past life remembered as being highly emotional, in order to recreate in the actor the feelings associated with that experience."*

After that fine description he referred to it later as simply *"an exercise, a great boon for the ego, a classroom toy and a ginger-peachy parlor game."*

Another comment by Marowitz: *"It's an artificial and disruptive technique which can produce stunning results in the classroom but is chemically unsuited to the needs of performance. No technique which encourages an actor to introduce an emotional non sequitur into his performance can be anything but misguided."* Eight pages of his book are devoted to arguing against its use in performance moments.

Among the more critical comments about the use of *Affective Memory* in the Strasberg manner toward performing acting roles' moments are Harold Clurman's, that *"It's therapeutic, not artistic,"* and Elia Kazan's comment, *"It's false. You see the worst misuse of emotional recall in actors who are really playing with something in themselves---not with the person in the scene. There is this glazed, unconnected look in their eyes and you know they're somewhere else."* Kazan's comment was seconded by director-teacher Robert Lewis, who delared that *"One senses that the actor is really feeling something, but that the emotion is a personal one, not necessarily related to the character or the particular play."*

There is Phoebe Brand's comment also, that *"It makes for a moody, self-indulgent acting style"* and Stella Adler's, that *"It's polluted water,"* and that *"Lee always thought it was the cornerstone of the Method,"* and leading New York acting teacher and practicing psychologist Michael Schulman's, that *"It takes you totally out of the moment and out of the scene,"* and teacher-director Robert Lewis's even earlier critical comment from his Group Theatre years with Strasberg (before it was discarded there, after setting off battles among some of the members that still exist today), that *"Unless used correctly, what can happen is that the emotion that you get from the exercise, if you do get it, feels marvelous---as you know if you're an actor . . . You've got this feeling. It somehow blinds you and deafens you so that you don't really see, you don't really hear, you don't really play the action of the moment, but you hang on because it's a marvelous feeling. You don't want to let that feeling go. But you're using emotion for its own sake, and that is no better than using characterization for its own sake. That is one of the dangers."*

And the noted teacher-actress Uta Hagen issues her own warning: *"To work for an involvement for its own sake on stage bogs down the movement of the play, disconnects you from the play, makes you blind and deaf to the play. Beware."*

It's true that Stanislavsky originally taught its use to his actors. But it's equally true that he summarily stopped using it, partly because he detected an alarming and undesirable hysteria in the performances of some of the members of his theatre and felt that that hysteria emanated from the acutely felt desperation to make the memory work each time.

He noted that that hysteria was most pronounced in moments when the actor was trying to overcome the undependable nature of such a memory; knew that such an unhealthy tendency violated art and any truly creative bringing of a character's life; and, worse still, observed that too frequent and extreme use of emotional memory as an acting approach had brought some actors of the First Studio of the Moscow Art Theatre to serious mental illness!

It was Stella Adler who, upon her return to the Group Theatre after her 1934 sessions with Stanislavski in Paris, brought word that the founder of what by then had come to be relabeled "the Method" and was sweeping American acting circles by then had much earlier abandoned the Affective Memory approach.

An issue of *The Tulane Drama Review* of some years ago was devoted to a group of noted teachers' judgments about the process. In it, Ms. Adler opined that to go back to a feeling or emotion of one's own past was believed by her to be unhealthy; that in her estimation it tended to separate the actor from the play, from the action and circumstances of the play, and from the author's intention. It seemed to Ms. Adler that the approach was lacking in artistic control and she stated that she could not support the use of such a methodology. She was agreeing with Stanislavski, also with the many, many others who have always shared the same judgment.

In the same issue, Vera Soloviova, a noted coach who taught in America after studying directly with Stanislavski at the Moscow Art Theatre, offered her own strong objection to affective memory---especially for use in the actual performance moments of roles.   Ironically, during the Moscow Art Theatre's exploration with it, it was she, when having difficulty crying in her role in *"Cricket On The Hearth"* at the MAT, who had used an affective memory of her mother's death and tears flowed dependably at each performance.   Those many years later---perhaps realizing that too many theatre people had heard of her widely publicized use of it on that occasion at the MAT, was uncharacteristically mild in her own public criticism of it when she stated that she preferred to encourage her students' creative imaginations to *"go further in unknown spheres of more creative imagining."*   She's said to have been much more graphic in her condemnation of it before her class members and friends.

Robert Lewis, also, in his book *"Method---Or Madness"*, argued that any actor worth his salt has stored up within himself memories of all sorts of experiences and feelings and should be able to evoke the memory of similar emotions in his life without his thinking about them consciously at all.   Many of us would disagree with only Bobby's last sentence.

He attributed a great deal of the nonsense that had been voiced about the Group Theatre in the 1930's to this particular, highly controversial item.   He laid the blame for that nonsense and its source squarely at the door of its leading proponent (although considerately not naming him), agreeing with those who were critical of that increasingly celebrated teacher's approach as an acting tool that it was untrustworthy in that teacher's manner of use and was dangerous territory to tread, in any case.

As mentioned earlier, Strasberg learned of the item while attending the American Lab Theatre, studying with Richard Boleslasky there.   Boleslavsky had been with Stanislavsky when the latter first experimented with it, and long after Stanislavsky had discarded it Boleslavsky continued his own experimenting, and Strasberg picked it up there.

Yet, in the book *"Strasberg At The Actors Studio"*, documenting his own work with actors, Strasberg voiced, in his own words, as recorded and reported in that book, some rather significant observations and reservations about it:

As quoted in that book, his recorded comments point out some discouraging problems.   He commented that out of a hundred *Affective Memory* attempts (imagine how many weeks, perhaps months, those would take) perhaps six might work; that even if the actor were to perform the Affective Memory exercise correctly it might not work the first time because of a counter-conditioning which may have taken place causing the original experience to have lost its emotional force; that, moreover, the emotional value of the experience might even have changed substantially in the period since.

224

He stated that an actor might be planning to reevoke a happy experience and wind up weeping because the happiness might at that later time be gone, or the same actor might be seeking to recall something sad which would suddenly, at that later time, strike him as a joke.

Mr. Strasberg steadfastly maintained, however, that by attempting *a lot* of affective memories the actor might gradually obtain a stock of memories which would be permanent and which would become easier to invoke for use in moments of roles, as he continually advocated they be used.

The foregoing describe as nearly as possible the comments of the most publicized proponent of the exercise that he so determinedly maintained in his work as an approach for actors to use in roles, calling it on many occasions *the cornerstone of his Method!*

An actress who learned this procedure from Mr. Strasberg and who publicly maintains that she relies upon it in all roles once made the comment on a late night television talk show that *she never knows whether it will start on time or at all upon call; how long it will remain effective; or whether it will end when she wants it to!*

There's one more question about this item as taught by Strasberg: In "*Strasberg At The Actors Studio*" the editor states that in the cases of those people who needed certain psychiatric treatment Mr. Strasberg refused to allow them to use it at all.

What an overwhelming obligation this must place squarely upon the shoulders of anyone teaching its use . . . . the determining with any accuracy *which* members had need of psychiatric treatment and---after exposing them to the "How-to-do-it" procedure (even if only as an observer)---also assuming the responsibility of making sure that they wouldn't do it privately at home!

Since many readers have heard about this item, and may have explored it under a coach's direction in an acting class somewhere, I feel it's important to note the foregoing comments and opinions about this highly publicized item which most of us prefer to not use in our own teaching (at least in the Strasberg manner) and not recommend.

I feel it's important for the reader to differentiate between the Stanislavski-based and other approaches and this item which---even though tried for a time by Stanislavski and others of us as simply one of many explorations---were discarded for the foregoing and other reasons.

In addition, it's disastrous for actors to feel they need the sequential "preparation moments" the *Affective Memory* requires of some actors to summon forth deep feelings---even if it requires

225

less each time. Imagine the actor trying to find time for even a few of them under film conditions, for instance, where pushbutton involvement with feelings is invariably required in those few last seconds just before and after a director yells "Action!"

One of my main objections, also, is that an actor depending on such an approach might be so locked into one feeling level for the duration of the use of this item (as Bobby Lewis once cautioned)---if it's working at all that time!---that the scripted changes of intensity are missed. The actor simply isn't there---in the right place or even in the person of the character---to note them and respond more truthfully to them.

I've chosen to not explain in elaborate detail in this chapter the more involved procedures of the recommended manner of exploring this item because I have no inclination to encourage its testing. There are some teachers and coaches who, having learned it and practiced it, find this exercise a handy time-killer, in some cases a confidence-destroyer and study-prolonging item, who would be happy to explore the *Affective Memory* in the Strasberg manner with any reader over a nice long period.

What's so handicapping to actors who adhere to the publicized manner of seeking affective memories---even before the planned use of them during performance---is the ritualistic, step by step, sense memory after sense memory procedure it involves, and, along the way, the determined *resisting of the very emotion being sought* when it's triggered by a particular sensory stimulus.

In Strasberg's own classes those fully emotional moments might come because of a particular sensory stimulus which was in fact the most powerful "key", but Strasberg would often abruptly snap the actor past that key sensory moment with the admonition to *not go directly to the emotion!* People in Strasberg's classes watched this happen on many occasions.

It's so simple---if a conscious memory is in fact of sufficient affective impact for an actor ---to go moment by moment through the same sensory steps and recognize the "key" moment forcefully and easily---the sight, touch, smell, sound or physical action that produces the reexperiencing of the emotion. It's simply up to the actor's ability to observe his own inner experience to catch that moment. To be urged by a teacher to *pass it by and avoid the very emotion being sought* seems self-defeating.

It's been reported by some in Moscow in recent years that in the final months of his life, while confined to his home by illness, Stanislavski decided he was right all along about *affective memory* being important. No one can argue with that. It should be involved in all the work of any fine actor. That's not what has been the bone of contention in the battles over this item.

The battle has been over Mr. Strasberg's advocating that, once found to be effective, an *affective memory* should then be used by the actor *in actual performance*, substituting the actor's reexperiencing of it in substitution for the character's experience---as many have commented, *being somewhere else.*

That individual, totally conscious, sense memory moments that were part of past experiences can be reconstructed along the way to finding the most powerful "keys" is irrefutable, but the process can be much simpler than some make it out.

For example, on one occasion in my distant past, preparing the role of Jimmy in *"Big Fish, Little Fish"*, and not being completely confident that the desired inner emotional experience would come in a moment with Matthew (a lack of confidence that I kick myself for now), I decided to seek an affective memory.

In direct opposition to Mr. Strasberg's insistence that an affective memory should always be something the actor has experienced over seven years in the past---which I grant may be true in many cases (because so many of the most affective were experienced in childhood and teen years), I chose the moment of delivering my dog Tiny to the vet to be put to sleep, which had happened quite recently.

I remembered vividly that in the exact moment of swiftly handing over Tiny's leash to the nurse and turning away from my last look at Tiny tears had come gushing; that they remained during my hurrying out to my car; that they remained as I sat for a long time crying uncontrollably in the car; that they finally abated, but had kept coming for many minutes, making it impossible for me to drive away until the emotion subsided.

I knew the "key" instinctively when it came---the hurried, tear-blinded handing over of the leash and avoiding looking back at Tiny. Nevertheless, I reexplored the few last moments before and again the crying came on cue. I went past the moment and the crying abated. I retraced just two of the last steps leading up to the handing over of the leash and the tears gushed again. I had seen actors in Lee's classes rushed past those moments impatiently and criticized for too soon seeking the very emotion toward which the exercise was directed.

Had my own involvement in the character's own experience in rehearsals failed to produce the emotion, I might have resorted to using that "key"---not to maintain it but simply to trigger it in a brief, conscious thought before returning to the character. I wouldn't have needed to retrace several sensory steps to lead up to it, as Strasberg insisted was often necessary. The "key"---*Tiny's leash*---would have produced what I wanted in the very first moment of thinking it. (Note: *Tiny's leash* is an *Object!*)

227

I'm happy to add that I found I didn't need it after all, but I'll admit that I filed it away afterward for use in a similar moment if ever needed, since I'd gone through the exercise and found a workable "key" so easily.

But, like those who feel *affective memory* can so easily come *subconsciously* for the actor through involvement in the character's own experience---rather than needing to step out of the character and substituting *Tiny's leash*, for example, I'm one of those teachers (like the critics of the approach quoted in earlier paragraphs) who recommend an *affective memory substitution in actual performance* only as a "last resort" for the less than ideally emotional actor who shouldn't be in the role in the first place.

I want to mention something about my late friend Geraldine Page: It has been thought by some that, since she worked with Lee Strasberg over many years and deeply respected him, she must have often used an *affective memory* in the achieving of her stunningly brilliant role moments. Not true. She said she never tried for them.

On only one occasion, by accident, one came to her by itself during a performance of *"Summer And Smoke"*, and she used what it gave her in performance afterward. That's how many affective memories can and do come for actors---*through the character's experience!*

■ **Do you have difficulty concentrating? Do your thoughts flit uncontrollably from one focus to another? Are you impatient with maintaining continuous attention? If any of these apply, you probably should consider a profession other than acting.**

Attention and Concentration

The Actor's Control Mechanisms

Stanislavski himself may have confused actors as to what he considered the most important area of development for actors. His emphasis on *action* was afforded more comment in so much of his writings than his apparently just as deep conviction that *attention and concentration* were equally important.

The confusion that still exists today as to which must be more important probably stems from the fact that *action* (the most highlighted item and the stated basis of Stanislavski's System) involves *desire*, while *attention and concentration* involve *objects*.

228

Going to the root of the difference between the two, there would be nothing to create a desire to take action if it weren't for, first, attention and concentration upon some *object*. *Actions and Intentions* should therefore be open to argument as being *"the actor's primary control mechanisms"*.

First, a few little anecdotes to illustrate why I call *Attention and Concentration* the actor's *control mechanisms:*

One concerns Sir Laurence Olivier, when he was playing the tragic King Oedipus in *"Oedipus"* at the Ziegfeld Theatre in New York. Don Richardson, in his book *"Acting Without Agony"*, relates an incident indicating Olivier's supreme control of his attention and concentration.

He'd just played the final scene wherein he electrified the theatre audience with an animal howl after hearing the news that he was married to his own mother and had gouged out his eyes with a costume buckle. When he was helped to his feet and led off-stage, arriving in the wings Sir Laurence saw a friend and immediately, with blinded, bloodied eyes, whispered to her *"Cocktails, Babs?"* The king was no more.

Another example: When José Ferrer was playing *"Cyrano"* on Broadway some years ago, my girlfriend Addie Tinder and I were standing in the wings one night when Ferrer made his exit after his long soliloquy's last line.

He had held the audience spellbound with his customary long pause before his last words, then, coming offstage he whispered to the stage manager---instantly out of character, *"How long?"* The stage manager pointed to his watch, smiled and told him *"You held 'em eighty-five seconds tonight, Joe!"*

It's been written that the celebrated Italian actor Salvini, at the end of a season's final performance of *"Othello"*, collapsing in death, spoke the last lines, *". . no way but this, killing myself to die upon a kiss,"* then whispered to the actress playing Desdemona, *". . for the one hundred and third and last time this season."*

Another time comes to mind out of my own early professional years. It illustrates the importance of maintaining concentration during performance:

Prior to joining the cast of *"A Goose For The Gander"* (an utterly ridiculous, short-lived farce starring Gloria Swanson) during its summer theatre tour following its brief Broadway run, I had my first meeting with Miss Swanson. Fortunately I'd already been hired by the producer. She looked me over and said, *"He's too young."* I think I smiled as I said *"Not when I'm in makeup."* I remember her smiling back---with gritted teeth.

229

Next, I was denied even a single rehearsal with her. I hadn't reckoned with Miss Swanson's resentment at a so young character man having been hired to play her ex-school boyfriend. She later chuckled when she told me she was doing everything she could to scuttle me! Her opportunities came.

At my first performance, in my one and only entrance when I was to come in and embrace her, instead of laying her head against my chest (as she had done with my predecessor), the diminutive star (whose head barely reached to my chest!) suddenly grabbed my head and pulled it down---all the way down---to her own bosom! For a moment I went blank, but then I managed (shaken) to straighten up and improvise, laughing, *"You haven't forgotten! You used to do that."* Her head jerked up and she fixed me with that startling, luminous green, steely-eyed glare which was her trademark. (She wasn't noted for staying in character.)

Next, when she was expected to stand next to me playing with my tie, she walked far up center to the back of the set and instead played with the drapery, to force me to work upstage toward her. Instead, through sheer concentration on what was happening, I faced front and chuckled *"Aha! Trying to get away from me!"* She immediately came downstage to where she was supposed to be and again (I think by then furious, totally out of character) speared me with those green eyes.

Somehow, shaken but determined, I got through my long scene and was exiting up the stairs to the door with my exit line, *"That's the most coldblooded thing I've ever seen!"* I had two more words to get out at the top of the steps, but before I could say them, from across the stage where Swanson stood came a loud, obviously fake sneeze *"Kerchoo!"* that I later realized was intended to "kill my exit". (I hate that phrase from old theatre, but I suspect that's how she would describe it).

Without thinking, but because I was *paying attention* and believing as best I could, I immediately yelled *"Gezundheit! "*. . . then my two last words, *"Goodnight, all!"* I'm sure the applause at my exit was larger than it would have been otherwise.

I had to pass her dressing room door later on the way upstairs to my own. She was waiting for me. *"You don't add lines! . . . even in a play like this!"* she growled. I'm sure, looking back, that I stuttered as I responded *"I had no choice. You sneezed."* She looked at me for a moment, then smiled. From that rocky start, we became friends.

An example of the opposite---*lack* of attention in an acting performance: As Tobin the Texan in *"A Great Big Doostep"* in New York, after a fight of my character with another character had been carefully choreographed so neither of us would get hurt,

the other actor, J. M., was so keyed up on opening night and totally out of control that his attention failed and he lost control . . .
and broke one of my ribs! I've read that J. M. 's begun teaching
actors in Los Angeles in recent years. I hope he's learned and is
teaching *control through attention and concentration.*

The first, last and always prerequisite for an actor or for the
young person desiring to become a professional actor or actress is
concentration of attention. Anyone whose attention wanders uncontrollably or can't be focused meaningfully in the first place
would be well advised to consider another profession.

Attention to something, concentration on something, complete involvement with something in an intensified degree is necessary for the focusing of sufficient concentation that feelings
and emotions can be kindled.

Stanislavski once said that *"An actor's concentration affects all of his senses; it embraces his mind, his will, his emotions, his body."* He came to the conclusion that the first requisite for creativeness is the complete concentration of the entire
nature of the actor.

Concentration of attention is the primary ingredient in any
truthful experiencing of a moment which can be expected to have
any meaning for the person experiencing it or to convey any truth
to an observer. It must be alert to detail, sensitive to nuance and
easily directed from one focus to another at will. Its function for
the actor begins long before he begins to act.

The capacity for observing reality and evaluating it, while
important for upward mobility in any profession or walk of life,
is required to a more urgent degree for actors.

In the case of a would-be business executive, observation and
evaluation of a reality generally leads to the next step of documenting that reality for future use in either its existing form or
with some improvement or change to be determined later.

However, that reality as viewed by a would-be actor should
more often be not only stored away in an available file cabinet of
life observation in its pristine form but also transformed by the
actor's imagination---even in the moment of observing it---into
the wider spectrum of its own organic meanings and suggestions.

■ Attention to Surroundings

Objects of all nature---sights, sounds, forms, substances and
compositions---for the actor should be observed with added atten-
tion-magnetizing and feeling-evoking interest. The ability to
focus attention to the point where something is consciously and
meaningfully experienced can and should be self-educated by the

future actor from the earliest age when the desire to seek such a career is experienced.

There's perhaps no other profession or calling which so urgently demands that the total of past observations and experiences be filed away and ready for use upon call. Observations and experiences without sufficient attention given them as they occur are expensive wastes for the actor.

Sounds can hold myriad meanings if they're life process sounds. If they're other *environmental sounds* they constitute the musical accompaniment to fantasies. *Form and composition*---so much a part of any art form---should demand and receive the would-be actor's close and continuous study.

The irritating (for most of us) nextdoor piano attempts of a child can be observed with not only their faults but also with their dedication to tomorrows. The lonely bleating of a calf separated too soon from its mother should be heard with the spirit and understood in all its tragedy.

The rippling of a happy, carefree stream at the winter snow's melting can be musical rather than ignored in passing. The nightsounds in forest clearings can suggest to the fertile imagination the society and culture of the insects, small rodents and wild things they truly are. Even the bustle and clamor of a busy city intersection can be observed to be a symphony (not only for George Gershwin), rather than dismissed as an irritating cacophony of many dissonances. The dense, heavy air in the outer office of a psychotherapist can be listened to with sensitive registering of the silent outcries behind all the fixed smile masks of the patients in chairs across the room.

All these surroundings---sights, sounds, aromas, tastes and touch experiences, if filed away early in the actor's right brain sense and affective memory bins, will more surely be there to imbue theatre, film and television role moments with their completenesses *if the actor has concentrated sufficient attention upon them in those past moments.*

■ **Attention to Other Characters**

One of the most interest-magnetizing objects for someone destined to be an actor should always be the *personalities and behavior patterns of other human beings.* They should be one of the forever continuing studies of the actor ---not simply how people look, how they conduct themselves and how they interact with others. The actor should look more closely with an inner eye.

Most actors, by the time they're developing their careers to the point where they may expect important roles, perhaps even by the time they're first appearing in lesser roles, have experienced enough and sufficiently varied behavior patterns of their own under different conditions that they have a fairly extensive catalog of such moods, feelings and role behavior patterns in their awareness out of the pasts of *their own lives*. They need only to have given their *controlled attention* to those times when they were experienced.

However, there are many personalitiy traits and patterns with which they won't have had first-hand acquaintance---behaviors and traits which they can only have observed in *other people*. In observing those other personalities, it's important for the would-be actor to be able to maintain a form of *controlled attention* that's as free as possible from the bias and conditioning of his or her own personality filters.

Most human beings are by nature and to at least some degree neurotic, as present day psychologists and therapists confirm. Some are only mildly afflicted with such conditioned response while others, behind masks, border upon the psychotic degree.

The problem for the actor, then, is that, like other neurotic beings, it's possible that when encountering others who may present some problem or threat or affront, those other persons may be viewed in terms of their threat (whether real or imagined) to the actor's conditioned self, rather than as the *separate, distinct and unique realities* which those other persons truly represent.

The filtering process of the neurotic is known to be impaired to at least some degree, and if the actor himself is inclined through his own neurotic conditioning to experience *guilt*, for example (even when it's not justified), then another person who by hiw or her own personality causes him to feel guilty once more is triggering some facet of his *guilt moment* mosaic and could be difficult to study without a fierce *control* applied to attention so that the actor's own conditioned response can be short-circuited.

If another actor is conditioned to feel *inadequacy and self doubt* through neurotic conditioning and at some point encounters someone who by some action or comment occasions the *inadequate and self-doubting* moment for the actor, that other person may also become simply a part of the actor's brief experience and not really be seen in the light of his or her own complex nature.

The actor should try to understand the importance of seeing other people and their differences from him in their innate truths. To do it, he needs to *short-circuit his own conditioned responses* and see that person who causes him an unpleasant experience as simply a *different* version of neurosis and *different personality* from the actor's own.

The neurotic too often overlooks the fact that other people are problem-experiencers also. If he can exercise the *controlled attention* being discussed here and bypass his own conditioned responses, he can usually observe that the other person is simply acting out his or her own form of conditioning and is available as *a clinical specimen* for documenting purposes; that the other person, upon strictly objective observation (rather than subjective), may be discovered to be simply going through what they must go through and doing to us what they would do to anyone else. In all probability it has nothing to do with us.

This is so hard for actors to remember sometimes, but it's important to bear in mind whenever possible.

Remember, we're still discussing *Attention.* And we're not discussing the *accidental* attention which attracts and holds us for a brief moment in spite of ourself and then is quickly forgotten. We're discussing its more important aspect . . . *directing it!*

The two examples given are provided as a manner in which the actor may begin early and ideally continue throughout a creative life studying not only what result is occurring in *our own mind and feelings* because of what other people may do that impacts upon us, but also *the unique personalities of those others.*

It isn't easy to bypass one's hurt at another's hands and simply look more closely at the perpetrator of the hurt, but the actor can educate himself to do just that. There's no other way to so effectively study those *other personality categories and their behavior patterns.*

But, after all that observing of other personalities and documenting of them for possible use in roles, there remains the question of where the actor should *direct his attention*. . . even when a role suggests one of those other personalities that we've so carefully documented.

■ Attention to Our Characters' Own Experience

While those behavior patterns of others are valuable in roles for which they apply, the actor should remember that---even when our character is involved in a moment that in the dialogue or action suggests their use---the focus of our attention can more ideally be riveted and remain upon the *experience of our own character* as its (and our own) primary concern.

It's a violation of human nature to afford others too much of our attention. In the moments of a role we should often be *focused on our own character's experience more than on others'.*

Since we're discussing *attention* still, this should be emphasized: The word "attention" is too often applied to only *exter-*

234

nals. It's my strong conviction that, for the sake of *total charac-terization* and the *total experiencing* of our character's own life, the attention of our character---even when it's any one of those characters we've so closely studied in the past---should be direct-ed more to *the experience of our own character!*

In other words, our character---like others it confronts---should whenever possible be acting out its own fantasies and neu-rotic pattern missteps, and whenever it can be justified be focused on *its own experience*, rather than be so continually focused on others' behavior toward it that its own processes remain less con-scious, therefore less experienced. The constant returning of di-rected attention to *our character's own experience* is a natural oc-currence in life and should be the same for our characters.

■ The Ability To Shift our Attention

The actor must also be able to shift his attention from one focus to another at will. Acting roles demand this, and the degree to which this ability is developed is the determining factor as to how effective an actor can be in his truthful experiencing of indi-vidual moments, as those moments change, move from one focus to another, deepen and become more intense here or there, and re-quire sufficient concentration of attention at the threshold of the immediately subsequent moments to transport the actor to the fantasy of the character in the new moments.

Not only alacrity with change, and adjustment to ever-changing focal points for the attention, but also the perception and experiencing of the stimuli causing such changes and adjust-ments, needs to be developed.

Whether it's something seen or overhead or sensed, or some internal, more personal change within the character itself, the actor must educate himself in the art of remaining alert to what's of sufficient importance that it should cause the character to ad-just its concentrated attention to a new focal point, a new object, which then holds the attention for a time.

Each such stimulus, in its own way and by its own occur-rence, demands that the actor either drift easily or leap precipi-tously to the new point of attention. The need for that ability lies waiting around every moment's corner.

An often heard phrase---usually one of the first admonitions of parents and teachers---is *"Pay attention!"* Literally, the actor must learn to *pay with attention* for the many values which can be received from doing it.

By paying attention to highway signposts, accidents are avoided. By paying attention when announcements are made, opportunities are perceived which lead to more opportunities or sig-nal pitfalls or setbacks that can be avoided. By paying attention, living things survive and actors grow more swiftly. In the Lawbook of Acting, *Paying Attention* should be one of the first laws!

Nowhere in the actor's preparation and later experiencing of a role is *attention* more important than in the role's separate liv-ing moments. An actor whose attention is focused on a thought, an object or some other definite item---for the duration of the timespan for which that item is ideal---and then is easily moved to focusing upon a different item as suggested by the writer in a next *Beat* as a situation progresses . . . that actor will be ideally involved in the character's experience.

■ **Next is an item that's so important in actors' work but it's the exact opposite of what some probably inexperienced and certain-ly wrong directors may demand, and what all actors should fight for when the opposite is brought up by one of those directors ...**

Between The Lines

The Actor's Gold Mines Are There!

Have you ever been told by a director to "*Pick up your cues?*" It was probably at an early stage in your acting career, maybe in a local community theatre, when you were still working with fairly amateur directors who didn't know any better.

That admonition probably came from a director who could-n't understand why there was *no life* in what he or she was direct-ing. The assumption was probably made that speeding up the ac-tion and dialogue would create more life. It's a common miscal-culation of nonprofessional directors. The "life" that's hoped for isn't ever in the dialogue in the first place.

Marlon Brando, in a magazine interview some years ago that's mentioned in this book's shortly upcoming item about *Dialogue's Role in the Illusion of The First Time,* pointed out that *"if you watch people's faces when they're talking, you see them search for words, ideas, concepts, a feeling, how to phrase what they're saying."*

Between the lines is where living moments are found. The actor who brings *silent, personal experience between the lines* lit-erally breathes life into any performance, whether it be high drama, comedy, musical theatre or even opera.

236

The *between the lines experiencing* is what the film camera especially looks for and exploits. In proscenium acting---being more distant from the audience, it's often less demanded by directors than it is by film directors. The latter appreciate the continuing closeness with which the camera looks *behind the words and actions* for the personal experience of the character.

Film acting is more *reacting, taking in, being done to by incoming experience, private struggling with thoughts and feelings and other personal experiences behind the lines.* Directors interviewing actors for film especially look for actors with that awareness for any role that has some story importance.

The *"Pick up your cues"* director is, after all, concerned with dialogue exclusively. For the film actor the dialogue, although it may progress a situation, is not what the camera's concerned with. More than any words that appear on the pages of a script, the camera's watching the mind and the body, both during any dialogue and *between the lines.*

If a film director ever admonishes you to *pick up your cues* you may be sure that director is new and inexperienced as to what film is. When a director admonishes you to, you haven't much choice. You'll probably have to do it, even though you know better . . . or head for the nearest exit.

■ **Are you one of those actors who presume to tell their bodies what to do and how to do it every minute of their performances? If you are, as quickly as you can, learn to *listen to your body!***

The Body

is The Actor's Key to The Right Brain

and All Complete Experience!

The body is the actor's instrument. Like any other instrument, it may be neglected, mistreated and long forgotten in the closet of unconsciousness, lying out of tune and without all its parts in functioning order, when unexpectedly needed to join the orchestra and play the music of the actor's mind.

Or it may be maintained in mint condition, constantly tuned and kept ready for the call for its service. It's the only instrument the actor has. It must be available and capable of interpreting the actor's experience under the baton of the right brain.

237

Although it should be a cooperative coworker at all times as well, it's important to realize that the body shouldn't be considered as simply an obedient servant. It's one of the actor's most expert consultants for advice when the actor's searching through the file cabinets of experiential and emotional memories in the right brain for things the left brain might overlook, indeed might be totally unaware of.

Psychologists discuss the two basic behavioral stimuli--- *Unconditioned Stimuli* and *Conditioned Stimuli* in terms of *Unconditioned Stimuli* being things to which the body responds with natural reaction because there's simply an automatic response that fits the situation, and *Conditioned Stimuli* being things to which the body responds in a unique manner because of some preconditioning in the right brain from past experience that's been recorded as being meaningful.

Whenever in the actor's past the mind has experienced something it considered important *the body was moved in its own unique responsive manner.* Often the conscious mind hasn't even observed these small or large behavioral responses at such times, being so riveted to the experience itself in purely *"what's happening"* and *"what to do about it"* terms.

In real life the other, more affective phenomenon occurs with regularity---the full participation of the body with thought and feeling moments of whatever substantive nature. It's a pity that one is denied the alertness to observe what the body does in those moments, since it could otherwise be observed to repeat *fairly similar behaviors over and over again* in fairly similar experiencing moments of the right (subconscious) brain while the left (conscious) mind is ignoring it.

The observation of what the body does---the considering of why it expands, contracts or contorts in a similar manner when impacting moments of similar natures recur is a fascinating study focus. And the need for the actor to try to observe the emotional body more closely in such moments, and to remember those moments later with respect to their physical responses, extends far beyond the fact that it's an engrossing study.

While the left brain of the conscious mind may *direct* the body into conceptual movements as logical manners of handling emotional and feeling moments and escape from them---with such direction being based in the main on observation of *reasoning and even other people's* observed patterns, the body itself---if consulted in a productive manner to gain its more accurate and more personal contribution---can lend far more organic and more unique truth of its own *while the experience is occurring, without conceptual direction.*

This phenomenon lay undiscovered by all but the more scientific minds for decades, in fact centuries. The period when the phrase *"Seized by the devil"* was applied to contorted, twisted, demented poor souls should have produced deeper inquiry into why the body so skillfully signaled to all that someone was *"out of his mind" and "into his body"*, where experience and conditioned response ruled more mightily than any logic or coordination the individual might have attempted to engage.

It remained for the passing of time and the research of Ribot, Charcot, Freud and Pavlov's *"conditioned response"* discoveries to begin to reveal some of the separate functions of the left and right brains and the different manners in which the two relate and interact with the body.

As important for actors as were the codifications and eventual system contributions of Stanislavski and others, were those in scientific quarters involving the researchings and findings of scientists involved with furthering the new investigations into those *two separate worlds* inside human beings' heads, where two countries situated so close to each other nevertheless live two so different lives and speak two so different tongues.

We now understand that the left brain stores data and information, knowledge of how to coordinate, organize and exercise logic, etc. It can theorize, assess, manipulate body events, handle tools and call forth all nature of information and step-by-step procedures for accomplishing desired results.

That it can also *feel* (in its own limited way, mostly physical) is understood, but its feeling experience is limited to the intelligence spectrum. It more feels *about* than truly *feels* in any degree of depth experiencing terms.

Relating this inadequacy to acting, the intellectually conceived manner of directing the body as to how to handle itself as accompaniment to an important feeling experience is based more on *observation of others' behavior* than on the *combined right brain and body experience* of the actor.

Acting which preceded the emerging awareness of the two separate brains and the different behavioral stimuli was much of the time based purely on the interpretation of generalized, universally accepted and observed movement patterns of others.

Acting teachers of the present period often refer to such miming as "representing"---which it truly is; "playing results"---the results of observation of others; and "manifesting"---demonstrating on the surface pretended feelings and body participations which the left brain has judged to be appropriate.

But it's the *right* brain that contains the file cabinets of all truly emotional experience in its dusty repository.

Seldom visited by exclusively socially oriented people whose lives are adapted to their environments to such a degree that their capacities for feeling are drawfed, the *right* brain's file department is literally the repository of *all of our meaningful past experiences,* whether they were considered important or unimportant by the left brain when they were experienced.

So many actors past and present have believed that they were using all that was available out of their own lives when they accessed only the data and information, perhaps also the logic, in the left brain files. They were not.

Unfortunately, the left brain can't ideally communicate with the right brain because it speaks in only data, logic and "formula-speak" words, no matter how very reasonable and appropriate-seeming those words may be. So the left brain isn't able to access the same wonderful secrets the right brain can. There's a high, forbidding wall of language barrier between them.

If the left brain should even attempt to consult the file clerks in the right brain and knows that, for instance, a certain feeling should be filed under the logical word "sadness", it can't possibly know that the right brain clerks have filed "sadness" over and over again under perhaps "yellow" or "satin". Ridiculous as this may seem to some actors, these disparities between the two brains have been determined to exit, and the single means of bridging the language gap between the two is *the body!*

The body works almost full time with the right brain clerks, filing away experience after experience as each occurs and responding in physically visible patterns to everything the right brain experiences.

It works only part-time, and not as intimately, with the left brain, because the latter file clerks treat it as a servant. It's told by the left brain people when and how to do certain things physically and treated as a mere functionary able to provide hands, feet and muscles for the doing of things the left brain can't do without it. The left brain works only *through* the body, not *with* it.

The body is the simple answer to involving both brains in the acting process. It's the only intermediary who speaks the language of the right brain and still understands what the left brain people are calling for.

If encouraged to choose the words which hold any hope of communication between the two, the body can easily find those words which have data and information relativity for the left brain and which also have experiential and emotional memory preciseness for the right brain.

It's interesting to observe some actors preparing their characters' experiences, beat after beat, in roles:

One actor sits, eyes tightly squinted, in an almost catatonic stillness, trying to focus on what the character *should be* thinking and feeling, while trying to decide the content of a beat.

That actor is mentally thumbing through file folders of almost exclusively *left brain, consciously observed* behavior, often even of others' more than of his own. In the end, that actor will find that what was planned and what was hoped would produce a kinetic experience for both the character and himself produces nothing more than carefully orchestrated and laboriously guided *"acting"* that's judged to be *right* for the moment.

■ The Body Is The Key To The Right Brain

Now, watch another actor preparing. His body contorts, his eyes close tightly, his hand pushes on his forehead in despair and his mouth hangs open. *He knows instinctively* what his character must be thinking and feeling in the moment being planned, and knows that by putting himself through a *"body-searching"* process---fragment moments of the desired focus on the beat's most affecting aspects, as *he knows them personally*---the body's habit responses to his own right brain experiences will touch and crystallize many of those *uniquely personal, feeling-related stimuli words* that lie in the dusty memory bin of the right brain. Those are the depth-experiencing words---the keys---he needs to find ---and can find---in the *"body-searching"* process, once he learns how to use it.

For some actors this *"consulting the body"* procedure appears too complicated to even try, until they've tried it and observed the amazing results of the best way some of us know for consulting the body for its miracles.

What's especially remarkable is that even when certain words are telegraphed back by the body we can't understand why they've been produced. Unfortunately, the snobbishly logical left brain file clerks think the right brain clerks sending those messages back to the body are in utter confusion and malfunctioning.

Here's what the "body searching" process is hoping to---and more often than not really can---produce kinetically for the actor's use out of the *Affective Memory, Experiential Memory and Emotional Recall* files of the right brain:

In a childhood moment of anguish over the killing of a barnyard animal friend for the family's food during the winter, the child---experiencing the anguished moment mentally and emotionally---didn't notice the contortions of its body, one after another. The body, triggered by the altered mental state and the agitation of the total being, participated in the moment with extreme contortion and a definite reactive behavior pattern of its own.

241

Always more observant to sensory surroundings than the crying child's left brain could notice as it lay crying desperately on the old patchwork quilt of its bed, *the body*, filing the incident away, did notice vividly and remembers its most vivid impression as being the old patchwork quilt. *"Patchwork"* or perhaps simply *"Quilt"* became a key word.

Later in life the child (by then an actor), in seeking to recall that terrible moment for its product in preparing a role, remembers the anguish and may attempt to utilize that feeling, expecting the body to respond as it did originally. Unfortunately, in trying to reevoke that remembered moment of *anguish*, the actor doesn't understand that the body's total responses are filed in the right brain under *"Patchwork"* or *"Quilt"*.

Another example: A child may have been separated from its twin at a very early age, with the resulting traumatic experience at the point of separation. The crying, hysterical child of that moment may not even have consciously noticed the heady, sickening *"Lilac"* perfume of the woman who came to take away the other twin for adoption.

Later in adult life, the actor can remember with the left brain the details of the separation moment, the extreme mental desperation experienced, and the fact that the body reacted wildly in some forgotten manner throughout the event. He'd like to rekindle the body's participation.

He hopes the desired participation of the body in an adult acting moment can be rekindled and ignited through reconstructing those pieces of data that are still consciously available in the left brain files. Pehaps the actor tries to reevoke the desired experience in a class devoted to the *Affective Memory* exercise described earlier.

Unfortunately, the important keyword *"Lilac"* that would elicit both the body's total participation and the right brain's emotional reexperiencing would probably not be found in that manner, since the perfume itself may have hardly if at all been noticed consciously in that long ago moment. The actor, even in an *Affective Memory* exercise , might recall every sensory item *but* the perfume. The exercise would be a failure. The body, unfortunately for the actor, could only respond totally to the single kinetic key *"Lilac"*.

Whatever mood, feeling, emotion you're seeking to reexperience, your *body* and the *right brain* are where it has been previously experienced. The left brain has simply documented the fact that it occurred . . . then probqbly even lost the file folder or computer data disk where the event's moment by moment outline was recorded.

When any experience is sufficiently meaningful it *moves the body . . . and the body remembers!* It's in the reexperiencing of the *physical* moment---*with the body fully involved*---that the complete circuit of *mind / body / feeling totality* can become reinvolved as it does in our real life moments.

It's really quite easy to *"consult the body"* and persuade it to supply those important key words that will involve the full responses of the right brain!

The *"body-searching"* process, described in the earlier *"Creative Psychological Objectives"* chapter and being discussed again here, isn't at all the same as the Affective Memory exercise of Strasberg and others. Even when that exercise is conducted by a guide continually prompting the actor to remember the sensory objects of some long ago experience one after another, the often predictable failure of that exercise approach occurs because it's still too often the "documenting" clerks of the left brain that are being consulted.

The right brain clerks---the keepers of the keys!---often simply watch and chuckle as the actor struggles with only conscious memory of the event (the total the left brain clerks' files can provide) with little if any awareness of the *body*, which is the only intermediary that could so easily bring the desired result!

The process of memory-consulting simply needs to be reversed. There's enough knowledge of *logically appropriate* body movement patterns in emotional stress moments of all kinds stored in even the *left* brain that some actors can achieve continuing success without ever finding those important key words which the total body recognizes. Yet there's only one step further which those actors would need to learn and take in order to involve the *body and the right brain* in their processes.

Mere *logical appropriateness* for such moments isn't the same as, or nearly as effective as, the far less generalized, more personally specific body responses which apply to the specific actor involved. The phrase *"One size fits all"* doesn't work for actors' individual and unique emotional resources.

But those *intellectually applicable* body responses at least offer that much to start with as the actor begins to search for what will involve the body in an exciting manner and---via rekindling the body's experiential memory---also access the wonderful resources of the right brain.

■ **Body-Searching**

Employing a *sequence of body movement progressions, one after another, each very briefly,* and the conscious directing of the body into those many patterns, moment after moment, while maintaining *a self-willed, intensified degree of the desired feeling*, is the step needed to seek the miracle of the body's exciting word keys for accessing the right brain.

Prompting the body through an ever-changing movement experience instinctively associated with the feeling patterns and varied peaks of such moments, while (to the degree possible) continually experiencing the desired sensations of the moment in an intensified level of experiencing them, there remains the single step of *"asking the body"* to crystallize the words that, one after another, are occurring to it.

Almost immediately, the body begins reaching into and finding the most potent associative memory fragments that lie filed away but forgotten. Those fragments of impressions that occur during this *body-searching* are uniquely *yours!*

In the process, with the left brain's clerks observing as they will be, should the body produce a very clear impression of a *wavy rainbow*, or perhaps *Kilroy* or some other seemingly abstract item, sound, texture, aroma or whatever, the logic with which we and the left brain clerks are observing the process and its result might deny, doubt or even ridicule whatever the body is so clearly suggesting.

A wavy rainbow? . . . or Kilroy? How could either possibly mean anything important to us? How could either possibly have any pertinence? We're of course responding to the whispering in our ear by those doubting, ever so logical left brain clerks.

It's those actors who learn to respect these strange-seeming results who have the answer. It's the actor who understands that somewhere, in some distant and forgotten past experience, a very clear association with the combined emotional and physical experience he's looking for in that moment was filed by the right brain clerks *at the direction of the body*, not the left brain, under *"wavy rainbow"* or perhaps *"Kilroy"*.

The actor need not and probably won't even remember that when he was four the family's big dog broke into his pet Kilroy's rabbit hutch and the last of Kilroy was a mortal squeal. He *needn't even try to remember* those source moments!

When an actor comes to trust this process and employs it with increasing effectiveness through practice, that actor will find so many heightened degrees and colors of feeling and emotion which have been reevoked by the *body* becoming the finding agent instead of the far less effective left brain file clerks.

Whatever manner the actor may be taught for putting these word keys to use for their emotional result, the fact that they can be so easily discovered through the body itself is the miracle!

■ The Body . . . As Social Marionette

If one aspires to a career as a businessman or businesswoman, or is planning a life as a socialite, a club president or a politician, there are behavior items to be learned and cultivated . . . social norms and rules of etiquette and protocol that are primary ingredients in the recipes for success in those milieux.

What those norms and rules are, ultimately depends upon the precise parameters within which they're designed to function, also upon the kinds of people within those circles to whose norms and etiquette standards we're expected to conform.

It's so easy for actors to generalize themselves into logically appropriate images, to such a degree that they appear more as marionettes than as unique personalities. Whatever kind or degree of self-conscious norm-courting may be advisable or judged to be necessary for success in some other professions, it's self-defeating for the actor to follow such a dull body-adapting course.

The *learning* of common etiquette, social poise and acceptable behavior under social conditions is of course a good thing for all. There are occasions in any profession when they're requisites. For the actor, though, they should be viewed as characteristics of behavior required for "public roles" of brief duration.

Just as they're learned by Social Register debutantes in finishing schools or by young men from wealthy families in academies for those later roles in society, they should be viewed by actors and actresses to be the same mere "roles". They seldom have much to do with inner thoughts and feelings. Like dark suits and dinner dresses, they should simply be hung in actors' closets ready to be put on for cerain public events.

■ The Body . . . As The Actor's instrumental Entertainer

The actor should devote himself or herself more to the *private, much more personal* body patterns, always consciously expanding the resourcefulness in employing the body and its behavior patterns in emotional and feeling moments more closely tied to *experience* than to social norm.

To help cultivate this habit of always looking for more interesting manners of doing things---thereby gaining added experiential values in each such moment as well as appearing far more personal---in addition to simply, always and very consciously, noticing those moments when the body is "sleepwalking" dully through what it does, and easily turning the same moments into some kind of self-entertaining, there's the acting class exercise mentioned earlier that I've often used in class, called *"Find a Different Way"*, involving simply doing what's done in a different and unusual manner . . . picking up a telephone, sitting down, walking across a room, opening a door, reading a book, hugging a mate, sitting at a desk or table, emptying an ashtray, even simply standing. Even outside classes it's a manner of constantly training the body to enjoy everyday things.

Not mentioned earlier, when conducting the exercise in a class, at different moments of the exercise, as the actor does some ordinary task in a different way, I've called out *"What you is this?"* to prompt them into recognizing a type or personality or mood the different way has produced. *"My impish me,"* one actor might call back, or *"My balls to the wall me"* another once yelled back. *"My sneaking in the house me,"* another. In this manner they're prompted to experience more consciously and enjoy the personality and mood variations which might not be part of their accustomed manners.

Theatre and film directors often encourage actors to *find a different way* to do some of those ordinary tasks, to bring the body of the actor into more interesting participation. Any of those small tasks can be deadly dull if done in "sleepwalking" manners. All that's required to make them more interesting is *finding a different way* to do them. It needn't be extreme. Just enjoy having some, any kind of momentary experience with it. Nothing's more attractive than seeing somebody enjoy doing what they do.

In that class, one of the inspiration-producing exercises might be a *"Hi, Honey, I'm Home"* exercise for two people. Either the husband or wife enters the front door---of course in an unusual physical manner, and calls out the *"Hi, Honey, I'm Home"* second step of the improvisation. From the other door of the set comes the mate---in an unusual manner from the very moment of entering. They then go toward each other---each in a different, unusual way, and meet in the center---in a different way, and do whatever comes next in a different way too.

The work of an actor who does most things in a distinctly different (from usual) and unique way becomes increasingly interesting to observe, and it's probable that if there's the option available for the viewer between watching such an actor and another actor in a scene who does everything correctly and simply in a purely functionary manner, the former will be given far more attention by the viewer!

■ **Avoid Those Strictly "Centered" Positions Whenever Possible**

Another item of which actors should be aware is the difference between *obviously social* positions and *private (personal experience)* positions. Becoming aware of the difference, and doing something about it, is another way of encouraging the body to give us pleasure.

There are actors, as well as other people, who by habit and from social training almost always sit erect and "centered" in most situations, looking like self-conscious job applicants in employment interviews more than anything else. Those actors have probably never noticed how stiff they appear, how automatically focused on another person their attention appears, how robotically impersonal they appear, and how robotically impersonal they in fact feel.

"Centering" is the problem. Nice for social and formal situations, "Centering" is a straitjacket that kills or at least inhibits personal experiencing for the actor.

What is *Centering*? Sit in your chair now. Lay both your elbows on the chair arms with your hands both hanging over or clasping the front of the chair arms in the same position. Sit erect, with both feet in front of you squarely on the floor in the same position. Don't you feel totally *centered*? . . . like the job applicant mentioned previously, trying to make a good impression?

Also, don't you feel you're *aimed directly at someone across from you*? Of course you are. Try to imagine the kinds of scenes and situations where the position feels right. You won't think of many. Notice that any you do think of are probably simply *talking* positions having little to do with any *personal experience*.

Actors hoping for the optimum of personal expriencing in their work should in all possible moments *work in off-center positions!* This recommendation probably demands some explanation for the immediately skeptical actor whose acting training may have been primarily classical:

It's true that in earlier centuries and even as recently as the Edwardian and Victorian eras so many theatrical characters were socially correct, stiff and proper in most role moments. But how often do you see these characters (except as stereotypes or cartoons) in contemporary drama?   I'd venture not often.

We've come out of the *"dialogue"* and *"talk about it"* acting eras. There aren't that many drawingroom scenes anymore. In contemporary drama and comedy the characters actually go home and relax or have domestic squabbles, or if they don't play out their dramas at home or in some private arena they relax their social behaviors in most other locations as well, whether in athletic gyms, workout spas, on park benches, in skid row doorways or alleys, in airport waiting rooms or even in executive offices and ritzy salons.

Contemporary roles are more often *psychologically* oriented. Dramas are *far more personal* of nature. A habitually "cen-

247

tered" actor usually doesn't even get past the first reading interview for most roles these days.

Now, try something different in your chair: Loll sideways. Lean your head sideways onto one hand. Let each leg do whatever it wants to, as long as it's different from the other leg. Now, with no part of your body in a centered position, again give some thought to the many situations where you'd feel right. There's no limit to the number you'll come up with this time . . . because your new position takes you out of the stiff, social feeling into all kinds of potentially *personal experiences*.

Now, one more step: Staying in that position, imagine yourself in even the job applicant role mentioned earlier. Of course you might want to take your foot off the desk (if that's where it felt like going to a moment before), but stay lolling to one side, maybe even still leaning your head on your hand, still essentially off-center in every detail.

And suppose you're the Personnel Manager conducting the interview . . . which applicant would you probably give first consideration to? . . . the self-conscious, ultra-correct person who's totally centered, trying so hard to make a good impression and appearing so insecure, judging from its maintaining of such a stiff, "communication only" position? . . . or the apparently self-assured person who's confident enough to be himself or herself without stiffness, and whose manner of sitting before you suggests that working with them would be a much closer, more personal relationship? Doesn't the latter's position even suggest more the confident person you'd want sitting behind a desk in any important position with your company?

The point for the actor is that there aren't that many purely *social* roles written these days.

With some exceptions of course, even top executives and other professionals are now expected to appear as more *"personal experience"* types than as the stiffly social types of those earlier decades.

And don't fail to notice that *working off-center* is a much more enjoyable experience for you, the actor, as it prompts a feeling of total relaxation and unguarded openness that the stiff, centered folks will never experience.

In your private life too---to the extent you can without offending the sometimes socially self-conscious matriarchs and patriarchs among your relatives who may still be living with and observing the social norms of earlier times, try to remember to practice and enjoy more *"off-center"* body use.

■ You, I---all of us---long ago developed fictions about our bodies; felt them imperfect in one way or another. Imperfect though they may in fact be, or be simply imagined by us to be because they're not like others' bodies, they're what we must work with.

Body Habits Correction

Freeing The Body From Image-Connected Obstructions

There's a manner I've used for dealing with body concerns of actors and helping them become aware of how in the past they've obstructed some of their process freedom, created unnecessary limitations in their characterization and performance experiences, and formed habits and mannerisms that don't work to advantage with otherwise excellently prepared characterizations.

The phrase *"Body Habits Correction"* might suggest that only the body is concerned. But the fact that body habits are vitally connected with *self image* concerns is the big problem in any attempt to help actors overcome those habits which were formed so long ago in the interest of presenting socially acceptable selves.

The actor who exhibits certain body habits which often recur and constantly get in the way of and obstruct some of his processes generally has some psychological problems of identity, self image or desired social image type creating those habits.

Such problems---even if conscious, which they most often aren't anymore---are probably very well hidden, but the body habits they've helped create are not.

Rather than attempt to discuss any of the many individual psychological problems that can and do create body habits and mannerisms, I'll save time by getting quickly to a form of body habits therapy I've found helps focus the actor's attention on the body and movement mannerisms, illustrates the manner in which they affect his work and, after bringing them out into conscious awareness, offers a manner of working through the problems they've created.

First, let's assume that we're already conditioned to think certain things about ourselves in our manner of relating to our environment, as mentioned in an earlier chapter, by the time we've reached those formative years when we're persuaded to believe what parents, friends, teachers, relatives and neighborhood friends tell us we are (over and over, in much the same words). That would be enough, but it doesn't end there.

Also in those childhood years we've encountered other people's pronouncements about certain *physical* aspects of our being.

We've probably spent hours of worry in front of mirrors hoping to convince ourselves that those things others are saying about us and about our body are groundless. In most cases, those attempts at self-persuasion have failed.

Unfortunately, standing there before our mirror, instead of telling us those other people are wrong, our mirror confirms what we've been told. There really is that problem---that telltale clue, that imperfection of some part of our body that's bound to hold us back as we approach adulthood and strive for life goals.

Of course it doesn't occur to us at the time that those physical differences between us and others around us wouldn't seem so terrible if they weren't by this time closely connected in our minds with things that are bothering us about ourselves in purely psychological identity terms as well.

For example, if too many people have told us that we're *"lazy and good for nothing"*, then, looking in the mirror, we'll also note that our body which has been called *"weak"* or *"sickly"* is indeed *"lazy and good for nothing"* also. Or if we've been constantly scolded for being *"dumb"*, looking in the mirror, our body which has been called things like *"pimply"* or *"scarface"* is also very apparently *"dumb"*.

Those completely unjustified associations are formed, and we immediately go to work to calculatedly develop body positions and movement patterns that are intended to cover up those physical shortcomings and lessen the chances of being rejected because of what we imagine they tell people about us.

For people who later go into other professions this curious association of carefully projected image with apparent and unacceptable or at least unfortunate aspects of our body would matter less. For actors, though, the resulting (even though imagined) association matters. It really does.

The actor is called upon to play many different kinds of roles during a productive career. Those many roles demand an instrument that's as free as possible from any limiting conditions and unshakable mannerisms, whether they be real or imagined.

As actors, we may have a whole catalog of unconscious mannerisms which result from those long ago found solutions which seemed at the time ideal cover-ups for whatever bothered us about ourselves, whether psychological or physical.

Those mannerisms will remain with us throughout our lives if they aren't consciously dealt with. For actors, they come back to plague us in moments when directors make perfectly innocent demands or suggestions that feel vaguely or acutely uncomfortable for us. In the end we of course have to do what the director says, but we're either vaguely or even agitatedly upset as we force ourselves to do what's been requested, without any clear understanding of why it's upsetting to us.

Later, in performance, we approach those moments with a conscious dread because of the discomfort and embarassment they bring with them. We're self-conscious as we go through those moments. They'll simply never be comfortable for us, and we try to find manners of sneaking past them. We may not succeed.

There are more of these *"body habit problems"* in each of us than we realize until someone---perhaps an observant acting coach---can help us bring them out of hiding into conscious awareness and provide some prescribed work to overcome the acting instrument restrictions they produce.

Here's the exercise which I designed years ago and have used in my acting classes from time to time with many remarkable results:

Each actor is asked to prepare a list of, say, three or four parts of his or her physical body that s/he doesn't like. After some moments each individual sits before the class and mentions the first of the three or four items and is asked to show the class clearly what s/he's talking about.

The slight flabiness around the middle might be called a *"fat blob middle"*; the hump in a nose might be called by the actor a *"groundhog nose"*; the receding hairline might be called a *"clown makeup forehead"*; two larger than normal ears might be *"rabbit ears"* or *"donkey ears."* Actors will probably grin sheepishly as they point out the characteristics they're talking about.

After they've stated and demonstrated their first item (before they proceed to the second), they're asked by me (1) *"What's wrong with having a . . .?"*, to which the reply (after a brief moment of thought) will probably be an unpleasant adjective or character label that *"What's wrong with having a . . . (the item)?"* suggests. Perhaps it's *"dumb"* or *"ugly"*.

Immediately, then, they're asked (2) *"What does it make you feel to have dumb donkey ears* (or whatever)*?"* Again there'll probably come another adjective or unpleasant label, a different one, maybe *"Hicky."* Then (3), *"What do you think other people automatically think someone is who has dumb, hicky donkey ears?"* Again, an adjective or unpleasant label will come. (Each of those adjectives and labels needs to be jotted down.)

Finally, they're asked (4) *"Show us what you do to keep people from noticing your dumb, hicky, stupid donkey ears."*

The answer comes, with a physical illustration (or maybe two or three different physical devices). It's exciting to an entire class made up of friends who've watched each other's work and

251

have been aware of certain repeated body positions and manner-isms---this moment of finding out *why the actor walks the way he walks, sits the few ways he customarily sits, uses his hands in certain ways time and time again, etc.*

The person being interiewed feels little or no embarassment as he goes through this questioning and comes out with all those unflattering labels and adjectives with deepest honesty. Even in the next step of demonstrating for the onlookers precisely what he's talking about, he still feels no threat because the realization of the connection between the habit mannerism and its source is in that moment fascinating him too.

And when he's showing them the special walk he uses or the way or ways he customarily sits to keep people from noticing whatever he's talking about there's usually warm, friendly recognition laughter from those who've seen that special, sometimes slightly strange walk or sitting position so many times before.

Because of the manner in which the questioning is conducted and the unthreatening atmosphere made possible by the fact that the discussion is---or so it seems to him---purely *physical*, whenever there's chuckling at something (which is sure to happen as details are shared) he can easily share in it.

After thoroughly discussing that first item that he doesn't like about himself the actor is asked to move on to the second disliked item, and so on, with exactly the same procedures and sequence of questions asked for each of the second, third and fourth items.

Of course there may be those two or three people who *"don't dislike anything"* about their bodies. Pressed a little, there are usually a few things that *"used to bother"* them but *"don't anymore."* They feel they're being completely truthful, and probably are to the extent they can be. The resulting physical devices have become so unconscious that they can't be thought of.

While the others---more conscious in varying degrees as to what physical items still bother them---have been able to come up quickly with those adjective and label associations, the person who *"isn't bothered anymore"* will have to reach back into distant memory not only to come up with what used to bother them but also to remember why those items bothered them long ago.

These people's mannerisms and frequently repeated body positions are probably just as fixed and are often as easily observable as those of the folks who still remain more conscious of them in the present. Once pressured to remind themselves of the items that *"used to bother"* them, and giving their *raisons d' etre*, the *"not anymore"* actors can glean just as much benefit from the interview's reexamination of them.

In addition to the fact that this area is possibe to be dug into in a spirit of sharing and unthreatened self-exposure in this manner, there is also a manner of achieving some very interesting and effective results afterward.

During the itemizing and discussiing of those items the actor will have amassed a list of some twelve to perhaps sixteen unflattering labels and adjectives in responding to the questions that are designed to elicit exactly those many responses.

The response words will be read back to the actors, one after another, they should jot them all down, and each person will then be asked to take a few moments and pick *the word or label that they most dislike.* Normally, it'll clearly apply to the mannerism and source which is the most pronounced in the actor's work. But, if the actor seems suddenly evasive and picks a word which very apparently seems less confronting to him, the coach should persist in helping guide him (willing or not) to the more obviously affecting label.

After all have their most disliked labels chosen and are aware of their sources, there's the step of indelibly etching into the actor's consciousness the discoveries and what they create in physical limitations (even if not also in mental inhibitions).

There's seldom enough time in the same class for even one improvisation per person to allow the next step to be taken. For most productive taking of that step, it should be taken in the next subsequent class. Two improvisations, minimum, should be scheduled, but three are ideal for that next step.

■ **"Body Habit" Characters**

Each actor is asked to prepare *three different characters* whose personalities are to be constructed in the following manner: (1) a character who *hates, but has to live with being* that labeled personality; (2) a character who is *proud of being* that labeled personality and flaunts it; and (3) a character who is *the complete opposite* of that label. They're asked to *prepare* the characters in that sequence, but when presenting them they're later told to present them, for good reason, in the opposite sequence. The actors should be asked to jot down those exact guidelines, to make sure they prepare correctly.

The actors should bring each character to the next class replete with appropriate wardrobe, props, hairstyles and whatever else they'll require for the bringing of each of those personality types. They should be asked to improvise first meetings in a place where strangers meet. Conferences, resort hotel lobbies, airport lounges, railroad or bus waiting rooms and similar locations that can serve ideally.

They should be told to prepare every possible manner of *"showing and telling"* and *"broadcasting"* that they're the kind of personality they are in each label's case.

They should plan what to talk about that will "broadcast" who and what they are---business, home, foods, names to drop, places their characters would brag about, books they'd have read and would recommend, types of activities their kind of character would like, etc.

In any serious acting class it'll offer a nice change of pace and the people will probably look forward to it, anticipating the comedy that will obviously result in one or two of their "body" characters and the stark drama that will result in one or two of the others.

For the teacher it's a very serious result that can be achieved. In observing the resulting work from three different angles, the coach can judge the best steps to help eradicate the actor's body habit problem---at least the one chosen, but often several, since they're often related. It could on the other hand clarify how the coach can help the actor comfortably utilize some imagined imperfections and their sources in some constructive manner, now that they've been brought to a more conscious awareness.

Two other benefits of this exercise are (1) that the actor will have found that those kinds of characters and role moments which have caused body-use embarassment in the past are easily within comfortable experiencing, and (2) there'll probably have occurred a significant breakthrough on the part of the actor into some new and possibly important characterization areas that otherwise could never have occurred to him.

■ **The other inhibitor of actors' freer experiencing is one that's quite similar but for best curative work needs to be presented to actors as being something else entirely...**

Desired Images And Their Opposites

...For Coming Out From Behind Ourselves!

Desired images can be just as limiting for actors as those real or imagined body imperfections. These too need to be dealt with.

So the following is another class exploration of my own devising for opening the actor's doors to wider characterization horizons---while accomplishing signifantly more than that at the same time.

No matter how we spent our very earliest years---and sometimes precisely because of how we did spend them, at some point we began "role playing" in our daily lives. As our goals and concerns changed, their achievement demanded new masks, new costumes and new behavior patterns to complete the newly embarked upon *performances.*

You might pause for a moment at this point and think of the image you currently want to project socially. As you read this, observe the way you're sitting. Are you sitting that way because that's how an *actor* sits, or how an *honest person* sits, or how a *people-pleaser* sits, or how a *king of the mountain* sits?

Now, if you've just changed position, look at that new position you've unconsciously settled into. Isn't it just one more of the limited few that spells (again) *actor, honest person, people pleaser* or *king of the mountain* or whatever? I'd wager it is.

Examine what you wore in public today. Wasn't it calculated to present the same image? And your hair style? And the way you walk? The car you drive? The colors and fabrics and styles you wear? They're all there, aren't they?---as if you've made a list, studied it, memorized it, to be the *very picture* of what you want people to see you as, rather than what you know you are inside.

What actors---more than people in some other professions---can benefit from observing is that all those surface calculations, all those bits of *"window dressing"*, have probably blended together into a hardened, shell-like outer layer of limitations, obstructing many natural impulses and richnesses which can't break the surface shell to come out.

The *"Desired Image"* is a lifeless cocoon that holds too many actors in its hardened casing. A perceptive teacher, upon noting that an actor is so imprisoned, should immediately find some manner of helping to break the cocoon surface and encouraging the actor to either discard it and walk away from it or at least climb back into it only when necessary for some social purpose.

If an actor is continually observed to be bringing little more than conceptual work to characterization, with each attempt producing little more than carefully executed ideas with little or no true inner experiencing behind those "character pictures", it should be a clear sign to the teacher that there are parts of the actor's inner truths and emotional experience which are being denied and laid aside from any amount of use either in the planning of characters or the performance of them.

It should also be recognized by the teacher that there can never be true feeling experience brought by these image-playing actors until they explore and fall in love with their own inner truths than with the cardboard characters they otherwise bring.

255

Like the title of this discussion, I call one of my class explorations the *"Desired Image and Necessary Opposite"*.

All members of the class are instructed to spend some length of time considering specifically what their own current *desired images* are. Each is instructed to jot down a list of personality labels which they'd like people to view as attributes of their totality, then to combine the most evocative labels into just one label of about two or three words.

For example, a gregarious and attention-seeking class member might ponder for a time over words like *likeable, interesting, friendly, Good Joe,* maybe even *stimulating*, then decide to add still more and different words such as *attention-needing, sophisticated, athletic* and maybe more which seem unrelated but are all still part of what the actor wants to be recognized to be.

This will take each member some time, but eventually each might decide all those labels can at least peripherally be combined (because the teacher has instructed that they shall be) in a fairly all-inclusive label such as *"Hotshot team prodder"* or some other label, and be pleased with the image this label implies. All class members will be pleased. All labels are of course pleasant!

The next step in such a class is to have all members come forward individually and state their individual labels, then explain what the adjectives and labels mean to them personally.

There's usually considerable insight to be gained as to the individuals' psychological orientations through this step alone, but in addition it brings clearer self-observation to the individuals themselves through having to bring into conscious awareness and put into words their desired images' makeups and their component parts.

When all class members have stated and discussed their image labels they should then be directed to form into words what would be *"The Exact Opposites"* of those labels.

Some class members will come up with labels which are precisely that---exact opposites of their desired images. But some will inadvertently come up with labels which they personally feel to be opposites but which to other ears, hearing those labels, seem unrelated.

Those apparently unrelated opposites shouldn't be changed, because in some such cases they will be what the individuals believe themselves to more truly be, behind their desired image masks.

It's common for, say, the *"Hotshot Team Prodder"* to come up with a *"Stupid"* or *"Clumsy Deadbeat"*; for a *"Hypersensitive Extremist"* to come up with a *"People-Hating Injustice Collec-*

tor"; etc. It's unusual for the *"Mysterious Elegant Lady"*, on the other hand, to come up with a *"Self-Centered Rat Trap"* or an *"Identity Hitchhiker"* or something else seemingly unrelated. Either of those latter labels might, though, be exactly what the actress secretly thinks she is inside, and should be accepted without question.

This exploration, like the *"Body Habits Correction"* one, will probably require two separate class sessions in a row for optimum effectiveness. For the second session, the same procedure is followed in the preparation of at least two characters for two separate improvisations to be located, again, in a place where participants are strangers meeting for the first time.

They should be asked to prepare (1) a character totally based on the *desired image* label and (2) a character totally based on the *opposite* label, with (in addition to the emotional tools chosen to bring such personalities) the previously listed items as well--- wardrobe, props, hairstyle, catch phrases, topics of conversation, appropriate sitting, standing and walking manners, etc., all again planned to "show and tell" and "broadcast" for others the exact personalities they are (as either their #1 or #2 character) and make sure others get their messages in every way possible.

It's remarkable to see that, for fairly obvious reasons, the *Opposite* and normally disliked image characterization will be *so rich and full of beautiful highlights, shadings and feeling experience!* This often happens because the actor is working on what he 's personally ashamed of being inside. Sometimes it's because he or she has studied the undesired image categories so thoroughly in the process of avoiding any association with them, as a result has a full catalog of those adversaries' patterns.

I've found that the *"Desired Image and Necessary Opposite"* exploration is a quick device for introducing actors caught up in image-presenting to a whole new gardenful of personality experiences, and often it's a means of quickly bringing into their work many of those more deeply felt inner experiences and impulses which have long ago been laid aside and hidden.

Following the encouraging comments of the actors' peers for what occurred in those *"negative"* characters, some dynamic changes in the actors' work patterns begin immediately!

■ **Are you one of those actors who's pleased with critics' and others' comments that you're *"very interesting,"* *"fascinating to watch,"* *"entertaining"* or some other word or phrase that's nice to hear? That may be all you are as an actor.**

Depth

The Expanding Of Reality

There are some actors who achieve success *without* depth of true feeling or emotion, because of such actors' perhaps otherwise expert use of their own interesting personalities or their unique qualities as strictly character actors, but it's seldom that there'll be that quality that evokes sympathy or even much empathy on the part of the observer.

We watch such actors and perhaps enjoy the creative qualities they may bring to their performances, but we experience little from watching them save amusement, admiration for their theatricality or fascination with their intellectually contrived *petit pointes* as they present us with attention-attracting mosaics of personality and surface details.

Such actors are frequently developed in prolonged periods of being "teachers' pets" in college or university Drama Departments and early community theatre performances. From the start they're usually seen to have interesting personality traits which entertain onlookers, and those qualities encourage their being cast often in roles which can best profit from those interesting qualities.

There's usually the unfortunate tendency on the part of their instructors and director friends to exploit those benefits for productions by limiting those actors' role-castings to precisely those kinds of characters.

The actors so categorized, and so regularly appreciated for their work within those parameters, sometimes tend to neglect possible developments and techniques for achieving greater depth, eschewing the latter because their personalities seem to offer their best assets for continued approval and favoritism.

Others around them may consider acting study in its deeper aspects and assiduously dedicate themselves to achieving far deeper experiential growth while the "personality" or "character" actor is probably molding any further development to fit what's already there in abundance. Later, there'll be many occasions when more depth is needed in order to obtain certain roles that require it, and such an actor will probably never be more than very briefly considered for them.

Depth in the actor's personal life---whether it's apparent on the surface or not---is probably experienced by its host personality most hours of every day of his life. There are few human beings who escape the childhood traumas and the blockages and thwart-

258

ings that plunge them into lifelong conditioned response and at least somewhat warped perceptions of life around them and their own relationships with their enironment.

The foregoing is usually and especially true of actors---from childhood, later throughout professional lives and into old age and retirement. Most fine actors contain in abundance all those conditionings which provide richest mineshafts of hidden ore for feeling and emotional experience.

It's unfortunate that these mineshafts sometimes lie buried far beneath the surface and require acting class exploration of their tunnels and passageways in order to find and bring to the surface their rich deposits. Under qualified guidance, an acting class is often the place where this has to be accomplished.

Before acting study, though, the would-be actor---from the earliest age in life which is possible---should try to be acutely aware of his own feelings and emotions and what he feels may be the cause for their being experienced. While others who don't aspire to acting careers can as well simply go through such moments observing only their content, the actor should observe the effect within himself at the same time and try to understand its cause.

There are those who believe, as I do, that a young person destined to become a fine, richly deep and moving actor later in life is probably one who's experienced a greater than normal amount of brooding, a greater than normal sense of solitary and troubled isolation from the social environment, and probably a greater than normal amount of absorbing himself in studying his own experiences and their meanings in their broadest and most deeply affecting aspects.

While his more socially active and group-oriented peers are playing games, excelling at sports and debates, and going to parties, this kind of young person is often less athletic---at least in those teen years when the BMOC's (big men on campus) are the athletes; is shy in the bubbly social circles; turns down invitations to parties (later wishing he'd gone); and, although feeling deeply about many important issues, doesn't even enter debate tournaments to argue as fact those important issues which he knows are true.

The early life of a future artist is usually a lonely life, with a plethora of opportunities for the deeper experiencing of moments, which forms the ironically ideal basis for later depth in what is, equally ironically, a very public art form.

Depth of any kind---in feeling and emotion terms---requires its moment for full experiencing, and that's the reason some of us expect to find this paradoxical-seeming pattern in the early years of someone destined to bring vast audiences the greatest degrees of depth experiences through his or her acting performances.

There are of course all types of depth. What we're discussing here isn't so much degree as it is those qualities associated with vulnerability, suffering, caring and being vitally affected rather than being only slightly concerned with the *personal experiences* resulting from external, environmental and other rather ordinary causes.

It's the *dramatic sense,* in whatever level of depth or shallowness it may be experienced by an actor, that determines the depth result which can be brought to the characters he plays.

The process of nurturing and intensifying what dramatic sense the actor has from the beginning is a life-consuming activity for the actor who recognizes its vital role in preparing and performing characters whose experiences are meaningful enough to provide audiences and viewers with important vicarious experiences of their own.

For the actor who seeks the greatest depth possible for his characters' lives and for their separate moments, it's important that unhappiness can easily be expanded into pain, that frustration can be expandable into agony, that joy can be exploded into ecstasy or wafted into Nirvana, and even a humdrum reality can be turned into something far more worthy of an actor.

The vulnerable, open to hurt character is most often the character which will involve the viewer's empathy and vicarious support throughout its travails.

But we need to distinguish between *emotion* and *emotionalism.* True emotion is generated within an actor who can easily believe in his character's experience, who always has inside a deeply felt *Object, Action, Intention* or *Objective* that crystallizes for him the depth experience, and who has access to his own past experience. *Emotionalism* is self-induced for effect.

There's no common manner in which the different personalities of different actors can find the ability in themselves to cry, whether the crying is allowed to surface or is held tightly suppressed inside. Luckily, however, there are a few things that are shared by most actors, as well as most human beings, with regard to moments when crying---whether inside or outside---is easy.

While some personalities do cry while taking some action---whether that experience or action be violent and accompanied by violent emotion or may be softly and tenderly experienced in appropriate moments, the vast majority of people (including actors) who cry for whatever reason should notice that *actions* are less frequently accompanied by any kind of crying experience, and *crying* is seldom accompanied by *action.*

There have been literary titles in the past which---perhaps with knowledge of this phenomenon on the part of perceptive writers---have made reference to and used this difference:

Some years ago an actress named Lillian Roth, describing her years of troubled life problems that ended her film career, wrote *"I'll Cry Tomorrow"*. The significance of the title was that she had gone into action to cure her problem, putting off the crying until later---at a moment when she could take time for it. She knew there was no time for crying while taking action.

More recently, in the early nineties a television drama produced by MTM Productions and starring Mary Tyler Moore bore the title *"First You Cry"*. It traced the aftermath of being told of breast cancer and clearly separated the initial reaction moment of crying at the news from the later moments of taking action.

Similarly, in earlier literature about the Irish seamen and their grieving families there was the keening of the women upon hearing of their husbands' deaths in the angry seas. There was no action taken during the rite of keening. Burials or religious rites and the actions they involved came later.

Little children whose toys have been broken or whose pets have died cry first, without any action being taken or even possible for them, then later begin the attempts to fix their toys or do what has to be done with their pets.

These are just a few examples of the source for the theory that helps at least many actors find their abilities to bring tears in whatever manner (let out or held tightly inside) when desired. It's surely more often than not in *non-action* moments that any experience related to crying is possible for them.

People cry not only when they're hurt or sad. They often cry out of anger, sudden gratification, nervous agitation, resentment, happiness or even the observing of beauty. Crying comes from attention to something, not from taking action.

Actors desiring the ability to generate tears (again, whether externally or internally) need to perceive the types of moments that can bring tears to most human beings. And they should search out what their own particular touchstones are, what kinds of moments should be simply more deeply experienced, to bring those kinds of moments in all their truths.

Professionally speaking, it's not so much that directors will always foresee the possibility of crying in some moments of roles where the actor might find them . . . yet some directors might and in fact do.

Therefore, it's of some value for the actor, when reading for roles in interviews, in order to be cast in them to begin with, to be able to surprise and excite directors and producers with their ability to go past ordinary depth (even in the reading interview) and, through bringing tears or true inner crying to a moment, assure the observer / potential employer that they can perceive even simple moments in deeper perspectives. The word "deep" is used forever after by those observers in speaking of those actors.

Crying of either kind is of course only one result of depth experiencing that goes beyond less affecting experiencing. If fear, desperation, anger, despair, hate, threat and other passions and strong feelings lack convincing depth there's little chance that the actor can succeed in any meaningful role.

All such feelings---whether caused in the character by other characters or conditioned in the total personality of the character by its own processes---need to be recognized by the actor as being *highly personalized* experiences. The degree to which those experiences are possible with regard to another person is often one-dimensional, being related to a simple event or action.

On the other hand, the degree to which they can be experienced in depth as *the character's own personal experience* has as its determining factor the depth-experiencing facets that should be available in any survival-oriented real life personality and can be more surely found and experienced by the actor if they're sought in *the character's own personal experience*.

■ **Are you one of those actors who's always praised for *"beautiful line readings?"* Don't take it as a compliment of anything except perhaps your hard work and a nice background in grammar!**

Dialogue
and Its Role in The Illusion Of The First Time

William Gillette, the actor and playwright who long ago played *"Sherlock Holmes"* to packed houses for many years, wrote this much quoted observation about *"The Illusion Of The First Time in Acting"*. In it, he stressed the importance . . .

" . . . for an actor who knows exactly what he's going to say to behave as though he doesn't; to let his thoughts apparently occur to him as he goes along, even though they're there in his mind already; and to apparently search for and find the words by which to express those thoughts, even though those words are at his tongue's very end throughout."

There are many characeristic traits among the manners in which human beings communicate with each other verbally that are missed by so many actors. These characteristics need to be thought about, consciously incorporated in the actor's handling of dialogue, and practiced until they become habit.

They offer the actor so much! They relieve the actor of the obligation to give perfect (therefore not really human) line readings. They eliminate the nervousness that usually accompanies and results from that obligation. They provide more opportunities for the character's feeling experiences behind the lines. They create *The Illusion of The First Time* for the actor himself in the process of delivering someone else's words.

They duplicate more faithfully the manner in which someone in real life would search their way through the same sentences. And there's potential joy for the actor in the multitudes of little experiences which result from observing and using as many as possible of these human characteristics.

Actual *repunctuation of sentences* shouldn't be overlooked! Most people don't successfully speak in very short, terse, capital letter to period sentences, because they haven't thought that far ahead and must find their words as they go.

They don't stop so often at commas (because their thought processes don't think commas), especially when the following phrase may begin with a *"but..."* or an *"and..."* or *"because..."*, as just a few examples. They continue past such commas, knowing there's more to say, and then, after one of those aforementioned words or a similar confident start, they must briefly search for and find the way to continue through the point they're in the process of adding. Most of us, in real life, when we come to a period, unconsciously ignore it too, and start into the next sentence's first words and then, not at the period, have to form the manner of saying what we want to say.

Not only in final performances of roles, but also in those important reading interviews to obtain those roles in the first place, the actor needs to form the habit of *experiencing the life behind the words* rather than the words themselves. There are some items to help accomplish this, also reasons for their use.

An actor may go for years on end reading for roles in offices, perhaps being hired for some tiny roles now and then, but always cursing his luck for never rising above those tiny supporting roles and walk-ons. He wonders why. So does his agent. Neither is aware that while he may be a "good actor" and give "excellent readings" (those being casting directors' customary reassuring words to actors' agents following failures, to avoid hurt feelings), he actually brings little beyond those very well delivered lines.

263

Perfect, capital letter to period dialogue readings can actually mark the actor with the "bit player", "day player" or "walk-on" label in producers' and directors' experienced judgments during those very first moments of reading for roles. The reason is that a "bit player" (with only a sentence or two of dialogue) is a mere function, a necessary bridge between the more important actors' moments. "Bit players" are ideal if they don't distract for even a brief moment. Giving "perfect line readings" is the best manner of not distracting in the least!

Actors should watch the *leading role* players in film, television and theatre more closely. They should notice---even if for the first time taking the trouble to---that the top stars' dialogue lines sound convincingly original; that the actors seem to *search for words and phrases to express themselves* (words and phrases they of course know, but their characters don't); that they seldom speak full sentences in capital letter to period outpourings; that they don't treat punctuation like a religious obligation; that they hesitate and struggle for brief moments, affording their characters moments of seeming inadequacy at finishing sentences . . .

. . . that there isn't nearly as much eye-to-eye communication as other actors might be habitually using; that they seem to be concentrating on their characters' problems (as Marlon Brando advised) more than on perfect dialogue delivery or communication; that their moments are varied and interesting because of all those items; and that our attention is riveted on them and their characters' experiences rather than on what they're saying.

Starring actors and actresses have usually cultivated the art of duplicating these human processes faithfully, and at some point in their careers have become courageous enough in readings for roles in offices to bring those processes into their readings.

At that precise point, perhaps, or soon thereafter, when called in to read for a small role they may have been sent back to the outer office with the complete script and told to look over one of the very top roles. That's how some get their first starring oportunities, in fact. In willingly making their reading less than ideal for a tiny role they impress the producer and director with their leading role potential by bringing *the total human being* rather than an actorishly perfect version of only the dialogue.

Actors destined to rise into top roles quickly are interesing to watch as they focus more on their characters' struggles than on the words they speak. They avoid the melodramatics that result from seeking the emotional experience in the words themselves.

They seem to not know what they're going to say next. They pass periods and commas and (as mentioned before) hesitate, after starting next phrases with confidence, to become hung up then, rather than at the grammarical punctuations---just as most humans do.

Their bodies become involved interestingly in those between-the-lines moments. Their own personalities are afforded moments to involve their own highlights of character experiencing.

Even their moments of listening to other characters are more interesting, because they're brave enough to enjoy those tiny, important reactions as they listen---unlike the worried actor who, because he's focused on how to "act" the next line of dialogue, is nervously preparing its perfect delivery while he should be still experiencing the current moment. The leading player knows the next line will be there when it's due, not before. He doesn't rush, therefore never feels rushed and nervous.

A curious and beautiful thing happens inside the actor when he's employing some or all of these human characteristic items in his readings, also in his performances, quite apart from the role-getting advantages they offer:

The carefully incorporated searching for words and phrases, especially, brings the actor the feeling that he's actually saying things which *haven't been written by someone else*. He, too, is having an *"illusion of the first time"* kinship with his caracter's truths in all its moments.

Work on this approach to dialogue should start early and continue until all these charateristics beome firmly imbedded habits and fairly automatic, thereby making both reading and performing of writers' dialogue a gratifying adventure instead of a worrisome obligation and an ulcer-aggravating nervousness.

Opportunities for the bringing of the character's subtext and the actor's own personality and talent exist in many, many big and small moments of all roles. The actor who misses them, or who fails to create them for himself if they're not easily apparent in the author's style of writing, misses the prime ingredients which constitute *the illusion of the first time* and distinguish good and true acting from bad and false acting.

The more truly characteristic of normal human speaking patterns the actor's delivery of dialogue becomes, the more true to life will be the experiencing of moments for both our characters and ourselves.

■ **Is your acting teacher difficult to get along with, always defensive, constantly demanding strict obedience, maybe even constantly taking members out of classes following innocent questioning of one of the teacher's approaches? There may be a reason. I'm personally embarrassed to explain this, but the...**

Early Years of Acting Teachers

Can Be Hard on Their Class Members

This item was brought to mind during this book's writing by something one of my brilliant ex-students, James Gammon, was quoted as confiding in an article about him in recent years in *The Los Angeles Times.* He's one of today's most beloved, slit-eyed, gravel-voiced character actors (who amply deserves and should someday be at least nominated for an Academy Award, having already received a Tony Award , a New York Drama Critics Circle Award amd a Los Angeles Drama Critics Circle Award.

During the time about which he was reminiscing---his first years of studying with Lawrence Parke (in this author's first years of stopping everything else in Hollywood to return to teaching fulltime)---he was a wet-behind-the-ears Illinois 25 year old who'd recently been a television cameraman in Florida doing community theatre there, and was a stark naked newcomer to Hollywood and the pursuit of a film acting career.

The article brought me some amused but sympathetic embarassment with his description of me as a teacher at that time: *"He was a very strict, knowledgeable acting coach, very much the disciplinarian. Quite frankly, he terrified us students. We were actually afraid to breathe."*

Jim was to later begin teaching actors himself, at his, Tim Scott's (another of my alumni), Alan Vint's and Nick Nolte's and other now starring actors' *Met Theatre* in Hollywood. I'm told he too was *"very strict, very much the disciplinarian"* in that early period of teaching. That's what prompts this discussion of the early, self-proving (because of self-doubting) years of coaches who may become important later . . . but start with insecurities.

As I now look back on them, prompted by Jim's comment, my own first years of teaching, after stopping everything else to return to what turned out to be my calling, were ridiculously nervous and edgy, militantly defensive and continually driving my actors to just short of their cracking points (probably to prove myself). The nickname applied to me (even though lovingly) by some of those early students was "Mongoose!" A mongoose eats snakes alive, snaps and glowers at the slightest annoyance, and isn't very nice company ever.

I'm embarrassed to say that I often threw actors out of class summarily if they simply questioned my approach. (Several of those folks later became stars.) I once threw a coffee cup full of coffee at the same Jim Gammon because (even though it was his habit) he was again three minutes late arriving for rehearsal! I even accidentally knocked over the Stage Manager stand of young Roger Ewing (later "Thad" on *"Gunsmoke"*) before raging to the stage to yell into poor Gammon's face.

I once brought big Richard Moll (who became the hilarious "Bull" in the *"Night Court"* series) to tears with an unnecessarily scathing critique comment. I made one of today's top comedy series actresses cry, telling her after a dramatic scene that she should do comedy (which she has certainly done on an Award-winning level later).

Those are just a few examples of how tyrannically defensive a teacher of acting can be, out of his or her own insecurity, in those early teaching years when a teacher isn't yet totally secure in the knowledge that he or she is on the right track.

Looking further back, I now realize that when I studied with Strasberg, and regularly annoyed him with my questions and was called *"Clurman"* by him, it was in Lee's own still developing period (although I doubt he ever admitted he had one). Worse, it was in the early decade after his frictions involving acting technique with Mr. Clurman and others of The Group Theatre.

That was probably why Clurman, told of Lee's resentment of my questions and my being called his name, advised me to keep asking and take Lee's impatience in stride comfortably because in having to more clearly explain what he meant Lee was forced to further clarify things in his own mind for communication.

I'm sure most other teachers too, after they develop more self-confident security in their teaching, are supremely grateful to the many talented students whose already developed talents aided in the further developments of their coaches!

I doubt that any acting teacher's early ads ever say anything like *"I'll teach you and you'll teach me,"* but that's what happens. It's difficult to create an aura of being all-knowing and secure in one's teaching approaches and ever admit that you've just learned something from one of the actors who---if they're continuing to study with you---have probably come to look upon you as already being some kind of supreme being.

It's a heavy, constantly challenging and frightening responsibility in those earliest teaching years to be expected by our class members to already hold the answers to all the mysteries, to see deep into their inner souls and know precisely what each needs to make them brilliant.

My personal development of approaches such as my *Neurosis Provoking Moment, Creative Psychological Objectives,* my manner of (I believe) further refining Vakhtangov's *Object* concept, etc., would not have been possible without the enduring patience of my students---in spite of my shameful treatment of some of them---during that time.

Because of my own admissions of my early ridiculousnesses in these paragraphs, I honestly wouldn't advise new, vulnerable, easily freaked actors to experience their first acting study with any of the new, still probably self-doubting teachers.

My own recollections of having been so defensively hard on my students in that period now pain me in their recalling.

Always a determined innovator searching new acting approaches, I've discovered in later coaching years that, although it's a fine and stunningly effective approach item, my *Neurosis Provoking Moment*---even though I understand it's now credited to me at the Moscow Art Theatre School---is something that not too many actors need that often. I've since found other manners, simpler ones, for helping actors achieve equal result.

Similarly, although I taught in a so furiously determined manner my version of the *Creative Psychological Objective*---in much the same manner as Strasberg's determined conducting of the *Affective Memory* experience, I've come to realize that excitingly formed *Objects* can produce equal results in most actors and accomplish that equal result more quickly and easily.

The point is that as they continue teaching most teachers discard some of their more complicated and time-taking approaches and themselves learn how to simplify and quicken the processes they teach. It's probably at those later times in the development of teachers that new actors can make the swiftest development strides in their classes.

If the actor can't afford the classes of those teachers who have come to be renowned based on many, many years of contributive teaching, he should as an alternative at least seek out a teacher who, perhaps less renowned and universally respected, has at least taught for many years and is known to be excellent.

"Has taught for many years" is one of the most important assurances that the actor stands less chance of encountering a self-defensive, nervous and professionally insecure teacher who may (even though unknowingly) put the actor through months or years of the coach's own insecurities.

■ **In real life we can often get by with only half-experiencing. That doesn't work for actors. The next item's title itself is one of the biggest, most vitally important words for actors. Check what shape your over-all personal development is in. Use as your most reliable guage...**

Experience

The Inner, Not The Outer, is What the Actor Should Always Seek!

Nothing else---no personal charisma, no ingenuous appeal, no artifice or cleverness, no reliable gimmick---qualifies someone to be called an actor!

Here we're not discussing the amount of acting background an actor may have. The experiencing dealt with here is that ability to focus so intently upon something that depth feelings are generated by that concentration for the actor and a clear and definite experience is shared with the spectator moment after moment.

Acting is a very public art. Theatre audiences pay admissions to view it. Television viewers remain tuned to a program if it holds their interest. What they're all seeking, without exception, is something they can *experience*.

What they're hoping to watch and experience vicariously is an interesting character's or an interesting group's *experiences*.

While some viewers attracted to an outer space fantasy or an adventure or crime story will be satisfied with intragalactic collisions, close calls, car crashes, blood and gore or earthquakes, what they seek in a dramatic story involving human conflict is no less than a clear and involving *human experience* on the part of any character seeking to hold their attention.

Actors chosen with regularity for starring roles in the former categories are kept busy with the vehicles, guns, screams and special-effect bloodlettings that are more important to the viewer than the experience of any one character.

Not so in the latter category, where scenic or equipment spectaculars aren't what attract and rivet the attention of theatre, film or television audiences. In human dramas the audience expects to find at least one (but hopefully more) deeply involving experiences shared in all their naked facets by one, hopefully more, of the leading characters. Actors cast in those roles need most vitally the ability to create and bring those involving experiences. To do it, the actors themselves must be continually involved in deepest experiencing.

In stressing and repeating the word *experience* so importantly, there's a book that comes automatically to mind---maverick psychologist R. D. Laing's book *"The Politics Of Experience"*. It's a thought-provoking book dealing with the *uniquely personalized* aspects of true experience and the convincing theory that we can experience *only our own experience* and none other.

Dr. Laing's theory---which good acting affirms as fact---is the most sound principle possible to be cited for the growth into brilliance on the part of actors. It's an important awareness to which all actors should evolve quickly, to save themselves years upon years of floundering in trying to experience anything nearly so completely by focusing upon other characters and what they can use from those other sources.

In real life, the actor should observe that most of his own moments are *self-concerned, self-observing and self-experiencing* upon closer examination. It simply stands to reason that this should be equally true of any character he expects to play in any human drama.

Perhaps an example or two will help at this point:

An always irritable, ovrburdened mother who causes her only son to adopt street gang life rather than stay home and enjoy her always unpleasant company doesn't merely rant and shout at her son when he does come home. She also stomps through the sixth floor walkup hallway out of irritation with her husband, the neighbors and the slum landlord.

She pushes in front of others in shopping lines and demands service ahead of others in the supermarket at the end of the block, bangs the dinner plate on the kitchen table out of the same never-abating irritation with her factory worker husband, screams at the collection agency on the telephone, and on Sunday slams a half-dollar loudly into the collection plate at her church out or irritation at how much God asks from her and how little He has given her.

As a *self-concerned and self-experiencing* person, she has one basic experience at all times and in all places, and therefore qualifies as a character in a human drama.

As Lajos Egri says (in that quotation from his book *"The Art Of Dramatic Writing"* mentioned earlier), *"It is the dramatic character who creates the dramatic situation . . . not the other way around."*

Now, consider the confusing secondary facts which would be encountered by an actress preparing the same role if that actress isn't aware of the overriding importance of *self-experiencing* and the clear conditioning of response which experience provides:

The mother obviously loves her son deep in her heart; one can see it in certain actions, dimly discernible through the rasping and screaming on the surface but nevertheless clearly there in small hints the author has provided in a few brief moments that appear as non sequiturs and might be easily missed. She simply loves him in *her own self-experiencing way.*

She's a devoted wife, although her tired husband is often driven out of the small apartment at night because of her constant complaining. Her devotion is simply limited by *her own inner experience.*

She does believe in God, and doesn't deny Him her half-dollar every Sunday, even though she resents having to pay for things she doesn't get. She appreciates her own supermarket's quality even though she complains while shopping there. The author indicates that she would never shop anywhere else. It's not the supermarket; it's just *her manner of experiencing everything.*

The actress who doesn't catch the small, almost hidden hints in the author's presentation of the woman---and *doesn't look behind the behavior for the single conditioned experience that prompts it*---will in all probability prepare her inadequately. It's easy to miss some details that may be important.

Human experience has for many decades been known in scientific circles and most lay terms as well to have as its always present core at least some degree of neurosis.

All human beings, without exception, are subject to at least some levels of conditioned response as a result. Behavior patterns in real life are the keys to our understanding of the personalities behind them, and for actors those keys---observable in any well written character---become golden if they're perceived and used in the preparing of dramatic characters.

It's the *type of conditioned experiencing* chosen by the actor in preparing the character which determines the quality of the later performance. Obviously, in order to perceive the subtleties and nuances of personality types in written characters the actor should have at least a layman's knowledge of personality types.

The latter needn't entail years of scholastic specialization. It's fairly easy, if we think as we observe, to realize that the behavior of someone toward us or toward another person is probably not based upon us or that other person, but rather upon a conditioned response personality that would behave in the same manner no matter where or with whom it might be.

If we can appraise other personalities around us with logic--- even though perhaps in the first moments we feel a personal assault on our own conditioned sensibilities, we can usually categorize them at least in general terms and use their behavior as a study opportunity rather than experience them as attackers.

In past centuries the subject of neurosis and conditioned response were not often dealt with in dramatic literature in more than a surface manner, but there came the time when leading dramatists began to base more and more of their important roles on those emerging awarenesses.

Henrik Ibsen's works remain important to this day, primarily because they achieved dramatic impact through clearly neurotic personalities and the types of continuous *self-experiencing* by their leading characters which were recognizably appropriate for their personalities and also intensely experiened.

Chekhov, Griboyedov, Dostoevsky and others among the late 1800's and early 1900's playwrights made conditioned response the bases for enduring characters as well---even though they may not have yet read the writings of Ribot, Charcot or Freud.

By the 1920's and 1930's there was no question as to the value of clearly defined, neurotic source characters. In the contemporary entertainment literature there are few works, except those of the horror, thrill, jeopardy and spectacle genres, which are not based on such personality cores.

The actor who can easily distinguish between the character's own experience and the less complete and less true experience of *playing the situation only* can always find depth experiencing which is woefully unavailable to other, less insighted actors.

The *personalizing* of experience, then, is the answer---just as Stanislavski and Vakhtangov decided. If the actor can glean such clear insight from the writer's descriptions, behavior nuances and manners of relating attributed to the character ---and has the persistence and intelligence to decide the logical emotional core and preconditioning of the character, the most important first step can be taken---the determining of *what the character, deep inside itself, is constantly experiencing* that causes its apparent attitudes, its recurring behavior patterns and its actions toward other characters.

A surface behavior is not an experience. *Experience is uniquely individual, stemming from a uniquely individual conditioning.*

Three businessmen might be meeting in an office for an important discussion. One, perceived by a shallow actor to be simply a forceful organizer and leader admirably capable of taking important action, could easily be determined by one with deeper insight into the *personal experience* of that character to be a desperately driven identity-crisis case. The latter would be more interesting and, more importantly, deeper.

Another of the three might be seen by some actors as an obsequious, self-abasing hanger-on, while an actor with greater depth perception might easily categorize the man as one who can't assert himself out of fear of hurting others and offending with his own personality's guilt conditioning.

The third man could be judged by some to be an ambition-driven young man as he argues strongly in the face of his superiors' opinions, while to the more perceptive actor, upon closer examination of his behavior's hints of the *inner experience*, he would emerge into far more engrossing life as a slums-escaper conditioned to criticize any environment current around him because of his childhood in the slums and the resulting conviction that nothing around him will ever escape the smell of the gutter.

Similarly, three mothers might witness the crisis of their three sons almost being run over by a passing car as they play ball in the street while the mothers visit on the sidewalk.

The first mother, running out and picking up her little boy and hugging him to her breast, might be judged to be loving and protective. On the other hand a highly sensitive actress might discover (through observing more of her recurring behavior patterns throughout the script and recognizing their significance in terms of the character's *inner experience*) that the mother is constantly afraid of failure and in that moment is afraid of her own neglect and its possible result in other people's eyes more than relieved at her little boy's escape from injury.

Another of the three mothers, as she runs, yanks her son back onto the sidewalk and proceeds to spank the living daylights out of him, might be judged by one actress to be a stern disciplinarian because of that one act. However, an actress alert to the *recurring behavior patterns* throughout the role and understanding their significance in the character's *inner experience* would more accurately see the violent and angry attitude about her son's close call as one more manifestation of her inner resentment at the whole world for her feelings of being trapped in responsibilities and obligations.

The third mother, simply standing and screaming, unable to move to her son as she watches him sheepishly return to the sidewalk, might be judged by one actress to be an eternally frightened person, while with a deeper penetration of her *total role behavior* the conclusion might become clearly apparent that she doesn't trust herself to act logically in any moment, whether in such a crisis as the one desribed or in simple conversation or everyday behavior of any kind.

A mere personality label is too simplistic for the creating of *experience*. While most actors realize that one must be formed in the early stage of preparing the role, it alone can't provide the actor with the optimum basis for any *depth experience* throughout the role. It remains an intellectual judgment until the actor supplies the specific and varying degrees of the character's *self-experience* of its own particular kind as that experience is impacted by events which occur in the course of the character's scripted experiences.

The actor's truth depends upon what he *selects to experience* and on his ability to *experience what has been chosen.*

For so long in the distant past of the human experience, egoism, selfishness, self-centeredness and similar personality attributes were looked upon as undesirable traits. It required the resolving of contradicting theories about the *inner experience* of human beings to bring such lepers back to social respectability.

Fortunately for humankind, behavioral science did eventually discover that without such previously condemned aspects there would be only repression of survival instincts, suppression of self-evolving experience and empty social masks with unpainted expressions continually consulting psychotherapists to learn why their lives were unhappy and incomplete.

The actor must be egoistic! His processes must be observed by him. His relation to his environment and the society within which he must function is important if he's to develop *a sense of being.* His body is his instrument and his mind is his tool for playing upon it. He must constantly observe and file-cabinet *his own experience.* It's his greatest natural resource.

If also an artist in any spiritual sense, the actor has *experiences that are uniquely his own.* Down through history those who've had the courage to share those unique, sometimes revolutionary *personal experiences* have made great contributions to the evolving of new thought, new concepts and new approaches in the world of acting.

■ **I'm so tired of hearing film actors make putdown comments about theatre actors and theatre actors (which is probably more often the case) making derogatory comments about film and television actors.   Such snobbish, elitist comments are usually made by amateurs . . because professionals are busy commuting back and forth among all three!**

Film And Television Acting
vs. Theatre Acting

Good acting is good acting, whether in theatre or before the cameras of motion pictures.

The actor simply needs to know the different manners of working and the adjustments in styles of performance required by the different performance mediums. Those adjustments are really the only problems.

274

For someone whose early professional background is exclusively stage---with the luxuries of several weeks of rehearsals, the contributions of directors' suggestions and plenty of backstage preparation time before and when needed even during continuing runs of theatre presentations . . . the first film role can be pure torture.

There's usually little time for preparing characterization, learning lines and planning of complicated approach items between the moment of receiving the script and the moment of being called before the camera. The experienced stage actor feels the crush of time devastatingly in first film role experiences.

Sometimes the actor is told he has the role at ten o'clock in the morning; receives the script and plane ticket by messenger at eleven; is hustled to the airport at eleven-thirty and zipped to God knows where the location may be by late afternoon; is allowed a short few hours of Screen Actors Guild required rest period upon arrival; then that evening is suddenly in wardrobe and makeup and playing the final wrapup scene of the film instead of the first into the late hours of the night.

The resonant projection developed for stage performance will probably be too loud for the boom mike. The physical performance and facial exaggeration must be reduced and tightly caged within the limited frame of the camera's closeup lens. The art of hitting marks exactly to accommodate prepared shots (and not cover other actors) must be quickly learned, and the director is too busy to take the time to teach that technique.

There's a whole new vocabulary to learn! Several different angles of various types---master shots, medium shots, over-the-shoulder shots, closeups (in the many different takes that are repetitions of the same scene)---that have to match in the most minute details or be cut out of the picture in the Editing Room. The actor has to note and remember in each take exactly when and how he did something in the first filmed version and repeat each action exactly in each of the later shots.

His own closeups may even be shot at the end of the day, with a Script Supervisor (not the other character) feeding the other's lines because the other character, perhaps one of the stars, has been released earlier to go home.

There are just one or two brief rehearsals before each take. The director will expect your best performance, fully prepared and brought from home, and won't have time to contribute many of his own suggestions to help. Most of what he'll contribute are movement cautions about weaving, bouncing or drifting in the frame (which were never objected to by theatre directors), specific directions in which you must look (because filming involves specific camera angles), perhaps one or two suggestions for your hands, maybe a request to *"do less"* or hold a prop higher so it will be in the frame, etc.

The first take may be finished and there may be literally several hours of waiting before lighting, sound and camera angles are readied for the next take---even when there's nothing involved but simply relighting and repositioning of the camera for the other person's medium shots and closeups of the same scene.

Theatre actors, accustomed to nightly performances, aren't used to morning calls that require being at *"Makeup by five-thirty"* and being *"Ready on Stage 8 by seven."* It's a whole new ballpark!

But there's the other side---the happier one---that the stage actor will experience in film: Stage technique (voice production and projection, expanded body communication, etc.) can be laid aside more easily than some think. Film thrives on intimacy. The camera doesn't look *at* the actor; it looks *inside* him. If the actor makes sure there's something important going on *inside* he'll be happily surprised at how much of it the camera will have recorded without any necessity of the projection a large stage requires. That's often a luxury that's new to the theatre actor.

For the actor making the transition from film to theatre it's easier---as long as the actor has a resonant voice that can sound natural and unforced when required to be projected to the second balcony, even if it's had to be modulated for film's boom mikes for a long time.

As long as he's learned to "cheat" toward the camera some of the time he'll be equally comfortable "cheating front" on stage. And as long as he's comfortable expanding his body's participation throughout long shot scenes for film he should be able to project the body's messages to the rear of the balcony.

There'll be the luxury of three or four weeks of rehearsal, receiving a director's guidance and suggestions in ongoing rehearsals, later the exhilaration of a live audience's response, and plenty of rest-up time between performances.

Film being mostly centered in a small number of production centers, the film actor will normally have had quite a bit of stage experience, whether on Broadway, in small Off Off Broadway venues or in the resident company of a regional theatre, before being brought into film and should experience the return to theatre quite comfortably. Unfortunately, the stage actor will probably arrive for a first film role without any equal acquaintance with its demands.

The best advice this author can give the stage actor is to at least *learn* all the film processes possible---film set vocabulary, technical requirements, etc., well ahead of time, in preparation for the moment when the first film or television role comes without any warning, as it usually does.

If you're a stage actor, don't waste time criticizing film actors as being inferior. Get some books about film acting and camera technique, so you'll be ready. If you're a film actor, do the same to be ready for an unexpected theatre opportunity.

■ **Are you a bundle of nerves before or during acting performances? Do your hands shake, your cheeks twitch, your mouth feel dry, your neck feel tight or actually feel pain? Do you find yourself constantly watching every movement of your arms, hands, legs, sitting and standing positions, and worrying about them? Get help!**

Freeing The Instrument

After So Many Things Have Tightened It

Don't delude yourself that you'll ever be able to do your best work as an actor if you're aware of tightness, tension or any other sign that you can't work *"with a feeling of ease,"* as Michael Chekhov recommended---able to experience that body condition that Stanislavski, Vakhtangov and, yes, Lee Strasberg even more, taught as being profoundly important for actors. *"Never happen!"* most of us would say.

Learn the manners of *freeing your instrument.* Honestly, you'll have to. You have no choice.

We're taught from earliest childhood that there are certain correct manners of doing what we do. They're presented as social laws and we're constantly admonished to obey them.

"Sit up straight!" our mothers told us. *"Stop slouching!"* . . . *"Don't play with your fingers!"* . . . *"Get your hands out of your pockets!"* . . . *"Look at me when I'm talking to you!"* . . . *"Stop fidgeting!"* Who hasn't heard some or all of those in their formative years? They're among the least harmful, but they begin the body-tightening process. Nobody enjoys being constantly criticized, and the inhibiting process begins.

There are others: *"Act like a man!"* . . . *"Sit like a lady!"* . . . *"Big boys don't cry!"* . . . *"Bite your tongue!"* . . . *"You're embarassing me!"* and a few hundred other criticisms directed at our young sensibilities when they aren't yet able to cope with what society (at that early point, still mostly familial) throws at us.

In our early school years it becomes even more assaulting to our emerging egos: *"Stop looking at me!"... "Sissy!"... "Tomboy!" ... "Don't stand so close to me!" ... "That's dirty!"..."Don't be so dumb!"* At that point we're commencing to be told who we are and given little appreciation when we attempt to be otherwise.

By that time we're starting to respond in some direction---either acommodating our environment by attempting to change and conform to the accepted norms or else flaunting our bad points for all to see and deride for whatever satisfaction it can give our developing neuroses. Either response, in its own way, tightens the controls we apply to our bodies.

The teenage years do the rest of the damage in most cases: *"Why can't you be like Tommy?" ... "Mama won't let me go out with you because you're poor, Italian, Irish, German, Jewish, Catholic, Protestant, or from the West Side, or something else, or because your mother or father is or isn't something!"...*

During those years---sensing the urgency of approaching adulthood and the need to conform to social acceptability or peer approval criteria, we've adopted certain behavior patterns and image projection designs.

We've diligently tailored our bodies and our demeanor in appropriate, goal-directed manners to become exemplary symbols of our social group. Then we've allowed the modeling clay to dry and caged our body and our behavior inside the hardened surface of the effigy we've created!

Certain moods, feelings and emotions which didn't fit our societally demanded presentations have been hidden, and our bodies--denied the stimulus of free expression of our true feelings---became resentful servants of our image performances.

We put aside our childhood spontaneities because they were too dangerous. We limited our behavior paramaters and our personal expressiveness to those accepted within our peer spectrum. In effect, we put part of ourself to sleep and for years kept much of ourself tightly closeted and mildewing behind tightly locked doors of acceptance-seeking.

Then one day we decided to become an actor. We assumed that we could satisfy both society and our acting career with our assumed image manner and style while easily achieving depth of feeling and emotion whenever desired.

Our first attempts to do so---looking back on them at a later time---were ridiculous, contrived and false. We were suddenly faced with the realization that our body responded only in its practiced and educated manner, and that our feelings and emotions in our early acting classes were judged to be false, represented and conceptual without any basis in true experience.

278

We were called "stiff" and "inhibited" by a possibly less than sensitive acting teacher. We were admonished to *"Loosen up!"* and let our body move with our feelings. We hadn't realized we were stiff and inhibited. And we had no idea where to start toward *"loosening up"*.

The process of *freeing our instrument* was recognized by the teacher as being the most urgently necessary first classwork, and it was probably pressed upon us over a long period by a teacher who knew the importance of our learning to cope with it.

Unfortunately, most of us don't even realize we have recurring tensions, don't realize how inhibiting they are in the mind/body processes of acting, and only when it's pointed out that we have many neural muscle tensions that recur time and again and limit our control of our instruments do we become serious about such freeing of our instruments.

Suddenly, when a teacher skilled in detecting and dealing with tensions explains what they are and why they often recur, we understand why our temples occasionally ache, our brow and the bridge of our nose feel tight, our cheeks feel stiff and we realize that our jaw is seldom relaxed.

For the first time really concentrating on other parts of our body one after another, we find our neck, our shoulders and our stomach feel tightly controlled even as we sit or stand in our most customary positions. Even our lower extremities---our legs and feet---can be detected for the first time to actually be tight, as if somehow controlled. We notice that our wrists are tight, our stomach is controlled.

We may not realize that all those years of concern with our projected image, constantly controlling so many muscles in all parts of our bodies, has caused those body parts to be obliged to function counteractively with the particular nerve circuits to which they should ideally relate in harmony.

There are many favorite *relaxation* exercises conducted by different teachers. There are teachers who, like Chekhov, recommend the sending of messages through the nerves that control tight muscles to relax either single muscles one at a time or to let *"a feeling of ease"* consciously flow through the whole body. It actually works very well and is so simple.

There are teachers who recommend the violent shaking of parts of the body one after another to loosen them individually, rotating the head and neck about a dozen times, doing abandoned marionette-type "body dances" involving the total body, or simply sprawling in a chair, checking where tension is felt, and consciously relaxing any tensions detected through messages conveyed by the applicable nerves.

279

There's the *Song and Dance* exercise conceptualized and conducted by Lee Strasberg. There are the many *instrumental block* exercises of Hollywood teacher Eric Morris, the *Theatre Games* approaches of Viola Spolin. There are hundreds of other manners teachers use to help actors with this important task.

There are *"Abandonment"* exercises conducted by some teachers who feel that the random movement patterns of the body as it's thrown in disjointed manner in all directions with no form or control, if encouraged to become habit as a manner of relaxing the instrument, increase expressiveness and also create ephemeral, moment after moment experiencing of a variety of feelings.

The *Sensitivity Training Centers*, such as those conducted at Esalen in California, also at the several Ford Foundation Sensitivity Training Centers, specialize in this very same *freeing of the instrument* for not only actors but also for business executives and others from all walks of life.

At Esalen there are regularly conducted group exercises designed to relax the participants' self-delusions that they need so much control, such as the *"passing in a circle"* experience, in which one person goes to the center of a tight circle while seven or eight others form that tight circle with arms and hands tightly interlocked.

The person in the center simply lets himself fall sideways in one direction, becoming increasingly confident that his body will be caught easily by the interlocked arms of others and be tossed easily toward other interlocked arms, caught, and sent in another direction. Knowing he'll be caught, not dropped, brings a relaxing of his own tight control.

Many of these experiences are conducted nude. In fact, there's one tension-eliminating exercise conducted at some Sensitivity Training Centers for which many actors aren't ready. It's a *Nude Sensitivity Training Exercise* wherein one person lies nude first flat on his stomach and others (whose turns will come later) first do what's called *body-slapping* to awaken the pores of the one lying there. Then, on signal, the others, eyes closed, lying around him in a circle, explore with their hands the many parts of his body.

Of course warts, old wound scars, fatty deposits are found by those hands, but they're explored nonjudgmentally. Those are the most telling moments for the one lying there. The experience of being accepted without judgment is taking its effect. The one lying there turns over on signal, and the same exploring is conducted. What's especially remarkable is that the male who fears he'll become aroused down below by the touching finds that it doesn't happen. The blissful relaxation that comes from having our body explored and feeling no judgmental response in the many fingertrips makes it impossible.

At the end of this experience there's such complete relaxation for the one who's been handled that he or she hates to get up and become one of the circle exploring the next person. No one who hasn't been through this experience (at Esalen or elsewhere) can possibly understand its lasting effect in freeing the instrument.

Some teachers simply have their class members adopt *non-talking* positions---positions in no way associated with talking to other persons---and then proceed, while maintaining those positions, to carry on situation dialogue and relate with others in the manner in which they unconsciously do those things in life.

Whatever approaches may be used by a teacher in the effort to relax and free the actor's instrument for the fullest use and easy control of mind/body functioning, it's usually one of the first things a qualified acting teacher must help the actor learn to do.

What most often causes tension to return varies with the individual. An extended period of experiencing stress is one of the surest to produce tension. Even brief periods of social insecurity can cause tensions to recur.

Freeing of the instrument sometimes involves the correction of body habits developed to cover imaginary body faults, or is needed to eliminate image projection devices that have perpetuated a limited use of the body for the sake of presenting a chosen image---both discussed in earlier chapters. Freeing the instrument must almost always deal with problems that are produced by imagined inferiorities. Sometimes they're difficult for the actor to detect and it's still more difficult to change those habits. But all of those common contributors cited have usually created the tensions that actors must learn how to ease and to hopefully eliminate.

■ **If the actor fails to develop his or her own manners of relaxing tensions, those tensions are often what produce the next item...**

Mannerisms

A Few Have Helped Careers . . . Many Have Hurt Them

Webster defines "mannerism" as *"excessive use of some distinctive, often affected, manner or style in art, literature, speech or behavior; a peculiarity of manner in behavior, speech, etc., that has become a habit."*

Who among us hasn't enjoyed Jimmy Stewart's faltering and stuttering speech, John Wayne's uncoordinated shambling and shuffling, early films' Zasu Pitts's fluttering hands and widly orbiting eyes, Bette Davis's and Gloria Swanson's stiletto-pointed stares, James Dean's off-center slouching, Sandy Dennis's jagged anxiety attacks and tics, Marilyn Monroe's slithering and undulating, Geraldine Page's and Billie Burke's fluttering hands flying like wild birds, Gene Wilder's eye-popping, etc.?

There are some professional careers that have been perhaps helped become indelible, certainly have become identified with mannerisms that were considered to be charming, cute, mesmerizing or somehow at least unique and attractive. But there have been those whose careers have dwindled away when their mannerisms have become obstructive to the clarity of characters or have caused problems for theatre and film directors.

In early films, the hands-fluttering Zasu Pitts managed to remain a star of her period even though she caused the coining of the item called *"Zasu Pitts cutaways"* in film. Her constantly fluttering hands could never possibly match from one shot to another, so there had to be constant "cutaways" to total non sequiturs like an old dog scratching fleas outside a screen door, or some ducks on a pond or whatever, before cutting back to her scenes in editing them! Her mannerism---totally wrong for film---might have killed her career, but it didn't.

Jimmy Stewart's constant stuttering, stretching simple dialogue lines out ad infinitum, was simply coped with---because many found it charming---by reducing the words of his speeches.

John Wayne's constant shifting from one foot to another, causing him to "drift" from one side of a shot to another, had to be coped with by more medium shots and fewer closeups. Some later actors of great talent (several names fly to my mind) weren't so lucky. Their constant bouncing, weaving and drifting in close film work have caused their fine talents to be passed over sometimes in casting.

A number of stars, past and present, whose unique mannisms have been the most pronounced, and whose performances are continuous displays of those mannerisms, include many Academy Award nominees and winners---Gloria Swanson as *Best Actress* (1929, 1930, 1950); Bette Davis as *Best Actress* (1935, 1938, 1939, 1940, 1941, 1942, 1944, 1950, 1952, 1961); Billie Burke as *Best Supporting Actress* (1938); James Stewart as *Best Actor* (1939, 1940, 1946, 1950, 1959); John Wayne as *Best Actor* (1949); Kim Stanley as *Best Actress* (1964) and *Best Supporting Actress* (1982); Sandy Dennis as *Best Supporting Actress* (1966); Edna May Oliver as *Best Supporting Actress* (1939); Geraldine Page as *Best Supporting Actress* (1953), as *Best Actress (1961,*

1962), as *Best Supporting Actress* (1966, 1972), as *Best Actress* (1978), as *Best Supporting Actress* (1984), as *Best Actress* (1985); Robin Williams as *Best Actor* (1987, 1989); Michael J. Pollard as *Best Supporting Actor* (1967); Gene Wilder as *Best Supporting Actor* (1968); Una Merkel as *Best Supporting Actress* (1961); James Dean as *Best Actor* (1955, 1956, 1957); Margaret Rutherford as *Best Supporting Actress* (1963), etc.

But there have been many---including a few of those listed above---whose so often repeated mannerisms have caused their careers to eventually come to a halt.

Gloria Swanson's mannerisms were only right, later, for her 1950 *"Sunset Boulevard"* role of caricaturing herself. Bette Davis's mannerisms were able to survive the ages. Billie Burke's fluttery naiveté worked for many years. James Stewart's mannerisms would still be welcome today. So would John Wayne's.

Geraldine Page, Sandy Dennis and Kim Stanley---three of Lee Strasberg's favorites---are examples of proclivities being used to produce characteristically larger than life external pyrotechnics which appeared to be beyond the three actresses' control.

Actually, all three of those actresses were very much in control of their performances. They worked in those jagged-edged, anxiety attack manners in most roles by choice. For example, Geraldine Page was first persuaded to work in that manner as Alma Winemuller in the Circle In The Square production of Tennessee Williams' *"Summer And Smoke"* (the role which immediately skyrocketed her to starring roles in the New York theatre) by director José Quintero.

It was upon being cast as Alma Winemuller and being encouraged by Mr. Quintero to add those mannerisms for Alma that she fell in love with the experience of working in that manner and continued it throughout her roles in both theatre and film.

Her first film, *"Hondo"*, with John Wayne, nearly discouraged her from any further film work after 1953, although she received an Academy Award nomination for her role in that film. Her mannerisms were a source of annoyance to John Wayne, and he often ridiculed her, even in her presence, on the set.

Page and Wayne were like oil and water, complete opposites in their manners of working---she with those sharp-edged mannerisms always anxious to surface, and he with his quiet, shuffling manner. After that first film she retreated to the large proscenium stages in New York where she felt more freedom.

When more of her mesmerizing, flamboyant Broadway starrings again brought her to Hollywood, she brought all those same mannerisms back with her, flaunted them, and proceeded to be nominated for Academy Awards in every appearance. Miss Page was a veritable catalog of eccentric mannerisms throughout her illustrious career, but her brilliance as an actress allowed her to get away with all of them time after time.

Kim Stanley---whom Lee Strasberg stated he considered the *"the epitome of all he worked for"*---has worked even closer to the breaking edge of collapse. Her performances in both film and theatre have been so outrageously enlarged that they have limited her for film casting.

Her first film starring role in *"The Goddess"* was so extravagantly theatrical! You could well imagine that most of her moments were actually *Affective Memory and Private Moment exercises* reproduced in wild hysterics, and that they had little to do with her role as Rita Shawn in that film.

Miss Stanley was said by Strasberg to be *the epitome of all he worked for,* probably because each acting role was apparently used to inspire hundreds of *affective memory* searches and used as another opportunity for her to go totally out of character to indulge herself in those different *affective memories.*

Although to Strasberg she was a beloved example of what he worked for, to Stanislavski she would have been an example of why he summarily stopped using *affective memory* as an acting approach when he detected an alarming and undesirable inner hysteria in the performances of some of the actors and felt that that hysteria emanated from the so acutely felt need to make the memory work each time. He had also observed that too frequent and extreme use of emotional memory had even brought some actors to serious mental illness. Miss Stanley did eventually have a nervous breakdown.

Her perhaps best career work was under Bryan Forbes' very strict hand in *"Seance On A Wet Afternoon"*. He had seen her performance in *"The Goddess"* and, although smitten with her talents, at their first meeting is reported to have said to her *"Kim dear, shall you be conservative with your hands, or shall we use handcuffs?"* His keen eye and soft-spoken control throughout her performance as Myra and her own (in that case more controlled) talents won her the *Best Supporting Actress* Award.

Following her real life nervous breakdown---as Stanislavski feared for actors overindulging in affective memory work---and almost twenty years of retirement from acting, Kim has since had two noteworthy film roles---as Jessica Lange's monster of a mother mother in *"Frances"* and the tough barkeeper in *"The Right Stuff"*. All the mannerisms were there still, simply sticking out from the surface of an older woman.

Sandy Dennis---even though she won *Best Supporting Actress* in 1966 for *"Who's Afraid Of Virginia Woolf?"*---has always had to be carefully cast, and carefully controlled by a strong director to limit her excesses, as she was by Robert Altman in *"Come Back To The Five And Dime, Jimmy Dean, Jimmy Dean"*.

Mannerisms have been around forever. They're not solely of the kind that have been criticized (whether deservedly or not) as being products of Strasberg's Method. Buster Keaton, Edna May Oliver, Margaret Rutherford, Una Merkel, Marjorie Rambeau, Zasu Pitts and Billie Burke, in those old films, were simply caricatures in most roles they played.

With their lovable eccentricities always there as expected for us to laugh at, their unique mannerisms kept roles coming and kept many film audiences laughing for many years. And there are more recent examples of mannerisms that audiences have enjoyed:

James Dean began his career imitating what for the early Marlon Brando were more manner than mannerisms, and continued those mannerisms throughout his theatre and film work, but was always cast in roles that turned those mannerisms into assets. To his immense credit, they were always skillfully incorporated in deeply thought out characterizations, and they were physically appealing as well, so he got away with them admirably. Some others have been less fortunate.

The bottom line seems to be that obvious personal mannerisms, if always consciously and skillfully incorporated in actors' characterizations, can be stunning hallmarks of actors' work, distinguishing their careers. If they're unconscious, uncontrollable and distracting, on the other hand, they can shorten actors' careers. If an actor has mannerisms it's a good idea to make sure they're of a type that endears him to audiences without limiting him from a broader variety of important characterizations.

■ **One of today's leading film directors, discussing some of the actors of early films (and theatre of those earlier times also) before an audience of actors at one of my *Actors' Seminars*, named a few examples of what he termed "Toothpick actors" . . . always so properly erect in most of their moments. He advised that the time when that was acceptable is long past.**

He had everyone in the audience stand, totally centered, for a moment and observe what they felt like. Then he told them to slouch to one side, perhaps lean on something or someone, and observe what they felt like in the new positions. It drove home the point that actors should whenever possible work in positions that are much more personal, less socially proper. He strongly recommended that actors should much more of the time work . . .

Off Center

That's Where Feeling Experience and Relaxation Thrive!

This item is covered in more detail in the Chapter *"The Body"* . . . but this additional chapter is being devoted to *off center* use of the body to fix it more firmly in the actor's consciousness as the highly productive manner of working that it is.

I had for years thought that it might be one of my teaching secrets. But I learned that Strasberg had also discovered this in his work and often recommended it.

Many of his *Movement to Aid Relaxation* exercises, as described by Dr. Lorrie Hull in her book *"Strasberg's Method As Taught by Lorrie Hull"*, utilize off center emphasis---for example, with one limb at a time used in some off center manner to break the *habitual parallel position* of tension-producing social behavior. Dr. Hull reports that he admonished students *"Do not remain in a habitual parallel position. Wiggle and move about so you are sometimes shaped like a pretzel."*

While not seeing a pretzel shape as being very often desirable in the performance of a role, relaxation certainly is. And the body positions most conducive to relaxation are more often *off center* than socially erect with both hands in similar positions and doing the same thing, both legs planted on the floor straight in front, and the head held erect and facing straight front.

The latter positions are so straitjacketedly social! As stated earlier, they belong if anywhere almost exclusively in employment interviews where the attempts are being made to be proper and well-mannered. Those positions aren't relaxed. They also inhibit an actor's *personal experiencing,* a character's as well.

In relaxed moments---especially when we're with close friends, but also when we feel no social behavior demands with others less close, how many of us sit or stand in those self-consciously erect and body-paralleled positions?   Not often, I think.

And have you noticed that most people in real life who do sit or stand in those body-paralleled positions usually talk with their hands so much of the time? They have the tendency to illustrate, punctuate and emphasize with their hands almost every sentence they speak, actually defeating their communication through those physical distractions.

The reason for all that hands-flailing is that those everything parallel positions are usually *communication* positions, nothing more. They're usually directly aimed at other people and usually concentrated on response, rather than being conducive to any *self-experiencing.* Have you also noticed how bored (even tired) you've become after any length of time in the company of one of those *everything parallel, hands-flailing* people?

The appealing qualities of actors like James Dean, Marlon Brando, Dustin Hoffman, John Wayne, Gary Cooper, John Garfield, Jack Nicholson, Montgomery Clift (among many other male stars) and Geraldine Page, Sandy Dennis, Sally Field, Lee Grant, Julie Harris, Jessica Lange, Cloris Leachman (among many other female stars) have included the regular preference for *off center* positions that relaxed and emotionally conditioned their instruments while presenting their characters' personal experiences in more visually appealing manners.

There are myriad references to *off center* work in Stanislavski's discussions of characterizations. It was the very essence of dancer Martha Graham's movement and Isadora Duncan's flowing patterns. Vakhtangov recommended it as being important in exploring for the embodiment of characters. Michaelangelo's, Rembrandt's and Reubens' paintings, among other artists' masterpieces, used it to enhance composition and form. And Michael Chekhov's *Psychological Gesture* requires it for the complete body-searching for characters' physical forms.

Two or more actors in a scene, if all standing erect and totally centered in every respect, present not an ounce of composition or focus. A director must supply whatever composition and focus he wants by coaching one or more of them into *off center,* angled positions with their bodies. If the same two or more actors were comfortable with working *off center,* most of the time the director wouldn't have to do a thing with them!

The justification for repeating this approach under its own Chapter heading is that it's so bloody important to remember!

■ **Many of us laugh and exchange anecdotes about actors we've known who go through the next painful, amusing to observe and in the end often futile process which some actors insist they need. The sensible, productive alternatives are available, but this fiction is sometimes picked up in an acting class and trusted as "the way" by some actors. It needs to be discussed.**

Preparing To Feel

Some Actors Go To Ridiculous Extremes!

There have always been and still are actors who believe they must take considerably more than a moment to *"prepare to feel*

287

something". Some are always insecure; some simply misguided.

Those ridiculously long "preparing to feel" moments are most often required by actors whose acting approaches involve stepping outside their characters' realities to prepare the use of non-character items such as the *Affective Memory* substitution or some other approach that is of a more personal experience nature than the character's continuing life would be for them in those same, easily available moments of the character's own experience.   I've felt sorry for those actors and wished they could discover the vastly more constructive manner of "preparing".

The "preparing to feel" approach that is so much simpler and so much quicker is that taught by most leading teachers in whatever manner is preferred---simply *becoming the character* and concentrating on *what has been prepared for it to experience, based on the circumstances and other justifications of its (the character's own) reality of the moment!*

Mr. Strasberg continually recommended to actors working with him that actors need to *"take a minute to prepare."* That's right . . . he often specifically recommended *a whole minute.*

One would hope he meant that when an actor has carefully prepared a moment's involvement and feeling with specific thought-focus and any other preparation tool, he may need a short period of time, when the moment of its use approaches, to remind himself of the preparation chosen and to kindle the desired feeling experience.   Check your watch.   The director has just called "Action!" A minute? . . . . that's sixty long seconds!

A *very short* moment could be needed, perhaps---if the actor has allowed himself to be totally distracted from his character's experience by perhaps exchanging gossip offstage during a theatre performance or playing chess in a corner of a film soundstage when he could have been staying in character, but . . . *a minute!*

A teacher offering the actor this advice may offer it because he or she isn't known for contributing enough *instantly activatable involvement for actors based on simple belief* but instead advocates a step-by-step reviewing of place, time, weather, etc., or perhaps *reevoking a personal experience* to substitute for the experience of the character, when the very circumstance and nature of the actual role moment would be easier to believe quite quickly and easily.

Sandy Meisner offers this anecdotal explanation of the *preparing to feel* moment: *"Long ago I owned a car. When I got into my car in the winter I had to pull out the choke to give the cold motor extra gas. A warming-up process. For an actor, preparation is a warming-up process."* He called it simply what it truly is---*self-stimulation of our imagination to create in our-*

selves what we've determined is our emotional condition (as the character!) before we begin a scene. Simply "pull out the choke."

Sandy's comment was being made in theatre terms. In theatre performance, a minute, as recommended by some teachers. . . fine. If the actor needs some time to *"prepare to feel"* something he has that time, backstage between scenes.

But what about film? A minute is much longer than it sounds like, and with twenty-two soundstage union crews on a film set (or perhaps more now)---each union crew comprising two or up to maybe four members and all on union salaries, a minute is a lot of money! The actor who needs a minute to *"prepare to feel"* something is expensive---and probably not worth his salt in the first place.

An actor who has an expert technique for experiencing the moments of roles doesn't need to *"prepare to feel"* for any longer than the length of time it takes to simply think a prepared thought of the character, the surroundings and the situation that has in its simple, single thought alone the feelings that are quickly tapped by thinking it!

The author was a casting director during an earlier period, assigned that position by NBC, CBS and a television production company because of my fairly extensive knowledge of actors and my judgment of talent. On one occasion an actor who had worked with the teacher who most often proposed and taught that *"one minute to prepare"* postulation came in (at the director's suggestion, not mine) to read for a role.

When called into the inner office to read for the producer and director, he sat in the chair indicated to him . . . then immediately laid back, closed his eyes, hung his arms over the sides of the chair, and began breathing deeply. The producer looked at me, questioning what to do. (And the director who had suggested calling him in was becoming red-faced with embarassment.)

After a moment the director asked the actor *"Robert, are you alright?"* For a moment the actor didn't even allow himself to be interrupted! The room was deathly quiet. Eyebrows were raised still higher.

Eventually, Robert abruptly sat straighter in the chair, opened his eyes, smiled, and said *"I was taught to take a minute to prepare."* Needless to say, Robert didn't get that paricular role, and to my knowledge hasn't gotten all that many since.

Marlon Brando, once in that interview for a magazine article mentioned elsewhere, hit the nail on the head nicely. He described what could be called *"preparing to feel"* as simply *"pushing a button."* In Mr. Brando's excellent working techniques, the "button" has always been carefully prepared ahead of time.

By experiencing the preplanned thought---the *button*, with its prepared feeling content as an automatically available property, the feeling could always be produced instantly by Brando, as it can be by all ideally professional actors.

Too many actors who require a minute to *"prepare to feel"* something probably have no expert technique and---even after that minute---may not feel all that much.

Sadly, those who've used some *"preparing to feel"* ridiculousness have probably also experienced its worst faculty: Most of the time spent in *preparing to feel* is actually spent experiencing the awful realization, moment after moment, that what's being prepared to be felt *isn't yet being felt!* If whatever the actor has prepared to aid the process doesn't produce it easily and instantly, then the conscious effort to *make it work* and the conscious observation that *"it isn't working yet"* negates any emerging truth it could possibly have when it finally if ever comes.

A director may as well give that actor as much time as he or she thinks he or she needs . . . then make a quick call to the casting office for a replacement.

■ **Actors preparing roles should bear in mind that writers aren't either actors or directors. They do get visualization ideas, though, and those visualization adjectives and phrases go into their dialogue and action descriptives. They need to be registered briefly, thereafter ignored !**

Punctuations and Parentheses

Consider Them Suggestions, Not Acting Text!

In almost every scripted role ever handed to an actor, a great number of speeches are preceded by a word or two enclosed in parentheses indicating the author's feelings as to how the speeches are to be delivered . . . *(shyly), (with tears in her eyes), (desperately), (on the verge of madness), (stifling a chuckle), (angrily), (sobbing now), (a queer expression on her face),* etc.

Actors should of course note those recommendations and suggestions of the writer. Often they contain important nuance that doesn't appear elsewhere in the dialogue or action description. But more often they're simply the imagined visual performance in the writer's eye . . . and the writer isn't often an actor.

Some of the same "directions" (that's what they appear to be) show up in action description as well. Again, they're there because of how the author has visualized the scenic action. At least

when they're in the action description they're more surely important to the progressing of the character's moments. Even there,
though, they should be questioned if they indicate a specifically
limited manner of the actor's experiencing a moment, which they
most often do.

In either case, they offer conceptual ideas of how the writer
thinks a moment should appear in performance. But, more often
than not, if the actor observes all of those conceptual recommendations and follows them to the letter the actor will be limited to
a totally surface, and perhaps very poor, experience.

Following those "directions" explicitly, the actor is denied
the process of creating. And the director---if he or she doesn't
know better---is reduced to the equivalent of a stage manager of a
touring reproduction who has to direct a replacement member of
the cast during a cross-country tour. Following those directions
explicitly leaves no opportunity for original work.

No director enjoys being denied the opportunity to bring his
or her own concepts to the production over all and to persuade
from his or her cast members in turn the ultimate of their own
creative contributions. In many cases the brilliance of a director
or an actor far surpasses the original concepts of the writer.

Most coaches and teachers, and directors as well, recommend
in strongest terms that actors cross out all of those parenthetical
suggestions before any homework on the script. If they're not
crossed out, actors are admonished to at least ignore them in
planning, in rehearsing and certainly in performance.

Actors come to scripts with first observations of their roles,
but immediately there commences their own creative analysis,
and what evolves in their preparation results sequentially from
their own analysis. Their own contributions may very well go
beyond the writer's. The writer has supplied the palette and the
paints, but it's the actor who visualizes the form, selects the
brushes and lays in the colors of his or her own choice.

As characters are planned and come to life in the hands of the
actor, inspirations come that may have eluded the writer. In
many instances actors, through dedicated preparation of characters' short or long sequences within their totality, can discover
behavior more consonant with their characters' inner lives than
that prescribed by the writer in those many and varied parenthetical suggestions.

And if the actor's inspired by one of the role preparation pro-
cedures---the Six Qestions research, for example---to bring ideas
and justifications for a character's behavior, activities that are
appropriate for it that don't appear in the script, etc., many of
those parenthetical suggestions of the writer must go.

The best advice one can be given is to of course register and perhaps give consideration to what the author's asking, then, whether the author appears to be making an ideal suggestion or not, cross out the parenthetical direction---perhaps also the similar (at least what are totally) *"how to do it"* directions included in action descriptions---and proceed, continually avoiding all those possible detours. That's what so many of them would truly be . . . detours.

■ **The next item is up to the individual actor's taste and judgment. My own feeling is that the choice between utter simlicity in acting and a more "busy", agitated manner of working depends on many things---the character itself, the production style of the director's choice, the nature of situations and what they involve, etc. However, there are cogent arguments for...**

Simplicity

The Elimination of Excess

It's ironic that during my own earliest years of development as a teacher some of the approaches which I devised for my classes were so complicated and time-consuming in their attempts toward achieving more of what Vakhtanogov labeled *Theatrical Realism*---an enhanced, more creative version of simple involvement on the part of the actor.

I say this because I had myself gained an early respect for simplicity in acting. Harold Clurman's, Robert Lewis's, Kazan's and others' recommendations didn't go unheard or ignored. And the absolutely "bare bones, 1-2-3" recipe for playwriting of Robert Anderson (*"Tea And Sympathy"*, *"I Never Sang For My Father"* and other plays), when I studied playwriting with him, was *"What do I want? . . . What do I have to do to get it?"* . . . *"Who or what is standing in the way?"* had left an indelible impression.

And the admonition of Lajos Egri, in *"The Art Of Dramatic Writing"*, that *"It is the dramatic character who creates the dramatic situation"* became a cornerstone and foundation of my teaching and remains a basic tenet.

In the late sixties, in New York, in conversation at one of the rehearsals of *"The Cherry Orchard"* with the Russian teacher-director Yuri Zavadsky of the Moscow Art Theatre, he voiced the same precept with the words *"When simplicity is beautiful all else is excess."* There was a brooding simplicity in all the performances in his finished production, but in at least this author's estimation there was too much of it.

There's an amusing anecdote Jack Lemmon tells about his experience in the filming of *"The Apartment"*, the 1960 film directed by Billy Wilder. These many years later it doesn't embarass Mr. Lemmon to remember the many, many times that Wilder stopped his performance to repeat the words *"Less! . . . Much less!"* and other similar admonitions.

Finally, when Jack felt he couldn't possibly do less than he was doing, he complained to Wilder *"If I do any less I won't be acting at all!"* Wilder smiled happily and responded *"Good boy! You're finally getting it."*

Director-teacher Robert Lewis, in his 1957-58 lectures before audiences of actors in New York, remembered a talk the great Laurette Taylor gave before actors in which she described what she felt to be the ingredients of fine acting. After standing perfectly still on the stage throughout her talk as she spoke of the many things she felt were important, at the very end, after beginning a sentence, saying that she felt the most important thing to remember was . . .she suddenly assumed a grand, theatrical pose and ended her final sentence of advice with *" . . . simplicity!"* The maintaining of utter simplicity throughout her talk, then that abrupt transition into grandiloquent theatricality, had driven the point home with utter clarity!

But there have been and still are today many actors and actresses whose personal acting syles couldn't be simple even if they made Herculean efforts to change their ways of working.

Geraldine Page, one of the greatest actresses of recent times, was never accused of simplicity. In fact, her constantly racing mind found those moments that obviously suggested simplicity her most difficult. In an early moment of her masterpiece performance in *"The Trip To Bountiful"*, instead of simply sitting and brooding, she insisted on a rocking chair, rocked in determined rhythm to a hymn she sang softly to herself as she schemed. It was a long, mesmerizing moment. To her, that was simplicity.

And as Alexandra del Lago in *"Sweet Bird Of Youth,"* if there may have been even one single moment of simplicity in any of that play's (and later film's) original script, it became charged with her characteristic arcing electricity in performance. For her, simplicity was simply not natural.

Simplicity in acting is an available choice. It fits some actors' personalities and their manners of working. It wasn't something Gerry Page could have lived with and she didn't try to. You must decide for yourself where your own realities and tastes must take you.

■ In today's acting world, the biggest name remains *Stanislavski,* because more than anyone else he wrote about his work so continually. The name *Strasberg* comes in a close second, because of the hundreds of stars and leading players he persuaded to join the Actors Studio and the turbulent waters of controversy that have generated continuous publicity for his work.

The names of so many other great teachers who brought the Stanislavski System to America aren't even known to the majority of today's acting community---Vera Soloviova and her husband Andrius Jilinsky, Tamara Daykarhanova, Leo and Barbara Bulgakov, Raikin Ben Ari, Miriam Goldina among them.

They all taught the Stanislavski and Vakhtangov Systems but none were prolific writers and none courted publicity. So today's new actor is too often familiar with only the two names, *Stanislavski* and *Strasberg.* Consider the following simply a history lesson.

The Stanislavski System(s)

There are So Many Now! . . . and They're All Different!

The *Stanislavski System* was formulated by Stanislavski commencing in 1907, when his first theories about *Concentration* and the development of *The Inner Character* became firmly fixed in his mind. Between 1907 and 1921, in the First Studio of the Moscow Art Theatre, he continued adding the parts of it, working side by side with and continually inspired toward next steps and their defining by his close friend Leopold Sulerzhitski.

The first exposure of American audiences to the Moscow Art Theatre ensemble style and the Stanislavski System on which it was based was in the New York appearance of the theatre company in January of 1923 and its subsequent tour of Chicago, Boston and Philadelphia before returning for more performances in New York.

American audiences were stunned, and a second American season of the theatre was quickly booked, opening in New York in November of the same year, later including appearances in Chicago, Boston, Philadelphia, Washington, Pittsburgh, Detroit, Cleveland, Hartford and New Haven. The tour continued into 1924, with its last performance in New York on May 11th of that year.

From 1923 up to the present, the Stanislavski Sysem which stunned American audiences in those appearances has become the cornerstone of American acting and acting throughout many of the other theatre capitols of the world.

Actors who buy and read Stanislavski's *"An Actor Prepares"* and none of the other books of his writing probably don't realize that the notes that appear in that book---not available in the United States until 1936, published by Theatre Arts Books--- document exclusively those earliest interesting experiments which contained the early items of the later System attributed to him. Important items of what came to be known as The Stanislavski Sysem (still later, *The Method of Physical Action*) will be found in that book. However, that first book deals almost exclusively with only *the work of the actor on himself.* It included little of what later was to be his System.

Yet today, in many Drama Departments of colleges and universities throughout America, that very first book of his writings---containing little of the characterization approaches that appear in the two other books of his trilogy---is used as a study text and is misconstrued by many as representing The Stanislavski Sysem's total!

By the time that very first book, translated by Elizabeth Reynolds Hapgood (who never actually studied with him, worked only from his notes, and it's now determined edited faultily), reached bookstores in America, his System had already moved forward. That book should now be called "first year class work", as it literally was when he made most of the notes it contains.

Then his continuing notes---again translated by Mrs. Hapgood---resulted in the second book to reach America, *"Building A Character".* Its notes, devoted in the main to the preparing of characterization and embodiment, were held up by World War II, were received piecemeal from him by Mrs. Hapgood, and were finally published and distributed in America in 1949--- nearly forty years after much of his System had been formed!

Its edited notes were from the period when he was spending six to eight months preparing a single production or sometimes a single character, and he himself found later that the approaches in that book would not be simple or rapid enough for the standard commercial theatre preparation periods.

Like his earlier *"An Actor Prepares",* this second book *"Building A Character"* was already close to thirty years behind time for Americans, insofar as reflecting his own continued evolving of his approach, and again apparently faultily edited.

It had been Stanislavski's plan to combine the internal truth-seeking (of *"An Actor Prepares"*) and the susequent external characerization work (of *"Building A Character"*) into one large book, but this was not to be.

295

Moreover, it wasn't until 1961 that Mrs. Hapgood, editing from notes his family furnished her after his death, finally---after years of collating so many of his later notes, and without his consultation (because he had died twenty-three years prior to that)---got "Creating A Role", the third book of the trilogy, into American bookstores, again not available to American actors until thirty-three years after his death!

In other words, *many years after his death* what is so broadly thought to be his "final system"---which he himself felt wasn't really final at all, and which he was still modifying in 1937 when he suffered an angina attack and in 1938 when he died---reached American actors!   And the planned new Russian editions (in English) will contain many corrections of material that reportedly distorted some of his views and theories in English earlier.

No wonder the confusions and contradictory interpretations. What was already history was always being "caught up with" in America many years behind time.

Also, under the very roof of the Moscow Art Theatre he founded and headed there were other teachers who had been taught by him who had begun teaching, and who had themselves begun modifying and adapting his teachings with their own innovations and concepts, while still being accepted by their students as teaching *"The Stanislavski System"*.

Michael Chekhov, the actor-teacher Stanislavski had once pointed to as the one who most epitomized the results of his teaching, was already teaching his own innovative approaches, at first attributing them in the main to Stanislavski and certainly at least identifying his approach with Stanislavski in spite of its vast differences. He finally at one point boasted that *"If Stanislavski's System is high school, then my system is university."*

Vsevolod Meyerhold, early recognized as a brilliant director and leading pupil of Stanislavski, had also broken away earlier and formed his own acting and production style which---involving what at the time was called "the grotesque" and his *bio-mechanics* concepts---was much closer to Bertolt Brecht's *"Living Newspaper"* concepts than to Stanislavski's.

The director-teacher most often referred to as his real heir, Eugene Vakhtangov, was considered by all (including Stanislavski) the most faithful to his master's teachings.   It was Vakhtangov, however, who recognized that the many bits and pieces of the system codified by Stanislaski still lacked some contributive items.

It was Vakhtangov who formulated several "missing links" in the approach; established a clearer manner and sequence for the use of the many approach items; and modestly and loyally stood aside as his contributions were credited to Stanislavski.

It was Stanislaski's former student and by then his most respected teacher, Vakhtangov, to whom both Stanislavski and Michael Chekhov regularly turned later for coaching on their own Moscow Art Theatre roles!

It was Vakhtangov, in those private coaching sessions, who is known to have attempted to persuade Stanislavski to recognize the importance of establishing the *stimuli and causes* for all physical actions *before* seeking to form the actions themselves. He labeled the tool he postulated for that purpose the *Inner Object*---which Stanislavski had at various points in his own writing called the *Object of Attention* and/or *Object of Concentration* but had thought of the item as most often being simply *physical and external.*

Vakhtangov continually urged the foregoing modification of the Sysem's use of *Inner Objects* and *Thought Objects.* There's evidence that his persuasions succeeded to some degree with Stanislavski, but it must be remembered that Vakhtangov died in 1922, and Stanislavski's System had by then become known as *The Method Of Physical Action.* There was simply no going back.

Up to the time of Stanislavski's death, his Sysem---labeled by him *The Method Of Physical Action* and officially recognized by the Moscow Art Theatre and throughout the theare world by that title---was still missing the important conceptual adaptation of the *Objects'* use which had been urged upon him by Vakhtangov and which was to be further suggested by the publications of others including Sigmund Freud and Pavlov's *conditioned response* findings.

In the end it was perhaps those emerging theories of Freud and Pavlov which persuaded Stanislavski to observe that more consistent and more meaningful result *definitely could, as Vakhtangov had urged, be obtained by the actor if conditioned by a stimulus of a more tangible form, incorporated early in the preparation among other given circumstances, than could be realized by a simple Action.*

It can be observed from his writings and notes to his actors that during the last years of his life Stanislavski was constantly seeking those manners in which actors could create such "stimuli" and apply them to their own responses to bring deeper and more truly emotional experiences than *Actions* alone could evoke. He continued to give them his own original labels---*Rhythms, Motive Forces, Justifications,* etc., but more and more often he referred to them with Vakhtangov's term, *Objects.*

Several of Stanislavski's own pupils emigrated from Russia to America in the 1920's and early 1930's. Richard Boleslasky (who wrote *"Acting---The First Six Lessons"*), was a member of the Moscow Art Theatre from 1906 to 1920, during the earliest period of Stanislavski's formulating of his System. Although he had directed the first production of the First Studio of the MAT, he had not taught there, and had not worked with Stanislavski after 1920---a time when Vakhtangov's influence on Stanislavski was occasioning at least some reexamination of the System.

Maria Ouspenskaya, after three years of training with Sulerzhitsky, Stanislavski's trusted associate, joined the Moscow Art Theatre in 1911 and she too went through some of those same earliest explorations. When she relocated in America (after the Moscow Art Theatre's two tours here in 1923-1924), she joined Boleslavsky and Germanova teaching at the American Lab Theatre, then established her own studio in New York for some years, finally relocating her studio in Hollywood in 1936 because of her own film roles.

There followed many years in which the early Russian teachers by then teaching in America continued to teach in the same manner, while Stanislavski and his System went forward with continuing developments about which those teachers from the early MAT work were reportedly unaware.

It is a fairly acepted fact among historians that those teachers apparently "fossilized" the early experiments and explorations into being thought of in America as *the final Stanislavsky System,* while the years between 1920 and 1938 represent some eighteen years of continuous, fanatic developments and adaptations in Stanislavski's work.

When some of the American students of Stanislavski, Vakhtangov and Michael Chekhov---Tamara Daykarhanova, Vera Soloviova and her husband Andrius Jilinsky, Leo and Barbara Bulgakov and the previously mentioned Germanova, all trained in those early years at the MAT---visited Stanislavski years later, they observed the later developments and the emerging of the more complete System. They brought back those advances, and those American actors who were fortunate enough to study those later developments with them profited from the System's many advances.

But those teachers who brought the newer developments---including the total abandoning by Stanislavski of the *Affective Memory* approach---could not reverse the tide of supposedly authoritative teaching approaches of the American Actors Lab. The *Affective Memory* approach was still being taught there by Boleslavsky, and in 1924 and 1925 Lee Strasberg learned of that approach that would later bring controversy and criticism to Stanislavski's System through his determined emphasis on the approach that Stanislavski himself had abandoned years earlier.

Like Strasberg, some of the teachers who had migrated from Russia later added adaptations and modifications of their own devising, thereby widening the gap between the original source material and the scores of increasingly different techniques existing today which claim the Stanislavski System as their source or in some cases their totalities. Being less prolific writers, however, some of their explorations and discoveries have never been documented.

The truth is that by the 1930's most of those mentioned and scores of others had begun to drift farther and farther away into their own systems.

That drift continues to this day, with the people taught by those early teachers, and later with the people they taught, as they too turned to teaching, still drifting ever outward along separate networks and tributaries of widening differences.

In many cases they've claimed to teach *"The Stanislaski System"*, or they teach their versions of *"The Method"* of Strasberg. Many are primarily of Stanislavski System or Method persuasion, perhaps, but all are different. This has been so confusing for American actors for so long!

During Stanislavski's lifetime, of course he too passed through several stages of development. First came the early *truth-seeking explorations* published in *"An Actor Prepares"*.

At the same time, but with more concentation upon them as time went by, came his early codifications of *role analysis and characterization approach items,* as published in *"Building A Character"*, which explained more of the System which was to become known as *The Method Of Physical Action* and which is more defined in that book and (still as a work in progress, according to him) in *"Creating A Role"*.

Finally, there were the later years of intensified exploration ---inspired by Vakhtangov's continuous urging up to the latter's death in 1922---toward a means of effectively incorporating the use of *Inner Objects and Thought Objects* (which Stanislavski still called *Objects of Attention and/or Objects of Concentration* on different occasions but more often by then, simply *Objects*).

The last years of his life were much more involved with psychologically conditioned *Inner Objects and Thought Objects* than is generally known. He was moving closer to Vakhtangov's adaptations than can be easily detected in the available published records, since so many of his notes were made before those last years of his life.

The confirmations of his late life searchings in the new area have come in the main via actors who studied with and worked with him during those last years. But this aspect of his continuing search, during the period when those adaptations were inspired by Vakhtangov and later, is certainly there---if one seeks it out---in *"Building A Character"*, in *"Collected Works, Vol. II"*, in *"My Life In Art"*, in "Stanislavski's Legacy" and in other more recent books edited from his notes or discussing them.

In those last years he's reported as having more and more often asked students *"What is it that disturbs your character?"* ...*"What's on your character's mind?"*... and *"What is your character's problem?"* Those questions, as worded by him, obviously solicit other than *action-worded* responses. They can quite clearly be seen as inviting his actors to consciouly define what this book and a number of other teachers call *Objects*.

In Stanislavski's own recorded directions to the cast members of the opera *"Werther"* in Paris during those years is a quote from his directions to his cast in which, in his own words in that recording, he stated that *"If the attention of the actor is constantly moving from one Object to another, then the constant changing of the Objects of His Attention creates the unbroken line of the character's experience."* Where in that quote is the word "action" mentioned?

Although Stanislavski and his System are so frequently mentioned in this book (because they're mentioned in most discussions of the acting art as common reference), contrary to what many teachers would claim, there are few contemporary actors or acting students who've actually studied *The Stanislavski System* in all its originally recommended phases.

And Stanislavski would have approved, at least with respect to the continued searching for a final system. He recommended it. His life was dedicated to progressing the principles of the actor's art as far as he could and simply passing his discoveries on to others to aid their own continuing searches.

So the American actor who is assertedly being taught *The Stanislavski System,* in whatever form, is at least (if the teacher's assertion is honest) being taught what that particular teacher believes to be the main elements of that System, even if consciously deleting a few of the earlier exercises which no longer apply with as much pertinence as they did in Stanislavski's time, and even if adding a number of the teacher's own discoveries that that System will have helped inspire.

There are many current versions of the Stanislavski System. But, even though they're taught in adapted forms and different vocabularies adapted to contemporary tongues and continually experimented with in different manners, the main body of their technigues began with Stanislavski.

■ Many of today's actors look upon their teachers as psychotherapists, partially because the mind processes are advancing so
rapidly today and, more and more, acting teachers find it necessary to continually adapt their teaching approaches to accommodate those discoveries.

Teachers As Behavioral Scientists

Qualified or Not . . It's Required in The Teaching Experience

With only a few distinguished colleague exceptions, most of
us who have spent the major part of our lives teaching actors are
mere journeymen in the fields of human behavioral sciences such
as psychodynamics, psychology, psychiatry, psychoanalysis,
psychotherapy, neurobiology, neuromuscularity and other sciences involved with the study of the mental, physical and emotional processes and even the science of the human nervous system's ability to react and learn.

But, because acting in its highest concept involves every one
of those fields in the actor's analysis of characters, finding of
means for conditioning his characters' behavior, learning to cope
with and control his own nervous system and the conditioned
stimuli of his left and right brains, in the teaching of actors it's
inevitable that one must study, experiment with, and teach to the
best of one's ability as much of those still evolving sciences as one
can. Acting involves them.

The compulsion toward becoming an actor strikes early in
those destined for professional acting careers, most often before
the young person so afflicted has any desire to study those human
sciences. The need to become knowledgeable in them becomes apparent almost immediately when the decision is finally arrived
at to become an actor. It's then---not as an original career goal---
that the student actor begins to avidly study those fields. Out of
acting career needs, that study never ceases.

Later, should an actor be sought out by other talents to teach,
that actor-teacher is catapulted into the chair of a behavioral
science practitioner, most often insufficiently prepared.

Stanislavski himself was the son of a wealthy Moscow manufacturer of gold and silver threads. His early life included purely
amateur theatricals. It was later, as he began directing and teaching, that *he began studying human behavior.*

Vakhtangov was the son of a wealthy tobacco farmer, later a
law student at Moscow University when he turned to acting and
within just a few years began teaching.   Just five months after

being admitted to the Moscow Art Theatre, Stanislavski suddenly assigned him to teaching a class. Like Stanislavski, *finding himself involved with not only the psychologies of characters but also with the psychodynamics of his individual students, he too sought all the behavioral science resources he could.*

Strasberg as a young man was first a wig salesman in his family's business, was persuaded by a friend to join an arts organization, which he did as a purely social activity, then became involved with the deep feelings for acting that, in his case too, led to teaching within a few years. Not even a high school graduate (many don't know that), Lee made the sciences of the mind a dedicated lifelong study. *Behavioral science, and more particularly neurobiology and neuromuscularity, became all-consuming studies for him, to which he dedicated the rest of his life.*

Sanford (Sandy) Meisner's father, a furrier, expected his son to be a clothing manufacturer. For a time Sandy worked as a stock boy in a pants factory, but at 19 he obtained a scholarship to the Theatre Guild School of Acting. In 1931 when he was one of the actors chosen for The Group Theatre company and there became more excited about acting, he studied and began the development of his talents for teaching. Sandy has always vehemently denied any abilities as a psychotherapist, but *the recordings from his class sessions clearly indicate his ability to modify his actors' personal lives as they relate to acting.*

Other noted teachers---Robert Lewis, Stella Adler, Uta Hagen and many more of us in America and still scores of others---have all had to become at least entry level behavioral scientists *to interpret the often complex natures of different characterizations demanded by writers, to diagnose the many different instrumental blocks of our students and offer remedies, etc.*

The Hollywood teacher Eric Morris is perhaps one of the more deeply involved with human behavioral sciences in his teaching method. He graduated from the Northwestern School of Drama. He too was not a Psychology major. After years of finding in his own theatre, film and television acting what he considered an insufficiently affecting relationship between the Stanislavsky and Strasberg approaches for actors and the personal realities of the actor himself, he began developing his "Being" theories and approaches in his own acting classes. *He continues determinedly searching for manners of expanding the actor's consciousness, to not only be affected by the impact of internal and external stimuli, but also to create the opening through which communication from the unconscious can occur and flow into the actor's behavior.*

All teachers of actors who are serious about developing the mind and body channels for actors' fullest use of their talents are inevitably drawn into involving with most of the behavioral sciences to one extent or another. Some teachers observe the need, bemoan it, but assume no obligation to do anything about it through the expanding of their own knowledge.

Other acting teachers perceive what depths still remain inaccessible to actors---even many actors possessing wonderfully effective techniques, and joyfully embrace the responsibility of participating in the continuing search for precisely those mysteries stored in the unconscious and manners in which actors may open the portals of access to them.

■ **These *"Straight Talk"* items would be incomplete without a detailed biography of Eugene Vakhtangov. He is perhaps the best kept secret in all of the history of The Stanislavski System and its later evolution in America, at least through inspiration, into *the "Method(s)"* of today.**

He didn't write as continually as Stanislavski. He kept himself too busy. The important modifications he contributed to the use of the System were known mostly to those he taught. And some of those whom he taught were hesitant to offend Stanislavski by including Vakhtangov's specific reformulations in their written descriptions of his work. Like most of the culture, myths and stories of the Native Americans in our own country, much of Vakhtangov's specific revisions have had to be handed down verbally by some of those who worked directly with him.

He deserves his own place, perhaps more than most others, in the *"Straight Talk"* section of this book.

Eugene Vakhtangov

His Immense Contribution to The Stanislavski System

Although considerably less known than Stanislavski to American actors, it was the brilliant Eugene Vakhtangov who first studied the System of Stanislavski; then within just five months after joining the Moscow Art Theatre was delegated by Stanislavski to teach his own classes at the Moscow Art Theatre; was soon told by Stanislavski *"You, Eugene, teach my System better than I do,"* and was regularly turned to personally by Stanislavski and Michael Chekhov for private coaching in the preparing of their own roles.

But the more significant heritage left by Vakhtangov---exceeding in importance even his *"theatrical realism"* adaptation of the System in his directorial concepts---is the understanding he postulated and urged upon Stanislavski for the use of *Inner Objects and Thought Objects* as the missing link in the System for which Stanislavski himself was continually searching.

While working with his actors in his first period of work, Vakhtangov followed the Stanislavsky System religiously, step by step. But later he came to a new understanding of the laws of dramatic art, while still resting on the principles of psychological realism and still thoroughly studying and passionately propagandizing Stanislavski's System.

It was he who observed the difference between *action* and the *stimulus that causes* action. It was he who revolutionized, as much as he could, the perception of the source of true experience for the actor. It was he who proposed that true experience depends upon the actor's ability to be stimulated, incited, by *scenic problems.* He once said to his student, Ruben Simonov, author of *"Stanislavski's Protege: Eugene Vakhtangov,"* and another student, Miriam Goldina, who translated and adapted Simonov's book into English for its printing in America, *"In life, our feelings are the reaction to what happens to us. It is less easy to recall what we felt and what action we took in a truly important moment. What happened to us, not what we did, is marked indelibly in our memory. It, not any resulting action, is what we remember with the most feeling."*

And Raikin Ben-Ari, one of the other former members of the Habimah Theatre whom Vakhtangov directed in *"The Dybbuk"* in the last months of his life, confirmed in great detail (in a meeting with Miriam Goldina and me in Hollywood in the late 1950's) what Miriam had spoken about to me many times---the more *Thought Object*-oriented manner Vakhtangov had utilized in directing *"The Dybbuk"* with a cast composed of predominantly inexperienced actors, which was to mightily impress the American audiences who saw that production. Vakhtangov's variation on Stanislavski's System was a manner Ben-Ari, another American coach Benno Schneider, Miriam and others used in coaching top stars in their later Hollywood coaching years.

The main variation on the System that Vakhtangov taught to Ruben Simonov, Miriam Goldina, Raikin Ben-Ari and others, and taught them to use, brought some other essential additions and specifications to the interpretation of the System with some of his own discoveries and with the theories that evolved from them, but the most important addition and adaptation remains his fervent proposal that *Inner Objects and Thought Objects* should become more central in all aspects of the System's preparation processes.

He was only partially (and belatedly) successful in persuading Stanislavski, and the available printed references to his variation are few and must be specifically looked for. While he added them to his work with his own classes and used them in his direction of productions, he finally abandoned his effort to persuade Stanislavski to incorporate his modifications in the System.

But Stanislavski, later in life, more specifically taught that the actor should think *"first of all about what he wants to obtain ---and then (not first) what he is to do."* Very clearly, *"what he wants to obtain"* suggests an *Object*, and *what he is to do* clearly suggests the *Action... in that order!*

Had he lived beyond his late thirties, Vakhtangov would surely today be credited by a broader sector of the acting art world with *the final key* to the more total and more facilitative use of the System---the key that could be used by actors either with, or even instead of, action.

Born February 1st, 1883, the son of a wealthy tobacco farmer, he gave up that rich life, left his home, and began to make a living for himself. He began as an actor and director in small theatres in Moscow while attending Moscow University as a law student. Joining the Drama School headed by the Moscow Art Theatre actor, Alexander Adashev, in 1909 he studied under Leopold Sulerzhitsky, Stanislavski's closest friend who had inspired much of Stanislaski's early formulation of the System.

His talents quickly attracting the respect and close friendship of Sulerzhitsky, he was taken with the latter to Paris in 1910-1911 when "Suler" was invited there to direct Maeterlinck's *"The Blue Bird"* at the Rejane Theatre. Upon return to Moscow, "Suler" recommended him to Vladimir Nemirovich-Danchenko, Stanislavski's co-director at the MAT. Nemirovich-Danchenko was impressed, and he and "Suler" recommended him to Stanislavski, who had already heard about his work.

He met with Stanislavski and joined the MAT on March 15th, 1911, receiving forty rubles in subsistence salary (just ten less than the already established Richard Boleslavsky) because all three of the Moscow Art Theatre heads---Sulerzhitsky, Nemirovich-Dantchenko and Stanislavski---by then already knew him to be brilliant.

Stanislavski assigned him to teaching in a conversation on August 3rd, 1911 and raised his pay to sixty rubles immediately. His first directing results at the MAT---Gerhard Hauptmann's *"The Festival Of Peace"* in 1913, Henning Berger's *"The Deluge"* in 1914, Henrik Ibsen's *"Rosmersholm"* in 1918--- firmed his position there.

Throughout those years he was also teaching classes elsewhere, extending Stanislavski's System to many actors outside the MAT---at the Gunst Drama Studio, the Chaliapin Drama Studio, the Armenian Studio and the Tchaikovsky Motion Picture Studio.

On September 13th, 1920, the Vakhtangov Studio at the MAT was renamed the Third Studio of the MAT, with Vakhtangov installed as its head.

During those last years of his so active life (1920-1922) he directed Chekhov's *"The Wedding"*, *"The Miracle of St. Anthony"*, Strindberg's *"Erik XIV"*, a second version of *"The Wedding"*, Carlo Gozzi's *"Turandot"* and the premiere of S. An-Sky's *"The Dybbuk"* at the Habimah Theatre. In those last years of his life he continued working frenziedly in spite of excruciating stomach ulcer pain, pneumonia in his left lung and terminal fatigue from his self-driven, overworked spreading of himself in too many directions.

It was Vakhtangov who demonstrated in his productions and his concepts of their form that Stanislavski's System could be used by actors and directors in all forms of theatre and was not limited to the purely realistic style most often associated with Stanislavski's own productions.

He passed away at 9:55 the evening of May 29th, 1922. The history and chronology of his important work with Stanislavski and his contributions to the Stanislavski System can be found in the book *"Stanislavsky's Protege: Eugene Vakhtangov"* by one of his students, Ruben Simonov, published for America in 1969 by DBS Publications, Inc., as translated and adapted by another of his former students, the former wife of the founder of the Habimah, my own very dear friend Miriam Goldina, with whom I taught side by side for a time in Hollywood. A photo of her on my wall is inscribed *"To Larry, the joy page in my book of life."*

It was my friend Miriam's often stated and firm conviction that, born just seven days after Vakhtangov's death---June 5th, 1922--- I was (and if it were so then, would in her conviction still be) the reincarnated spirit of Eugene Vakhtangov. I never shared Miriam's firm belief in reincarnation, but her statement (made on many occasions to many people beside myself) was a beautiful and treasured compliment. No one could be more supremely gifted by fate.

A Money-Saving
Library For Actors
On Tight Budgets

Some Outstanding Books For Actors

That Can Provide A Fairly Broad Perspective
And Quick Access to Research When It's Needed

I'll preface the following list of books with Michael Caine's comment about books: *"I read books like mad, but I am careful not to let anything I read influence me."*

I suspect Michael's amusing comment may apply to books in general for many people, but I'm sure it doesn't apply for actors---who continually spend much of the little money they may have on books about acting, continually searching those books for truths they haven't yet found and ideas that will suddenly and blindingly illuminate the path toward brilliance in acting.

Actors---even those studying with teachers they respect and who are sure they're making progress in the development of their talents---*"read books like mad,"* like Mr. Caine says he does, in their never-ending search.

And there are *so many books* about acting--sometimes two, three or four by the same prolific teachers. Often one of a teacher's books intrigues the actor and he buys all of that teacher's books as well, only to find, as is often the case, that there's either much duplication or (in one or two of an author's published works) some basic concepts and approaches that abruptly cause loss of interest in that teacher.

There's a plethora of books written by some that simply exploit the broad interest in Stanislavski and a score of others---books which present nothing original that hasn't been written about more effectively by many others, and books that offer perhaps only one or two original thoughts if any at all. And the actor has gone without something he needs to buy those books.

The following list of available books comprises my own selections for recommendation of the most complete, the most important and the most helpful books (in my own estimation) by multiple-book-published teachers and other writers that I feel are (or state that I don't feel are) important for the actor on a limited budget to have. A few books are included only because they're recommended by some others---with my own reasons for not judging them to be equally important.

308

The majority of those comprising this list offer, in single or perhaps two books of their celebrated writers' writing, most of those leading teachers' complete teaching methodologies in the clearest presentations possible, along with hundreds of stimulating, original ideas of their conception.

I realize that in offering even slight criticism of some books, or in omitting some teachers' books from being listed, I must spark some resentment on the part of even some close friends who teach and write about their work for publication . . . but my obligation in this chapter is to my readers.

So . . . here's a list that can simply save money for the reader in the gathering of a library that can provide what I feel is the broadest overview available of valuable descriptions of leading teachers' approaches in their own published words, the most complete and accurate histories and chronologies of the evolution of the acting art and related crafts, and the most complete (single volume) research resources on subjects with which the actor may (and probably will) become involved during a meaningful professional career.

Most of these books are handily available at Samuel French and other actors' bookstores in major cities or can be ordered from either Samuel French Trade Books, 7623 Sunset Boulevard, Hollywood, California 90046, or Samuel French Bookshop, 45 West 25th St., New York, NY 10010, or the Applause Theatre Books Catalog, 211 West 71st Street, New York, N.Y. 10023.

Books On Acting

■ **"A Challenge For The Actor"**, by Uta Hagen
---(Charles Scribner's Sons, Macmillan Publishing Co., 1991-$22.50.

In this, her more recent book, following the deservedly best-selling success of her earlier book *"Respect For Acting"*, Ms. Hagen expands on her own manner of using *Inner Objects*, among other of her approaches, taking all of them to still higher levels of understanding and artistic creativity. Those and other theories are also discussed in her book *"Respect For Acting"*, described later in this list of recommended books.

Here, in this book, is further evidence that Ms. Hagen is one of the most coherent and enlightened teachers of the actor's art, and this, like her other book, should be in every actor's library. Both of her books are outstanding, as is her teaching.

309

■ **"Acting: The First Six Lessons"**, by Richard Boleslavsky
---(Theatre Arts Books, 1933) - $16.95.

I've never recommended this little book, discussed here only because some people do recommend it. The reason for a lengthier discussion than some other books is simply to justify not recommending it, when quite a number of college and university Drama Departments do include it in their recommended lists. For their students it's at least written entertainingly.

It's impossible to disagree with Boleslavsky's statement that the actor's art cannot be taught; that he either is or isn't born with ability; but that the technique for expressing his talent and his art is something that can be taught . . . technique being something which is realistic and possible for the actor to make his own.

I feel the book owes what importance has been accorded it by some to the fact that Boleslavsky was one of the first emigrants from the Moscow Art Theatre to teach the Stanislavski System in America.

But some of us feel that his book gives a pocketful of desired results inspired by the author's years of working with Stanislavski during only the latter's very earliest explorations. It offers its *"how to do it"* advice in a coy, facetious form too often hidden behind the sense of humor for which Boleslavsky was known.

This book isn't for the actor specifically seeking more how-to's regarding the preparation of *characterizations for roles*, especially. In the chapter headed *Characterization* Boleslavsky only briefly mentions that characterization is important, then devotes almost no paragraphs to what it is or how it's accomplished. His book was published before Stanislavski's *"Building A Character"* was even known to him.

Although he was a member of the MAT from 1906 to 1920 and played many roles there, he didn't work with Stanislavski after 1920---the beginning of a time when Stanislavski was daily making adjustments and adaptations to the early version of his System. He hadn't yet discarded the *Affective Memory* as being a potentially harmful approach, as he did soon thereafter. It's believed that Boleslavsky, throughout his teaching in America, thought it was still being advocated as important in Stanislavski's teaching.

Boleslavsky migrated to America in 1920 and (with Germanova and Maria Ouspenskaya, two others from the Moscow Art Theatre) taught at the American Lab Theatre in New York until 1929, when he moved to Hollywood to direct.

310

At the American Lab Theatre he taught the *Affective Memory* (in this book he calls it *Memory of Emotion*) to a young, impressionable 23-year-old acting student named Lee Strasberg during 1924 and 1925, presenting it as (and believing it to still be) one of the main items in Stanislavski's evolving System. Stanislavski himself had summarily discarded its use in teaching, which most believe Boleslavsky didn't know.

Boleslavsky was Strasberg's only teacher. And Strasberg grabbed onto *Affective Memory* and continued to claim it as one of the dominant items in his own work until his death.

With respect to Boleslavsky's ebullient personality, as it assuredly affected his writing in this book, some interesting comments about his personality and the always present sense of humor that obscures so many of the points in this book appear in the private diary notes and correspondence of Vakhtangov. They explain the caprice with which Boleslavsky probably wrote that hides important concepts and advice behind fairly amusing dialogues with "the Creature":

On March 2nd, 1913, after the twenty-fifth rehearsal of Gerhard Hauptmann's *"The Festival Of Peace,"* Vakhtangov, directing Boleslavsky, wrote a note in his diary bemoaning the fact that Boleslavsky was admiring himself all the time, unconsciously playing around with 'bon ton'; that verything was wrong with his manner of working on his part and his working with his fellow actors; that he paid little attention to his work and that everything he was doing was dry and uninspired.

And from a plaintively frustrated letter to Leopold Sulerzhitsky (Vakhtangov's first mentor at the MAT), on March 27th of the same year, some of Vakhtangov's comments while still working with Boleslavsky on the same play included a frustrated outcry that what he labeled Boleslavsky's unethical behavior was making the Studio's work appear more like amateur, home theatricals and that his entire manner and way of conducting himself during rehearsals, his attitude toward his work, his way of working, was disturbing. Vakhtangov described him as always careless, always frivolous, always superficial, always disrespectful towards his partners on stage.

This author feels that that same personality is easily apparent to the insighted in his small book. Boleslavsky's wit and appreciation of his own ever present cleverness are there on every page. It does state desired results, and it offers clear manners of accomplishing some of those results---*only* if one has the patience to sift through the distracting dialogues, allegories, anecdotes and somewhat vague illustrations to get to the practical and explicit "how to" guidance actors probably hope they'll find if the book has been recommended to them.

311

■ "Acting Without Agony---An Alternative To The Method"

by Don Richardson--- (Allyn & Bacon Inc., 1988) - $16.95.

This book is unusual, certainly, in this time when most books are Stanislavski or Strasberg oriented. It's to the point, fiercely, without a lot of wasted words. Presumptious, many might feel, because it asserts that role preparation and the summoning of feelings *need not be so complicated* as it is in the teachings of many other teachers. He has a point, an important one.

The title clearly states the author's viewpoint. In his very easy to understand book---which is full of helpful suggestions as to an attractively simple manner of working on roles, Don offers his own version of *Actions* (in that respect not unlike others, calling them *Objectives* out of personal preference), but offers them in a more vivid and up to date form in contemporary terms than are available in many others' teachings and writings.

The differences between Don's recommended approaches and those taught by Lee Strasberg, Stella Adler, Uta Hagen, Sandy Meisner and others of us are vast, just as his book's title implies. He proposes, not unlike the more celebrated teacher Robert Lewis, that there are much simpler manners of finding and using productive acting approaches.

Readers of his book will find his suggestions simple, time saving, and designed objectively for the contemporary actor's manner of working as demanded by today's shorter rehearsal periods in theatre and by the quickened pace and unique requirements of film and television acting.

Don't look for complicated approaches like *Justifications, Personalizations, Particularizations, Atmospheres or Substitutions* in this book. The remarkable thing is that they're there if the reader stays alert, but their manners of use, like the rest of his approaches, are so simplified.

A gifted actor will find Don's way of working a great shortcut compared to the three-years-student approaches so often taught in conservatories, academies, institutes and other long term programs of the postsecondary education type. It quickens the pace of developing the actor's instrument as well as the pace of preparing roles for today's professional acting demands. It's his claim that his approach is as ideal for the newer actor as it is for one who's more experienced. He may be right.

It lays out excellent suggestions for breaking down separate scenes with simplicity and supplying the actors' highest concepts of what their characters should be doing, why they should be doing those things, *how*, and with what *Emotion* (Don's word) those things can be done.

He shares my own enthusiasm for and teaches many items of his (and my) selection from the Stanislasky, Vakhtangov and other experiments of the Moscow Art Theatre, but that's where any similarity to the *"Stanislavski guru"* group of acting teachers ends. The outstanding merit of Don's book is the *simplicity and freedom from much of the dogma* that it offers the actor in the achieving of desired results.

■ **"Actors On Acting"**, edited by Toby Cole & Helen Krich Chinoy
---(Crown Publishers, Inc., 1949; revised 1970) - $15.00.

In this book the actor can have *a complete library of all the histories of the acting art!* In the 20th anniversary, 1970 revision it updates the history of actors' legacies to include many of those of more recent years as well. Every page contains the words of the actors themselves or the comments of eyewitnesses that have been disinterred to help us obtain illuminating descriptions of those early actors' art.

Most of the actors whose greatnesses have remained uchallenged by time will be found here. And the 20th anniversary, 1970 edition includes the recent innovators of the last half of this century---Grotowski, Peter Brook, Julian Beck and Judith Malina, Joseph Chaikin, as well as some of the debates about the "Method" between Lee Strasberg, Robert Lewis and others.

It's a marvelous, thorough book. Actors owe it to themselves to include it in their library.

■ **"Advice To The Players"**, by Robert Lewis
---(Theatre Communications Group, 1980) - $8.95.

Here, in his own words, one of America's most important teachers details with his characteristic clarity a respectable number of his teaching approaches. And those approaches are shared totally, with his characteristic openness exemplified by a comment in his own Preface to the book, stating that he, like all others, has stolen and stolen, from his Group Theatre days forward, from others. He acknowledges that most teachers take, alter, update, add to, subtract from others' exercises. *"Grab what you can,"* he advises. *"It's all in the family. Be my guest."*

"Bobby" Lewis's celebrated teaching is admittedly eclectic, drawing from the theories and innovations of others of earlier and his own time, as his longtime friend and fervent admirer Harold Clurman points out in his Introduction. The book includes many exercises that he's tested over a long period with a host of students and which have produced unmistakably valuable results, plus his characteristically direct-to-the-point lectures.

313

His book, like his exercises and his always gently amusing lectures, simplifies and demysticizes many of the approaches that some others teach but are known to teach in more complex, less down to earth manners. What Stanislavski and others took total chapters to express, Robert Lewis can and does, again in both his lectures and this book, present directly and clearly in a few easily understood words.

His book is full, chapter after chapter, of some of the most provocative ideas and suggestions regarding the best manners of using them. Every actor owes it to himself to have this book!

■ **"An Actor Prepares"**, by Konstantin Stanislavsky
---translated by Elizabeth Reynolds Hapgood (Theatre Arts Books, 1936) - $15.95.

This was the first of the three book trilogy of collected notes made by Stanislavski and later translated and adapted by Elizabeth Reynolds Hapgood for printing in America. This is the book (of the three) most referred to and most broadly used as source for the *original* versions of the individual approaches for the *developing of the actor himself* rather than many of the approaches for the *developing of roles*.

It's unfortunate that Stanislavski couldn't combine this first book of the trilogy with the second book, *"Building A Character"*, as had been his initial plan. This first book's appearance in America---so many, many years before the second book appeared here---led many to believe that this first book comprised all his teachings, which it did not. To this day, there are Drama Departments that present this first book as the total of the Stanislavski System. That's unfortunate, also very wrong.

That some of the approaches recommended in this first book may have been improved upon by others who've come later notwithstanding, many of the exercises written about by Stanislavski in this first book have transcended time and influenced modern acting more than any other writings yet published about the acting art. It's simply important to remember that this book deals mostly with *the actor's work on himself*.

■ **"Building A Character"**, by Konstantin Stanislavski
---translated by Elizabeth Reynolds Hapgood (Theatre Arts Books, 1949) - $15.95.

The second of the books translated by Mrs. Hapgood from Stanislavski's notes, it's devoted to the *external characterization* aspects.

The misapprehension that Stanislavski neglected much of the externals of characterization is understandable. It had its origin in the huge time differential between the appearance of *"An Actor Prepares"* and this book in America---*thirteen years*.

He was still working on this, the second book of the trilogy of *"An Actor Prepares"*, *"Building A Character"* and *"Creating A Role"*, as late as 1937, just a year before he died. The manuscript didn't reach Mrs. Hapgood, its translator, in America, until after World War II.

Readers can gain from this collection, translation and editing of his notes a clear perception of Stanislavski's own struggles to find external theatrical forms both based on and emanating from inner truths and also those imposed on external characterization for their strictly theatrical value.

Through the ignoring of so many of these items in the *Method* training of some American teachers there has been the common misconception in some quarters that Stanislaski himself wasn't concerned with such externals. This book can clear up that misconception, and the lengthy discussions from Stanislavski's own notes might trigger some ideas for the actor that the other two books of the trilogy might not suggest.

However, for the preparing of *the character itself*, one of the most enduring and most valuable books adapted from Stanislavski's own notes on the subject of *characterization* remains . . .

■ **"Creating A Role"**, by Konstantin Stanislavski

---translated by Elizabeth Reynolds Hapgood (Theatre Arts Books, 1961) - $15.95.

This, the third book of Stanislavski's trilogy, was written by him around 1934, but not translated by Mrs. Hapgood and published posthumously until 1961---almost a quarter century after his death---by Theatre Arts Books, after the manuscript was finally sent to Mrs. Hapgood by Stanislavski's son.

In this book's early pages appear his advice to *List The Facts* (with a clear example of how to do it); his recommendations about *Appraising The Facts;* discussion of his versions of *Super Objectives* and *Through Lines of Action* for creating the continuous psychologies of characters throughout roles. Also, his own versions of *Creative* and *Psychological Objectives* are explained.

Here is discussion of *Objects of Attention* in a form he describes as *"a new quality of his method"*, stressing that new quality. He states that *Actions* should be carried out for the sake of the *Objects of Attention*---exactly as Vakhtangov had urged up to the time of his death!

Vakhtangov would have been pleased to see his suggested adaptation of *Objects'* use finally given that much recognition by Stanislavski in print.

This book, for many of us, represents the crowning achievement of Stanislavski's printed teachings. And that's fitting, since it was the last of the three books of his great and enduring trilogy of advice to actors.

■ **"Experimental Theatre"**, by James Roose-Evans
---(Universe Books, 1970) $8.95

For actors and directors seeking the most exhaustive and most authoritative history and chronology of primarily *experimental* theatre (but more than that, a history of *most* theatre--- with an incredible amount of detailing of the innovators' lives and their specific innovations), here's the book! It circles the whole globe down through history with its huge cast of innovators and their approaches.

As a history of *theatrical innovation and experiment*, I can't think of a more total pesentation of the revolutionary concepts of earlier times that are still experimental and revolutionary today.

This book may of course be more for the director and the conceptualist than for the actor, but it can fascinate and inspire the artist in the actor, page after page, too.

■ **"The Film Actor's Complete Career Guide"**, by Lawrence Parke
---(Acting World Books, 1992; 4th Edition, 1994) - $24.95.

This 304 page book, by the author of the book in your hand right now, offers clear, concise, fully detailed *how-to* advice for every step of the film actor's career-building ladder---from preparing to come to Hollywood, through the early period, through the manners of advancing a career, all the way to top stardom.

It details the right and wrong ways to start; newcomer traps to avoid; how to survive and stay; publications and services the actor should and should not rely upon; the right kinds of professional materials and what to do with them; self promotion, self advertising, self publicizing that the actor can do; how to work with press agents later; getting and keeping the right agent; what small and large agencies do and how they do it . . .

Audition tapes and audition scenes; interviewing for roles; mistakes actors make in interviews that hold them back; casting directors---what they do and how they do it; the performing unions the actor must join . . .

The film job, step by step---what to do before, during, after; details of working with the camera and film crew people; how roles and billing and salaries are adanced by agents and actors; the different contracts and what their small print means . . . and much more.

The book is full of behind-closed-doors, inside information that many actors never learn until it's too late. Every aspect of successful career-building is covered in this totally candid, recipe-book-detailed, career building textbook.

As its author, I certainly recommend this book. I also consider it appropriate for recommending in a book entitled *"Acting Truths And Fictions."* Its truths and its fictions-blasting are simply more involved with the professional talent marketplaces of film, television and theatre.

■ **"How To Start Acting In Film And Television Wherever You Are In America"**, by Lawrence Parke---(Acting World Books, 1993) - $19.95

This is another of Mr. Parke's books designed to give actors all the information they need to prepare for, start and advance in professional acting careers.

In this case, he's writing for those who live in other parts of the country, who aren't planning to come to Hollywood to begin professional film acting careers, but, being actors, want to obtain film and television roles in location projects filming near their homes, also national and local commercials filming in their areas or close by.

Filming in the 90's takes place everywhere. Many of the smallest towns in America have served as locations for the biggest boxoffice successes. And most of those faces in small roles and walking through or standing behind counters as extras live in those small towns. The book offers clear, concice, fully detailed "how to" advice for the steps actors can take to begin film acting careers wherever they are, often right in their own states.

There's a complete list, by states, of all film commissions, talent agencies and location casting directors throughout the United States, to help the actors find those offices nearby.

There's a chapter on auditioning and reading for roles; how the actor should conduct himself at interviews; what to expect; the differences between auditions for dramatic roles and commercial roles; etc.

Also, page after page, it offers a lot of behind-closed-doors, insider information that many actors never learn until it's too late---the kinds of photos and résumés that attract attention and interviews; procedures for getting agents; how to impress their areas' casting people; a complete education in how to act for the camera; what to do before, during and after film jobs; everything the actor will need to appear professional in first film roles.

In addition, there's a complete vocabulary, with definitions, of the terms film actors need to know on film sets.

So many actors living in remote areas feel they must be satisfied with just doing local theatre. This book will show them how to get location film and television work too!

■ **"On The Technique Of Acting"**, by Michael Chekhov---(Harper Collins, 1991) - $12.00.

This is the amended and more complete edition of the shorter 1942 version of Chekhov's book that was originally titled *"To The Actor"*. It contains many more of the exercises recommended by Chekhov than appear in the earlier version.

I'll give my honest opinion about it only because I feel as a book it couldn't possibly (and I feel doesn't) succeed in teaching what was so personal a technique of that brilliant man. I feel the actor wanting to study Chekhov's techniques must study with one of the present day teachers who understand them and can present them in the classroom environment much more effectively than they can be conveyed, even by their creator, in any book.

I've personally listened to the tapes he made at the request of some of his students in 1955. They're in simple language, for the most part lovingly reminiscing about his relationships with Stanislavski and others, including his former roommate Vakhtangov. When talking of his teaching, those tapes are much clearer and simpler in the discussing of his approaches. The book doesn't equal them (at least in my estimation).

Chekhov himself was a gifted, consummate artist. But, like many other artists, his ability to communicate his own art and its processes to others---in spite of the many exercises he formulated in the attempt---was during his liftime and is still today, in this book at least, less than ideal for most readers.

Chekhov's teachings were also difficult, often impossible, for many of his students at the Moscow Art Theatre to grasp. His classes were always diminishing in numbers of students as his actors tried time and again and failed to succeed with his complex, esoteric approaches.

His own eccentric and fascinating characterizations remain the hallmark of his career in theatre and films. His ability to teach the processes he himself used was less impressive.

The actor who'd like to explore the approaches of Chekhov should more ideally seek out one of those who was most closely associated with him. Of the two who come immediately to mind are, first, certainly George Shdanoff, who was associated with Chekhov throughout much of his life, who still currently teaches his approaches in Hollywood as this book is written, and whose name appears as the person to whom Chekhov dedicated the 1942 version of his book *"To The Actor"*.   George is a friend of this author. We were associated in the founding of the Acting Coaches And Teachers Association. I hope he'll forgive me for the foregoing comments about his beloved friend's book.

■ **"Respect For Acting"**, by Uta Hagen, with Haskel Frankel ---(MacMillan Publishing Company, 1973) - $18.95.

Here's a veritable gold mine of exciting ideas and personal advice for actors. It's ideal for the working professional as well as for the insecure newcomer seeking assurance and encouragement just as much as clear, inspiring guidance toward finding the keys to the mysteries of the acting art. Many of those keys are in Ms. Hagen's book---her earlier work with *Inner Objects* included.

Every page of her book offers sensible, practical and feeling-kindling material that can penetrate to the core of today's actor's sensibilities.

Her theories are generated in not *losing ourself in the part* but, rather, *finding ourself in the part*.   Her book goes far beyond the simple hypothesizing of that simple but stunning difference into a whole bookful of manners (all copiously detailed) through which that can be accomplished.

Ms. Hagen has continually taught acting at the HB Studio in New York, for years beside her late husband Herbert Berghof and continually since his passing away. Many current stars have profited from her teaching. It's the firm conviction of this author that anyone who reads her fine book, even without actually studying with her, will come away a better actor.

■ **Sanford Meisner On Acting"** , by Sanford Meisner and Dennis Longwell---(Vintage Books, 1987) - $11.00.

There's no American teacher more beloved than "Sandy" Meisner who still today, with a voice that for years has required amplification, a body wracked with pain from accidents, and cataracts in both eyes that require thick glasses, continues teaching in New York, in Los Angeles and some of the time on the island of Bequia in the West Indes where he goes to rest, taking a few students with him and conducting leisurely classes on the island.

He's been teaching his classes at the Neighborhood Playhouse of the Theatre, at 340 East 54th St. in New York ever since most of us can remember, in more recent years offering a two-year training program. Of the faculty of fourteen at the Playhouse, four teach acting under Sandy's supervision.

For a time, following a falling out with the Playhouse, he was Head of Actor Training for 20th Century-Fox Studios in Hollywood. Actor Jim Brolin and some others wanted to study with me during that period but 20th Century-Fox insisted they work with Sandy there, so I remember that time.

Sandy eventually returned to the Playhouse and has remained there, with occasional periods in Hollywood more recently, conducting classes there.

The book is mostly in the form of recordings made in many class sessions as new actors were first introduced to his basic approaches, then taken step by step into the further developments he recommends and has taught to many of today's top stars throughout the many years of his celebrated teaching career.

■ **"Since Stanislavski And Vakhtangov:The Method As A System For _Today's_ Actor"**, by Lawrence Parke ---(Acting World Books, 1986, Revised 1994)

I offer no apology for this book being among those I recommend. In describing and discussing the items of the Stanislavski and Vakhtangov approaches, I feel (as Laurence Olivier stated in a letter to me) this book presents one of the first clear manners of step-by-step combining those approaches and others which have been discovered since, while adapting them to the requirements of today's professional actor in film, television and theatre.

The step-by-step, sequential approaches for preparing roles, manners of accessing the resources of the right brain and involving the body in the creative process, and many approaches and exercises of my own devising, are included.

In the 1960's, during one of her return visits to the Moscow Art Theatre, my approaches were lectured on before the current students and faculty of the MAT School by my friend Miriam Goldina, former student of Vakhtangov.

Readers of the book you're reading at this moment will find some of the approaches described earlier in "Since Stanislavski" reprinted or less lengthily described in this book, simply because those are some of the "acting truths" in which I believe so wholeheartedly that I feel they belong in this book as well, in somewhat revised form, for those who haven't read my earlier book and by their inclusion here won't have to buy it.

■ **"The Stanislavski Heritage---Its Contribution To The Russian and American Theatre"**, by Christine Edwards
--- (New York University Press, 1965)

For the actor-historian who wants to trace the progress and use of the approaches of Stanislavski in relation to the changing environments, political upheavals and others' discoveries that affected it, there's no finer, more thorough or more fascinating book than this one.

Ms. Edwards has done a staggering amount of research into not only Stanislavski's work but also the approaches of literally hundreds of others who were contemporaries---whether other actors of the world stage that preceded him by a few years, peers with whom he never worked, admired acquaintances whose work and opinions about acting he valued, close associates with whom he worked daily, or students---of the man whose work has shaped or at least affected the work of actors throughout the world for decades.

There are few leading actors' and directors' work, down through history, that are not mentioned and described in detail in this book. The theatres that antedated the Moscow Art Theatre are detailed. Stanislavski's own early beginnings are there. Names, places and dates are all there and documented.

The book is doubly fascinating because---sprinkled throughout among the descriptions of authors' works, theatre productions, related activities, explorations and discoveries---appear direct quotes from lectures, writings, correspondence and conversations of those being written about.

Even criticial reiews of the period between the early 1930's (when Stanislavski's System was beginning to be popular in America) and the time of her book's publication, about that System and it's "American Method" adaptations, also notes from Seminars discussing the latter, are quoted expansively.

For any actor, director or theatrephile of whatever interest area---acting, directing, scenic design, costume design, theatre history, this is perhaps the most complete book of its kind. I recommend it highly.

■ **"Strasberg's Method---As Taught By Lorrie Hull"**, by S. Lorraine Hull---(Ox Bow Publishing, Inc., 1985) - $17.95.

Probably the most complete review of the life and work of Lee Strasberg is this book by Dr. Lorrie Hull, who first studied with Mr. Strasberg for many years, was one of the earliest members of the Actors Studio he headed, later taught for him, also for many years.

On page 2 she explains that Strasberg's Method *"seeks to add new elements to Stanislavski's basic principles by means of experimentation. This is accomplished by making use of our expanding knowledge of human psychology, the process of conditioning, the role of habits, the interaction between the conscious and the subconscious and the process of creative imagination."*

Her book traces Mr. Strasberg's childhood, his early acting study, his emergence as a teacher, the history of his teaching, the Strasberg exercises of all kinds (in lots more detail than I've found in other books about his work), etc. There's a section on directing actors which suggests manners in which directors and actors can most objectively and effectively work together. There are suggestions of scenes for actors to work on for their unique values in development of different facets of the actor's experience.

In discussing the *Affective Memory* approach that was so emphasized in Mr. Strasberg's work, Dr. Hull traces the early explorations of it by Stanislavski---not mentioning (out of deference to Lee) that Stanislavski discontinued use of it for several reasons. She describes many of Mr. Strasberg's exercises for *Relaxation, Concentration,* use of *Sense Memory,* use of *Affective Memory,* and many other instrument-conditioning approaches employed by him in his continuous teaching career.

Mr. Strasberg's teaching approaches concentrated on *"the training of will, intelligence (thought), emotion, imagination, and the stirring of the unconscious,"* as described by Dr. Hull, also on *training the actor to relax and to concentrate* so that the actor could use those faculties.

However, Dr. Hull also describes in detail the different manners Mr. Strasberg recommended for beginners', intermediate and advanced actors' work on roles for their scenes in classes, in all cases structuring their work with seeking out *units, intentions and actions,* with sensory work in addition to create more personalization for the actors, and with inner monologue work when actors seemed to need deeper identification with their roles.

For those interested in the authentic details of Strasberg's approaches, rather than hearsay, there's no more thorough book in my estimation. And it's written by a teacher who worked with him personally for so long, taught for him, was one of the earliest members of the Actors Studio Directors Unit, and for so many years headed the teaching program of The Lee Strasberg Insitute.

Chapters 8 and 9 of her book---*Preparing And Learning A Role* and *Class Scene Studies*---present the approaches Mr. Strasberg recommended and she teaches for use in role preparation. Certainly, those who felt Strasberg neglected *role preparation* in his work should read those two chapters!

■ **"The Technique Of Acting"**, by Stella Adler
---(Bantam Books, 1988) - $14.95.

It appears that this record of Ms. Adler's long and illustrious teaching career is more devoted to her manner of serving the beginning actor than to her manner of working with advanced professionals. Many stars of today have praised Ms. Adler's more advanced work with them in areas not covered in this book.

The exercises and other material in this book are ideal for actors seeking early guidance and growth, expanding of their imagination and perception of the many variations available through different modifications of the basic actions and intentions advocated by Stanislavski. Anyone who is familiar with the Stanislavski System is acquainted with most of the approaches put down in this book.

Ms. Adler began her teaching career at the Group Theatre while acting and directing there. By 1940, feeling her teaching calling strongly, she developed the Dramatic Workshop at the New School For Social Research and taught there for two years. Then, in 1949 she established the Stella Adler Acting Studio in New York. By 1960 (renamed the Stella Adler Conservatory of Acting), there were a dozen faculty members. In 1986 the Stella Adler Conservatory of Acting West opened in Los Angeles. She has occasionally suspended her own classes in New York for trips to the Coast and conducted short courses there as well.

Books (and Tapes) On Dialects

■ **"American Dialects"**, by Lewis and Marguerite Herman
---(Theatre Arts Books, 1947)

There are no more thorough books on so many dialects than this and the other book *(Foreign Dialects)* by the Hermans.

In this book are *The Three Southern Dialects (Del Marva Peninsula, Tidewater and East Texas), the Louisiana-French Dialects (Cajun and Creole), the Mountain Dialect, the Negro Dialects (Gullah, Virgin Islands), the New York City and Upper New York State Dialects, the Pennsylvania Dutch Dialect and the Middlewestern Dialect!*

The book uses a system of phonetics that's non-technical and very easy for the actor. It's a very handy book to have ready for when the occasion comes and the actor needs quick study.

■ **"Foreign Dialects"**, by Lewis and Marguerite Herman
---(Theatre Arts Books, 1943)

In this other fine book of the Hermans are the following foreign dialects: *Cockney, British, Australian, Bermuda, India; Irish; Scottish; German; French; Italian; The Spanish Dialects--Mexican, Filipino and Portugese; Japanese; Chinese; Pidgin English; Hawaiian Beche Le Mar and Australian Pidgin; Swedish; Norwegian; Russian; Middle European Dialects, including the Lithuanian, Jugoslav, Czech, Finnish and Hungarian; Polish; Greek and Yiddish!*

This, like the Hermans' *"American Dialects"* book, is important to have ready on the actor's bookshelf!

■ **David Alan Stern's Dialect Tapes**, available for most dialects on individual tapes, sold in Samuel French and other actors' bookshops through the country. They're excellent, and are taught by one of the leading present day dialects teachers.

For Period Research of
Customs, Wardrobe, Styles

■ **"Everyday Life Through The Ages"**, edited by Michael Worth Davison---(The Readers Digest Association, Ltd., 1992)

This fantastic book presents *the people, their appearance, their wardrobe, their props, their customs and activities and more. From 100,000 BC up to the Hunters as They Turned To Farming; Cities in the Mesopotamia and Indus Valley; Ancient Egypt; the Minoans and Mycenaeans; theBible Times---the Civilizations of the Near East; Ancient China, Imperial Rome . . .*

The Iron Age Invaders; the Medieval World; the Byzantine Empire; the New Europe of Saxon, Celtic, Franks and Vikings invaders; Western Europe's late Middle Ages; Early America; China and Japan; Western Europe's new Nation-States; Russia in the Middle Ages; The Modern World of AD 1776-1900---the Revolutionary Years in America and Europe; Western Europe in the 19th Century; Eastern Europe Empires at their Sunsets; Africa---Warriors, Slaves and Settlers; India's Hindus and the Raj; The Great South Lands---Australia, New Zealand and the Pacific Islands; China and Japan in the later periods!

There's no more thorough or ideal book I know of for an actors' quick researching of particular historical periods!

Some Acting Marketplace
Straight Talk about
the Film, Television and Theatre
Worlds of Today

■   **You're talented. All you need is the opportunity to show how brilliant you are. You just need the chance to "audition". You can still audition sometimes for theatre in New York, but in Hollywood...**

Audition Tapes

Are The Going Thing Now!

Years ago casting directors and agents as well, if interested in actors, would offer the opportunity to do scenes in their offices. The office phones rang incessantly while the actors were doing their scenes. Hurried telephone or drop-in conferences constantly distracted those auditioning the actors. It wasn't the best condition for either the actors or the auditioners, but it was the only way for newcomers to show their talents.   Almost nobody holds office scene auditions anymore.

Now, they offer to view actors' *Audition Tapes*. If the actor doesn't yet have a half-inch or three-quarter-inch audition tape for the agent to look at or, having an agent, a few audition tape copies for his agent to offer to the casting directors who don't know his work, it's probably the end of the line.

At least the audition tape manner of becoming acquainted with actors' talents has vast advantages over the old scene-watchings. But a good audition tape can be costly; if the actor's new what goes onto the tape has to be short scenes (not monologues!); the material has to be intelligently chosen; and the quality of the taping has to be good to avoid being turned off quickly in an office after two seconds.

Three to five minutes is a fairly long tape. Whoever's viewing it has a pile of them to get through. Put your best work in the first brief piece. Continue with others of your best. The least effective goes last. (They may not get to it.)

No big shouting matches. They not only distract from your natural qualities, but also aren't the kind of work for which somebody new would be considered anyhow. Don't do a popular scene they'll have seen a million times before. Don't work eye-to-eye with your scene partner all the time (that's not even good for theatre auditioning, and it's death for an audition tape).

Choose pieces that offer some variety---an angry piece, a self-kicking piece, maybe a love scene; whatever shows your different areas of special talent and personality.

There are companies that advertise in actors' publications, offering to tape a single scene for between $300 and $500. They won't care what you bring in to do. They'll often produce poor quality tapes with little concern for camera angles, good lighting, good sound and enough closeups. You'll probably be rushed into the taping, without any camera rehearsal, because another couple will be waiting.

The best audition tape is one composed of "film clip to tape" and brief clips from previous television roles that show you in different aspects of your talent. But by the time you have enough of those for a good audition tape you may not still need an audition tape anymore.

A fairly inexpensive audition tape preparation is easiest to get in a class or workshop where there's top quality, late model, color videotaping and a director or coach directing the scene tapings who has a knowledge of film and television, so the scenes taped won't be just stage-style scenes with periodic zoom-ins for the few closeups. If you do some excellent scenes on tape, make sure ahead of time that you can take the tapes to a tape-editing facility and for not much money have a master tape and several copies made from clips of your best scenes.

The best manner of taping scenes for audition tapes is to (if possible) use what are primarily monologues or heavy with your own dialogue, with another actor in one side of the frame, in what's called an "over the shoulder" shot. In that manner---even though there's exchange of dialogue---only one actor (you) will be clearly featured. Also, lighting can be carefully set; sound will be perfect; you'll be in fairly tight closeup work.

To be fair to your scene partner, the shot can easily be reversed with you "framing in FG" and the other actor featured in closeup for his own audition tape.

When you have the tape in the shape you want it and have a number of both half-inch and enough three-quarter-inch copies ready so that copies can be provided to more than one office at the same time, print on the cassettes "Audition Tape", your name, your agent if you have one, and---this is important---be sure to print somewhere where it will stand out "For Pickup, Call (your telephone number, not your agent's)." Agents hate the responsibility of not only having to deliver your tape in the first place (you should offer to always drop them off yourself when your agent tells you where), and they also hate the responsibility of having to pick them up. They might even lose them.

Then, somewhere on your résumé print *"Audition Tape Available for Viewing, Half-Inch and Three-Quarter-Inch"*. It's about the only way you'll get to audition these days.

■ **Are you ready for an even more disenchanting fact about the Hollywood of today? Read on.**

Agents of Today

Are Now Either Power Brokers or "What's Left" Accepters

It's one of the Hollywood myths that all agents have power and "clout" in the film and television industry. Whether they represent actors or writers, the rule of thumb these days is that a talent agency must almost always be giant, many departmented, staffed with at least fifty but preferably one hundred agents on its staff, or it most often has very little real power or "clout".

Once, most agencies represented talents of a broad spectrum of professional levels from the biggest stars down to some talented newcomers. That isn't generally true anymore.

The advent and growth of what is called *"Packaging"* changed the face of the agency world forever.

A "packaging" agency is most often awe-inspiringly large, with hundreds of top clients---Starring Actors earning many millions for each motion picture, Top Writers earning millions for each film screenplay their agency sells, Top Directors who, like the others, are often paid upwards of a million for each directing job and Top Producers whose track records at America's boxoffices increase their position with each picture, one after another.

The packaging agency has literally scores of agents in each department, each agent personally, hands-on handling only a handful of the agency's top clients in a particular category. One agent at CAA (Creative Artists Agency, continuously one of the most powerful of all agencies if not *the* most powerful) might handle just Tom Hanks, Tom Cruise, Jack Nicholson, Meryl Streep and Macaulay Culkin for acting, while another agent in another department handles those stars' own production companies for their personal producing ventures.

At the same or another powerhouse agency, one agent might handle as few Directors as, say, Sydney Pollack, Robert Altman and one other director for directing, and another agent in another department would handle those directors' and a few stars' production company ventures.

Yet another agent might handle a handful of the agency's top Producers and Writers because of his or her ability to demand the highest salaries in the industry for them. More, in the other departments, handle Top Cinematographers, Top Art Directors and

Scenic and Wardrobe Designers, Top Composers, Top-of-the-chart Rock Groups, etc.

Such a giant agency also employs a full time legal staff of entertainment attorneys, a huge bank of accountants, film investment counsellors and bank financing experts for arranging the financing of motion picture projects of the agency's own clients.

The only real power anywhere in Hollywood is there, in the towering skyscrapers and penthouse floors of those behemoths. The reason is that most top stars, top directors, top writers, etc., are now also production company heads of their own production companies and can obtain those multi-dimensioned representations there more effectively than they could be handled by a smaller office.

A "package" is started when a writer at one of these giant agencies writes the screenplay. Next, an executive producer or producer client at the same agency is assigned to develop the project. The producer (or sometimes two producers assigned to the same project if it's hot enough) gather the rest of the package---the director (one of the same agency's clients), the stars (also clients), the scenic and wardrobe designers (clients, too), the composer (also a client) and probably even the cinematographer (ditto). That's a package.

At that point the decision is made to present the package to a studio intact, simply for the tedious details of proceeding into filming (sic), or the project may be offered to one of the committed stars (who've promised to appear in the film) for the star's own production company.

Bank financing, if needed, is of course easy on such a project with so many top ("bankable") names already committed out front. Investors pound at the door of the agency to get in on the deal and consider themselves lucky if they manage to be allowed to invest.

What's left, in such a package, for the other agencies? Supporting cast roles (there might be a few of those left), hundreds of purely "bit" roles for some two hundred smaller agencies to fight over on their clients' behalf, "below-the-line" staff and crew members . . . little else!

A casting director is eventually hired to complete the cast. Then comes the humiliation for former stars and constantly working top featured actors. If not with the giant agency from whence comes the package, they mustn't expect their usual salaries. All the decent money's committed up top in advance.

They can't expect their established billing positions, either, because the agency that controls the package affords its own clients those top billing positions and even some stars with other agencies must accept billing positions underneath the hot new clients of the packager---many "new discoveries" who may have no previous film credits but will be billed as "Starring" or "Also Starring" in the credits.

The other, smaller agencies don't even hear of the upcoming project, probably, until they receive the list of still uncast roles in the morning delivery of the Breakdown Service.   At that point the scramble begins---and desperate that scramble is!---to obtain at least interviews and readings for their clients for some of those "trickle down" smaller roles.

Similarly, most television series now, whether dramatic or sitcom, are normally conceived of in the network offices, assigned as projects for development to Development staff people, progressed "in shop" up to the point of casting of the leads, and only then handed to independent production company producers to executive produce and line produce the actual series.

In these cases too, the stars are already cast (by the network) in most cases; even top supporting roles are tentatively set under the cloak of secrecy before the smaller agencies even hear of the projects and can offer their clients.

"Packaging" has been responsible for upping top stars' salaries into many millions while at the same time reducing less impressively connected talents' salaries and billing positions to bare bones. The less fortunate actors with other agencies can either accept what's offered and suffer the humiliation or turn down still another offer and remain out of work.

It's tough for the many actors who've loyally remained with the smaller agencies (or haven't been courted by one of the giants) to understand why their careers, their salaries and their billing positions have sagged so devastatingly.

The foregoing is explained because those hundreds of smaller agents---perhaps with a few lesser stars on their client lists, probably totally dedicated to every client on their lists, barely scraping by on the ten percent commission incomes from clients' employments that keep getting smaller and smaller each year---are often doubted and criticized, often abandoned out of acute frustration by clients whom they've worked so hard over years of association to build to where they are by then.

This isn't a very pretty picture of where Hollywood stands now for actors who aren't clients of the behemoths, but it's a true picture. And it's not going to change in the near future.

So the best advice one can (with great regret) offer actors who have any promise of upward mobility these days is to become signed by one of the giant agencies as soon as possible. In today's talent marketplace, there's no real power anywhere else.

330

But for the newcomers and others still struggling to get bit and small speaking roles, the best advice is to consider themselves lucky to even have an agent, no matter how small the office; to not sit back and expect the agent to do all the work; to help promote themselves in theatre roles in or near Hollywood toward attracting attention with their talents; to at least stay with the small agency long enough to help pay back the agent's tremendous investment and time in helping them start . . . then perhaps someday accept the first offer of representation that comes from one of those large "packaging" agencies.

The last preceding paragraph is advice I profoundly hate to give, because there are so many wonderful, caring, hard working agents in those smaller offices who are longtime friends of mine and nothing hurts them more than to build a new talent---with all the hard work it takes---and then see that client take off suddenly to one of those towers and penthouses. But it happens.

■ If you're with a smaller agency, some insight into your agent's daily grind might help you understand why you should show your appreciation and affection in every way possible!

An Agent's Typical Day

It's Not Easy!

For actors who don't know how talent agents function, it may help to profile a typical day in the life of an agent, for example, who operates a small, one agent office. Although some of the activities vary in offices where there are several agents (with each agent and sub-agent delegated to handle individual aspects of the agencies' operations), the details described here have to be handled by someone, and in a small one agent office they're all handled by that one person. We'll follow a "one person office" agent for a typical day.

He's up early so he can read the previous day's *Daily Variety* and *The Hollywood Reporter* over a hurried breakfast (hoping to find some advance news about a production), then before leaving home probably make a couple of desperate calls to catch clients who haven't returned phone calls the night before about appointments for the coming day. Then he takes the fastest streets to his office to check the *Breakdown Service* (casting information) sheets that have arrived in the early morning hours, to see what he can send clients out for or at least make phone calls about.

Checking all of the many roles at the many studios and production companies in the usually many pages of the *Breakdown* takes time, along with making lists of whom to submit from his client list for some of those roles. Perhaps gathering of photos and résumés for some clients he'll submit will be necessary if casting people don't know them and he can't afford a secretary.

If he has nobody to do it for him he'll be delivering those submissions to several offices (unless he's one who works primarily with faxed submissions), hoping they'll be among the first on the casting directors' desks.

He has to "lay out his rounds" so he can cover the most offices as quickly as possible---at least those offices that still allow agents' visits and where such a visit might be of some avail if he gets there quickly enough. This all has to be done by about 9 a.m.

Most Breakdown Service lists caution *"No Phone Calls"* to keep most of the agencies from tying up the casting office telephones. And most (not quite all) of the smaller agencies without clout know they must respect that request. The larger, "clout" agencies disregard it, and get away with it because of importance.

Most agents have beepers and cellulars. During their rounds they get many calls and have to return calls while driving. Actors shouldn't expect immediate callbacks from agents except in emergencies because the agents are hurrying through their trips, covering many miles, interrupting only for urgent calls, getting to clients with quick appointments, making deals, etc.

The small agent has to wait perhaps twenty minutes at Universal before getting inside for maybe a three minute talk with one casting person, then wait twenty more minutes to get in to talk to another. The same happens at Columbia and other studios and production company offices where there are more than one casting person.

Sometimes he's told the person he wants to see is "unavailable" or "in a meeting", then watches one of the large, clout agency people sweep imperiously into the same inner office. There's a definite "pecking order" among agents. The large agencies, with many stars in their client lists, are seldom told *"Not available."*

On a studio lot at noontime, agents have quick lunches in the commissary hoping to run into production people. Then it's off again on more rounds throughout most of the afternoon.

Around four in the afternoon agents start streaming back to their offices to get the late afternoon deal-making and next day interview calls. By five, most are back in their offices, kicking themselves for failing at a lot of the day's plans, checking the mail and salary checks; doing their paperwork and calling clients to tell them they can come in and pick up their checks.

If they're currently scheduling any interviews, this is the time a few are scheduled, even though they're tired and disheartened at the day's unsatisfying results. It's the time for calling clients about interviews the next day, and many of those clients can't be reached. That means the agent sits on hot coals throughout the evening and sometimes late into the night wondering if the clients will be located in time so the interviews can be kept. Sometimes a client calls back at 3 a.m. after a late party!

By bedtime agents are totally exhausted. Many of the small agents have urgent financial problems that pursue them into those bedtime hours and keep them from sleeping at all. The only agents actors are likely to see in the stylish star-hangout night spots late at night are those with larger agencies who have to be there because that's the only time they can meet with their stars.

So . . . all these things considered, be a little patient with your agent---especially if he or she isn't one of the agents at a large "packaging" agency. Appreciate your agent, and show it in any ways you can!

■ **Have you thought a Casting Director's job was a power and glamour one? It's not. Many are often out of work, and when they're working it's a twenty-four-hours-a-day job!**

Casting Directors
What They Do, How They Do It

Contrary to what many actors think, Casting Directors don't cast actors for roles. Producers and Directors do that. Casting Directors suggest actors for interviewing or simply setting by a phone call or two; call actors in when they've been okayed to be seen; make deals by phone when actors are wanted; have contracts typed and signed; give first work calls to the actors or their agents. It's really not the power position many actors think it.

That's why it took until the 1980's for Casting Directors---by forming a strong Society (the Casting Society of America)---to get separate card billing in the opening credits of motion pictures for many of their members. The Casting Director, even so, still isn't one of the power figures. Maybe that person can hurt or help an actor to some degree, but not much.

As to hurting an actor, I'm reminded of an incident that happened when I was casting a pilot for NBC: I'd prepared my list of suggestions. My list included a well known actress's name.

Sitting in the Paramount office of the director, with the Assistant Head of Casting for NBC present with the director and me, when I suggested the actress, the director smiled broadly and nodded.

But the NBC Casting man (who I later learned simply didn't like the actress and had often tried to hurt her chances) started, albeit so apologetically, with *"Uh . . . you know, she has that problem."* There's a potential killer if there ever was one! But this time the director's eyebrows lifted and he asked *"Oh? . . . What problem?"*

The NBC man had to stutter an explanation, after which the director responded, *"My god, I didn't know! I haven't known that in all the time we've been going together."* The NBC man was never again allowed to sit in on our casting sessions. He was in fact soon fired from NBC. It could have hurt that star at some other time. This time it was the Assistant Head of Casting for NBC who hurt himself in the attempt.

Casting Directors, in earlier years employed on permanent staffs at major studies, are now hired to handle individual, temporary jobs mostly. (1) They're hired; (2) they're given a "day out of days" and budget breakdown of how much is planned to be spent on individual roles; (3) they make up a preliminary list of suggestions of people to be considered for mostly supporting and bit roles (because the top stars are already cast and committed by the producer or the "package") . . .

(4) they meet with directors and/or producers to compare their lists; (5) make first calls to check availability of actors at the times when needed; (6) make phone deals for many of the larger supporting roles that are pre-cast in the directors' and producers' minds, and immediatly firm those deals if they can . . .

(7) again meet with the director or producer to discard actors who can't be gotten at the right time or at the right price or billing; (8) search their memories overnight and prepare more lists to talk with the director; (9) get okays for those of the casting person's own suggestions who can be brought in for interview; (10) call the agents to set the interviews . . .

(11) hold the interviews---usually in the producer's office; (12) immediately afterward, have long discussions to find out which roles the producer will okay to be set from the people seen, and which roles require more interiews; (13) attempt to firm deals for those okayed, and sometimes are unable to do so at the billing and salary available. . .

(14) call in more people for the roles not cast yet; (15) finally get the last roles cast; (16) finalize those deals with the agents; (17) with the total cast list in hand, call "Station 12" at SAG to check for Station 12's okay of everybody; (18) if some SAG member is

delinquent in dues, make sure they pay up at the Guild before they can work; if one of them isn't a member or is perhaps a "must join" in order to work, make sure they join, and if they can't, have to recast the role . . .

(19) after SAG has approved and everybody's okayed to work, publish the Cast List; (20) have all actors cast by then come in to pick up their scripts or have them delivered (for top players especially) to their homes; (21) coordinate "wardrobe" situations . . .

(22) have all contracts typed up, have top players' agents sign the contracts for their clients, and have the contracts for the smaller role playrers ready for delivering to the Second Assistant Director for the actors to sign upon reporting to work; and in the late afternoons of the days before the individual actors are to first report, give the agents their clients' "morning calls" . . .

They also have to keep their own careful records of actors' salaries and required billing, so they know what the actors and the actors' agents will probably accept on susequent job offers. They keep voluminous files of photos and résumés for desperate searches.

They're always on the phone talking with agents or meeting with them briefly when the agents come to their offices. And at the end of their day, tired and beaten down by producers, directors and clout agents they've had to kowtow to, they may be one of those who've committed themselves to appear at "Casting Showcases" for fees to tide them over between employments. Those folks barely have time to eat before going out to those "jobs" that last till almost midnight.

And, casting these days being the temporary employment it usually is, most casting people spend daytimes in production offices distant from their own "independent casting" offices (for temporary assignments), and have to head back to their own offices after working days elsewhere to handle more details there!

For a currently working casting director to go out at night to see people in a theatre production, be generous enough to appear on a discussion panel or a seminar to talk casting processes before actors, or even make that $300 or so for appearing at a "Casting Showcase" (for bank account help when they're not on a temporary casting assignment) is something just this side of Hell if they're also working on a production at the time.

And actors wonder why casting directors don't have time to sit down for little chats (general interviews) with hundreds of actors every week (as many did in former, less hectic years) or come to see them in a theatre production! Show your appreciation if one of them does one of these things. That casting director probably won't be sleeping that night, will be making up another list.

■ **Don't let anyone convince you that it'll hurt your career to do some commercials!**

Commercial Acting

It Can Be A Wonderful Supportive Income!

At one time those actors who also did commercials were looked down upon. Not anymore! Now, beginners (especially talented newcomers whose faces aren't known yet, who are always in special demand for commerials), top stars and even internationally starring players all make commercials.

It doesn't matter at what point in your career you make that first or that one-hundredth Class A National commercial which can bring you anywhere from about $5,000 bare minimum for a short run up to many thousands more for good long runs that are repeatedly brought back because they produce results with network primetime viewers. Any commercial you can do, do it happily and without any qualms. You'll stand an excellent chance of making a lot of money!

John Wayne did no commercials until he was almost ready to retire. Sir Laurence Olivier waited till sickness caused him concern and diminished physical energy persuaded him to do those Polaroid commercials. James Garner and his TV wife Mariette Hartley didn't worry about doing those many, many commercials. Elizabeth Taylor and Sophia Loren haven't batted an eyelash about pushing their perfumes. Phyllis Diller, Farrah Fawcett, Suzanne Summers, Ivana Trump, Connie Stevens and others sell their jewelry and dresses on Home Shopping Clubs. Cybill Shepherd is "worth" that hair coloring. Bob Hope and even Frank Sinatra have done commercials.

John Forsythe and Lloyd Bridges are on television much more frequently than most people may realize---John with his voice-overs for any number of products and Bud Bridges with his mellifluously hearty voice for many others. Sandy Duncan's career started from scratch with her old Dodge commercials, and more recently, having moved into television starring, she's still happy to romp through a field or sit on a sofa avidly chomping on those thin wheat wafers.

If you could read the contracts of those stars and others for those many, many products you'd probably faint.

The actress who cha-cha-cha'd with a cat for so long, Patsy Garrett, became wealthy with her "cat dancing". Virginia Christine, who for years proclaimed that Folgers was *"the very best kind"* and the lovable character actor who squeezed the Charmin were all able to retire on their earnings.

The latter are mostly "exclusive" commercial contracts, running into seven or eight figures or perhaps more per year now, for those chosen to be continuing spokespersons for certain products.

Commercial acting is a wide open door, especially for new actors. It's much easier to get a commercial agent than a theatrical (motion pictures and television) agent, because they're not as concerned with your acting talent, are more concerned with your look and type.

It's much easier to actually get your first commercial, also, than your first acting role, because, again, it's your look and type that matter. Many of today's stars got their first jobs and their Screen Actors Guild membership cards by doing commercials! And, along the way, commercials are great supportive incomes.

There are excellent *Commercial Workshops* where actors are trained in all the technical and performance differences between commercials and dramatic acting. At many of those workshops' sessions there are commercial producers, directors and casting directors visiting and watching to discover new talents, and many first jobs have come from attending those workshop sessions and being "scouted" by those visitors.

To seek commercials, the actor only needs a *Commercial Composite* (a two sided photoprint with just a headshot of the face on one side and on the other side two, three or four shots of the actor in wardrobe, handling props, in locations that suggest what the actor might be best for).

Auditions are easy---signing in on the sign-in sheet upon arrival, getting the product's copy sheet, rehearsing the dialogue of the commercial quickly, being called in to be taped, doing the taping (which is made easy by the copyboard or copy sheet hanging just to the edge of the camera lens), and being released.

This author, having always vowed that I'd never do a commercial, was persuaded by an agent, in later life, to try for a Coca Coca "Class A" national commercial. I agreed to go, and to my utter shock I got it.

There are certain "types" that are especially in demand for commercials . . . *housewives, dads and mothers, sportsmen, Coke and MacDonald's kids and teens, senior citizens and grandpas and grandmas, high fashion, "Main street", comedians and comediennes with elastic faces, voice-over talents, etc.* Maybe you're one of those. Chances are a good commercial agency would be happy to add you to its list. You might have to read a piece of copy briefly, but again, it's not your talent they're concerned with.

It's best to seek for commercial agenting an agency devoted strictly to commercials, and for dramatic film and television an agency that works in the theatrical media. Regular acting and commercial acting are two different worlds, with their offices usually located in totally different parts of town. And the commercial world has its own casting people. The smaller agencies who want to handle actors for both film and television and also for commercials can't possibly cover the ground effectively.

Commercial actors must be prepared to jump when an audition appointment comes, because it's probably within the next hour or two. Go in with some idea of the character (which the good commercial agent will always tell the actor) and try for it. If you get it, it'll pay your rent and bills for some time to come.

■ **If you're headed for Hollywood, don't expect to find it anywhere near Hollywood and Vine...**

Hollywood Today

It's Not What The New Arrival Is Expecting!

There's no Hollywood in Hollywood anymore. Hollywood now is used car lots, one or two surviving dime stores, run down apartment buildings and small houses with weeds in their yards.

"Hollywood and Vine"---the mecca young people have read about, dreamed about and immediately rush to upon arrival---is actually no more than traffic lights, cars, tired, lost-looking people waiting for buses and bag ladies and bums holding their hands out begging from behind their shopping carts of trash.

Hollywood Boulevard is still dotted with souvenir shops, though, because "Hollywood" is still where tourists come by the thousands just as expectantly as they used to. Otherwise, most of the Hollywood Boulevard blocks have a couple of boarded up, iron-grilled fronts and sometimes only one or two "Going Out Of Business" businesses between one corner and the next. Iron-grilled storefronts are everywhere, and some of the businesses that have any kind of valuable merchandise inside have uniformed security guards in their doorways now.

The Pantages, Egyptian and Grauman's (nowMann's) Chinese Theatres newcomers and tourists have seen in gold and glitter photos in magazines haven't looked that way in years. Now they look like plain old hometown movie houses, two of the three in various stages of decay, with hot dog stands on one side and hock shops on the other, in one of the seediest city sections of graffiti-covered Greater Los Angeles that anyone has ever passed through.   The only shiny, glittering things left in Hollywood now are the gold stars implanted in the Hollywood Boulevard sidewalk---the Walk Of The Stars---with past and present celebrities' names on them, and some of those are reported to be sinking.

Sunset Boulevard, although it also cuts through the center of Hollywood, cuts through it as swiftly as possible headed west into West Hollywood and the tip of Los Angeles bordering the palatial homes and clean, landscaped streets of Beverly Hills.

The film studios that used to be in Hollywood are now far away in Studio City, Universal City, Culver City, Burbank and other cities, distant rides away on the freeways.   Paramount is the only film studio still in Holywood.   The television networks too are scattered over the horizon in all directions, although they announce their programs as *"originating in Hollywood."*

The stars, with few exceptions (mostly former stars, in cheap little houses) haven't lived in Hollywood for many years.   As soon as they could afford, they moved to Beverly Hills, Bel Air (with its guarded gates), Brentwood, Malibu and even farther away from "Hollywood" up the coast.   Some prefer Washington, Oregon, Maine and Connecticut.   Even fan magazine photos datelined "Hollywood" aren't really shot there anymore.

A few of the talent agencies still rent one room, upstairs offices down long, dark hallways in some of the oldest buildings near Hollywood and Vine, but they're about all of the industry that's still there.

The Hollywood to which a million actors migrate yearly has become a small "border town" catering to its specialized daily menu of tourists, transients and actors who live in the side streets because of low rent.   But it's still the postmark from which the first postcards must be sent to family and friends back home announcing a newcomer's arrival.

From the newcomer actor's viewpoint, at least it's one of the lowest rent areas of all the graffiti-covered areas within Greater Los Angeles.   Every backstreet has many old houses and apartment buildings with "For Rent" signs out front.   As soon as they can afford to, newcomers move to the Valley (San Fernando Valley), or perhaps a little farther west to West Hollywood, where the rent is a little higher but the apartments, houses and neighborhoods are newer and cleaner and the streets are less risky to walk around in at night.   Regardless of what the Hollywood Chamber of Commerce says, Central Hollywood streets aren't all that safe at night.   That's Hollywood now.   It's not what a lot of people expect!

■ **When your friends poo-poo modeling, ignore it. Many top stars owe their careers' starts to it.**

Modeling

Many Important Careers Started That Way!

So you're an actor, and you feel nothing but disdain for those professional modeling celebrities who, because of their hard-earned celebrity in modeling, are brought into starring roles in motion pictures so easily and abruptly. Behind your sneer, isn't there maybe some envy? Don't scoff at modeling.

Top film and television stars whose *modeling* careers brought them first recognition and sometimes quickly led them to starring careers in film have included Tom Selleck, Cybill Shepherd, Marilyn Monroe, Jennifer O'Neil, Maud Adams, Brooke Shields, Mark Harmon, Brigitte Bardot, Anouk Aimee, among those who first come to mind, but there are many, many more. Some still model and do commercials, happily.

Modeling isn't only for the beautiful and handsome. Many very offbeat-looking actors make a lot of money as "print" models---athletes slurping beer, complainers in department stores, rodeo riders showing their boots, supermarket shoppers holding up Pinesol bottles, etc.

All that's needed to at least investigate this avenue of supportive income while looking for other acting jobs is (1) finding a modeling agent who likes your look, (2) starting a portfolio (several photos) by working with as many photographers as possible (sometimes getting free prints for helping them with some test shoots) , (3) having some 5x8 "comp cards" made up (the only investment for some) with a headshot on one side and a number of shots on the other side, somewhere on the card listing your measurements, hair and eyes, height and weight, sizes.

Unless you're a fashion model and perhaps one of the beautiful and handsome folks, you don't need the standard "tote bag" that models must keep available for fashion show and runway calls or (for men and women both) "catalog" jobs that can run into many thousands of dollars---posing in many different pieces of wardrobe for the catalogs of major mail order houses.

After all, modeling is still *acting*, and working with cameras. And many times the same advertising agency bigwigs who are standing around watching the print shoots (for magazines) or billboard shoots of their products in your hands are probably also highly paid account executives connected with sponsor accounts that also produce or sponsor television programs and series. You'd be more likely to be spotted for a regular acting job at a modeling session than at a restaurant or beer parlor table complaining about industry conditions.

■ **Are you smart enough to see through most of the sometimes questionable advertising encountered in the fringe areas of any industry that attracts so many naive dreamers as does acting, whether it be film, television or theatre ?**

Newcomers Need To Walk Carefully

in both Hollywood and New York

There is no one more vulnerable and available to be exploited than an actor freshly arrived in either New York or Hollywood with a head full of dreams. The newcomer's ingenuous, trusting naiveté has been and still is more exploited in Hollywood than in New York, but a number of attractive and very questionable practices are out there waiting in both industry production centers.

The main difference is that actors who select New York for starting their careers are usually more aware that there'll be a perhaps lengthy period of study and preparing, while in Hollywood there are thousands more new actors who arrive every day with hopes of being "discovered" suddenly and being swiftly rocketed to stardom through someone's interest in them.

Someone's interest in them may not always be honest.

■ **The "Screen Test" Scam**

Most of these scams have now given up the ghost, but a few are still operating. In the first place, there are *no* real screen tests anymore. That long ago first step in the "contract player" process of creating stars at major studios faded away years ago.

Nowadays, it means that you've picked up a flyer somewhere with *"Free Screen Test"* or *"Are You Tomorrow's Star?"* or some similar catch phrase in big letters, or read those words in a Want Ad column, rushed to the address given or made the phone call, were shoved in front of a videotape camera, were told afterward in hushed tones that you were ideal star material and were offered the opportunity to star in an upcoming film . . . *if* you were willing to immediately pay a paltry amount (a few thousand dollars or whatever amount they could smell in your pocket) for a period of preparation with their acting coach, a complete and expensive makeover with their image consultant, a star's hairstyle by their hair stylist, face makeover by their makeup expert, etc.

There is *never* that "upcoming film" you were to star in. And if you're gullible enough to fall for this scam you probably don't have the makings of potential stardom to begin with. The magic for naive dreamers in the words *"Screen Test"* is unequalled by any other words, and those quick buck operators know that.

■ "Act While You Study" Ads

Most of these schemes have been put out of business now, but at least until recently there was still one in Los Angeles that continually ran those ads in Los Angeles papers' Want Ad sections until the papers were admonished by a civic bureau to refuse to publish them. From those enticing ads those worthless acting schools signed up many hundreds of new people for expensive acting class semesters on the pretext that its head could obtain casting opportunities for class members while they studied.

Nothing is farther from the truth in such cases. Newcomers soon discover that, but their checks have been cashed swiftly before they can discover what they've stumbled into. They simply leave out the back door in disillusionment, many dollars poorer, as hundreds more wide-eyed hopefuls come in the front door, lured by the same false advertising.

The head of one of these ripoff establishments still bears a bullet crease on the forehead, put there by a former student who after leaving that particular money plant discovered that it was still collecting his "GI Bill of Rights" study checks from the government, pretending that he was still attending the school. He simply walked in one day and, being a poor shot, left only that bullet crease.

A similar indication of how scurrilous these "Act While You Learn" organizations can be, and the outrage they provoke when they're detected by their victims, was the murder in the sixties or seventies (I forget which) of the head of a small (again mostly GI Bill of Rights) acting school / theatre in Hollywood. A former student walked into the office one day with a gun and shot the head of the organization! That actor had better aim.

■ The "Occasional Industry Showcasing" Workshops

Only a few of the acting workshops that feature that phrase prominently in their advertising in actors' publications such as *Drama-Logue* (Hollywood) and *Backstage* (New York) are honest. Most use the phrase as pure come-on to gain class members; thereafter, keep postponing their class members' showings (for

the "industry people" who seldom come anyhow) with the putoff
that the members simply aren't ready and need more tuition-pay-
ing coaching.

■ Exploitative Talent Agencies

There are many self-labeled " talent agencies" that are in no
way involved with legitimate agenting. They're strictly scam operators. Most are not franchised by the Screen Actors Guild (as
agencies must be to represent actors for motion pictures, television, commercials, etc.).

Regrettably, there are also a few talent agencies that actually
obtain Screen Actors Guild franchises (to imply more credibility)
and are able to continue operating their scams in exactly the
same manner until the Screen Actors Guild discovers their practices and puts them out of at least SAG-franchised operation.
Some still stay in business as non-Union agencies, aware that
many newcomers don't know the difference.

Legitimate, franchised agencies are prohibited from taking
any money from actors, either out front or later, except the ten
percent commissions on employments gotten for the actors by the
agencies.

But the crooked agencies (whether operating behind the
smoke screen of a SAG franchise or not) make their money not on
obtaining employments for actors but---until they're caught---on
one or probably more of the following scams:

Actors are often required to have all new photos taken by the
"favorite" photographer designated by the agent. The photos are
high priced, because the photographer "kicks back" most of the
fee to the agent.

Actors might be required to also sign with specific personal
managers of the agent's designation. Another "kickback" of fees
if the actor ever works at all, since the manager usually gets the
standard fifteen percent commission (over and above the agent's
legitimate ten percent), and at least a second ten percent of the
manager's fifteen probably goes to the agent.

Actors might be required to attend acting workshops and
classes specified by the agent. In such cases much of the class tuition is probably another kickback to the agent.

A still more questionable possibility (of the crooked agencies
type) is described on the next pages.

Agencies operating such scams almost without exception per-
petrate them on new, non-Union actors and would-be actors, for
good reasons: All those practices are prohibited by the Screen
Actors Guild. The agencies know that. But they also know that

343

SAG can't disenfranchise them until the Agency Department at SAG has received at least one or perhaps many more complaints from actual SAG members and has conducted an investigation to confirm the practices beyond doubt.

Complaints from non-Union newcomers---even though convincing and corroborated with supporting papers---don't fall within SAG's jurisdiction! SAG may be absolutely sure (from so many complaints that must simply be filed) that the agency is conducting some of those practices, but can't do anything to stop them until one of its own members complains. Then and only then, following an official investigation, the agency can be closed down summarily and usually is.

■ Something To Check Into Before Using

Actors might from time to time see ads in *Drama-Logue* and other actor publications stating that persons representing themselves as perhaps Casting Consultants, Producers, Directors, Production Company insiders of whatever kind or some other entity will help actors obtain talent agency representation. Some of them specifically offer their services to non-Union actors exclusively---probably for the reason (the Screen Actors Guild's agency regulations) mentioned earlier.

If such an ad states that the agent obtained in such a manner would have job opportunities for the actor's type, the actor should certainly be aware that not many agents have any acting job opportunities that they can offer without trying, as agent, to obtain them through casting directors of film and television projects and going through regular casting processes.

And it's easy to determine whether the advertiser is a Casting Consultant, Producer of whatever. A casting office would surely be listed in the telephone book as just that and at least be known to the Casting Society of America (of which most but not quite all of the working casting people are members), also to Breakdown Services Ltd. (which distributes casting directors' available role descriptions to all subscribing agencies when they're casting). Similarly, a producer would probably be either a member of or at least known of at the Producers Guild of America, while a director with contacts and any directing history would be a member of the Directors Guild of America. It never hurts to check such advertising claims.

If an actor responds to the ad, in the interview the new actor might be assured that an agent would be obtained for them for a fee of between three hundred and five hundred dollars. A deposit against that amount might be asked, with the assurance that if an agent weren't obtained the actor wouldn't be obligated to complete

344

the payment, or perhaps even that the initial deposit would be returned.

But of course the actor might be fairly certain of getting an agent. In such cases one certain talent agent in an expensive highrise office on Sunset (fully franchised by the Screen Actors Guild so that the scheme could work ideally) might have agreed to sign every single newcomer referred by the agent-getter in return for an agreed upon share in the fee charged by the Consultant.

The actors would happily pay the rest of the fee, believing that they then had an agent representing them for acting roles. That might not be so. That agent might be satisfied with the steady income from simply signing the newcomers sent by his agent-getting associate and there'd be no reason for him or her to do any work.

The many thousands of dollars received in that manner each month would be lots more than the agent could realize by actually working for the actors for just one or two ten percent commissions from one or two low salaries for beginning jobs.

Most "agencies" that would be involved in this particular arrangement probably wouldn't sign agent/client Screen Actors Guild contracts with the newcomers. If there'd be any actual SAG contract signed the newcomer should realize that, as such a contract states, the agent is their sole representative for at least one year (a year of probably no employment, probably also no interviews at all) before the actor can seek another franchised agent.

There are hundreds of thousands of actual Screen Actors Guild members in Hollywood. At any one time, about half of that number of union members are trying to get agents. Some of those actors have lengthy credits, many past roles, and still must seek new agents from time to time and are often turned away because their established salaries and customary billing haven't reached a sufficiently promising level.

Agencies are supposed to make their money exclusively on the ten percent commissions of their clients' employments. They happily sign actors when there's assurance of employments and good, healthy commissions. They're loathe to sign newcomers that require time-consuming initial promotion and long waits before there's any hope of first jobs for those newcomers and any hope of realizing substantive ten percent commissions.

Any agency that accepts new, totally inexperienced actors for representation should be considered with caution by the newcomer, whether obtained through simply mailing the actor's photo and résumé and being afforded an interview or through the help of one of those advertising such help with getting them agents.

345

■ Sexual Impropriety in Agent Interviews

Unfortunately, this does occur. There have been agents who have used their positions to coerce young women (and young men, but less frequently) into trading sex for the opportunity to be represented. Several agents---including several fully franchised by the Screen Actors Guild---have in the past been jailed for such offenses when they were reported to Police Departments' Vice Officers, as they always should be.

The only effective manner of dealing with this kind of improper behavior on the part of an agent is to in fact immediately contact the Vice Division of the Police Department for the city in which the offense occurs and file a formal complaint. Chances are, there will already have been other complaints of the same nature and action can be taken by the Police. Such reporting has in the past resulted in the agent being at least put out of business if not also convicted and jailed.

Again, it's the naive, desperate, non-Union newcomer that such an agent dares to attempt to coerce by hints or outright, bald-faced demand of the aforementioned type as a condition for representation.

One such agent, when brought to trial in 1994, had twelve (count them!) young women who had filed official complaints! He is still, at this writing, serving a five year sentence.

Another, in the eighties, representing a few motion picture and television series stars and generally considered by the industry to be a decent agent, was reported by both young women and young men as requiring nude improvisations in his office. After a time he was accused of actually raping a young actress in an office interview; was tried and convicted; is now back on the street, we understand in another large entertainment center and conducting an activity there. At least such former agents can't again at any time become franchised by the Screen Actors Guild.

■ Even Some Publications for Actors Are Valueless

Actor newsstands' racks display some publications that on their covers promise important "Casting News". One or two of them are stapled shut, to make sure they're bought and paid for before actors find out there's very little or none of what's promised inside.

The only really reliable Hollywood publications we know of whose pages are full of film, television and theatre casting news, theatres' ads describing roles they're offering, etc., include *Drama-Logue* and *Backstage West*, both completely reliable weekly newspapers for actors.

346

There is one big, impressive-appearing magazine that's been in existence many years, raking in heaps of money from hopefuls' photo ads, those in the photos hoping to be "discovered" that way, even though industry people in Hollywood know that new talents are never discovered in the manner the magazine claims---at least for any kind of acting.

After many years of publication Variety has reported that one such magazine has just recently been sued in a class action suit which has named as defendants many stars and leading managers who've been featured in articles about them---articles which those celebrities claim they didn't even know about (their having been written by their press agents)---and which, the suit charges, have included tacit endorsements of the magazine's ability to get industry neophytes acting assignments.

At this writing, Variety also reports that, based on the assertion by the celebrities that they were unaware of the stories disseminated by their publicists, some fairly top stars have been dismissed as defendants in the court where the class action lawsuit is in progress. The publicity firm for the magazine and some of the stars featured in the articles remain defendants in the matter at this time.

How one of these magazines works: It sends small groups of employees to many cities throughout the country, placing large ads in newspapers a few days ahead of their arrival, heralding their coming to "search for new talents". People who want to be tomorrow's stars are invited to attend free one-day "seminars", usually conducted in large conference room spaces in leading hotels. Local hopefuls have sometimes been observed to be lined up two deep through the hallway and into the lobby hoping this was their chance to "be discovered".

Being aware of that particular magazine's history and manner of operating, I managed to sneak into one of its presentations one day in a city where its "seminar" was being conducted.

A host lecturer showed a videotape touting the advantage of the hopefuls paying to insert their photos in the magazine, either one time or continually. The illustrated lecture claimed credit for the career starts of some current stars through such advertising---claims that Hollywood industry people know are false. A second day's session, offered for the many people who eagerly signed up, represented as essentially a "career-building advice class", was another pitching session to hook advertisers.

The magazine started modestly years ago, mostly in Hollywood, before its expansion into continuing mnationwide campaigns, with its publisher seeking acting teachers' cooperation in advising their class members to insert their photos, paying a certain insertion price, part of which insertion price would be shared with the teachers! This author was one who was approached in that manner. Others told of the same approaches and shared the disgust of this author.

■ Mailing List Sources

There are also companies that advertise pressure-sensiitive labels of professedly up to date addresses for actors' mailings to agents and casting directors. Most of such labels are out of date. One very legitimate company so advertising is *Breakdown Services, Inc.*, which really does keep its labels accurately up to date because its other services are provided for the agents and casting directors themselves on a daily basis. It lists agency and casting office names, addresses and telephone numbers only, but it's always up to date.

One of the most up-to-the-minute sources for lists of agencies that offers more information---their addresses, their staffs, what kinds of clients they represent, and their reputations, is *The Agencies---What The Actor Needs To Know*, published by Acting World Books, available primarily at Samuel French Theatre Bookshops (7623 Sunset Blvd. in Hollywood and on Ventura Blvd. in Studio City), at Larry Edmunds Bookstore (at 6644 Hollywood Blvd. in Hollywood), and at Samuel French Bookstore, 45 West 25th St., in New York.

It's updated monthly with all latest information, through the cooperation of the Agency Dept. at the Screen Actors Guild, continuous contact with the agencies themselves and comments about the agencies by the members of a Casting Panel who work with all agencies on a daily basis and can judge them accurately.

There are some attractively covered paperback books which describe the agencies, too, providing addresses, telephones and staff listings, but the usefulness of such standard paperback publications for mailing list purposes is obviously less, since the agencies' information changes daily. New agencies are formed suddenly; others move suddenly; some cease operation suddenly; many change their types of representation without warning; etc. A book of this kind published even as recently as six months prior to purchase is woefully out of date as to probably about a third of the listings on each page!

Actors planning to use a purchased list in preparing mass mailings of photos and résumés to agencies can't go wrong by picking up the latest issue of *The Agencies---What The Actor Needs To Know*, picking out the most likely possibilities where there is announced interest in their type and their career level and then making up their own labels from those listings.

■ This next item comes to my mind because of how often I (and and other teachers) have been asked *"Do you think I should change my name?"* . . . also because I had to do that, myself!

Professional Names

Your Own Name is Probably Fine

Even Stanislavski changed his name! Born Konstantin Sergeyevich Alexeiev (an obviously Russian name), he chose to become Constantin Stanislavski, with the Polish surname ending and the Polish first letter of the first name. (The Russian theatre later changed him back to Russian wherever possible in the annals of history, but the two spellings of his first and last names have come down through the years in both forms.)

In 1948 I had been hired for a role, then was called by the diminutive casting director Liz Mears and told they couldn't use me anymore. I was "on the list." Because at the time I was still "Larry Parke", I was being confused with Larry Parks, who was involved in the House Unamerican Activities Committee hearings. I quickly became "Lawrence Parke"!

If you feel you need a different name for some reason---either professional or personal, simply think about it and decide. Any Municipal Court can, in response to a formal petition, change it forever. Remember, though, that you can never legally use your own birth name again. Change all official records quickly.

Professionally, there was a time when major film studios required their contract players to asume new professional names for various reasons. Since some of those same reasons apply today, the subject warrants a bit of discussion, although these days it's permissible to be Hispanic, Jewish, Chinese, German, Algerian, Italian or whatever.

The only reasons one can possibly think of now for assuming a professional name are (1) to avoid being categorized as only one ethnic identity that might limit one's casting opportunities, or (2) to make a name easier to remember or pronounce, or (3) to get rid of a name that you've disliked from early childhood, or (4) to create a specific image with the new name, or (5) because your agent or manager insists for some reason.

My own insight into this once fairly general practice of the old Hollywood studios came when one of my acting students was cast for an important role in Robert Wise's *"A Sound Of Music"*. On that occasion, the young actress, her parents, her agent and I met with Mr. Wise to adopt a new professional name for the young

349

woman because Mr. Wise insisted *"her family name was too long and hard to pronounce."*

In discussion with Mr. Wise he let us in on what he considered the "secret formula" for stars' names. He told us that stars' names should be one syllable first and last names, or one syllable first names and two syllable last names, or vice versa. At the outside, *no more than two syllables for either name.*

Although this formula might be laughed at today by many current stars, it was apparently used as a guideline in early years, and if we check out some of the name changes---changes made for whatever purpose---in more recent years as well, it may have been an intuitive consideration.

Before they achieved stardom, Edward Heimberger had become Eddie Albert, Leon Waycoff (already two syllables and one syllable) had become Leon Ames, Dominic Amici had become Don Ameche, Edward Asner had become simply Ed Asner, Anna Maria Louise Italiano had become Anne Bancroft, Milton Berlinger had become Milton Berle, Karen Ziegler had become Karen Black, Aaron Schwatt had become Red Buttons, Michael Gubitosi had become Robert Blake, Maurice Joseph Micklewhite Jr. had become Michael Caine, Tula Ellise Finklea had become Cyd Charisse, Kevin Joseph Connors had become Chuck Connors, and William H. Cosby, Jr. had become simply Bill Cosby.

Lucille LeSeuer had become Joan Crawford, Harry Lillis Crosby had become Bing Crosby, Thomas Mapother IV had become Tom Cruise, Bernard Schwartz had become Tony Curtis, Deborah Zerby had become Kim Darby, Doris von Kappelhoff had become Doris Day, Alexandra Zuck had become Sandra Dee, Issur Danielovitch Demsky had become Kirk Douglas, Vincent Edward Zoimo had become Vince Edwards, Raymond Cramton had become Chad Everett and José Vincente Ferrer de Otero y Cintron had (quite understandably) become simply José Ferrer.

Frances Gumm became Judy Garland, James Baumgarner became James Garner, Elliott Goldsmith became Elliott Gould, Archibald Leach became Cary Grant, Lyova Rosenthal became Lee Grant, Bettejane Greer became Jane Greer, Greta Gustaffson became Greta Garbo, Harlean Carpenter became Jean Harlow, Leslie Townes Hope became Bob Hope . . .

Roy Scherer Jr. became Rock Hudson (at his first agent Henry Willson's request), Arthur Gelien became Tab Hunter (at the same agent's request), Joseph Frank Keaton became Buster Keaton, Cheryl Stoppelmoor became Cheryl Ladd, Mary Leta Dorothy Kaumeyer became Dorothy Lamour, Jeanette Morrison became Janet Leigh, Joseph Levich became Jerry Lewis, Sofia Scicolone became Sophia Loren . . .

Myrna Williams became Myrna Loy, Malden Sukulovich became Karl Malden, Dino Crochetti became Dean Martin, Terence McQueen became Steve McQueen, Norma Jean Mortenson (or Baker) became Marilyn Monroe, Julie Newmeyer became Julie Newmar, Marilyn Novak became Kim Novak, Walter Palahnuik first became Walter Palance in New York and later Jack Palance in Hollywood, Eldred Peck became Gregory Peck.

Stephanie Federkiewicz became Stefanie Powers, Leonard Rosenberg became Tony Randall, Margaret Teresa O'Reed became Martha Raye, Virginia Katherine McMath became Ginger Rogers, Leonard Slye became Roy Rogers, William Penn Adair became Will Rogers, Carmen Orrico became John Saxon, Ramon Estevez became Martin Sheen, Rodney Steiger became simply Rod Steiger, Estelle Egglestone became Stella Stevens, Mary Louise Streep became Meryl Streep, Elmore Torn became Rip Torn, Julie Jean Turner became Lana Turner almost immediately after being found on a stool in Schwab's Drugstore.

The extra and stunt man Marion Morrison became the actor John Wayne, Raquel Tehada became Raquel Welsh, Susan Ker Weld became Tuesday Weld, William Anderson became Adam West, Jack Weinstein became Jack Weston, Mary Wickenhauser became Mary Wickes, Gerald Silberman became Gene Wilder, Shirley Schrift became Shelley Winters and Sarah Jane Fulks became Jane Wyman.

But there are also many of the early studio contract and later independent stars who refused to change their names and got away with it---some of whom were never urged to change because they were already starring on a sufficiently high level (in American or foreign stage and films) when the subject may have come up. Others simply liked their names: John, Lionel and Ethel Barrymore, Bruce Boxleitner, John, David, Robert and Keith Carradine, Montgomery Clift, Olivia DeHavilland (whose sister Deborah Kerr assumed that new name so there wouldn't be two DeHavillands), Geraldine Fitzgerald, Gregory Harrison, Earl Holliman, Kris Kristofferson, Marcello Mastroianni, Mercedes McCambridge, Elizabeth Montgomery, Edward James Olmos, Maureen O'Sullivan, Maria Ouspenskaya, Christopher Plummer, Victoria Principal, Sylvester Stallone, Maureen Stapleton, Donald and Kiefer Sutherland, Sam Wanamaker, Denzel Washington and Efrem Zimbalist Jr., among many others.

Whatever reason one might have for either wanting a new professional name or acquiescing when an agent or manager tells them they must adopt one (as some agents and managers do), it would probably be undertaken these days for a definite reason but not under orders from a major studio. There's usually some good reason for the suggestion.

A word of caution: These days a "theatrical-sounding" name like Lash LaRue or Ginger Whatever, even if it's the actor's name from birth, isn't all that wise. The error of trying to become more "theatrical" by a name change can be fatal. Consider that also.

■   **The biggest concern of actors in their "getting started" periods is how to promote themselves---how to get someone, anyone, to notice them, hopefully help them, represent them as agent or give them a chance at a role. It's a wheel-spinning, postage-wasting, mistake-making period for many. There are constructive and destructive manners in which actors can wrestle with the demon...**

Promotion
On Your Own Or Later With A Press Agent---Avoid Mistakes!

Actors often start sending out photos and résumés too early. Even the right kind of photo (head shot, 8x10 black and white glossy print) means nothing without enough decent acting credits listed on the résumé pasted on the back to prove you're an actor.

Don't make up a résumé until you check examples of résumés in the actor career guidance books at a bookstore and make notes as to what to include and how to include all of it in the right manner to appear professional.

However, if you don't have acting credits yet, don't waste money on a list or mailing address labels of agencies and casting offices, postage and photo money. You may think your photo's great, but after a quick glance at one more handsome or pretty face they'll turn the photo over and check to see if you're an actor. If you have no credentials to quote, into the wastebasket your material will go.   As in any industry, the people involved in hiring are only interested in workers with experience.

If you're without experience, don't delude yourself that your case will be an exception. *Get into a good acting class.* Your first promotion starts there.   If you're extraordinarily talented you'll get at least some help and advice. If you're not, and need a lot of study, look at the money you'll have saved on futile (too early) promotion.

If you have a goodly amount of acting experience, then on your résumé, after the names of the roles you've played (even if they've been small), use two or three words in parentheses to give them personality---*(The obnoxious bully)*, *(The crazy friend)*, *(The clumsy waiter)*, etc. That's subtle promotion, and gives the reader at least that much to attract their attention and to remember you by.

352

If some roles have been leading ones (in plays the reader may not know), indicate *(Lead)*, *(Co-Star)*, etc. Don't overlook anything that can add to the impressions those so brief readings can produce. But don't *pad your résumé with lies.* You'll get caught. Nobody likes a liar.

Get in as many plays, even in small theatres, as you can. And if you get nowhere in auditions in those small theatres, and you have enough experience and money to do it, rent a space, fix it up, open your own theatre. Star yourself. That kind of promotion will really help. So will any excellent reviews you get.

Enrol in a Commercial Acting Workshop. Commercial producers, directors and casting people visit the good ones, scouting for "new, unrecognizeable faces", and you might get your first SAG role that way.

Unless you know you're ready to be judged, don't pay to attend one of the many *"Casting Directors' Cold Reading Showcases".* The impression you'll make will be remembered. But if you know your talents are tops, if your résumé has a lot of credits on it, and you know you know how to read effectively, it's a good way to be judged, hopefully "discovered", by a casting director who might immediately call you in for something.

Don't write or call asking for an interview with a casting director. Almost no casting people hold those anymore. They're too busy either working or promoting themselves to get next casting assignments, because they're almost all "independents" now, often out of jobs themselves. You'd be wasting postage.

For mailings of photos and résumés to agents (when the time is right, not before), the only two mailing list sources I know of that you can count on being totally up to date---as mentioned previously---are (1) *"The Agencies---What The Actor Needs To Know"* ($10. at Samuel French Bookstores and elsewhere) or (2) the self-stick labels from *Breakdown Services, Inc.* Almost every other mailing list source I know of will be at least partially (if not almost wholly) out of date. Agencies open, close, move, etc., every hour on the hour. Those two sources named are always up to date. *"The Agencies",* updated every month, has full descriptions of the agencies, their well known hard work, respect, perhaps clout, who handles what, what they will consider, etc.

As you start inching upward---in roles, billing, salary and frequency of being called to interview, send thank you notes (very brief ones) to everyone. (It's a second impression, even tho' brief, and might remind them of you when there's another role you'd be right for on their desk that day.)

Don't write long notes to anyone! They won't be read! Just short, to the point, single paragraph notes.

Don't send gifts with your name on them---pens, ash trays, calendars, whatever. They're insults. Doors will bang shut.

Don't waste phone money trying to call agents and casting people. You won't get through to them. Your only early contacts with those who don't know you should be via your photo and résumé. That's what they want.

When you're in something, wherever, *send cards (not letters) inviting people.* Offer complimentary tickets (two), but ask that they call to reserve so tickets can be held for them.

The minute you have your SAG membership, insert your photo and your agent's name in the next upcoming issue of *"The Academy Players Directory"*. It's the "bible" for face and talent searching by producers, directors and casting people. It costs $20. The Directory is located at the Academy Of Motion Picture Arts And Sciences, 8949 Wilshire Boulevard in Beverly Hills.

When you have a decent, promotable role on television, go to *Variety* and *The Hollywood Reporter* and insert an ad asking people to catch your performance. Sometimes that works. Also *send cards* to casting people asking them to watch. Some might.

The minute you have a starring role in a film or a television series role, hire a Press Agent (Publicist). Probably not before. They're hellishly expensive. But once you have something they can really promote you'd better hire one to promote it so the next steps upward can come more easily. They have millions of ways to turn one lucky break into several more.

And later, continually working with your Press Agent, it's good to bear in mind that *you*, not that staff member, must be the one who always determines what kind of stories you want appearing in the press, what you will and won't do for publicity, etc.

It's devilishly hard to do, but you should always attempt to maintain control over your own career, even after you have your team---agent, perhaps personal manager, entertainment attorney, publicist, maybe business manager too. Stay in charge!

■ Organization Work And Joining

There's one kind of quick self promotion open to all actors, regardless of the current level of their careers. It's a kind of self promotion that doesn't occur to some actors . . . *Organization Work and Joining!*

Many excellent contacts and ongoing friendships that can speed career progress can come, believe it or not, from volunteering to work with and for industry organizations, industry clubs, industry charity fundraising groups, etc.---including of course Screen Actors Guild's, AFTRA's (American Federation of

Television and Radio Artists) and Actors Equity Association's Union committees and activities, if the actor is already a member of one or more of those unions.

Those other organizations (of so many kinds) have no membership requirements for their staff members, and most of them are always in need of cheap or totally free slave labor.

Most organizations of all kinds in Los Angeles, Hollywood, Beverly Hills, New York and other entertainment center cities---not just entertainment industry organizations but also civic groups of all nature---always have as many film, television and theatre luminaries on their Boards of Directors and heading their Honorary Committees as possible for their name value.

In New York the tendency in such organizations is more toward courting civic leaders, senators, social leaders, etc., but in Hollywood film and television celebrities are what most organizations seek---stars, production company heads whose names are publicly recognized, studio executives with the same recognition, etc.

Most of such organizations (especially in Hollywood and Greater Los Angeles) are heavy with names but usually short on "gofers" who are willing to "go fer" whatever's needed on a day to day basis. You can usually find one or two or many of them ready and happy to have your unpaid help in some "gofer" capacity.

The point---from the standpoint of your early (even later) self promotion--is that in an organization that has a number of entertainment luminaries in its committees or special activity groups you may be able to rub elbows and become acquainted with people who are in positions to help you if they happen to take a personal interest in you through working with your valuable (even though lowly) help.

One of the first avenues of this kind that should be considered, if you're a member of SAG, AFTRA or Equity, is to offer yourself as a volunteer to help the Union in any capacity where you can be of value. If you have some special ability or professional knowledge in a peripheral field that committees and projects often need---typing, wordprocessing, printing, envelope addressing, etc.---all the better.

You can rapidly gain a far broader overview of the industry and industry practices, and can meet stars, producers, directors, agents and others for the first time in a peer relationship, either on union business or socially, through this contributing of your valued help. If you have the time, the energy and an amount of intelligence to devote to such helping activities on a volunteer basis it can be one of the best investments in your career that can be imagined. What's more, you can start at any time.

Even as a lowly errand-running "gofer", you'd probably be in some of the photographs taken at special events, standing beside someone important and as a result appearing more important yourself than you yet are. You might be called to attend emergency meetings at stars' homes if they're chairpersons of committees having trouble getting things together and needing phone-calling or envelope-stuffing help.

You might even be paid (at least expenses, even in the "gofer" position) to go on jaunts for fund-raising, along with stars or other industry people. You might appear before City Councilpersons and have your picture taken in a group standing beside the Mayor in one of the shots made at City Hall. You'll be meeting people by the dozens that you wouldn't otherwise stand a chance of meeting for many years.

And even in running errands as a "gofer" you'd find out where many top people live, what their unlisted phone numbers at their homes are, where they like to eat, what film, television or theatre projects they're working on at the time which might offer an opportunity for you, etc. Your participation in their activities may feel calculated (as it is, of course), but you'd be earning many people's attention and gratitude at the same time.

Since it may be hard for some to envision how productive this volunteering can be as a manner of early (and even much later) self-promoting, I'm going to give some examples out of my own biography to illustrate how the many things you might involve with in this manner can mushroom into huge and unexpected results later.

In my own personal case, I rather got drawn into most of these things one after another than got involved in them with thoughts of what they could do for me. But in hindsight, I've certainly recognized the great richnesses they've produced in my life and my career, so I feel the benefits that can accrue from this kind of simply "pitching in and helping things" . . . volunteering yourself as a lowly "gofer" . . . should be suggested for others as a means of self promotion than can be of cumulative benefit over many years.

In New York in 1946---less than a year after being discharged from the Army at the end of World War II, my first professional "volunteering" occurred almost as soon as I had become a member of Actors Equity through my first lucky break with a role in the "Babes In Toyland" revival. A friend who was a Board Member of the Equity Library Theatre suggested I offer myself to be nominated for the Board. (Equity Library Theatre was and still is a special "showcasing productions" organization subsidized by Actors Equity Associaion.)

356

The Execuive Board Members receive no pay. It's strictly volunteer work and usually comprises a few stars, mostly known actors and one or two slaves for the "gofer" work.

I had complained to my friend about the awful feeling of having no connections yet and no hope of creating any. Or perhaps it was the words "Good Gofer Material" which were probably written all over the face of this energetic newcomer. My friend said the Board's professionally busy Members always needed slave help and I wasn't too busy. He nominated me and I was honored to be elected. I began meeting people suddenly.

Very soon there was the post of Assistant Executive Director to be appointed for the new Equity Community Theatre project which would be taking specially produced ELT productions to outlying theatres after their closings in New York. Since it was obviously a "gofer" job, who better than the newest gofer on the Board to do all the legwork and errands that the Executive Director, busy character actor Leon Askin, wouldn't have time to do?

My responsibilities beyond gofering included promotion of all kinds. Working my tail off on continuous liaison with promotion for the project put me into unexpectedly close and continuous contact with *The New York Times'* dean of New York critics, the late Brooks Atkinson, and *The New York Post's* theatre editor Vernon Rice, who were supporting the project.

Both of these gentlemen becoming friends, together they soon observed my hard work and results and together delegated me, as their representative, to go out and meet with many of the separatist, unconnected Off Broadway producers (then still operating in isolated aloneness without any central organization), to urge and foster the forming of an Off Broadway League with those two critics' support in their columns. (The Off Broadway League still exists today as the League of Off Broadway Theatres.)

Again working my tail off on those two worthwhile projects, I learned so much that was to benefit me tremendously many years later, in Hollywood, toward helping form the Equity Library Theatre West and the ANTA Repertory Theatre West in 1958 and being elected Co-Chairman for those organizations' inaugural seasons, still later forming the League of Los Angeles Theatres in 1972 and presidenting it for its first three terms.

It didn't hurt that among the first theatres to join the League as soon as I formed it were two (of the largest) that were headed by producers who had years earlier been part of the original cadre of the Off Broaday League in New York whom I'd come to know personally by then.

There were still more benefits to come unexpectedly from that very first (Equity Library Theatre) volunteering: Peggy

Wood, its president at the time, became a friend, invited me to join her and some other stars in the Episcopal Actors Guild---where I met and worked closely with (as an actor) more leading players that I wouldn't have met so soon otherwise. And almost eight years later, I'm sure it was Peggy who had me brought in as Papa's Office Manager, Mr. Jenkins, in the last season of her *"Mama"* television series!

But wait, there's more! From working closely with top critics Vernon Rice and Brooks Atkinson on the two projects mentioned came the surprises that Mr. Rice, in 1947---after confiding that he wouldn't have found time to come see *"A Doll's House"* Off Off Broaday if I hadn't been Torvald in it---honored me with his Off Broadway Award for my performance and, two years after that, while we were still involved with forming up the Off Broadway League, when he made a special trip to Keene, New Hampshire (where I was directing its summer theatre) to meet with me on details of the then rapidly progressing League and while there saw my summer theatre production of *"An Inspector Calls"*, awarded me one of his Summer Theatre Direction Awards that year.

And Mr. Atkinson, too, by then a supportive friend, after a meeting about the League, stayed to sit in on my acting class and, later commenting briefly about my teaching talents in one of his articles, afforded me one of the critical comments of which I shall always be proud.

And I firmly blieve that I must attribute a number of my early "Golden Age of Television" roles as an actor to contacts made and visibility promoted during the helping of those organiztions I'd volunteered to help earlier. (At least many more people had become acquainted with me than would have if I'd been simply "making the rounds" daily to casting and agency offices begging for roles.)

I've often wondered how many small roles I missed out on by not spending my days making those rounds. I was too busy!

By then I was "an experienced gofer" and one was needed at that time by the new United Cerebral Palsy Foundation headed by Leonard Goldenson---himself a Hollywood film producer. And someone suggested "Gofer" Parke to do the promotion and phoning to form up the National Sports and Entertainment Committee for the UCPF.

In setting that up and arranging its kickoff at New York's 21 Club, I became acquainted with world heavyweight champion Sugar Ray Robinson and noted playwright Ben Hecht, among others I persuaded to attend as Honorary Committee Members.

Thereafter, Sugar Ray and his then wife Edna Mae volunteered to help finance and later continually supported my first summer theatre venture as a producer-director, at Pompton Lakes, near his training camp. And in 1960 (ten years later in Hollywood) Ben Hecht had me work with him and Lotte Lenya (Mrs. Kurt Weill) toward adapting his stage play *"Winkelberg"* into its musical version *"Bodenheim"*.

Still more volunteer gofering followed, with similar results: By then a close friend, Peggy Wood (always a bigger star in London than in New York) "volunteered" me as official New York boat and plane meeter and liaison for Colonel Alexander, until his death head of International Artists and Artistes, a top London talent agency for stars.

Being honored with the responsibility of meeting Sir Laurence Olivier's ship as Col. Alexander's representative when Olivier arrived to play the *"Cleopatras"* and *"Oedipus"* at the Ziegfeld Theatre in the late 50's began an acquaintance with Sir Laurence which later made possible his fervent endorsement of my play *"The Cage"* during its commercial run in Hollywood at the Ivar Theatre in 1964-65, his almost (but not quite) obtaining a London engagement for it, his sending the play to Jean Paul Sartre which led to M. Sartre inviting me to come talk to him, and Sir Laurence's reading and endorsing of my first acting book.

In 1957---still helping London's Col. Alexander's agency on a volunteer, unpaid basis, my handling of English television star Terry-Thomas's arrival and early managerial details in New York put me in first contact with Ziv Television Programs, which eventually---I don't remember how now, but because Ziv knew that I was an actor ---led to my series role as "Luke" in Ziv's *"The Harbourmaster"* television series, filmed at Rockport, Mass.

And it was during the filming of that series that my volunteer help---as a New York actor who knew the people being proposed by the New York casting office for guest starrings---that led, when the series finished shooting, to my being brought to Hollywood by the studio's head and being afforded a hands-on education in all departments of film and television production out of a small office next to his with an always open door between us.

And the forming of New York's Off Broadway League and the later forming of the League of Los Angeles Theatres---the latter requiring appearances before the Los Angeles City Council, Chamber of Commerce gatherings, etc.---created friendships with two City Councilmen that in 1971 resulted in both of those gentlemen helping me obtain the financing for the transportation, salaries, food allowances (easily, with their help) for my theatre's invited trip to its European Festivals appearances as American entry that year and the subsequent European theatre capitols engagements of my environmental theatrepiece *"Minus One"* after it had been awarded highest honors at the French Festival.

359

I long ago stopped "gofering" to devote myself to my own activities. But the foregoing are presented here as indications of the many advantages which can accidentally and unexpectedly accrue from volunteering help, especially in an actor's early years, wherever you observe organizations needing it. Many such associations, clubs and industry or civic committees will greet your offer with open arms.

Just don't become so hooked into the "organizer", "helper" and, yes, "gofer" syndrome that it takes too much away from your time and the energies you need for promoting your own career in all the other manners available! That was a lesson it took me many years o learn.

■ **Most readers who have theatre experience will have experienced the turmoils and rigors of the following for one or more seasons. The advice and warnings here are for those who don't know how much has to be prepared ahead of time for...**

Summer Theatre

Performing One Play While Rehearsing The Next is Work!

There's one kind of actor employment that for many makes the use of too many of some more complicated approaches' individually brilliant preparation items almost impossible. It's an area of professional work where actors must pick and choose wisely as to what and how much of the preparation items they've learned are practical in terms of the available time.

One of the most demanding tests of talent, concentration, technique-on-call and readiness, a summer season in one of the many summer theatres that dot primarily the East Coast is something every actor should endure at least once, for good reasons.

Nowhere else is the actor's preparedness, versatility, stamina and creative imagination so tested.

The many summer theatre producers who present summer seasons in converted barns and city auditoriums in many locations throughout New England, New Jersey Seashore cities, Pennsylvania, a few locations on the West Coast and elsewhere during the summer come into New York in the Spring, announce their seasons' planned productions in *"Backstage"*, *"Drama-Logue"* and other New York and Hollywood casting newspapers, hold interviews, and cast their resident acting companies and "jobbers" based on the role demands of the productions they've scheduled.

Many producers seek leading and character people for seasons of totally "resident company" operations, wherein each player is hired because he or she fits particular roles in all (or all but one or two) of the planned plays. When they've announced their production schedules in those casting call items the actor can get the scripts at a bookstore and have a fair idea of whether it's worth going for an interiew.

In a "resident company" operation, each actor is usually rehearsing the following week's production during the day, then after dinner returning to the theatre to perform the current play at night. It's a continuous treadmill experience, except for the occasional (and much welcomed) "rest week" required by the Actors Equity contract---the week when the actor is either performing but not rehearsing or rehearsing but not performing.

Many "star packages" also tour summer theatres, featuring a publicly recognized name or two in the top roles and usually with some sufficiently recognizable Broadway or Hollywood people in the main and supporting roles in order to draw as large audiences as possible to the play in which they're appearing.

Sometimes a "star package" is booked by an otherwise "resident company" theatre for a week, in which case the minor roles are to be played by permanent members of the resident company. That's a bonus for the resident company member who can then claim on his or her résumé having appeared in a play with the play's star. In just one summer theatre season such a resident company member who has never worked with a star before might come away at the end of the summer with perhaps five or six new credits of roles played with some of the most famous stars! At least it's a great way to build credits of that kind.

In other cases, one or more "jobbers" are brought in to play one or more of those roles. Such "jobbers", not officially members of the "star package", may go with the company to one or more other engagements when there isn't somebody in each of those other theatres' own companies who's right for the role.

Also, there are some summer theatres which exclusively book those "star packages", one after another, throughout the summer months, maintaining no resident company.

The words "summer theatre" suggest the first category, however. And the actor who auditions for and is hired for an eight-to-twelve-week summer engagement of doing play after play after play should be prepared for a grueling summer of hard work.

Each week's Actors Equity contract salary will probably pay for a room, food and laundry, but little more. The actor supplies his or her own makeup supplies, his or her own wardrobe (at least all ordinary street wear) and his or her own transporation to get around (if there's any time to), in addition to those first three items mentioned. You don't do summer theatre to make money.

Summer theatre is where the actor especially needs a technique for quickly preparing and comfortably performing roles---one after another in rapid succession---that is dependable, fairly quick and easily adapted to the unique and often very different demands of the many roles to be played . Those roles may vary tremendously from week to week. There simply isn't time for the long drawn out role preparation processes some minutiae-suffocated approaches demand.

Once hired and aware of what roles he or she will be playing throughout the summer, the actor should start at once planning everything possible for each of those roles, as far ahead of time as is possible. Once at the theatre and involved with the very first production in the hurried (one week) rehearsals for it, it's too late for much else.

If even one role during the season is to involve a particular period's *style* with which the actor isn't acquainted---which is rather doubtful, since the actor's knowledge or lack of knowledge of that style will have been a consideration of the producer in the hiring process, that *style,* in all its aspects, as well as the paraphernalia of the period involved, has to be researched ahead of time. If there's a *dialect* required in one or more of the plays, be prepared ahead of time for it as well.

If you have in your wardrobe enough choices of purely contemporary wardrobe, take everything with you. If there's something obviously suggested that you don't have, go to a Good Will Store or Salvation Army clothing outlet and get it. The theatre is expected to (and will) furnish very specialized wardrobe, but if you want any say later in the more standard street wardrobe items, bring them with you.

If you've been taught to bring no character and no feeling to a first rehearsal, as some are taught . . . forget it! That's for four or more weeks of rehearsal if ever. Your very first rehearsal in summer stock will start an accelerated process. If you bring no planned characterization and nothing of your own planning for moments of the role to that first rehearsal, the director, in the rapid initial staging pressures, will be forced to let your character slip through the cracks and be unimportant in the continuing preparation as he concentrates on other characters that are interesting from the start.

In an earlier chapter there are those two quotes from two film director friends of this author, *"Bring something from home"* and *"Make from yourself something before you come."* That's important advice for the summer theatre actor too. But for summer theatre it's even more important, because there won't be time for all that after arrival at the theatre.

■ **The next item shouldn't be necessary in any book written for serious actors. But at the time when this book is written . . . just one day in a casting office would illustrate why it's included here.**

Those Temporary Fads

"In" is "Out" for Actors That Want To Work!

So you're one of the fellows who pays forty-five dollars or more for a shiny skinhead or crazy Cherokee haircut because two of your pals have them and you want to be one of the "in" crowd? Or you've kept that Santa Fe ponytail because your coffee house friends like it, even though your acting coach told you to get rid of it quick? Or you're one of the young women who thought a friend's tight African beaded braids were cute, and got the same?

You haven't heard from your agent recently, have you? There just aren't that many calls for Anglo Cherokees, skinhead cult members or White Afro-Americans these days, and there probably won't be for a long time. The next time your agent is purging the agency's client list you'll probably be the first to get a termination letter. And if would astound me if you even have an agent.

Go to movies. Watch television. See how many freakish counterculture roles there are. And realize that any leading roles with those distinctive facets probably spent hours in the studio Makeup Department getting them for those one time, special purposes. Woody Harrelson's shaved head in *"Natural Born Killers"* was gone the day after the film was finished. Forrest Gump's legless Lt. friend was cast with two strong legs. Robert DeNiro didn't walk into an office looking like Frankenstein's monster.

Just because you saw Sean Connery in his Barbara Walters interview some time ago with that ponytail he wore for a while (for a role), and just because Cher flaunts those outrageous styles (for fun) and Roseanne wears them (for publicity), and Anthony Hopkins was a skinhead for a while (for that sensational role), doesn't mean that you can get by with any of those same things as a beginning actor and expect to work as an actor or actress or even be sent on many interviews. Such roles come along perhaps once a year if at all, and when they're in a script they go to established players willing to adapt their appearances for specific roles.

The clodhopper and lumberjack shoes so stylish for women from time to time can kill any chance in an interview. A diamond stud or dingle-dangle in a young fellow's ear can offend some producers' tastes. Even producers and directors who sport them themselves (as some do) don't expect them on actors they're interviewing and often can't see the actor past them. An "A-line" or "Mother Hubbard" dress or the "layered look" on a woman can arouse suspicion that she has no waist. The glossy ponytail one actor might sport in an interview for a policeman role would cause chuckles.

If things of that sort do no more than simply distract (which they do), that's bad enough.

Actors and actresses are still categorized by types for casting purposes in both Hollywood and New York. That's how casting people remember them for possible call-ins when roles come up. If your physical or dress presentation of yourself is so unusual that you can't be thought of for a large variety of roles within a general category you're not going to be called for interview or even remembered as being otherwise right for anything at all.

Ninety-nine percent of roles for men, both younger and older, are still "straight" roles. If a script calls for something outlandish and you fit that nice role in every other way, the production is more apt to cast an experienced supporting role player and supply whatever's needed. If for one of those same outlandish roles an actor comes in for interview who's crazy enough to look that way all the time, that actor had better have a lengthy résumé of excellent roles of that general type and lie that the crazy appearance is in preparation for a low budget film the director and producer won't have heard of.

Roles for women are still subject to the age-old Hollywood belief that---except in certain "character woman" categories (usually older or at best secondary)---women should have attractive bodies and attractive faces. Too bad, but it's still generally true.

Renée Valente, until recent years one of Hollywood's leading casting executives at a major studio (more recently a producer), once in one of my *Actors' Career Guidance Seminars* in Hollywood warned actresses that those currently faddish, overdraped, low belted dresses not only hid their figures but also made her think more about what expesive salon or whose attic those dresses must have come from than about the actresses.

One of this author's female series stars, after her television series starring role at Universal ended, was having trouble getting important dramatic starring roles for a while. Everything she was cast for during that later period was light and devoid of any substantive depth.

In classes I had often called her "Bracelet Jangler", because of her new infatuation with the many jangly bracelets very popular at the time. I hadn't thought to advise her to get rid of her bracelents before interviews. Finally it occurred to me. She did. And today she again plays many top dramatic roles.

Look in the mirror. Make a list of the roles your current look and favorite wardrobe items are totally wrong for. Then make another list of the kinds of roles they might fit ideally. If the second list is very short when you're finished, first run to your hairstylist and get rid of that faddish do, and when you get home dig out those clothing items your "in" crowd friends would sneer at and have them ready. Then let your agent see the "new you".

If your agent has seen you with that weird hairstyle or seen you parading another of those "in" monstrosities, get back on the agent's "A List" quickly by showing up looking more conventional again. That's how you looked in first interviews to get an agent or you wouldn't have gotten an agent to begin with, and that's how that agent wants you to always appear.

■ **Some actors say they've come to Hollywood or New York to** *"give it six months, maybe a year."* **That actor isn't going to make it. The first disappointment . . . Poof! He or she will be gone.**

Tenacity
The Ability to Get Up and Go On With Determination!

Nothing's more important for an actor than the ability to presevere in the face of apparently insurmountable odds. There's probably no other profession that so continually places one's total being in the spotlight---available to be judged and summarily rejected on the basis of appearance, intelligence, talent, readiness for opportunity, behavior, presentation, characteristics or some other attributes that may be simply in the wrong place at the right time or the right place at the wrong time. Most actors are never told why they're rejected for something.

To *just keep going* is the biggest challenge of the actor. No one else cares whether his career moves forward or backward.

The pursuing of an acting career goal is endless. There are long timespans when that pursuit seems hopeless. Rejections are continuous. Opportunities come and go with ego-assaulting failures waiting around every turn. The actor who can take them in stride and go on may very well succeed.

Seldom will anyone tell us after a reading for a role that it was simply our height, or our look, or a script revision that's changed or eliminated the role, or that another actor with production company connections or public recognition unexpectedly became available, or some other totally uncritical fact that caused our failure to get the role. We most often blame our talent, or our failure to do as well as we could have and should have done.

We have to simply *get up and go on.*

This author, long ago in high school, was cast in the one-act play *"Afraid Of The Dark"* that was to represent the school at the upcoming District One Act Play Contest. Already at the time dreaming of becoming an actor but totally without any training or study, I was ecstatic. At the District Contest, first the play was announced as the winner. A few minutes later, my name was announced as Outstanding Actor! Suddenly, I was an actor, an "outstanding" one!

When the play was later presented at the State Contest and judged the winner again, I wasn't surprised when the announcement of Outstanding Actor began with the words *". . . and, from the cast of "Afraid Of The Dark," Wymore High School . . .".* I was out of my seat and edging toward the aisle when I heard *". . .Vern Owens."* (I'll never forget that name!) It was the blackest moment of my young life.

Suddenly, I realized that acting was something that must be studied. There were no books on acting technique in my small hometown Library, so I began hitchhiking twelve miles to a slightly larger town and borrowing books on acting, devouring them and borrowing more.

The play having won a second time, it went on to the Tri-State Contest and was again declared the winner. And when the Outstanding Actor Award was announced I was actually surprised to hear my name again.

I've often thought that that one teenage incident may have influenced my later turning to teaching actors in New York and Hollywood. I'd been shocked into the awareness that acting was an art that could be learned. At least it awakened in me the ability to *get up and go on,* as well as an appreciation of the actor's need to develop his talent through technique.

A leading soap opera star, in a recent magazine article, cited an article in one of the trade papers in the mid-1980's which stated that ninety-five percent of the people who go to New York or Hollywood leave within the first year, and the ones who stay aren't always the most talented but are the most persistent.

It's literally one of the hardest things to do, *getting up and going on.* Actors who continually fail to get first roles must do it.

Actors who receive embarassing critical comments about their work and who know that all their peers have seen those comments must do it. Actors who have accidents that leave them physically challenged in some manner must do it. Actors whose careers soar rapidly to great heights but then decline, leaving them almost penniless and agent-hunting again, must do it.

I've taught many hundreds of actors who, like those mentioned in the previous paragraphs, have gone to New York and Hollywood and succeeded quickly through determination and persistence. I've taught some who went to New York or Hollywood, studied, began working but couldn't face the many disappointments and who are now waiters, taxi drivers or carpenters.

No matter how talented, and no matter how many family connections or acquaintances actors may have to better their chances quickly upon arrival in one of the performance art centers, there are always up ahead those many times when they'll have to *get up and go on.*

Simply persuade yourself to view each failure the way one of my older actresses in classes, Pollyanna Houston, did. I sympathized with her after one of her failures to get a role, but she smiled and responded, *"That's alright, dear. Each role I don't get brings me one step closer to the role I'll get."* She kept cheerfully trying and soon after our talk became Mrs. O'Grady, the recurring upstairs landlady, in the *"Baretta"* television series!

■ **Are you still on one of the bottom rungs of the career ladder and worried because you're called in for only one type of role? If you are, and you're constantly grousing that nobody appreciates that you can play so many other types of roles, don't put down...**

Typecasting

It's Not Going To Go Away . . . And Be Grateful That It Won't!

It's rather ridiculous for actors to criticize *"Typecasting"* as being something evil and professionally limiting for the self-judged versatile actors who are sure they can play any and all roles ever created by writers.

Even if it were true, actors should realize---at least throughout the earlier years of their careers---that "typecasting" has assuredly been responsible for casting directors remembering them, envisioning them as ideal candidates for certain categories of roles (even if not yet any other kinds), and putting their own careers on the line by daring---out of all the actors in the New York

367

and Hollywood talent pools---to call them in for judging by the producers and directors who pay the casting people's salaries because of their judgment of talent.

Only when actors reach the highest pinnacles of respect and admiration for their recognized talents should they expect to be able to persuade producers and directors that they can bring some extraordinary brilliance to a role for which their past performances don't immediately suggest them.

Dustin Hoffman wouldn't have been allowed to play Willy Loman in *"Death Of A Salesman"* or Shylock in *"A Merchant Of Venice"* or even *"Tootsie"* in his early years.   Marlon Brando would have been laughed out of the office if he'd asked for the role of Marc Antony in *"Julius Caesar"* the week after he closed as young Nils in *"I Remember Mama"* or as Marchbanks in *"Candida"* or, even moreso, after his long run as Stanley Kowalski in *"A Streetcar Named Desire"*. Tom Cruise's surprising the film industry by being starred in *"Interview With The Vampire"* and receiving highest critical acclaim for it (even from the author, belatedly) couldn't have happened in his earlier years. Tom Hanks was limited to comedy for a long time before *"Philadelphia"* and *"Forrest Gump"*.

All those wonderfully diverse opportunities are completely out of the question for actors whose talents and outstandingly creative versatilities haven't yet been proven beyond question.

But actors should look on the brighter side: In those early years, to be thought of within some particular casting category, some "type", is insurance that there's a particular niche---an area of casting potential---that's helping casting and production people remember to think of them and possibly call them in for readings simply because they're the right "type".

A "type" isn't really all that limiting in the first place.   It's usually just a matter of *adjectives and labels*. Casting directors simply think of some actors as *"blue collar"* (that covers a lot of ground), or *"suave"* (lots of other ground), or *"brooding"* (more), or *"take charge"* (still more), or *"gentle"*, or *"down home"* or some other adjective or label that isn't really limited to just a few roles.

"Typecasting" is simply a marvelous boon to new, less experienced actors until they've achieved wide recgnition and earned the opportunity to break out of the molds that they consider so tight and binding but that, through *typecasting,* will have been what initially suggested them for every single role they'll have had until they're in a higher career level.

So . . . don't knock *Typecasting*.   If you're working as an actor, it's probably *Typecasting* that you have to thank for it.

*Some Stars, Top
Players, Agents and Others
Talking About . . .*

...Early Studies With Leading Teachers, Career Matters and Problems Actors Encounter in Their Early and Later Professional Lives

The following comments on a wide range of subjects were elicited from some current and former stars, other established actors and leading Hollywood agent friends with promises to all of anonymity, to encourage the utmost in naked candor.

Their comments are presented here as examples of actors' early study experiences as they've contributed to later successes; examples of the problems often faced throughout professional careers; examples of career missteps and mistakes that aren't all that uncommon; and examples of how different actors must learn to deal in their own manners with problems common to all or at least most professional actors.

One group of top actors (mostly, but not all, people who had worked with me) met with me for the specifically understood purpose of candidly sharing their experiences for inclusion in this book.   Other of the following comments were obtained on tape in private conversations with a number of stars and others whom I've been privileged to call friends.

■ Acting Study and Starting in New York or Hollywood

A character actor who got a quick start in Hollywood and has been in New York only for two plays, winning a Critics Circle Award for one:

"Half of the cast was from New York, four of us were from Hollywood by then.   I listened to some real horror stories of the New York kids . . . years of starving, doing Off Off Broadway for no pay just to be doing something . . . living in cold water walkups. . . some real horror stories that made me happy I came west to start.   I had my hard times out here at first, as you sure remember, but nothing like what those kids had gone through, what they probably went through again sometimes after the play closed."

An older actress (now) who had won a Tony Award on Broadway before moving to Hollywood:

"Hollywood wasn't the place for a singer. I was a singer first, and teaching singing to pay for acting classes. They don't do musicals out here anymore. It had to be New York. I worked at Macy's, taught singing, whatever, to stay there. It took forever, but finally it happened. When the play closed even some people out here knew my name because of the Tony Award and knew I was an actress as well as a singer. You got me started more easily here in Hollywood because of the Tony than you could have if I'd started here.

"Out here I've been able to work in acting roles, probably more than I would have in New York. There's not that much production in New York anymore. If you're in a flop you're out of work again. And if a production's successful it runs and runs forever, so other productions can't go into rehearsal because they can't get a theatre. When there aren't a lot of productions there aren't a lot of jobs. If I moved back I'd need to teach again just to stay alive. And I'm too old now for Macy's."

A leading character actor who stars and guest stars regularly in television roles, costars in motion pictures, and from time to time returns to Broadway; winner of several Tony and Obie Awards and a two times nominee for Supporting Actor category Academy Awards:

"No comparison. In Hollywood I go from one thing to another. My salary keeps going up. I get decent billing. People all over the country recognize my ugly face and ask for my autograph. You can work on Broadway all your life without anybody outside New York knowing you're alive. More important, I'm an actor, and here I 'm able to do it all the time.

"Besides, all my friends are out here ninety percent of the time now, for the same reasons. How many Broadway productions in a year? Compare that with the number of films. And television. Like I said, there's no comparison. I like to act."

An actress who's been nominated for an Academy Award for each of the few film roles she's done but so far has never won, and who definitely prefers New York theatre, hates Hollywood:

"I just don't like film or television. I've been talked into doing a few things, but it's not the same as theatre for me. I like knowing there's an audience experiencing something right now, right there while it's happening on stage. The camera's so cold, impersonal, and you never know whether audiences will enjoy what they see months, maybe a whole year later. In theatre you know. You can feel it.

"A film set feels so false to me. Hundreds of crew people standing around doing things they have to do, close enough to

371

breathe on you when you're supposed to be alone.   Doing the same scene over and over, with no spontaneity possible because you have to do everything exactly the same again and again. In theatre you can keep growing in the role each performance. That's such a wonderful feeling, finding more and more. In film, the first time they shoot a scene, that's it.   You can't change a thing. I always know I could do it better. I hate that.

"And theatre, even in New York, is so warm. A play is a fa- mily. Hollywood's a cold place.   You don't even have a chance to get acquainted with the man who's your husband or father or something. A scene's finished, they run to their dressing room and call their agent.

"Even friends who are out here now, when I'm here I call them, maybe have lunch or visit with them, but most of them change when they stay here. They sound rushed, worried to stay on the phone too long, calling up to cancel things because some- thing's come up. Everybody seems so, I don't know, restless, in- secure, not happy. New York's such a happy place.

"I'd never come to Hollywood if it weren't for the money. They pay me lots more than I'm worth, lots more than I'm paid on Broadway, but they do that with everybody out here if they want you badly enough, so I take the money and get back to New York as fast as possible."

On the same subject---New York / Hollywood, add to the fore- going two comments made to me some years ago, before I moved from New York to Hollywood:

Chico Marx, when we were touring summer theatres with *"The Fifth Season"*: *"Why Hollywood?   More work than any- where else, more money than anywhere else, more happening than anywhere else."*

Barry Sullivan, when we were location-filming *"The Harbourmaster"* series in Rockport, Massachusetts: *"I live in Hollywood so I can work all the time and live the way I want to. I'd only come east if I could afford to do a play."*

And this one, after a studio brought me west:

The noted playwright/screenwriter Ben Hecht, when we were working together at his late life home in Oceanside and in his of- fice suite at the Bel Air Hotel (both of course California): *"New York hasn't been the center of anything since the forties. Everything's out here now."*

■ **Later Years' Work Being Made Easier by Early Acting Studies; Adaptations Made By Actors To Fit Their Particular Professional Needs:**

372

An older character actor, veteran of Broadway theatre, several television series and over two hundred motion pictures, also a leading acting teacher in Hollywood now:

"Gadg Kazan gave me the key long ago: 'Read all the books; boil every chapter down to a single sentence that says what they took twenty pages to say; use what you need in a role.'

"Stanislavski was a talker. He wrote like he talked. Lots of words. Made your head spin with words. I started doing like Gadj suggested and everything was suddenly simple.

"Finally, after all those early classes, trying to put everything but the kitchen sink into every character, I learned what Gadj meant by using what you need in a role, no more. Keep things simple. You don't need every tool in the book for most roles. At least not consciously.

"I tell my classes that now. At least they're going to know what's available if they feel like complicating, but I tell them to pick and choose, 'Use what you need in a role, no more.'"

The male star of a top-rated television crime series:

"When I started out in New York I bought every book about Stanislavski! I studied with some of the best coaches, lived on Chock Full O' Nuts hamburgers, took every kind of odd job so I could pay for classes.

"At the first rehearsal of my first Broadway play . . . (Name) was the director, and everybody knew he was Method, so I used some of the words from Stella's and Sandy's classes, to let him know I knew what I was doing. (The Director) took me aside afterward and said, 'I know you're an actor. Don't keep reminding me. When you walk in here you're Tony.'

"On the set sometimes now, I look around and see some of those worried young faces, actors talking to themselves in corners, reminding themselves of all their planning. I feel sorry for them. They're still doing some complicated homework. I know when they're in a scene with me they're going to be half with me and half back in somebody's acting class.

"Actually, I don't do much homework myself anymore except usually deciding what's on my mind---the character's mind, then I come up with something, who knows what, to make it different from the cliché, to bring something special to it, but still make it honest. And I never talk to anybody, period, about what I'm going to do. Makes them deal with it spontaneously like Sandy used to tell us, makes them more interesting too.

"See, I haven't had a single role out here (Hollywood) that I had to do much thinking about a character for. I read a script, get a hook on the character's insides, and I know why they want

*me.   Like (the aforementioned first Director in New York) said,
soon as I open the script, I know I'm Tony. I've played every
kind of Tony there is, but they're all me. All those classes back
then and yours here made me see how many Tonys I have in me."*

An older member of the Actors Studio who works all the
time, in usually "separate card" starring roles:

*"Tamara Daykarhanova, now there was a teacher! None of
the ego bullshit, all the how-to's that really worked.   She, Vera
Soloviova, Jilinsky and a few others understood Stanislavski,
could simplify everything, make it stick.   They taught me everything I've ever used since. Strasberg gave me a lot of suggestions,
but not much how-to that I could ever get a hook on.*

*"I'm still a member of the Actors Studio out here. It's kind
of a fraternity, a private place to get with friends out here (in
Hollywood) that you don't run into often outside.   A lot of important projects came out of the Studio. They do out here too. That's
what it was in New York too for a lot of us."*

■ Studying With More Than One Teacher

A leading female star who studied with Uta Hagen, Robert
Lewis and attended Lee Strasberg's private classes in the early period of her career:

*"The thing about Uta and Bobby . . . they always amazed
you, always brought up something you didn't think of, and always made your mind spin with suggestions of what you could
do. I never found that kind of excitement with Lee.*

*"I'm sure all those years of study are what make it so easy
for me to work now.   Oh god, if I tried to do all that preparation I
did in New York!   But if I hadn't been through all that 'way back
then I wouldn't know where to even start on a character like (the
role she had just finished filming). Don't tell anybody, but it
took me just one reading, one morning, to really find her, and
find myself in her, as Uta and Bobby used to say to us.*

*"The way I prepare now is so simple.   Actually, I find myself
using some of Uta's teaching and some of Bobby's every time I'm
preparing, but funny, the ideas come before I remember where
they came from originally.   Some things just pop into my mind
without my looking for them. I think all those classes got filed
away up here (she touched her right brain) and now they just sit
there waiting for the next chance to turn on light bulbs for me."*

A beautiful actress who's equally at home in a Midwest farm
role and some classical, period pieces in which she's starred:

*"It's too easy to fall into single patterns that become clichés
if you stay with one teacher forever.*

"First Stella (Adler) knocked all the ego and ham out of me fast. She let me join her personal class. She made me get down to basics, start from scratch. She was tough, brutally straight with all of us, and by god we learned!

"But what we didn't get into with Stella, and for some reason I felt drawn to, was classical work, style. So when I heard that Bobby (Lewis) was teaching styles at Lincoln Center I was there in a flash. I knew he was Stanislavski-oriented, like Stella, and I knew he felt style work belonged in Method teaching, which most of the others didn't. The combination sounded right. I went to him to study style, but I found my confidence finally with the whole System in his class. Thank God for Bobby Lewis!

"Actually, those two, Stella and Bobby, are as unlike as two people can be. Stella was hard; Bobby's soft on the surface, but don't get him upset. The two of them, that's an example of what I say . . . actors should study with more than one teacher. Stella laid the groundwork and Bobby put it all together for me."

A young female star of a long-running soap opera:

"I studied acting with three other coaches for a while before I came to you with that problem. I never felt really confident, like I was learning much, so I kept looking and finally found you. But I picked up some things, different things, from each coach I studied with, so I guess it all adds up.

"Plus, dance classes, the Shakespeare work with Peggy Feury before she died, finally the work at FIWI. I'm glad I had that behind me too before I got this show.

"So I guess I'm one of those who'd say study with more than one coach, get what they can give you, and move on."

Voicing the opposite view, a young male star who leaped into top roles immediately when industry people saw him in one of this author's Hollywood theatre productions:

"I made the rounds of a bunch of classes when I first got here (Hollywood), mostly names in those Drama-Logue ads. I audited for free wherever I could, then I saw a review of one of your plays in the Times, called you, joined your class.

"I don't think I missed out on anything by sticking with you. When you know your coach is for you a hundred percent instead of blowing off ego steam like some I audited . . . that's why you were my only coach."

■ Actors Talking About How They Work

An actress who came from a singing background but who had years of early acting study in New York first:

"God, I made such a fool of myself when I was first looking for an agent out here. I wrote long, five, six page letters to some agents talking about my theories about acting! I hope none of them ever kept those letters.

"Finally (the agent) at (one of the giant agencies) called me in. I was ecstatic! But when I walked into his office he had one of those stupid letters in front of him! He said his agency couldn't handle me, but he'd seen me sing and from my singing he knew I could act. He wanted to help me, but he tossed my letter into the wastebasket---a letter I'd slaved over a whole night, laughed, and told me nobody wants to know what kind of acting approach you use; that producers and lots of directors are like the general public---they want to believe in the miracle of talent.

"He got me an appointment with another agent, one he knew could consider handling me in spite of no actual acting credits, just my reputation as a singer. He actually picked up the phone and got an appointment for me! Nobody better ever tell me agents out here are mean.

"The other agent asked me what approach I used as an actress. Really. One of his first questions! I was scared to answer, but following (the first agent)'s advice, I said something like 'If I ever find out, I'll tell you.' He said 'Great!' and I walked out with a good agent."

A male actor whose roles are usually physical action, jeopardy, special effects thrillers:

"How you work is homework. Before you get on the set. Keep it secret. No director should ever suspect that you work any special way. It might suggest that you need to be handled with kid gloves, in some special way. No director has time for that."

A top star who almost never discusses his manner of working, about an interview comment that was later printed in a magazine in spite of his request:

"I talked too much in the interview, she went ahead and printed the thing I said I used, and that was the only time I've used anything like that. Forgive me, Lee. Every time somebody brings that up I'm ashamed of myself. Even at the time I felt it was a copout. Keep your secrets, like (the previous action star) says. They come back to haunt you if you don't."

A Universal Television series star:

"Apparently it's an unwritten law with studios' P.R. people. I asked him why he took your name out of the story. He said 'Never talk about who you've studied with. The public thinks talent's God-given and it's best to leave it at that.'

A Tony Award winning actress:

"I never discuss my work. I wouldn't know how. I'd be lying if I said I use any system all the time. I never know where inspiration will come from, something out of the past, your class, Sandy's class, whatever. Once they come, they just pick me up and carry me. All I do is put them into words that work for me, objects, things I can use. I hate to worry things to pieces. Sometimes the longer I think about something the more confused I get.

"I think every role should be a happy, totally new spiritual journey . . . not a straight highway I've traveled a hundred times before in an acting class. You said that. It's true."

■ Insisting on Personal Choices Among Different Types of Roles

A male star whose career has included many stunningly different types of characters in England and later many more in Hollywood, but not until a recent first time (in the actor's more advanced years) included even one romantic leading role:

"I'm a frightfully dull person, actually. I've avoided the few simple romantic things offered me like the plague---and there weren't all that many, even in England when I was young. I never really wanted them, because I knew there was nothing that special I could do with them that the good-looking chaps couldn't do better, until (the recently completed role).

"Now, at this age, I decided somebody like me with some mileage on him could be fairly amusing and a little sad going through all those teenage tortures. Somebody else thought so too. They sent it to me. So I did it. Now they're sending me more of the same. But I never repeat. Helps keep me thinking. (His agent) thinks I'm a little off for not doing a couple more like that quick again, but what I do is my choice, not his."

One of the "macho" male stars:

"I got brave, tried to break out of the mold with that one. (His top agent) told me I was crazy. I wouldn't listen. I did it. Even helped finance it. Boy, what a mistake. The critics and everybody else laughed me right back into my cubbyhole! Even (his wife) said I should have known better. Maybe if I hadn't done so many pictures of the same kind, one after another, for so long . . . if they hadn't all been pretty successful . . . if I'd done some different things earlier . . . maybe they'd have accepted me better. You make your choices, later you have to live with them."

An actress who is equally known for dramatic and comic leading roles, is determined to maintain control of her own career, is demanding and strong willed enough to get by with it:

"My first agent gave me my walking papers because I turned down the first two things he wanted me to do. I did, honestly. Nobody'd ever talked back to him before. He said I'd never get started and threw me out. Well, I stuck to what I wanted and got lucky. They call me temperamental, just because I make my own choices and don't do everything they throw at me."

An older, longtime star:

"Those days under studio contract you didn't say no. You did what the studio told you to whether you liked it or not. I think Bette Davis and I were the only ones who ever said 'no' time after time and got away with it. And nine times out of ten when we wanted a role they said we were totally wrong for, by God we fought for it and got it!

"Young Gerry Page, when they brought her out, same thing. They did everything they could to make her glamorous, like they did Bette and me. It wasn't her. She felt ridiculous. She showed me that photo you have, the first photo the studio took. She practically cried. After we talked she got her dander up and had the balls to make them reshoot her without all that goop.

"In Hollywood everybody will tell you who you are, what you are. If you're smart, don't listen. Make your own decisions and stick to your guns. They'll call you hardheaded, but you'll sleep better."

But a former female star, who appeared in some of the early films that became classics, later retired after appearing in 102 motion pictures in a career that ranged from silents into the '40's, gave a reply that more actors might be inclined to agree with:

"Oh god, I made so many poor choices. (Title) with Cagney and those other two are the only ones anybody remembers. I envy the people who always make the right choices. If you know you're smart enough, fine, but who ever knows they're smart enough? That's the most important thing for actors, making choices, and some of us really screw up!"

■ The 'Being Discovered" Myths And Realities:

One of the talent agency heads of an agency that has offices in both Hollywood and New York:

"As you know, we mostly sign new people in New York, from Broadway and Off Broadway, when they've attracted attention in something there. It makes it so much easier to start them here on a decent level. Hollywood still has great respect for Broadway and even Off Broadway. Casting people, producers, are all happy to meet those new people who come with enough New York credentials."

Another (smaller) agent who likes to help new people, but scouts for them exclusively in Hollywood:

"I try to see every single 99-seat theatre play in town, even productions at colleges and universities. I read the reviews in Variety and The Reporter, Drama-Logue or wherever, and go if they sound promising.

"Some of those 99-seat theatres are great opportunities. New talents can be cast and work in good roles with well known stars that attract audiences. If somebody's interesting enough I leave my card for them. That's where I get most of the new folks I sign. A good review or two opens doors. I rarely even respond to pictures and résumés in the mail. I feel sorry for them, but if actors want to be noticed they should be working somewhere in theatre instead of wasting postage.

"And forget workshop showcases. Those are usually ripoffs . . . workshop directors advertising 'industry showcases', getting actors to pay for classes in hopes they'll get into one of the show-cases.

"'Showcase' is a dirty word to me. If the workshop does plays, that's different. They get reviewed, and their producers and directors know they'd better be good. Brings us back to the-atre. There are ten or fifeen, maybe more, very good small the-atres here. I mean really good. Producers that know what they're doing, give new playwrights a chance, know talent when they see it. Good actors know they have to keep acting. Serious actors should try like hell to get into one of those. People go to those because they're always good. If a new actor in one of those is good, somebody'll find them."

A former talent executive at one of the major studios, now an agent, who still helps new peoole get started in Hollywood, and who has shepherded many careers to stardom:

"When the contract players and term contracts died out at the studios, it was the end of 'making' stars in the old sense. Universal was the last studio to stop. We developed a bunch of people. You mentioned (name). He got on the lot one day some-how, found my office, came to me because he'd heard of me some-how, and I knew with some preparation he could have a series or a multiple contract. He had something fresh, he was handsome in a cocky way. We coached him, got him ready, and it worked. But that's yesterday. No studio wants to spend the money now to make stars.

"All those television movies of the week, with 'guest stars' you've never heard of? Maybe not even any background. That one 'guest star' or 'also starring' credit, gotten by a good agent with enough clout to demand it, starts them in a high enough po-

379

sition in billing that they're an 'instant star'. Other starring things come easily after one good credit.

"I turned to agenting because that's where it's at now. The top agents control things now. Actors have to get the best agent they can, not compromise on somebody with no clout unless they have to. I can help actors better as an agent, demand billing, salary, that they couldn't get with a lesser agency than ours.

"Like I say, nobody 'discovers' actors anymore but the agents. The names you don't recognize but up there in guest-starring roles are 'blackmailed' into those roles and billing by top agents with enough clout to browbeat producers into seeing them and by god or else casting them.

"Nobody should hope that a casting director is going to 'discover' them these days. Casting people have no clout. And there are no more on-the-lot New Talent Heads. Agencies are the only ones that make new stars now."

An Executive Producer of an independent production company which specializes in crime and mystery television Movies of The Week, and often shoots them on location throughout the U.S., offered another possibility:

"We found her on location She came in through the location casting director. In her reading, man, she blew us away. In filming too, she was wonderful! When we reshot some of it in Hollywood we brought her out to repeat the role, paid her transportation, upped her salary, even paid the difference in her SAG membership so she could work in Hollywood.

"Actors don't need to come to Hollywood to get started. In her case, for instance. Chances are she wouldn't have even been called in for interview here. We would have called for somebody both of us knew. On location, we didn't know anybody. She got lucky.

"Get a good role, doesn't even have to be that big, in a location film shooting near where they live, do a sensational job, someody in the Hollywood contingent's going to want to help them---producer, director, maybe a star, whoever. If they decide to come to Hollywood later, at least they've got a friend who knows they're great and may be able to help them."

■ Actors Can Hurt Their Careers in Many Ways

The Director of a fairly recent, important Off Broadway production:

"He called in 'sick' too many times and his understudy had to go on. Someimes he'd show up thinking he was in shape to go on but had to be sent home. I don't know where he is now. I *doubt he's working. And I'll never hire a known drunk again, no matter how perfect he is for it, or how big a name."*

The former agent and close friend of an actor taught by this author---a handsome young fellow who leaped quickly to costar-ring in one television series role, which role led to three more top series starring roles within a five year period:

"Nobody'll touch him now. He got into cocaine, remember, got violent when he was on it. After they fired him from (series name) he disappeared. Nobody knew where he was.

"Out of the blue he called me this summer saying he was ready to work again, I decided to give it a try. I told him on the phone, straight out, I was only doing it because of the commis-sions I deserved for those years when you and I were building him. He didn't even show up for the meeting, didn't call, any-thing.

"Then he called again in November, finally came, looked great, said the stuff was behind him. I wanted to believe him. I put him up for some things, but nobody wanted to take a chance. I can't blame them. Everybody knows his story. He's dead in this town. Dead! Now he's disappeared again, nobody knows where. He had it all, but he blew it."

A noted director of some important films of recent years, when a star with whom he'd worked before was suggested for his upcoming feature during our conversation:

"I thought of him. He's perfect for it, but I like happy people. He's a miserable excuse for a human being. Too bad. He's a bril-liant actor. Everybody knows that. But there wasn't one happy minute working with him on (film title) and that's what keeps him from some of the great roles he could be doing. Grumpy, jealous, complaining all the time. And that stuff spreads like wildfire on a film set . . . other stars, crew."

The top agent who represented a star of a top television series in the seventies whose career was almost ended (at least "put on hold", where it still is) when his series was cancelled:

"After the next to last season he demanded cast approval, script approval, director approval. I got them for him. That's why they eventually decided to not renew. Ratings were still good, it wasn't that. It was just him!

"He'd take the script into his dressing room in the morning . . . the script he'd already approved, mind you . . . and hold up starts to make a lot of last-minute changes. The actors got new dialogue a lot of times, with no time to get up in lines, causing re-takes that ran 'em over budget. He'd change dialogue, get more ideas right in the middle of a shot and yell 'Cut!' Drove the direc-

tors crazy! Twice he had directors replaced in the middle of shows because he didn't agree with them on something.

"I built him to where he was, dammit, but when I couldn't get him anything for a long time after that he fired me too!"

■ Some of My Own Actors' Career-Hurting Stories

Since talent agents, more than any others, know the details of how many careers have been killed by actors' mistakes, here are some out of my own brief period of agenting:

During the mid-70's, when the industry was averse to considering any new talents at all because of a production slump, and top actors were playing smaller roles because employment was down, I suspended my teaching for what I planned was to be only one year, and set up my own Screen Actors Guild franchised agency because I knew I was the only person willing and able to help some brilliant actors from my classes achieve starts on top.

Because my judgment of talent was widely respected, in my first two weeks as an agent I got one of my young actors his first ever film role---with guest-starring billing(!)---as Mary Ellen's boyfriend in four episodes of *"The Waltons"* series. (The actor, Robert Woods, is now an Award-winning soap opera star.)

Just as quickly, I got Don Reid his first series starring role in a Hanna-Barbera series pilot shot in Australia; got Pollyanna Houston the series role of Mrs. O'Grady in *"Baretta";* got German star Wolf Roth series starring roles in ABC's *"High Risk"* and *"The African Queen"* pilots (neither of which got network pickup, but they got him going in top roles in Hollywood until he returned to Germany); got others their first roles on guest-starring or at least starring or co-starring levels ; and word got around . ,

Soon I found myself representing not only those I'd suspended my teaching briefly to help but a number of already starring people as well, including a French actress who'd top starred in many Hollywood films in the forties and fifties and wanted to revive her career.

No one was interested, even old friends of hers, but no one told me why. Finally I persuaded a producer to meet her for a starring role (at first he said no), persuaded her to meet with him, went with her, and finally discovered why her career had faded. She criticized the role, insisted on changes she wanted so she could appear younger, insulted the producer's judgment every other word. Needless to say, the role went to another former star.

Another case, a really tragic one: One of my own most brilliant young men, for whom I quickly got two co-starrings to start his career, was rehearsing a small theatre production. As the

382

opening approached, the producer (who was costarring opposite him) suddenly fired him. His performance was already brilliant, but she was the producer, had the power to do it. She's one of my closest friends, so I won't say what I think was her reason.

The *very next day* the director of the next upcoming episode of *"The Quest"* series called me, offered him the *first position guest-starring* role because he'd been so brilliant in an "also starring" role in *"The Streets Of San Francisco"* for the same director. But . . . *I couldn't find my client anywhere!* The director waited patiently as long as he dared, then had to cast someone else. The role would have put my fellow securely into top starring!

Two days later, I finally heard from him. Upset about his firing from the play, he'd taken off for Mexico *without telling his agent---me!* (Had I known, I could have had the Highway Patrol stop him on the road and send him back in time!)   Your agent should *always* know where you are!   That was his one big break that he and I had worked toward.   He muffed it.

Another of my clients who stars and guest stars regularly now had been under contract to Universal but kept turning down roles and   finally Lew Wasserman, the studio head, had him banned from the lot as revenge. I managed to get him back on the lot for a starring role with a director who loved his work. I didn't know he was on PCP (angel dust) the day he went in to meet the producer. Casting should have detected something wrong when he reported in, but didn't.

In the meeting with the producer and his friend the director he went crazy, the guards were called , he was hauled to his car in the parking lot, the drug made him think his car could simply fly over the parking lot hedge. He spent the night in jail, and was once more banned from the Universal lot and word spread. (He's so brilliant that he's been back there in starring roles since, and his drug days are in the distant past. Only his tremendous talent, recognized by enough industry people, saved him.)

Another of my young actors became a series co-star in a top western series. A handsome devil, he started getting publicity and hired a PR man. He hadn't known that the star's ego had forbidden any of the series regulars' hiring publicists. He was fired. It was there in small print in his series contract. It pays to check.

Two of my young series stars decided to fight for impossibly large salary raises---even though it was a "low budget" series and I strongly advised against it.   The resulting hassle became very sticky.   They were both replaced summarily, and neither's had as much success since.

Another case: A very promising young actress with a wonderful quality for film (I'm ashamed to say, also one of my very special people), was given her first co-starring role (as her first role ever) in a Movie of The Week filming outside Santa Fe (which a longtime Hollywood producer friend of mine, Jon Epstein, was producing) and another longtime friend Milt Hamerman (for years Vice Pres. of Talent at Universal) was casting.

The young actress insisted that her boyfriend be allowed on the set at all times. One morning, because she was to be kissed by one of the young male stars of the picture, *her boyfriend insisted the young male star be tested for AIDS!* When her boyfriend was driven off the set the young actress left with him in a huff and didn't return---with most of her scenes already shot! She cost the film enormous budget problems in delay and recasting of her role. Nobody I know has even heard of her since.

One more: One actor, an established stock broker with many industry clients, had come to my classes because several of his film star clients kept telling him that with his hard-looking, pockmarked face he should be an actor. One of his brokerage clients even brought him to me.

A man of awe-inspiring intelligence and not an ounce of fear, he grew swiftly. He'd been one of the main reasons for my decision to temporarily become an agent.

I got him some good starting roles, and Kevin Tighe, then starring in *"Emergency"*, seeing his work in class, got him a role in his show. Then he got a running role in an upcoming series with Merlin Olsen (which unfortunately didn't make it).

When I closed my agency to resume teaching (as planned, but later than initially decided) I helped him get a different agent, a very good one. He soon left that agent out of impatience. I got him another one, another good one. He left that one too, again out of impatience. On his own, he later tried several more agents, had no respect for any of them, to this day has nothing good to say for agents. He probably isn't working much, because he probably hasn't found an agent he'd be willing to stay with.

These are examples of the types of mistakes that actors can make that often (not always, but too often) end their careers.

■ Some Random Questions and Answers . . . A Group of Four Top Players Gathered For the Purpose

I put the following questions about common industry practices to two women and two men, asking their comments:

■ How true is the saying "It's not *what* you know, it's *who* you know?"

Woman A: " Boy, have I got a story about that! (Name) *took me around, introduced me when I came out from New York. Finally I got my first role with one of his producer friends. First day on the set the sonovabitch producer asked me to come to his house that night! I said no thank you. He asked why I was obviously showing my gratitude to* (the friend's name) *and wouldn't do it for him! I found out my helper had a reputation. People can get the wrong impression when you let somebody help you out here."*

Man A: *"If you have both, great. But if somebody gets you in the door from then on it's up to you.*

Woman B: *"I didn't know anybody. I did a whole slew of plays here before any agent knew I was alive. It's hard not having any help, but when it happens at least you don't owe anybody."*

Man B: *"Dad tried to help, but nobody took me seriously. He got me my SAG card with a little thing in his series, remember, got me with his agent, but nothing happened till I did those plays. Help helps, but work 's what works."*

■ **How true is the Hollywood saying "You can't get a job without an agent and you can't get an agent without a job?"**

Woman A: *"How can you get a job, even meet casting directors, without an agent persuading them to see you? An agent's the first step. Some agents can know you're talented, but they know how hard they'll have to work to get you going. Keep hounding them till they take you."*

Man A: *"I kept after* (Casting Director name) *at Universal till he got me my first role. I did four or five scale jobs for him. He liked me, kept calling me in, so I figured I didn't need an agent. Finally I realized I was going nowhere, got smart, got an agent. I owe that to him. Without those first nothing jobs* (the agent's name) *wouldn't have touched me. I'd still be working for minimum, noplace but Universal, if I hadn't gotten smart and gotten an agent.*

"(The casting director friend) *stopped calling me in, got pissed off because I wouldn't work for scale anymore. I started getting some better things, better salary, started getting billing around town through my agent, but not with him. He won't speak to me now, but that's the only way you get better roles, start getting billing and salary raises . . . through agents."*

Woman B: *"It's understandable. An agent hates to take on somebody with no credits. That's all that saying means. You can't blame them. You know how hard they have to work to start*

385

somebody. And they know that after all their hard work if you start moving you'll probably leave for a bigger agent.

"Wonderful Alex Brewis. He started so many, got them into starring, and they broke his heart by leaving him for bigger agents. He finally got fed up and retired."

Man B: "No matter what you have to do, get an agent before you waste time with casting directors. An agent hits all the studios. He knows what's casting all over the place. A casting director's involved with just one company at a time. No comparison. Knock down doors if you have to. Get an agent."

■ **Here's a touchy one. How much "casting couch" still exists in Hollywood?**

Woman A: "Well, unfortunately casting directors, producers, agents are all human. They're like the audience, they respond just like anybody else if you have some special appeal. Up to a point, it's actually a compliment. If the question comes up, all you have to do is say 'No.' I think the one agent that ever tried anything with me actually loved me in his own way. I just said no. We've stayed good friends and it 's never come up again. I think he still loves me, and I love him. We respect each other. Just say no."

Man A: "Only time it ever happened to me . . . I did the lead in one of (a noted playwright)'s plays out here. Word came down he wanted me to come to his house. There was a role coming up in his next Broadway play. I didn't know about him. The director knew him, though, warned me, suggested I just kind of hint 'Maybe later, but now now.' It worked. That was the only time it ever happened with me. Naturally I didn't get called for the Broadway play."

Woman B: "Oh, it happens. Not that much, but once in a while. You know what I do? I laugh it off! I pretend they're kidding, even if I know they're not. It always works."

Man B: "Just once with me. She was a top casting director. Don't ask me which one. She'd helped me a lot. Then one night she had me go with her to a screening, had me in for a drink later, asked me straight out. I told her I had to get home to (name). She apologized the next day. We still play poker. Can't blame somebody for trying. Happens in all kinds of businesses just as much. But the decision's yours."

■ **How important is partying, socializing? Do you have to?**

Woman A: "My publicist hates me. I won't do it. He keeps calling me, saying one of his stars needs a date last minute, and I can use the publiciity, being seen with him. Maybe sometime if it's somebody I 'd like to meet . . . I just don't enjoy parties."

Man A: "I'm not a highlifer. I'd rather go to class, study lines, read, whatever. Who wants to get all dressed up, go out, spend a lot of money, pretend to have a good time just to get your picture in a magazine? Wouldn't get my face in a magazine anyhow---I'm not having a divorce, I don't get in trouble, I'm not gossip bait. I go out for a beer with a buddy sometimes when I'm not working in the morning. That's about it. Saves energy."

Woman B: "Nobody asks me anymore. I'm not what you'd call an easy mark. And I'm basically shy, a lousy conversationalist. I am. I'm dumb on everything but acting. I'm not a party girl. I'm an actress. I think everybody knows that by now."

Man B: "I'm a drag at a party. I avoid them. I'd rather play poker."

■ **Ethel Barrymore once wrote that *"For an actress to be a success she must have the face of Venus, the brains of Minerva, the grace of Terpsichore, the memory of Macaulay, the figure of Juno and the hide of a rhinoceros."* And Paul Newman, after a few years in Hollywood, said *"All they want is my blond hair and blue eyes."* How important do you feel physical beauty and handsomeness is for young people in film now?**

Woman A: "Oh my god, that was ages ago! Character's what they look for now. I think it's healthy, it's wonderful! My favorite star has acne scars and he's the sexiest actor in Hollywood. I think those beautiful pockmarks helped him get started. They sure haven't hurt him. "

Man A: "It'll always be important for women, but not for men. Producers still think women have to be beautiful, have great bodies. Men, they don't care what you look like. Yeah, I guess the old double standard's still in gear."

Woman B: "It's so unfair! Any other profession, who a woman is, what she can do, are what matters. For film, if an actress isn't at least fair looking she's a character actress from the git-go---a girl friend who listens, a frowsy neighbor nextdoor with kids, whatever. It's ridiculous. But it's still true too."

Man B: "(His wife) went into Abbey' Greshler's (her agent's) office one day, just to pick up a script, without her makeup on, hair looking nice and messy. Abbey gave her hell! Said if anybody saw her on the street that way she'd lose some things. Me? . . . Hell, Jack Fields (his own agent) told me once to dress way down, not shave so close, mess up my hair, wear dirty jeans or something when I went in to see people. I guess it worked.

*'Course now I have to wear 'star' outfits so they'll pay me more.
Back to the other . . . Women are women, men are men."*

■ **A big problem for new film actors is nervousness, because the
camera makes everything so important. Do you ever still get nervous just before a shot, and if you do, what do you do?**

Woman A: *"Of course I do! It's terrifying, all those people
standing around watching! That never goes away. All I know to
do is think about what happened with my character just before. I
see people do all sorts of things with their body to relax, but none
of that works for me. I concentrate on what's just happened in
the scene, what it's doing to me. Then I'm not nervous. At least
not as nervous as just standing there and getting self-conscious
would make me."*

Man A: *"Not anymore. In New York I was a wreck before
every performance. Stage, those early live television dramas . . .
you goofed up, nobody could save you and you felt like shit. Now
In film, I look for somebody to tell a joke to, laugh a little. I
know if something happens it's okay, it'll work the second
take. Don't get me wrong, I don't play around, I just need something to distract me from thinking of myself."*

Woman B: *"I used to be a basket case when I first came out
here. I was one of those 'minute to prepare' worrywarts till I realized what I was doing with all that preparing, I was 'acting.'
like you've said, using that time to keep telling myself I didn't
believe yet. Now I make myself believe what's happening. It
helps forget the camera's there. It's all in the mind, all those
nerves. I keep my mind where it belongs and my body behaves."*

Man B: *"I hate to admit it, sounds like ego but it's not . . . if I
get nervous . . . don't quote me . . . I think of the crazy money
they're paying me, so I must be okay. Okay, maybe it's ego. But
then it's easy to relax into my character. I tell myself I wouldn't
be there if I wasn't damn well worth it. In my case, nerves come
from thinking I may not be good enough. When I convince myself I bloody well am, the nerves go away."*

■ **There's lots more sex and nudity in films, even theatre, now.
How do you feel when you read a script and find your role includes
one or both of those? I know how at least two of you feel. I'm glad
you're here to answer this.**

Woman A: *"I think it's more honest than anything else. I'm
comfortable with both if I trust the director, and I wouldn't do
any of either if I didn't. I don't believe in exploitation, but if
there's good taste in handling it, why not?*

388

"At first I worried about my folks back on the farm, but after I did those two scenes in (film title) my mom just said she'd never noticed how skinny I'd gotten, and dad just started looking at me like I was a prize heifer when he thought I wasn't looking. Shooting those scenes is so complicated it's kind of fun."

Man A: "If it helps a picture make money I guess it's okay. In fact, I guess I'm for it . . . what's the big deal? It's part of life if that's all it's there for . . . and as long as it's somebody else doing it.

"Something young kids have to think about, though . . . If you've done nudity or sex stuff in a picture or on stage, you can't do commercials afterward. (Name) lost a commercial because they found out he did ' Oh Calcutta'. Something to think about."

Woman B: "I was surprised how easy it was in (film title). I thought I'd never even do nudity. And a sex scene! Whew! It took a meeting in the front office with (the Vice President, Motion Pictures, of her big agency) to talk me into it. I was still scared.

"(The director) closed the set, but nobody standing around the set treated it like anything special anyway, and both of us knew exactly what part of us was in those hundreds of quickie closeups all the time. Mostly heads and shoulders, you know, legs, his back some of the time, a lot of just rolling around.

"What a production's always worried about is the rating. Too much nudity, too explicit sex, even too much cussing, any bad taste in even one shot, it gets an R rating and won't make money unless it's a blockbuster like that one. The two of us were more relaxed all the time than (the producer) and some others there in black suits. They were so careful with how every shot was being set up, had a conference with (the director) every ten seconds. (Her partner) and I felt safe every minute.

"They even insisted both of us watch the dailies to see if anything bothered us, kept watching our reactions. I just sat there giggling.

"Those two days shooting all those brief little bits of that one long scene, everybody being so careful every second, were the easiest days I've ever spent on a film. I'm glad I did it."

Man B: "I think you know my answer. You know I'm a confirmed nudist ever since I went to Esalen that summer and went through all those nude sensitivity experiences. Blew my mind, taught me a lot. I believe in nudity, you know that, I know how healthy it is. I still go out to Treehouse when I can, but the only nudity I see in films, sex scenes too, are great looking, sweaty young bodies. That's exploitation. Nudity and sex are still exploitation in too many films, and I kind of resent it.

389

"NYPD Blue" exploited it for audiences, ratings. Demi Moore's beautiful pregnant body sold out on newsstands. That was exploitation too. When we get rid of some of the old Puritan crap in this country, nudity, maybe even sex in films, won't be exploited like they still are so far. "

■ **Now, I'd like you to think about this for a minute first. When you're ready, in a few words, what's the most important advice you'd give actors either just starting or working their way up the ladder in either film or theatre?**

Man A: *"Work. Act. If you make money, fine. If you don't, fine. Never stop acting. Somebody'll find you, help you. Even if you have to form your own theatre to do good roles, do it. Get enough good writeups in reviews, people'll notice. Anything else is just begging. Nobody likes a beggar. Just keep acting."*

Woman A: *"Know what you really want and what you're willing to do to get it. Don't step on people on the way up. You're going to meet the same people later, maybe when they're up and you're down. Acting's a small world. Keep your friends. All those actor friends are just as insecure as you are, they need your support, your reassurance, phone calls to ask how they are. Acting's a lonely world. Help make it a happy place. I think I probably work as much as I do because people like me, they know I like them, appreciate them."*

Man B: *"Don't be a wimp. Say what you think, not what you think you have to say. Agents, casting directors, even producers and directors. They ask you something, what you think, talk from your gut. They'll respect you. You want something, ask for it straight out, you may get it. You don't like something they're doing with you, tell them. Too many actors think they're less important than they are. Directors, producers, agents, they all need us. We're the talents, not them. We're what goes onto the film. If we respect ourselves enough they'll respect us more. Remember, without us actors, this whole industry's nothing."*

Woman B: *"I agree. You beat me to it. Agents need us to survive. Producers, directors . . . they're nothing without us too. Producers and directors know we'll do our best work if they keep us happy. You can be valuable to all of them long before you're a star. But you have to know that or they never will. On a set, if you just think you're lucky to be working they can smell that. They know they've done you a big favor, hiring you. You're nothing that way. Make them by God value you! Do it with your talent. Do your best work. Impress the hell out of them. Show them you know you're somebody. Place value on what you can do. That's when you're behaving like an actor."*

The Actor's Professional Vocabularies

Commonly Used Terms
in Actors' Study Phases

Acting Academies: Usually postsecondary education facilities offering many and varied study programs with which predominately beginning, aspiring actors become involved in preparing for later careers.

Action (or **Intention**): What a character is attempting to do (usually in moments, rather than in terms of the complete role).

Action Verbs: Verbs or verb phrases that involve the body in some specifically executable and exclusively physical manner (e.g., *squeeze* or *squeeze out, shove away, scrunch* or *scrunch in, knock off,* etc.).

Active Verbs: Although called this by some actors when they mean *action* verbs, an *Active Verb* is often less specific in purely physical terms---(e.g., *to persuade, to teach, to retreat, to tease, etc.)*---none of which specify any partiular body manner).

Actors Studio: The New York (later, Hollywood also) studio called "The Home Of The Method", where mostly top stars, writers and directors worked with Lee Strasberg at his invitation.

Actorisms: Clichés in actors' manners of working; some dating from earlier theatre; some representing misapprehensions as to the individuals' most truthful manners of performing roles; some formed by actors' psychologies.

Affective Memory: The memory of past experience stored in the right brain. As an exercise, a favorite of Lee Strasberg who dedicated his life primarily to promoting its use by actors through the experiencing of their own past moments rather than involving in belief in the character's experience. Explored by Stanislavski and later rejected for reasons. A hot potato that has always been the subject of controversy.

Animal (or **Animate**) **Images**: (1) A class exercise to awaken more areas of actors' sensitivities through miming animals and other animate beings; (2) A manner of obtaining characterization inspirations from animate beings, then translating them into strictly human ideas they can inspire.

Appraising The Facts: Considering the many facts presented by authors as to characters and their circumstances, to help arrive at the personalities of characters and their moments.   First, "Listing The Facts"; then "Appraising each individual fact listed.

Atmospheres: Location, present company, weather, social situation, etc., as they affect the character in specific moments.

Attention: Involvement with something by focusing upon it.

Auditing: Visiting and observing a teaching session, judging approach values and professional quality of class members.

Beats: Smaller moments of whatever duration, during longer sequences (Units), in each of which the character's concentration is focused upon an experience, a problem, an *Object,* an *Action* or *Intention,* etc. A new *Beat* begins when the character's concentration is caused by something to be refocused and the *Beat* ends when the character's concentration changes to a new focus.

Beat Object: What is on the character's mind, the focus of the character's attention and the generator of its feelings for the duration of the smaller moment (Beat) in a sequence of such moments. A *Beat Object* (Vakhtangov's recommended substitution for an *Action* or *Intention)* is the problem or other stimulus itself throughout a *Beat,* rather than a desired action resulting from it.

Behavioral Stimuli: Usually external events or impressions which cause responsive behavior of conditioned, preconditioned or unconditioned nature by the mind and body.

Being Done To: An alternative to the *"doing"* (action) choice, involving focusing more upon what is being done to the character rather than upon what the character is itself *doing.*

Between The Lines: For the actor, those *human experience* moments, perhaps brief and fragmented, that duplicate the human characteristics in speaking.   Dialogue is not experience. The experience of the character lies "between the lines".

Biography (or **History**) **Of The Character**:   An approach recommended by some teachers wherein the actor constructs details of the imaginary life of the character that has occurred before the character enters the script.   Prepared to afford the actor more personalization with, and justifying of, behavior of the character throughout a role.

Blocking: The moving of actors from one position to another, usually supplied by the director. (The other kind of *Blocking* is described as *Organic Blocking* later in these definitions.)

Body Searching: A manner of *consulting the body* for its help in accessing affective memories stored in the right brain, accomplished through random, fragmented, silent, purely physical improvisation.

393

Character Actor: Although every actor, regardless of age or appearance is essentially a *character actor*, the term is most often still used as applying to the actor or actress who, by reason of unique appearance of some type which doesn't suggest the standard, fairly outmoded concept of possessing handsome, pretty or attractive *leading actor* potential in casting terms. (It should be comforting to actors to note that in present day theatre, film and television many actors playing important leading roles are no longer of the cliché "leading man" or "leading woman" category.)

Character Comedy: That comedy which derives from skillful preparation of a character that is comic by itself, independent of a writer's comic situation.

Choices: The actor's decisions of approach items, characters' inner lives, objects of concentration or actions and intentions.

Circumstances: The facts, supplied by the writer, as to *who* the character is, *what* it is and *what* its situation is, *when* a given moment takes place, *where* it takes place, and *why* it takes place, also *why* it involves the character.

Cold Reading: The actor's manner of auditioning to obtain roles.

Comic Timing: (1) The actor's own sense of timing for comic result, also (2) The result of the actor doing *"takes"* about other characters and other characters doing *"takes"* in return.

Commercial Workshop: A workshop taught by a professionally experienced person who is himself or herself involved professionally with the unique acting styles demanded of actors when appearing in commercials.

Conservatories: Study facilities which generally offer training in two or more (usually three) semesters or terms and offer a varied curriculum of acting, speech, movement, theatre history and many other studies with which beginning actors may expect to be involved in later acting careers.

Conditioned Response: Usually combined feeling and body responses which are inextricably connected with past experience of an *affective, emotional* nature. Behavior that is conditioned upon, and caused by existing attitude about, something that occurs to the person.

Creative Psychological Objectives: A latter day manner of using *Action Verbs* in combination with right brain *sensory keys* (Similes) that the body remembers from past experience. Best found via the "Body-Searching" process.

Creative Work: The work of the actor on a role which may be desirable beyond and in addition to the purely experiential (perhaps emotional) involvement, for the purpose of a more theatrical realism for moments of a role.

Dialects: The unique manners of speaking---pronunciation of vowels and consonants, formation of sentences, intonation, rhythm and other characteristics of specific foreign or regional American peoples. Dialects are learned and duplicated, whereas accents are natural and may be either kept or eradicated.

Emotional Memory: See *Affective Memory*.

External Work: The actor's work on the physical embodiment of the character---manner, wardrobe and other externals.

Farce: Exaggerated comedy, most often involving accelerated pace and jeopardy of one or more characters and complications and exacerbations provided by other characters.

Form: The style elements suggested by the writer; also the actor's own aesthetic ability to perceive and interpret impressions.

Given Circumstances: See *Circumstances*.

History Of The Character: See *Biography Of The Character*.

Human Images: The use by actors of observations of selected human beings' physicalities, manners, speech, characteristics, etc., for the embodying of characters in acting roles. A concept originated by Michael Chekhov.

Illusion Of The First Time: The highly desirable impression for the viewer (and for the gifted actor as well) that what is happening is happening for the first time. In dialogue, it requires the involving of human imperfections in delivery of lines provided by writers, repunctuation, searching for words and phrases, etc.

Imaginary Center: Michael Chekhov's label for an imagined spot or item located in or on the body from which all of the neural muscle system flows and all sensory experience is centered, for the purpose of creating distinct characterizations.

Imaginary Characters: The imagining of several characters of the general type of a character, and imagining *wrong, unusual, distinctive* items, wardrobe, hair style, props, etc., for the producing of colorful inspirations.

Improvisation: Working without scripted action or dialogue.

Ingenue: A young actress designation most often used in the theatre and film world of England, somewhat outmoded in America.

Inner Dialogue: Unspoken dialogue, either with self or another character. As distinguished from *Inner Monologue*, most often considered to be desired communication addressed to another character which simply can't be or isn't spoken aloud.

Inner Monologue: A sequence of silent thoughts put into words but not spoken aloud, for the purpose of involving the mind of the character and resulting body participation in moments.

Intentions: Synonymous with *Actions* and *Objectives* in most actors' minds, perhaps only distinguished by the fact that *Intentions* can more easily be worded to include the *Justification* (reason) for the desired action.

Internal Work: The analyzing of the character of the author's intention, then laying out its goals, its problems, its tasks, its objects of concentration, etc., moment after moment throughout the life of the character.

Justification: For the actor who uses *Actions* or *Intentions*, the goal or reason for the action desired to be taken, most often dictated by the character's personality.

Juvenile: A term connoting a young male actor which, like its female counterpart, is more used in English theatre and film, having to an extent become passé in America.

Left Brain: The storehouse of logical thought and action, data, formulae. The left brain is entrusted with the directing of the body as to what to do and how to do it, also the amassing of intellectual and intelligent information of all kinds.

Listing The Facts: In Stanislavski's and Vakhtangov's recommended manner of analyzing the personality of characters presented by authors, this was and still is a highly recommendable first step of beginning the inner preparation of the character. After listing all the facts that relate to the character, the actor is advised to go back over the list and analyze each fact as it may shed light upon the inner life.

Living Sounds: Neglected or simply overlooked by many actors, the *Living Sounds* that accompany thoughts, body conditions, feelings, emotions, physical sensations, the executing of tasks, reactions, etc. As a class exercise, a manner of inspiring a more complete human experience as it involves dialogue and action.

Manifesting: Conscious *"representing"* of a feeling experience by the actor without any truthful inner experiencing of what is being pretended for an effect on the viewer.

Mannerisms: Characteristics that recur time and again in actors' work, whether they're conscious or unconscious. James Dean's off center slouch was a mannerism; Kim Stanley's jagged edged frenzies are mannerisms; Jimmy Stewart's hesitant stutter is a mannerism; Bette Davis's use of her bugging, piercing eyes is a mannerism.

Method, The: Often understood to mean *The Stanislaski System* as used by American actors; more accurately, the version of Lee Strasberg which, although inspired by a few of Stanislavski's and Vakhtangov's teachings, bears only partial resemblance to those Systems as he taught them to American actors.

Method Of Physical Actions, The: The name which Stanislavski applied to his System at the Moscow Art Theatre, after first calling it "The Stanislavski System".

Motivation: In either limited, temporary terms or in terms of the life and goals of the character, *Motivation* is the driving force suggesting and propelling the actions of the character.

Motive Center: Vakhtangov's adaptation of Michael Chekhov's *Imaginary Center*, centering the actor's total processes (speaking, listening, smelling and other sensations, as well as all neural muscle system movement) in an imaginary spot or item located on or in the body. Moving the spot or item immediately creates an entirely different embodiment, therefore an entirely different personality type.

Movement: For the actor, an aesthetic awareness of artistic form in bodily behavior to serve composition, focus and artistic ensemble effect.

Neural Muscle System: The intricate, circuited responsive system that generates body positions and movement patterns that have their stimuli in the nervous system, involved in the actor's seeking natural flow of body movement in attractive form.

Neurosis Provoking Moment: The moment in the formative years when the cumulative assaults and impacts upon a young person result in permanent damage or at least firmly conditioned response in the psychology.

"No Technique" Approach: An approach to acting which abjures all "technique" in the belief that the actor needs only *"get out of his own way"* (get out of his mind) to free the total of his talent.

Objectives: Literally, a goal toward which actions are directed. It is sometimes the word used by actors in place of *Action* or *Intention.*

Objects, Beat: The concentration focal points of the character during the individual *Beats* within the *Units* of the character's scripted life.

Objects, Inner / Thought: Objects other than physical (e.g., problems, relationships, worries, feelings) upon which the character's attention is focused.

Objects, Life: The ever present central concerns of characters that are the very cores of characters' conditioned response structures, creating and fixating their personalities.

Objects, Physical: Purely physical surroundings items that can be touched, observed, heard, smelled, tasted or otherwise experienced in their many aspects. They can be endowed with meaning to evoke sensory and sometimes emotional response in the actor.

Objects, Unit: The central concerns of characters, subject to the characters' personalities throughout entire roles, that are the characters' focal points of concentration throughout the larger divisions of roles, as those larger divisions (timespans) of roles are caused by changing circumstances (e.g., successes, failures, new obstacles, etc.) provided for the characters by their writers.

Obstacles: People, things, events, etc., that literally stand in the way of goal-directed actions.

Organic Blocking: The *Movement Blocking* and other suggestions that actors can present to directors as being appropriate for their characters from their own inspiration and research of their characters.

Parallel Behavior Patterns: The behaviors that are observed to recur time and again throughout the character's scripted experience which help the actor discover the personality of the character that continually motivates its behavior.

Personalization: Sharing of the character's feeling experience by associating it with the actor's own life experience, also the ability to fully experience vicariously what the character is feeling.

Physical Objectives: As generally used (and as originally recommended by Stanislavski), synonymous with *Ations* and *Intentions*.   Presented by Stanislavski as the tiny, very brief actions that, strung together in sequence, contitute moments of longer duration (perhaps *Beats*).

Private Coaching: One on one work of the actor with only a coach or teacher, conducted in private.

Private Moment: An an exercise in class, the exploration by the actor of some task or moment that in privacy includes many fragments of concentration or activity that actors might not think of (or might intentionally omit for reasons of taste and judgment) when the same task or moment is being observed (as in an acting performance) by others. (Originally labeled "Public Solitued" by Stanislavski.)

Professional Classes: The term most often used to describe the acting study programs offered by teachers (often in separate *Beginning, Intermediate and Advanced* class levels) in which most aspects of the actor's development may be anticipated as being taught (e.g., *approach items of a particular approach favored by the teacher, methods for preparing both the actor's instrument and manners of preparing roles, some scene study and perhaps also improvisation for the practicing of those items).*

Psychological Gesture: Michael Chekhov's *eurythmics*-inspired manner of discovering the personality core of a character by imagining its bodily behavior in moments of peak importance.

398

Relating: Maintaining communion with the character's surroundings, other characters, its own inner experience (less often its own experience when the term "relating" is used).

Repetition: The manner devised by Sanford Meisner for leading actors toward the use of other approach items, one after another, either proposed by Stanislavski and Vakhtangov or later formulated by Mr. Meisner.

Representing: The (usually chiché) manner of an actor's "performing" the character's and his own feeling experience as suggested by left brain logic and observation, intellectualized concept and little or no connection between the body and the right brain.

Right Brain: The feeling and experience files of a human being from whence *Affective Memory (or Emotional Memory)* can be accessed through stimulus and conditioned response of *Sense Memory* nature, rather than by left brain logic and intelligence.

Scene Study: The preparing and presenting of scenes by actors in acting class sessions for coaching suggestions and critique by teachers or directors.

Sense Memory: A memory of the body's prior experience in physical terms, stored in the left and/or right brain, often (but not necessarily) stored there because of its importance in connection with a feeling or emotional event in the actor's past.

Similes: In the actor's use, the mysterious (beause usually long forgotten) key words known only to the body and the right brain that can evoke stunning body participation in emotional or simpler moments from stimuli that have connected the body and the right brain in one or many such moments in the past.

Situation Comedy (Sitcom):   Comedy that depends for its comic result on the contribution of a writer of a situation that is comic.

Situation-Playing: In acting terms, generally accepted as meaning the experience of an actor when attention is focused exclusively on the situation without any involvement of a character's personality or other given circumstances.

Six Questions: In Journalism I, the first paragraph of a news story that encapsules the entire story in brief. For the actor, a checklist to prevent the overlooking of facts presented by the writer and for the providing of inspirations over and above the details provided by the writer, also for suggesting research by the actor of any items---professional activities, styles and customs, wardrobe, social influences, etc.---with which the actor is less than sufficiently familiar.

Social Mask: A *mask* performance of a character designed to cover that character's true feelings from other characters.

Standup: (1) A solo comic performer; (2) The type of comedy performance presented by a solo performer involving prepared "routines", personal "shticks" (amusingly quirky characteristics) and expert comic timing.

Stanislavski System: The System codified by Stanislavski for the training of actors and the preparing of acting roles.

Style: In dictionary terms, a manner of the executing of something.   In acting terms, periods have their unique styles, different national and ethnic cultures have their styles, and there are regional styles applying to different parts of countries. There are even styles dictated by status, calling, profession and urban or rural locations.

Substitutions: Uta Hagen's label for a manner of seeking more personal idenfitication for the actor in total characterization and in individual moments of roles.

Subtext, Analytical: The inner life of a character (in all its salient aspects) which must be analyzed and crystallized by the actor---from the facts about the character presented by the writer---toward motivating its actions throughout its written life.

Subtext, Directed: The self-conceived and self-directed further steps in whatever approach terms may be chosen by the actor in outlining the character's over-all and sequenced experiences throughout a role, as continually dictated by the personality and motivations previously determined to be moving those experiences.

Super Objective: The goal toward which the *"spine"* or *"through line"* of all the character's actions are directed.

Takes: Exaggeratedly comic silent comments of one comedy participant about another, to essentially make both the other participant's character, just prior action or assertion more comic than it would otherwise be, also to make the participant "doing the take" more comic as well through the exaggeration of his own reaction.

Talent Showcase: Technically, the presenting of a number of talents for exposure to industry people. Too often, also a ruse for enticing gullible acting newcomers to register for classes in a workship or acting class.

Task: What the writer has assigned for the character to do in a brief or prolonged moment of a role. A *Task* can be either simply physical or an act of interrelating with another character with a goal in mind.

Technique: A learned manner of conditioning an actor's instrument; a System of approach items for the actor's use in preparing roles.

Text: The written words of the script---dialogue, action description etc.

Theatre Games: Pioneered by Viola Spolin, an approach involving many types of improvisation, both silent and with verbal keys, toward sensitizing the actor's perceptions, awakening new areas in the actor's work portfolio, and inspiring characterization.

Through (Line Of) Action: The continuous goal pursuit of or negative escaping from something unpleasant on the part of the character, either (1) from first moment of appearance in the story to its final exit or (2) as the action desired to betaken through one of the larger sequences of a role.

Unconditioned Response: Behavioral response that is most often elicited by common stimulus and decided as to form of the response based on logic and intelligence by the left brain.

Workshop: A term generally understood in the acting world as connoting a training program or workout activity for actors that involves either scene study or improvisation, or both, under the guidance of a teacher or director, sometimes not even involving the continuous teaching of technique.

Film Actors' Terms

No actor should walk onto a film set before learning the many, many terms all film actors are expected to know. There's no teaching time on a busy film set, and there are hundreds of words and phrases the actor needs to know ahead of time. Even before a job, certainly during and again afterward, there are terms unique to film acting that the actor should know.

The following list is fairly complete. Actors new to film should study them over and over, have friends test them for their ability to remember them, and keep them ready in the mind from the first moment of hearing that they have a role, because that's when the the urgent need to know film actors' terms begins to be realized.

Added Scenes: Filming for which a cast member is called back for the filming of additional (new) footage after a picture is competed.

Assistant: The First Asst. Director, more often called **"The First"**.

Atmosphere: The "extras" who have no lines.

Backstepping: A method for the actor's hitting of marks, not all that dependable but some old-timers recommend it. (See **Sighting**, which is much more accurate.)

Background: Either actors, extras or scenery behind foreground players and action.

Bell: The loud buzzer or bell that with one long sound signals "Quiet on the set!" to prepare for a take, and with two short sounds signals "Noise okay again."

Blues: Blue (usually first revision) pages of the script. When actors receive them they're expected to substitute them for the like numbered pages in their scripts.

Boom: The Sound Crew member who extends the mike above the actors' heads; also the "boom" from which the mike is suspended.

Buzzer (sometimes called **Bell**): The buzzer on a set that with a long single blast quiets all noise in preparaion for filming; also with two short blasts signals "All clear" when the shot is finished and noise is permissible.

CU: This, in a script, indicates a "closeup" shot.

Camera Car: The car with a camera mounted on it for filming car chase and traveling car shots.

Cameraman: The **Director of Photography**, or **Cinematographer**: He or she sets up the shots with the Director.

Call: The actor's call with details of when and where and to whom the actor is to report for filming.

Call Sheet: Published by the Production Dept., showing all work calls for cast, crew, planned filming locations, scenes to be shot and equipment needed.

Chalks: The marks made around the actor's feet during a pre-filming rehearsal. His **"marks"**.

Cheating: A slang expression for what actors playing foreground must do when playing a scene with actors behind them.

Check Authorization Form: What you sign for your agent to send to the Payroll Dept. when you work, directing that your paycheck be mailed to the agency for deducting of the agent's 10% commission before issuing to you the agency's own check (from its "Clients' Account") for the balance.

Clapboards (more commonly called **"Slates"**): The two-boarded slates that are clapped loudly in front of the actor or an object just as a shot is starting, so the visual "marker" (identification information) on the work picture can be synced up in the Sync Room for the running of both work picture and dialogue track, synchronized, in "dailies".

Clean Entrance, Clean Exit: Being all the way out of the shot either before walking into it or when exiting a shot. Film actors learn to stop or start just out of the shot.

Closeup: A shot including little more than an actor's face.

Commercial Composite: The usually two-sided photo print of actors seeking commercials, with one large photo on the front and several "in character" shots on the back with the actor in wardrobe, using props, in locations that suggest what the actor is right for.

Continuity: The person who on a complex, many detailed shooting is responsible for the "matching" of all details in all sequences of shots.

Conversion Rate: A contract provision that can convert a "day player's" daily salary rate to a three-day or weekly rate which will not be as much as the same amount of work period at the daily rate would be. Actors receiving their "day player" contracts from "The Second" (Second Asst. Director) when they first report for work should check this item. It's a sneaky manner or paying lower salary if the actor is later needed for a longer period.

Co-Star: The billing level which immediately follows "Starring" in opening or end credits of films and television.

Coverage: Additional takes of scenes from other angles; reaction shots; closeups; medium shots; closeups of hands doing something; a clock ticking.

Covering: Accidentally covering another actor or something else.

Cut!: This is yelled to stop a shot still in progress or finished.

Crew: The technicians of all kinds---Sound crew, Lighting crew, Grips, Drivers, Makeup, Hairdresser, etc.

Dailies: The previous day's **"Rushes"** (all footage shot), synced up for early morning or sometimes lunch break viewing by the Director, the Producer and others.

Daily: The contract for an actor hired for either a single day of work or the type of contract for an actor who's to be paid at his daily rate rather than a weekly rate.

Day Player: An actor who customarily plays one-day or other small acting engagements.

Deal Memo: The draft of a series player's or motion picture star's contract sent by the producer to the agent representing the tentative terms of the contract being offered. (There are usually items still open for the agent to better in negotiation.)

Dialogue Director: The Director's helper who "runs scenes" with actors before their filming and reports to the Director any problems that the Director wouldn't yet know about, to save delays when the scenes are ready to be filmed. (Actors insecure with lines may have their lines cut.)

Downgrading: In a commercial, if someone expected to be a "principal" (face recognizable in the finished commercial) becomes unrecognizable in the final version, therefore won't get residuals.

Dupe Neg: The duplicate negative the Photo Reproduction Lab makes up from which 8x10's can be duplicated. Actors should know the term for use when ordering prints.

Dolly: The mount for the camera, or the movement of the camera when it moves toward, away from or with the scene's action.

Double: Does stunts and hazardous actions while made to appear to be the actor.

Drifting: An actor drifting from one position in a shot to another, usually blocking something by doing so. (John Wayne was a notorious "drifter", so many of his shots had to be "medium shots".)

Drive-On: Permission to drive the actor's car onto the lot and park near where shooting is planned.

Drop-Pickup: A Screen Actors Guild concession that allows actors to work one day, be paid, then be called back after a period of time to resume a decent-sized role. Must be in original contract.

Dry Run: A rehearsal before filming a shot.

Dubbing: The adding of music track, sound track and special effects track in the post-production work on a film. Also refers to an actor "dubbing" of a different language over the original track.

Editor: The man or woman who cuts the film together in the "cutting room".

End Credits: The lists of character names with the actors who played the roles; the crew members' titles and names.

Episode: A single show segment of a continuing series.

Est. Shot: A suggestion to "establish" a place, a building, etc.

Executive Producer: The head honcho of a production company or a top producer for such a company. He or she plans projects, assigns them to Supervising Producers for handling, then rides herd on the projects from inception through to completion.

EXT.: In the scene description, means "Exterior".

Favored Nations: This is the phrase guaranteeing that no other player will receive a higher salary than the actor to whom "Favored Nations" is contractually promised.

Featured: This is the billing given to the less important but still story-involved roles in film and television. It normally follows the "Co-Starring" billings in end credits.

Firming: The official hiring of the actor to definitely play the role.

Firm Start Date: The date a production company promises to an actor as the date of starting the actor's employment.

First: See "Assistant" and "First Assistant Director".

First Position!: The position where an actor is directed to be located for the start of a shot. When "First Position!" is called, the actor goes to that position.

First Team!: The call for the actors to return to their positions for filming, as the **Second Team** (their stand-ins, who've been standing in their positions) are retired after the setting of lighting for the shot.

Fitting Fee: Extra payment for having to go to the Wardrobe Dept. or elsewhere to be fitted for wardrobe. This fee automatically appears on the actor's salary check.

Force Majeure: The clause in a contract which allows the producer to stop or suspend production, whether expecting to resume or not, under certain unexpected and catastrophic conditions. Actors receive certain prearranged salary payments in lieu of their contracted salaries.

Foreground: Action closest to the camera.

Golden Time: That overtime which is still later than simple over-time, time-and-a-half and double-time hours used in figuring cast and crew pay. When a day's and evening's filming is extending into Golden Time, everybody sweats.

Grips: The crew members who move, hold and carry things.

Guarantee: The minimum employment period guaranteed the actor in a contract.

Hairdresser: Combs out and touches up women's hair.

Heads: What "closeups" are often called.

Headshots: Actors' professional photos, usually of just the head.

Holding Fee: A fee paid an actor to keep the actor available until something starts following a delay. (When the old *"Star Trek"* was being revived in the '70's, first planned as a series, then a mo-tion picture, again as a series, then again as a motion picture, to hold the cast members available each was paid a very large "hold-ing fee" by Paramount each time the plans changed---without even walking on a set.)

Honey Wagon: The portable john truck on locations.

INT.: In the scene description, means "Interior" shot.

Kill The Blowers!: The yell to turn off airconditioners on a sound-stage set before a take.

Lapel Mike: The small mike hidden on an actor who doesn't speak loudly enough or when it's impossible to have a boom mike hanging over the actors' heads, as in walking exterior shots.

Left Frame: To your right when you're facing the camera.

Lines: The speeches of your role in the script.

Lip-Sync: Actor lip-syncing lines synchronously with silent footage projected on a screen before him, as when "dubbing" into another language.

Location: Shooting that's anywhere outside the studio lot, even if on a nearby street.

Location Casting Director: The person who calls for interview the actors and extras, local residents of location areas where films are shooting, handles their casting interviews and first day work call details. Works in cooperation with the Hollywood casting.

Location Manager: When a film is to shoot at a distant location the Location Manager is in charge of the small cadre of personnel sent out to prepare everything---housing, use permits, location scouting, hiring of local crews, etc. During actual filming, the Location Manager is still in charge of such details.

Long Shot: When action is distant from the camera or made to appear so by a particular camera lens.

Looping: Re-recording dialogue while listening to a playback of the original track, to produce better dialogue, eliminate "overlap" problems, etc.

Makeup: Either the Studio Makeup Dept. or the man or woman on the set who does the job. (When actors are told to report to Makeup they should find out whether it's the Studio Makeup Dept. or "Makeup" on the set.

Marks: Chalk marks or tapes that mark feet positions where the actor starts, or walks onto, or stands on.

Master: A shot that usually includes large or moving action. One of the very first shots taken of a scene. The actor must remember all details of movement, position, prop handling, etc., because he must duplicate them skillfully in the additional shots of portions of the same scene when they're filmed later.

Matching: The duplicating of all actions, positions, handling of props, etc., in additional shots of the same scenes.

Meal Penalty: When meal breaks don't come after the number of hours of filming specified by SAG, a meal penalty is assessed over and above the actor's salary for the day. It's paid automatically.

Medium Shot: Shows much of the actor's body, sometimes with others in the shot also.

Merchandising: The series or film actor's contracted share in items sold or licensed by production companies that bear his or her likeness and/or his or her character's likeness. Usually an infinitesimal percent, but it can run into the millions on popular items if the series or film is successful.

Mileage: The amount paid an actor for gas mileage when he or she drives own car to location. Not often allowed, due to insurance coverage of production companies. When allowed, payment is made in hand upon arrival at location.

Minimum: The term used to indicate that the actor will receive the SAG-regulated minimum salary and no more. (It's standard for the actor to receive **"Minimum plus ten"**, so the agency can receive its ten percent commission.)

Mixer: The Sound Crew member who controls the volume levels of sound recording---to maximize dialogue and minimize other sounds and noise in sound recording. With the turn of a dial, he can make a soprano a bass or a bass a soprano!

Morals Clause: The clause that authorizes the firing of an actor (especially a series actor) if he or she does something just prior to or during filming that offends public standards.

Multiple Contract: A not often used contract now, employing a swiftly rising actor to appear in several pictures for a studio or production company over a period of time. (An upcoming actor who'll surely cost more later is often offered a multiple contract to do a number of films at the current salary.)

Must Join: Station 12 at SAG reports to casting people that a proposed cast member is a "Must Join", must come to SAG and join before being allowed to work. Actors are called "Must Join" by SAG if they've done their first film under the Taft-Hartley Law and must join SAG prior to their next employment.

(O.S.): When this appears with a character's speech, indicates that the speech is heard "off screen".

On A Bell!: Often the call called out when ready to make a take.

On Or About: This phrase covers the production, when setting an actor for a role, a little more flexibly as to actual start date in case of some problem delaying the employment start for a day or so.

Opening Credits: The credits---usually Producers, Director, Writer, Stars' names---at the start of a film or television program.

Operator: The Assistant Cameraman, who usually rides the camera dolly and does the actual filming after the setup and framing is readied by the Cameraman (Director of Photography).

Option: The production company's option to use the actor within a contracted period of time.

Outgrading: Removing an actor totally from a commercial in the final version.

Overlapping: Talking too soon after any other sound, or moving too quickly, leaving no room for cutting with scissors by the Editor. Actors are sent to the **Looping Stage**, usually at the end of a shooting day, for re-recording of the dialogue when either they or another actor have "overlapped". Speaking too soon after "Action!" is also overlapping.

Page Numbers: The numbers at the top right corner of script pages followed by a period.

Panning: When camera frame moves from one actor or object to another or when action is filmed in moves from one point to another and the camera follows the move.

Participations: The series actor's contracted (usually tiny) share in net profits realized by the series.

Per Diem: The meal allowance the actor receives for meals when on location if they're not furnished by the production company.

Pickup: The reshooting of a part of a scene wherein something wasn't satisfactory.

Pilot: The usually two-hour episode used to first obtain a series pickup by a network. Often telecast as a two-hour Movie of The Week or special two-hour program prior to the series start. Pilots that don't achieve network pickups are often telecast as Movies of The Week to recoup their production costs.

Pinks: The pink (usually second revision) pages of the script. Actors insert them, substituting them for like numbered pages, in their scripts.

Powder Down!: The call for Makeup to come to the set and powder the actor's face to eliminate perspiration shine.

Print!: What the Director calls out when a shot has satisfied him, to direct that that shot be "printed" for possible use in picture.

Process Stage (or simply **Process**): The two connected soundstages where a mockup car is filmed going along a moving street that is projected on a giant screen behind it, or actors cower before a leaping tiger that's actually on film projected behind them.

Producer: Sometimes the head honcho himself, in total control of the project; sometimes under the supervision of an Executive Producer, but in any event always the person most actively and continuously in charge of the project.

Props: The person who handles hand props on the set.

Recurring Role: A role which returns from time to time in a television series rather than being on a continuous contract basis.

Regular (or **Series Regular**): A series starring or co-starring role that appears in all or most episodes of the series.

Ready: This word, in a morning call, means completely ready for shooting , in makeup and wardrobe. "Ready on Stage 7 at 7."

Residuals: Repeat salary payments when actors' motion pictures, telefilms and commercials are rerun on television. Such payments are made automatically by responsible production companies, since the Screen Actors Guild keeps careful records each time a production is retelecast.

Rest Period: On location filming projects, the number of hours the actor must be allowed for rest between work periods.

Résumé: The actor's one page dossier of physical details, any union memberships, the name of the actor's talent agent, all acting credits and other information for the consideration of prospective employments by production and casting people.

Retakes: Shooting of some scenes again, usually due to problems.

Revisions: Script change pages to be substituted by the actor for similarly numbered pages in the script.

Right Frame: To your left as you face the camera.

Roll 'em! . . . Speed! . . . Scene Two, Take Six! . . . are typical last calls usually heard before the Director calls out **Action!** "**Roll 'em!**" means to roll camera and sound, interlocked. "**Speed!**" (or an electronic beep) signals that both camera and sound are rolling at the right speed for recording action and dialogue. "**Scene Two, Take Six!**" would be what "Slates" calls out hurriedly just before clapping the clapboards in front of the actor. All is then ready for the Director to call "**Action!**"

SAG Eligible: This means an actor is eligible to join SAG at any time he chooses, having done a picture without joining or being otherwise qualified under current SAG regulations for membership.

Scale: The minimum SAG salary for a day player is referred to as either "Minimum" or "Scale".

Scene Numbers: The numbers running down one or both sides of script pages.

Screening: Usually means the showing of a film with the producer, the director and many department heads present, for any suggestions or to simply show the film to department people and invited guests.

Script Supervisor (or simply **Script**): This person times each shot, checks all details for matching with other shots of the same scene, corrects dialogue errors, records data, then at the end of all filming hands that script over to the Editor as the record of all footage of all scenes available for cutting into the picture.

Second (or **Second Asst. Director**): The staff member who is in charge of the cast members at all times. Actors should never leave the set for any reason without telling the "Second". It's the "Second" to whom the actor should report in upon arrival, and who notifies the actor that they're released at the end of the day.

Separate Card: Actors' agents try to obtain billing for their starring players on *separate card*, with no other actor's name appearing in the frame at the same time.

Share Card: This means two or more leading cast members' names appearing in the opening credit frame at the same time.

Shooting Schedule: Production Dept. sheets showing scenes to be shot, locations planned for their filming, when they're planned, equipment needed, crews required and cast members involved. Actors can always request a copy, for their convenience.

Sides: Casting offices supply "sides" (a few pages of dialogue) to actors for their preparing to read for roles, rather than complete scripts. SAG requires that "sides" be made available for actors at least 24 hours prior to their reading appointents, so they can prepare at home before interviews.

Sighting: A most reliable manner of "hitting your marks" by finding intersecting points on both a nearby and a more distant object.

Sign-in Sheet: The sheet actors at commercial interviews sign upon arrival, indicating appointment time, actual arrival time, agent's name, sometimes also sizes, etc. Upon departure the actor must "sign out" indicating time of departure.

Slates: He or she holds the clapboards in front of your face and claps them when a shot is ready to begin; also rides the camera dolly continually, all the while adjusting focal depth.

Slopping: An actor "slops" when his role isn't finished on the day expected and he is to continue the next day or on another day. When actors "slop" they remain on continuous salary until their employment is finished.

Stand-ins: The folks who literally "stand in" actors' positions while lighting is being set. They're called **"Second Team"**, while the actor is a **"First Team"** member.

Station 12: The office at SAG which must be checked with by the Casting Director to determine that an actor is a SAG member and is paid up in dues and can be set for a role.

Stills, Still Book, Still Department: Still photography by the Still Photographer made on a set is printed for the film's **Still Book** and is available in the **Still Department** for actors to look at for the purpose of choosing prints they'd like to order.

Stop Date: The date the production company promises to be finished with the actor, especially used for stars committed to a **Start Date** on another immediately subsequent employment.

Storyboard: The cartoon strip-type board sometimes displayed at commercial interviews, so actors can see the planned visual progression of the commercial from start to finish before auditions.

Stuntmen, Stuntwomen: They fight, fall from buildings, get shot, etc., in hazardous sequences, while made up and wardrobed to look like the actors they represent.

Taft-Hartley: The Law which allows actors to do their first film roles without having to join SAG.

Take (or **Shot**): What's filmed between the words "Action" and "Cut!"

Temporary Fads: Most often the copying of a current style, manner or other "in" item that the knowing actor must abjure so that a broader spectrum of role suitabilities will always be evident.

Three Day: The three day contract for a television role. (There is no "three day" contract for motion pictures.)

Timesheet: What the Second Assistant Director has the actor sign on the set upon arrival to show time of arrival and upon release at the end of the day to show time of dismissal.

Top Of The Show: Television series announce to agents that there is a top salary figure beyond which no guest player will be paid.

Travel Time: The time during which an actor is required to travel to or from a remote location and be paid for same.

Trims: Pieces of film clipped out of footage by the Editor for alternating character's faces and their dialogue in sequences during the cutting together of the picture. The actor's closeups of dialogue or action sequences are each filmed in continuous takes, but in editing other actors' faces into the same scenes those moments when the other actors' faces are cut into the film will mean there are pieces of the first actor's footage that become "trims". (Sometimes the actor is permitted to obtain some of these after the picture is edited, to have 8x10 prints made of chosen frames of their performances.)

Turnaround: The period between completion of a television series' production for the season and the notification by the production company that it plans to continue or resume the actor's employment for the following season.

TVQ: This is the rating report that producers insist they "never use," but do, to determine who has a high "TVQ" (**Television Viewing Quotient**---an audience approval figure) and is therefore "bankable" (assuring banks' production financing and excellent boxoffice returns).

Two Shot: A shot, medium or otherwise, which includes two characters.

Typecasting: The act of considering actors for almost exclusively those roles which they best fit in terms of appearance, personal characteristics such as speech and manner, etc. Actors must anticipate being *"typecast"* throughout the earlier phases of their careers. It's the best way casting people can remember to think of the actor and call to have him or her come for interview.

Upgrading: When an actor has worked in less than a "principal" role in a commercial but is later "upgraded" into a recognizable face in the final version of the commercial and will therefore receive residuals as a principal player.

Voice Over: The profession of those whose voices are heard in television commercials usually praising a product displayed on the screen, whose voices are heard off-screen as narrators but whose persons are never seen, whose "trick" voices are used for dog barks, babies' cooings and children's playground yelling, passing race cars, animal sounds of all kinds, etc.

Wardrobe: Either the person who handles your wardrobe, or your wardrobe for the role you play. It's usually hung in the closet of your dressing room before you arrive, ready for you, and should be again hung in the closet at the end of the day for pickup to be cleaned or laundered during the night and returned to the closet for next days' filming.

Weather Permitting: The phrase used in issuing actors' work calls when the weather is questionable but shooting is still planned. A "Weather Permitting" call to work, if not cancelled by 6PM the evening before, is a day for which the actor will be paid, even if cancelled later.

Weaving: Drifting from side to side in a shot and causing problems for the cameraman trying to hold the actor in frame. (Again the John Wayne example.)

Weekly: The term for a contract when the actor is hired for one or more weeks on a picture, rather than being hired at his "daily" salary.

Western: Usually means the Western Costume Company. Actors are told to "Go to Western" for fittings of wardrobe which the Studio Wardrobe Dept. doesn't have available.

Whites: The original white pages of the shooting script.

Wild Lines: Lines said into a mike, on or off the set, as lines only (without picture). They're for adding to the track in a dubbing session.

Work Call: Usually all details of where, what time and to whom the actor is to report for the following day's filming. Such calls are received by actors or their agents by 6PM the evening before.

Wrangler: The horses' straw boss on western sets. The man or woman who checks to see whether the actor knows how to get on and off and whether the actor knows what to do when riding. If the actor doesn't know enough, a "Riding Double" is immediately on the spot demanded by the Wrangler to avoid accidents and injury to actors or horses.

Wrap: At the end of a day's shooting **"It's a Wrap!"** is called to signal going home time. At the end of the picture's final filming it's the signal for breaking out the Wrap Party champagne.

Wrap Party: Usually held on a soundstage with catering at the end of a picture's final filming day. The occasion for everybody to breathe sighs of relief and forgive everybody.

Stage Actors' Terms

Following are many of the terms which stage actors are expected to know. This special vocabulary is furnished with the thought in mind that there may be some actors (although probably few) who have done film and television exclusively, never having acted in theatre. Happily for those few, the list of special terms unique to stage acting is much shorter than the list actors preparing for first film and television roles need to learn quickly.

Acoustics: Either excellent or poor sound accommodation from the construction of theatres' interior walls, etc.

Actors Equity: The Actors Equity Association, the union to which professional theatre actors must belong.

Apron: The forestage that usually extends just out past the house curtain. People have fallen off aprons into orchestra pits.

Blocking: Actors' positions and movements from one position to another and accomplishing of physical tasks during a scene, usually according to the director's design. (Also see **Organic Blocking** which means the actors' own suggested blocking as being most appropriate for his character.)

Bows: The curtain calls after the final curtain when all cast members line up on stage to take bows.

Closing Notice: The notice required (by Actors Equity) to be posted on the Callboard backstage at the theatre as to the impending closing of the production.

Closing Performances: Those performances when disliked actors may anticipate capricious or vengeful props people substituting peanut butter (or something else impossible to deliver dialogue through) for sandwiches' contents and any number of other unexpected "tricks" designed to mar their performances when it's too late for them to do anything about it.

Composition: The final arrangement of two or perhaps many more actors and perhaps set pieces for scenic effect and appropriate focus of the viewer's attention.

Curtain Call: (See **Bows**.)

Curtain Warmer: The soft lighting that illuminates the house curtain for some moments before the performance is to begin, then fades out just before the curtain rises.

414

Down Center: Directly in the center, somewhat downstage.

Down Left Center: Not far from stage center but a little downstage and to the left as the actor faces the audience.

Down Right Center: The same, but to the right.

Downstage: Closest to the apron or footlights.

Downstage Left (or **Down Left**): Toward the front of the stage and to the actor's left when facing the audience.

Downstage Right (or **Down Right**): Toward the front of the stage and to the actor's right when facing the audience.

Dress Rehearsal: Usually the final rehearsal, with all effects such as lighting, sound, music, and full costuming and makeup.

Dressing Room: The small room assigned to the cast member for making up and wardrobe changing.

Equity: See **Actors Equity**.

Equity Deputy: The member of the cast who's elected by the cast to insure proper observation of all Equity rules and regulations by the production company.

Far Left: Midway from the apron to the back of the stage, far to the left side.

Far Right: The same, but far to the right.

Fittings: A special session, usually, in which cast members are assembled to first try on and have their wardrobe altered to fit.

Flats: The individual, stretched muslin, framed and painted set pieces that, lashed together, create the rooms, walls, etc., of sets.

Forestage: Quite near the footlights or apron.

Greenroom: A backstage area where actors relax and wait or participate in directors' critiques after performances and rehearsals.

House Curtain: The main curtain between the stage set and the audience which, rising, signals the opening of the performance.

House Seats: Actors are sometimes allotted a small number of seats which they may give to friends. Sometimes these seats are not charged to the actor; sometimes they are.

In One: A term used in musical productions when the actor is positioned forestage (practically out on the apron) or when in brief crossovers of the stage and short conversations the actors work in a narrow passageway between two downstage "travelers".

Jobbers: In summer or regional theatre, a *Jobber* is an actor brought to the theatre for the performance of just one or perhaps two roles in specific plays for which there is no *Resident Actor* in the theatre's permanent company who is qualified.

Jobber Contract: A one-play contract which brings a New York or other actor to a theatre for just one role.

National Company: The touring production, with its own cast, that tours to other cities either during or following the run of the original production on Broadway.

Notice: The actor's notification of impending termination of employment for whatever reason. (Producers usually post two week closing notices, since Actors Equity requires that termination of an actor must be paid for with two weeks termination salary.)

Organic Blocking: The actor's own contributions to his or her "blocking" in scenes, based on the character's personality, etc., rather than relying simply on the director's moving the actor arbitrarily.

Opening Night: The first public performance of a theatre production, for which actors stock up on antacid pills, headache pills and ego-strenthening maxims pinned beside their mirrors.

Pin Spot: The tiny spotlight area which illuminates a single actor when the rest of a scene is darkened.

Pit (or **Orchestra Pit**): The pit for the orchestra just down in front of the stage apron.

"Places!": After the actor has arrived as required by "Half Hour" and checked in, and after the Stage Manager has made the preliminary "Fifteen Minutes" and "Five Minutes" calls, knocking on dressing room doors for each, there's the last-minute "Places!" call to send the actors to their positions on stage for the start of the performance.

Production Number: Usually, in musical theatre, large song and dance numbers involving chorus members as well as principals.

Projecting: Clear and loud enough voice to be heard in the farthest seat of the audience.

Props: Hand props for actors' use in performance.

Rehearsal: One of the several kinds of rehearsals (run throughs) of dialogue and action under the guidance of the director.

Rehearsal Call: The time and place for the next rehearsal.

Rehearsal Schedule: A schedule of planned upcoming rehearsal times and places, sometimes indicating which cast members are required to attend.

Replacement: When an actor comes into a cast to replace another actor, the actor will have been required to watch the performance of the actor he's replacing and will be afforded at least one rehearsal in the role with the rest of the cast prior to first appearance as replacement.

416

Resident Company: The members of a company of "actors in residence" at a summer theatre or regional theatre, playing roles in most productions, continually or for the entirety of a season.

Resident Contract: The contract for employment as a permanent member of a company.

Rest Period: The period, in hours, required by Actors Equity for the actor to rest between some rehearsals prior to performance or between performances themselves.

Reviews: Following opening night performances, Broadway actors often congregate at Sardi's or another popular nightspot to wait for the early hours of the morning's reviews by critics, to read them before going home. It's not unusual for a production to post a **Closing Notice** (to tentatively close in two weeks) on the Callboard backstage prior to the second night's performance if reviews for the production are deadly. National touring productions' casts are usually out of town on the way to their next engagements before reviews appear in those out of town papers.

Revue (or **Musical Revue**): A production made up of unrelated musical numbers and skits, usually comic.

Run Of The Play Contract: The Equity contract specifying that the actor is unconditionally hired for the full run of the play.

Runthrough: A rehearsal other than one of the final (technical, dress) rehearsals.

Scrim: A diaphonous mesh drop which when illuminated from the front looks like a curtain but when a scene is illuminated behind it allows that scene to appear fully visible.

Set Piece: Some piece of furniture or a partial set.

Sides: The pages of the script wherein the actor's speeches appear but only the dialogue "cues" of other actors' speeches, between the actor's own speeches, may appear.

Sign In: The required signing in upon arrival at the theatre (no later than a half hour early) for performance.

Sketches or **Skits**: Brief, comic dialogue and action pieces, usually in musical revues.

Soliloquy: A character's talking to itself aloud when there are (usually) no other characters in the scene.

Stage Manager: The performance and stage crew manager whose responsibility it is to check in the actors upon arrival for performance and then to oversee (manage) all elements of the performance, give signals for light and sound cues, etc. The Stage Manager is in charge of each performance.

Stagehands: The electricians, set movers, etc.

Star Package: A production, complete with one or more recognizable stars, which is brought to a summer theatre, complete with cast, wardrobe and any special props required---everything but the scenery which is constructed according to a forwarded design by the theatre itself, for usually one week of performances.

Teaser: A fabric or other type of border at the top of the stage set.

Technical Rehearsal: Often the first rehearsal, sometimes one of several, where lights, sounds, music, etc., are first (or further) coordinated with the other performance elements.

Traveler: Any kind of curtain (usually decorative, sometimes painted to represent a scene) which either closes and opens in the center or "travels" from one side of the stage to the other.

Turntable: The platform which turns, with usually two or three different sets on it, to move the performance action from one scene to another quickly.

Understudy: All roles have "understudies"---actors ready to play when and if an actor in the role they're "understudying" is sick or otherwise unable to play.

Up Center: Stage center, farthest from the apron.

Up Left Center: Still fairly centerstage, but diagonally up and to the left of stage center.

Up Right Center: The same, but to the right.

Upstaging: The offense of distracting attention from another actor either by moving to a more prominent position or through distracting with physical activity.

Wagon: A moving set or large set piece, literally on a "wagon" that moves into place on stage and later moves off into the wings.

Wings: The side areas of the stage hidden from the audience, usually when "travelers" are used, as in musical productions. Actors enter "from the wings" and exit into them.

Acknowledgements

Excerpts from *"Advice To The Players"* by Robert Lewis, © 1980 by Robert Lewis, used by permission of Theatre Communications Group.

Excerpts from *"Strasberg's Method As Taught By Lorrie Hull"*, by S. Loraine Hull, © 1985 by S. Loraine Hull, used by permission of S. Loraine Hull and Ox Bow Publishing, Inc.

Excerpt from "Look, There's the American Theatre: An Interview With Elia Kazan", *Tulane Drama Review,* Winter 1964.

Excerpt from "At the Grave of Stanislavsky or How to Dig the Method", *Columbia University Forum,* Winter 1960.

Excerpts from *"A Method to Their Madness: The History of the Actors Studio"*, by Foster Hirsch, © 1984 by Foster Hirsch, New York: W. W. Norton.

Excerpt from interview with Marlon Brando reprinted by permission of *Playboy* Magazine.

Excerpt from *"Acting Without Agony"*, by Don Richardson, © 1988, Allyn & Bacon, Inc., reprinted and adapted by permission of Allyn & Bacon, Inc.

Excerpt from *"The Staislavsky Technique: Russia"*, by Mel Gordon, © 1987 by Mel Gordon, © 1987 by Applause Theatre Book Publishers.

Excerpts from *"Sanford Meisner On Acting"*, by Sanford Meisner and Dennis Longwell, © 1987 by Sanford Meisner and Dennis Longwell, Vintage Books, Random House, Inc.

Excerpts from *"Stanislavsky And The Method"*, by Charles Marowitz, © 1964 by Charles Marowitz, Citadel Press.

Excerpts from *"Evgeny Vakhtangov"*, compiled by Lyubov Vendrovskaya and Galina Kaptereva, translated from the Russian by Doris Bradbury, English transla - tion © 1982, Progress Publishers, Moscow

(Continued on next page)

Excerpts from *"Stanislavsky's Protege: Rugene Vakhtangov"*, by Ruben Simonov, translated by Miriam Goldina, © 1969 by Miriam Goldina, DBS Publications, Inc.

Excerpt from *"Respect For Acting"* by Uta Hagen, with Haskel Frenkel,© 1973 by Uta Hagen, reprinted with the permission of Simon & Schuster, Inc.

Appreciation is also acknowledged for the generous cooperation of the friends, many former students and associates, talent agents, producers and directors whose comments appear in the *"Talking About . . ."* sections of the book. Their promised anonymity is regretted because their candid comments contribute so vitally to the advice contained in those sections' discussions.

Index

424

425

behavioral science, 302
Moscow Art Theatre
   formed with Nemirovich-Danchenko,
   First Studio formed, 294; New York
   and American tour, 1923-24; 294
Motive Center
   Vakhtangov's adaptation of Imaginary
   Center, 78; examples 78
Movement
   chapter about, 172; Focal Leader,
   176; using Focal Leader, 177
"Murder, She Wrote", 69
"Murder Without Crime", 84
Musical Theatre Workshops, 194

"Ned McCobb's Daughter", 181
Negative Conditioning
   value for characters vs. positive
   goal, 92; in today's writing, 95
Nemirovich-Danchenko
   formulated the super objective, 2
Neural Muscle System
   use in Motive Center, 80
Neurosis Provoking Moment
   what it is, does, 73; finding super ob-
   jective with it, 74; lectured on at the
   Moscow Art Theatre School, 267
Newcomer Traps and Scams, 341
"New Generation of Acting Teachers,
The", 12, about Jeff Corey, 46;
   selective list of teachers, 201
Newman, Paul, 30
New York Critics Circle Award, 265
New York Post, The, i, 353
New York Times, i, 353
Nicholson, Jack, 28, 89
"Night Court", 266
"No Technique" Approach, 190
Nudity in films, discussed, 388
"NYPD Blue", 389

Object of Concentration
   first formed, 2
Objects
   Concentration on, 2; Vakhtangov
   urged prominent incorporation in
   the System, 2; Vakhtangov quote, 16;
   his recommendation, 26; self-experiencing, 57; Vakhtangov quote,
   98; Morris Carnovsky quote, 99;
   advantages of use, 102; how to

prepare, 103; examples of wordings,
   104; for units, 152; quicken role
   preparation, 208; Stanislavski
   coming to acknowledge, 300
Obstacles
   What they are, how to use them, 106
"Oedipus", 228
Off Broadway League, ii, 353
Off-Center
   for relaxing the body, 132; advantage
   of, 247; chapter about, 286; Strasberg comment, 286
   many stars known for it, 286;
Olivier, Sir Laurence
   use of Human Image, 75;
   concentration, 229; became friend,
   tried to help Parke's play, 359
"On The Technique Of Acting"
   describing Psychological Gesture,
   121; not simple, 122; graceful form
   exercises, 173; discussed, 318
Orben, Bob, 108, 167, 171
Organic Blocking
   What it is, 109; Six Questions, 109
"Othello", 148, 229
O'Toole, Peter, 89
Ouspenskaya, Maria
   at American Lab Theatre, 8, 215, 298

Packages, film, 328
Page, Geraldine
   mannerisms, 67, never accused of
   simplicity, 293; living sounds use,
   89; mannerisms, 283
Parallel Behavior Patterns
   as keys to personality, 112; examples, 113; use in forming character,
   141;
Parke, Lawrence
   biography, i; psychological games
   as exercise, 22; Self-critical personalities, use in classes, 23; many of his
   exercises throughout book; as
   industry organizer, i, 355
"Philadelphia", 367
Physical Objectives
   move the body, 55; description, 116;
   examples, 117; for comedy, 118
Pitts, Zasu, 281
"Playboy", 60
"Police Woman", 166

427